CHINA

Publisher:	Aileen Lau
Editors:	Irene Khng
	Zhen Ai Ling
	Catherine Khoo
Design/DTP:	Sares Kanapathy
	Sarina Afandie
Illustrations:	Eric Yeo
Cover Artwork:	Susan Harmer
Maps:	Hong Li

Published in the United States by
PRENTICE HALL GENERAL REFERENCE
15 Columbus Circle
New York, New York, 10023

Copyright © Sun Tree Publishing Ltd
1994

All rights reserved,
including the right of reproduction in whole or in part in any form.

PRENTICE HALL is a registered trademark and colophon is a trademark of Prentice-Hall, Inc.

ISBN 0-671-87896-4

Titles in the series:
Alaska - American Southwest - Australia - Bali - California - Canada - Caribbean - China - England - Florida - France - Germany - Greece - Hawaii - India - Indonesia - Italy - Ireland - Japan - Kenya - Malaysia - Mexico - Nepal - New England - New York - Pacific Northwest USA - Singapore - Spain - Thailand - Turkey - Vietnam

USA MAINLAND SPECIAL SALES
Bulk purchases (10+copies) of the Travel Bugs series are available at special discounts for corporate use. The publishers can produce custom publications for corporate clients to be used as premiums or for sales promotion. Copies can be produced with custom cover imprints. For more information write to Special Sales, Prentice Hall Travel, Paramount Communications Building, 15th floor, 15 Columbus Circle, New York, NY 10023.

Printed in Singapore

A DISCLAMER
Readers are advised that prices fluctuate in the course of time and travel information changes under the impact of the varied and volatile factors that affect the travel industry. Neither the author nor the publisher can be held responsible for the experiences of readers while traveling. Readers are invited to write to the publisher with ideas, comments, and suggestions for future editions. The publisher and the author expressly disclaim any responsibility for any liability, loss or risk, personal or otherwise which is incurred as a consequence, directly or indirectly, in the use of this book.

SAFETY ADVISORY
Whenever you're traveling in an unfamiliar city or country, stay alert. Be aware of your immediate surroundings. Wear a moneybelt and keep a close eye on your possessions. Be particularly careful with cameras, purses, and wallets, all favorite targets of thieves and pickpockets.

CHINA

Text by Frederick Fisher

With contributions from
Irene Khng
Catherine Khoo
Morten Strange

Editors
Irene Khng
Zhen Ai Ling
Catherine Khoo

Prentice Hall Travel

New York   London   Toronto   Sydney   Tokyo   Singapore

CONTENTS

INTRODUCTION

Welcome To China 1
Intrigue of China - Connoisseurs' Buffet
    Fast Facts 3

HISTORY, GOVERNMENT & ECONOMY

Kingdom and Dynasties – History ....
.... 11
Enter A New Era
    Chronology of Dynasties 13
    Qin Shihuang & the Great Wall of
        China 15
    The Soong Sisters 22
    The People's Republic of China:
        Principle Events 25

A People's Republic – Government ..
.... 27
    Mao Zedong, the Great Helmsman
        28
    Zhou Enlai - the Small Mountain ..
        30
    Saga of the Gang of Four 33
    Deng Xiaoping, the Survivor 34

Forward March – Economy 37
Industrial Economic Transformation - Fuel and Power - Industrial Mores - Communications, Transport, Money, Banking & Finance - Emerging Changes on the Industrial Scene
    Autonomous Economic Zones ... 45

PHYSICAL PROFILE

**Gorges, Glens & Greenery –
Geography & Climate** 49
Climate - Flora and Fauna
    The Mighty Shan - Mountains of
        China 53
    Birding in China 59

MEET THE PEOPLE

Tons of Hans – People 63
More than One Billion People - Ethnic Diversity - Minority Nationalities - South - West - North-central - Northeast - Other Areas
    Sex and Birth Control in the PRC ..
        66

Deeper Meanings – Religion 75
Confucianism - Taoism - Buddhism - Christianity - Islam - Judaism - Freedom of Worship
    Confucius 78

Treasures & Pleasures – Performing & Literary Arts 87
Beijing Opera - Acrobatics - Literature - Contemporary Chinese Painting - Architecture - 20th Century Contributions
    Mei Lanfang - Master of the Opera
        89
    Musical Instruments 91
    Tang Dynasty Poets 94
    Lu Xun the Writer 97

CONTENTS

Han Suyin - the Romanticist 98
The Folk Artist - Qi Baishi 100
The Painter of Horses - Xu Beihong
.... 101

**Trades & Traditions – The Crafts ......
.... 107**
Motifs and Symbols - The Fine Art of Chinese Ceramics
  Mighty Dragon, Creature of Good .
.... 112
  Jade, Virtuous and Valuable 114
  Cloisonne 118

FOLLOW THAT BUG

Grandeur & Splendor – Beijing .. 125
Orientation - Heart of the City - Forbidden City - Imperial Parks & Gardens - Beijing Environs - Chengde - Beidaihe the Summer Capital - Tianjin, Centrally Administered Municipality - Shopping - Dining
  Grand View Garden 135
  Oldest Observatory in China ... 136
  The Bell King 138
  Legends of the Great Wall 144
  Beijing (Peking) Duck 151

**Northern Hinterlands – Manchuria .
.... 155**
Qingdao - Yantai - Dalian - Liaoning Province - Shenyang - Changchun - Harbin - Other Acitivites in Heilongjiang
  Qu Fu, Shandong Province 159
  Yalu River Border with North Korea

.... 168
  Ice Carving Capital of the World ...
.... 170
  Heilongjiang Steam Locomotives ..
.... 171

Paris of the East – Shanghai 175
Shanghai Architecture - Shanghai Circuit - Shanghai Environs - Having Fun in the Big City - Delightful Dining - Entertainment
  Chinese Freshwater Pearls 185

Venetian Triangle – Suzhou, Wuxi & Hangzhou 195
Wuxi - Hangzhou - Cultural Hangzhou - West Lake - Hangzhou After Hours - Arts and Crafts - Environs of Hangzhou - Shaoxing
  Yangzhou 202
  Palace of the Prince of Shi Jinhua -
.... 210
  Hangzhou Dragon Well Tea 212
  Hangzhou Cuisine 213
  Huangshan 214
  Moganshan 216

Zhejiang & Fujian – Southeastern Coast 219
Ningbo - Wenzhou - Fuzhou and Fujian Province - Quanzhou - Xiamen - Gulang Yu Island - Overseas Chinese Contribution
  The Free Economic Zone of Ningbo
.... 222
  Lacquerware of Fujian 228

CONTENTS

    Porcelain Cities 229
    Village of Xunpu 232
    Wu Yi Mountain 239

Jade-Clasp Mountains – Guilin & Environs 243
Guilin Environs - The River Li, the "Green Silk Belt"
    Yangzhou 246
    The Three Treasures of Guangxi 251

Simmering South – Guangzhou, Guangdong and Hainan 253
Guangzhou - Shopping - Sightseeing - Guangzhou Environs - Shenzhen - Shantou - Nanning - Hainan Island - Around Hainan Island
    Eating Cantonese 257
    Guangzhou Trade Fair 258
    Hong Kong 266
    The Bountiful Coconut Palm ... 270

Artery of the East – Three Gorges, Changjiang & Environs 273
Chongqing - Chongqing Environs - Sailing along the Changjiang - The Three Gorges - Wuhan - Jiujiang - Nanjing
    On a Public Steamer along the Changjiang 279
    Cruise Ships of the Changjiang 284
    Jingdezhen 290

Pandas & Parks – Sichuan, Yunnan & Xishuang Banna 295
Chengdu - Chengdu Environs - Leshan - Emeishan - Kunming - Kunming Environs - Xishuang Banna, Dai Autonomous Prefecture - China-Burma-Laos-Vietnam
    The Giant Panda 300
    The Stone Forest 306
    Dinner at a Dai Farmer's 313
    All China Minority Nationalities Athletic Meet 314

Heart of China – Inner Mongolia & the Ancient Capitals 319
The Grasslands - Hohhot, the Capital - Datong - Datong Environs - Taiyuan - Kaifeng - Zhengzhou - Luoyang Loop
    The Loess Plateau 322
    Mongolia People's Republic 323
    Ningxia Hui Autonomous Region 326
    The Martial Arts of the Shaolin Monastry 337
    Jun Porcelain, Luoyang tri-colored Glazed Pottery 339

Cargoes & Culture – Xian & the Silk Road 341
Xian, Ancient Chang'an - Xian, the City - Xian Environs - Lanzhou - Xining - Xining Environs - Qinghai Lake - Jiayuguan - Jiayuguan Environs - Dunhuang - Dunhuang Environs - Mogao Grottoes
    Passage of Silk and Art Treasures 344

CONTENTS

    The Buried Terracotta Army 346
    Banpo Village 348

Journey to the West – Xinjiang and Environs 361
Turpan - Urumqi - Kashgar
    Journey to the West, Then and Now 366

Tangkas and Mandalas – Tibet .. 375
Lhasa - Lhasa Environs - Xigaze - Gyantze - Zhanang
    The Potala Palace 379
    River on the Roof 383

WHAT TO DO

Wok Culture – Cuisine 389
Beijing Cuisine - Shanghai, Center of Fish and Rice Land - The Deep South - Cantonese Cuisine - The Hot Stuff - Sichuan Cuisine - Yunnan's Smorgasbord
    Dim Sum Teahouse 394
    Chicken Culture 395
    Essence of the Wok 396

Endless Choice – Shopping 401
Cloisonne - Porcelain - Lacquer Products - The List Goes On

EASY REFERENCE

Travel Tips 406
Supplement essential for travel planning

Glossary 413

Directory 416
Useful listings

Photo Credits 422

Index 423

MAPS

China 122
Beijing 126
Manchuria 156
Shanghai 176
Shanghai, Suzhou, Hangzhou & Wuxi 196
Suzhou 197
Wuxi Environs 200
Hangzhou 204
Southeastern Coast 220
South Coast 254
Guangzhou 259
Chongqing 274
Three Gorges of the Changjiang ... 282
Nanjing 291
Sichuan 296
Yunnan 305
Inner Mongolia & the Ancient Capitals 320
The Silk Road 343
Xian 349
Tibet 376

"Drift by boat upon the Great River, Massed waters touching

the sky's very edge

"Sky and waves suddenly split apart..."

Attaching importance to its symbolism, the favorites

are the lotuses, water-lilies, plum blossoms, peonies, chrysanthemums and magnolias.

The Hans, Huis, Manchurians, Mongolians, Miaos, Kazaks

Kirgiz, Uygurs and Tibetans are some of the nationalities living in a seemingly homogeneous China.

WELCOME TO CHINA

Introduction

"So Messer Niccolo and Messers Maffeo and Marco, the sons of Niccolo set out on their journey and rode on, winter and summer, till they came to the Great Khan, who was then at a city called Kemenfu, a large city and a wealthy one. ...You need only know that they were hard put to it to complete the journey in three and a half years because of snow and rain and flooded rivers and because they could not ride in winter as well. ...When the Great Khan knew that the Messers Polo were coming, he sent his couriers fully forty days journey to meet them, and they were well served and attended." - **The Travels of Marco Polo.**

Actresses from the Chinese Opera shyly posing after a performance.

Thus, it was said, Marco Polo reached the Forbidden City within the walls of Peking in the 13th century to meet and work for Kublai, the Great Khan of the Mongols, in the glorious days of the Yuan Dynasty (1271-1368). Marco Polo's story, as related by the story teller Rustichello of Pisa presents a fascinating background to adven-

The Great Wall creeps like a concrete serpent across the difficult terrain.

turous travelers today.

Modern travelers to China jet to Beijing, Shanghai and Guangzhou, the principal entry points as well as to fast developing Chinese cities from all over the world and while Marco Polo stayed in China for 17 years in order to roam the country according to the whims of his liege lord, today's tour could take an average of 3 weeks. Hundreds of cities are now open, with aeroplanes, coastal steamers, trains, buses, and automobiles ready to transport you to the far reaches of this vast country, once a mighty empire.

China's ancient history rollercoasted along with the imperial dynasties which started almost 2000 years ago; indeed her modern history is still chequered by cultural revolutions and its modern transition from communist rule to a more relaxed socialist governing process.

Every political event has left its mark on this most populous nation of the world, but buttressed by a deep sense of culture and philosophy, as far back as Confucian times, the Han Chinese (the majority of the Chinese today), have taken the trauma in their stride. The Chinese have proven to be a practical people whose operating credo must be to survive it all and simply get on with it!

Not less worn down by time and events are the Chinese culture, philosophical tenets and practices. Trades and traditions seem only to modernise but never to change; intellectual

Fast Facts

Geography: China has an area of 9.6 million sq km (3.7 million sq miles) 70 per cent of which is mountainous covering majestic plateaus and extensive mountain ranges which crisscross her western landscape. Of the many long rivers which drain her mountains, the best known and most important are the Changjiang (Yangtse), 6300 km, and the Huanghe (Yellow River), 5464 km.

Highest Point: The highest point is Mount Everest (Mount Qolmolongma) in the Himalayas at 8,848.13 m above sea level. It is also the highest point in the world.

Climate: China covers 5 climactic zones. The climate ranges from semi-tropical in the southwest to temperate, cold and dry in the northwest. Along the coastal areas of eastern China, rainfall is plentiful and the 4 seasons are fairly distinct. In contrast, the Yunnan-Guizhou Plateau in the southwest is so high that the temperature is fairly constant and where spring is known to prevail in all 4 seasons.

Population: 1.1 billion at the end of 1987.

Capital: Beijing (Peking)

Government: Since 1949, with the establishment of the People's Republic of China (PRC), the country has been entrenched in a Communist system of government. Power resides in the one party, the Chinese Communist Party (CCP).

The National People's Congress (NPC) is at the apex of state authority and comprises some 3,000 deputies from all walks of life. Among a number of critical functions, they also elect the president of the PRC and the premier (on nomination of the president) and several vice-premiers. The premier and his vice-premiers control the government through the State Council which is the executive organ of the NPC.

People: Despite the seeming homogeneity that China projects, the country actually comprises 58 nationalities. The **Han** (and their Muslim counterpart, the **Huis**) predominate representing 94 per cent of the Chinese population. The other nationalities make up the remaining 6 per cent of the population and live principally outside the main cities in China.

Religion: Some religious freedom is permitted in China but subject to the regulation of the Religious Affairs Bureau under the State Council. Amid prevailing centuries old philosophies such as Confucianism and Taoism which presented some of the basic tenets of Chines attitudes and thinking on the whole, are some of the principal religions of today, Buddhism, Islam and Christianity.

Language: Chinese understandably is the most widely used language in China. The Hans, the Muslims and the Manchus use the language on a regular basis while the other nationalities, having their own languages, have, at least a working knowledge of Chinese.

Only 18 other nationalities in China have a written script; the government helped 10 of them create their own written languages.

Economy: China is basically an agricultural country with farmers constituting 83 per cent (1989) of the population. Long term plans for economic development, however, include improving China's industrial output four-fold by the year 2000. Over recent years China's economic growth has been gaining momentum as China opens her doors to foreign investments.

Currency: The unit of the currency, *renminbi* (people's currency), is the *yuan*. Tourists, however, are obliged to use the FEC (Foreign Exchange Currency).

indulgences of the scholars of today are not terribly different from the ancient Chinese *wenren* – they still treasure beneficial friendships, literary and artistic activities. Some of the durability of Chinese culture can be evidenced in its vast range of products today, such as ceramics, silks, bronzes, carvings, paintings, and countless else – modernized by today's technology, but still a touch ancient in spirit.

China, with its people, culture, poli-

The camel caravan is still a form of transportation in the far west.

tics, is impossible to dismiss, even in volumes; however, seeing is believing. China today is a far cry from Marco Polo's – the revered Khan has an equivalent in the great helmsman Mao or leader Deng. Today's visitor sees a burgeoning country, whilst parking at posh hotels in capital cities, whose facilities for sightseeing, shopping, eating and accommodation are magically flung open by the flash of credit cards and hard currencies.

In the vast tapestry of China's history, today's modernization may only

are officially administered by the Federal Government, comprising officials of the Chinese Communist Party. Over 5,000 islands are listed, from the largest, Hainan Island, to the smallest rock projections of undersea mountains. Hong Kong is due to be absorbed in 1997.

Those in search of wildlife will not be disappointed, for, due to its vast and varied land mass, China has a large diversity of flora and fauna from the cold north to the tropical south. Harbin and Manchuria offer great tracts of forest where bears, tigers, moose, deer and other trophy animals attract the world's game hunters. Bird life is exemplified in China's red-headed crane which has been depicted by artists for millenniums. Ducks, swans, bustards and herons are also common in the north.

The popular Eternal Spring province of Yunnan swarms with a wealth of flora and fauna, extending from Kunming to Xishuang Banna where giant bamboo forests provide incredible beauty, shelter for creatures living in its domain, serviceable building materials as well as favorite food for the rare panda. (Bamboo shoots are also a popular delicacy enjoyed in Chinese stir-fried cuisine). Wild elephants still range in southern Yunnan while domesticated ones become living tractors to aid in construction work and harvesting the forests.

Leopards and tigers are rare, at times illegally hunted, and an endangered species, existing in decreasing habitats somewhat like the plight of the near

represent a small transition, but in terms of its recent history in this century, "ten thousand" miracles (especially economic ones) must be taking place everyday, everywhere.

Today's national territory of China is divided politically into 21 provinces and 5 autonomous regions. Three major cities, Beijing, Shanghai and Tianjin

Enter the Three Gorges of the Changjiang.

extinct panda.

From the mysterious, fanciful Yeti of Tibet to the edible snakes of Guangzhou's famous restaurant, China houses a plethora of plants and animals. Biologists and ornithologists vie with geologists and archeologists for the vast amount of interesting research available within the borders ranging from the Himalayas east to the China Sea.

Intrigue of China

Mystery is the most common description of the "Middle Kingdom" (Zhongquo). Our world today fantasizes China in films like **Lost Horizon** and **The Last Emperor** recreating the old world of Mongol hordes, imperial palaces, temples and pavilions. Few travel to China to see the ravages of the Cultural Revolution or the new freeways interlacing Beijing. The most traveled destinations are still the Great Wall, Changjiang's (Yangtse) Three Gorges, Xian's buried terracotta army, and the widely-acclaimed beauty of Guilin.

Those who feel compelled to delve further into the vast array of history soon become China addicts. The first visit opens the door with a tour to one or all of the above areas. Thousands of books and travel articles suggest the triangle of the 3 most beautiful cities of Hangzhou, Suzhou and Wuxi. Then one hears about visiting the grasslands of

The imposing magnificence of the Gate of Heavenly Peace in Beijing.

Inner Mongolia, living in a *yurt* and slicing hunks of mutton off a roasted quarter of lamb. The Marco Polo syndrome then urges the traveler to venture further to Urumqi of the Uygurs, and Lhasa Tibet, the far-reaching points of the top and bottom of the world.

There are famous mountains that can be climbed by ascending thousands of stone steps which have been in existence for hundreds of centuries. The extensive waterways of the Changjiang, Huanghe and the Grand Canal tempt the boat traveler while train enthusiasts can ride the Iron Rooster for days on end to cover the length and breadth of the country.

Interlacing airline routes provide quick access to favorite sites for those who face time constraints. The resort areas of Beidaihe and Dalien in the north, Hainan Island and others in the south tempt the woofer (well-off old folks) generation to spend a week on the beach while tempting tours of the Silk Road, ancient capitals, cycling and trekking are on the menu for enthusiasts of history or adventure travel.

Connoisseurs' Buffet

Antique memorabilia, art works, and handicrafts imbued with intense, intricate, artistic labor are valuable acquisitions, enameled cloisonne, porcelain vases, or a dozen Ming-style blue and white rice bowls can be pur-

The Bund in Shanghai at night.

chased for a few yuan. Classic sculptures in jade, coral, lapis-lazuli, and other gemstones may be fairly expensive while a mass-produced porcelain figure of Ho Ti (Laughing Buddha) is modest enough to take home. A silk rug bought directly in Tianjin's famous factory is as tempting as a black and white painting of Xu Beihong's famous prancing horses. Papercuts, colorful posters,

street artist renditions of mountains and flowers make shopping a treat for the visitor.

Not least of Chinese delights is its cuisine which tempts the palate with its variety. The more adventurous can seek out special restaurants, sample varieties of eel, snake, vegetarian, herbal food and other exotic dishes like fried bees, bear claws, moose nose, and frog soup — tales to be taken back and retold time and again to unbelieving friends and family.

Beijing Opera needs a hands-on experience to enjoy. Acrobats can entertain delightfully and the movie fare is unique with Shaolin-trained performers jumping over houses, off pagodas and belting enemies with artful kicks and body movements.

The "Middle Kingdom" is now demystifying itself for the jet-age visitors, who are now able to satisfy their curiosities as China unshackles the locks of communist rule.

The intrinsic cultural reasons for visiting China remain; mandatory visits to communes and factories have been dropped in favor of the hundreds of historic sites now open for visitation. As interest in them grows, more of such sites are being uncovered and some are undergoing restoration work.

Special interest and longer term visitation are now common where, for instance, a course in Chinese language is offered at the People's University in Beijing in a package including air-fare, accommodation on the campus, classes and excursions around the country.

Whilst the majesty of her past is indeed unlikely to be matched, it is nevertheless exciting for the modern Marco Polo to witness the transition of today's Zhongquo, the ascending dragon of the 21st century.

KINGDOM AND DYNASTIES

History

China, home of one of the world's earliest civilizations has 4,000 years of written history and an immensely rich cultural heritage. The name, China, began only with the Qin Dynasty (221–206 BC), as it was known prior to this as Tschin, Tschina, or Tzinistan to the early travelers. It is today called Zhongguo in Hanyu pinyin.

Primitive man was thought to have lived here a million years ago. Fossils of Ape Man (*Yuanmou* Man) were found in Yunnan Province, while *Lantian* Man remains were discovered in Lantian, Shaanxi Province. They were supposedly walking the earth some 700,000 years ago and the slant-browed Peking Man, walked erect, used simple tools and fire, and lived in the caves of Zhoukoudian near Beijing.

Matriarchal clan communes were recorded in the Yangshao culture, in the village of Banpo near Xian, some 6,000 years ago.

One of the figures from the Ming Tombs, Beijing.

Zhoukoudian, incongruous site of Peking Man, said to have walked the earth 500,000 years ago.

Langshan culture revealed patriarchal communes 1,000 years later and showed the glimmerings of royal trappings and a class society. Archeologists determined the existence of these cultures from the remains of prehuman and human bones, weapons, tools, and pottery found in civilization sites.

The pre-dynasties and dynasties evolved in the central plains along the Huanghe (Yellow River). Among the earliest known, the Xia (2205-1766 BC) and Shang (1766-1122 BC) began dynastic periods before China became unified. During this period tribal communities existed and were constantly clashing with each other, striving for power.

The **Xia**, established under its first leader, Yu, were practical and innovative: they set up flood control and built irrigation systems. This period of pre-unified China saw the class society emerge; palaces and trappings rose in evidence and slave labor was imposed to facilitate grandiose projects.

Under the leaders of the **Shang**, the next dynasty, agriculture and animal husbandry grew and farming skills were developed. Sericulture, the silk enterprise, swelled from discovery to production on a large scale and as a result mulberry trees fed the worms who wove their filaments of fine thread. Workers sweated the threads from the cocoons and developed the reels and spools to make twisted strands for weaving and thence to the most-fabulous silks. Bronze

Chronology of Dynasties

Yuanmou Man	1.6 million years ago	- Eastern Han	AD 25–220
Lantian Man &	500,000 –	Six Dynasties Period	220 – 580
Peking Man	700,000 years ago	- Period of the Three Kingdoms	
Upper Cave Man	18,000 years ago	- Northern + Southern Dynasties	
Xia Dynasty	2205–1766 BC	Sui Dynasty	581 – 618
Shang Dynasty	1766–1122 BC	Tang Dynasty	618 – 907
Zhou Dynasty		Period of the Five	
(Western Zhou)	1122– 771 BC	Dynasties (north)	907 – 960
Eastern Zhou	770– 221 BC	+ 10 Kingdoms (south)	
- Spring + Autumn		Song Dynasty	960 – 1279
Period	770– 476 BC	- Northern Song	960 – 1127
- Warring States		- Southern Song	1127 – 1279
Period	476– 221 BC	Yuan Dynasty	1279 – 1368
Qin Dynasty	221– 206 BC	Ming Dynasty	1368 – 1644
Han Dynasty	206 BC–AD 220	Qing Dynasty	1644 – 1911
- Western Han	206 BC–AD 09	First Republic of China	1911 – 1949
- (Xia Dynasty)	AD 09– 23	People's Republic of China	1949 –

smelting and casting also developed under the Shangs. Oracle bones and inscriptions on the metal vases and pots revealed tales of life and the culture of the Shang. History was being recorded in pictorial and written form as language developed gradually from pictographs into stylized symbols. Slave struggles were evident in the social order and among their beliefs and practices tombs of the leaders also encased immolated servants and attendants along with the royal personage, in preparation for the afterlife.

The Shangs later lost their power to the Zhou (Western Zhou 1122 - 770 BC and Eastern Zhou 770-221 BC). The definition is due to the relocation of capitals, as the latter group moved from Chang'an (Xian) area to Luoyi (Luoyang, Henan Province).

This is a confusing period to casual readers of Chinese history, known as the Spring and Autumn period (770-476 BC), then the Warring States period (476-221 BC). It was a transitional phase in the social and economic order from the practice of slavery to feudal society. Smelting and iron-mongering developed, which led to the production of plows, axes, hoes and tools for the agrarian community. Class rule developed above the levels of slaves and commoners and a landlord group now emerged into the rebellious spirit of the rapidly changing times.

Historical records reveal the existence of over 140 princely states during the Spring and Autumn period which shrunk later to 7 such states as the Warring States period took over. Qi, Chu, Yan, Zhao, Han, Wei and Qin were

Cave carving of Sakyamuni outside the ancient capital of Datong.

the survivors in the intense struggle for power. The teachings of both Confucius and Mencius attempted to calm the warring in favor of peace and education. Different ideologies competed during this time: Mo Tse, the Mohist School; Lao Tse and Zhuang Tse, the Taoist School; and Shang Yang and Han Fei, the Legalist School; they all contested for a place beside the thrones of the developing dynasties.

Among the positive results of the struggles was an emergence of literature and the arts; poems and songs appeared in the south called Chu Ci (Ballads of Chu). It was obviously better times and more than 50 nationalities were identified as friendship and unity developed; the slaves became self-reliant peasants as the feudal society established and consolidated.

Qin Dynasty (221-206 BC) began with Qin Shihuang (self-proclaimed First Emperor of unified China). Qin ended the embroglio of the Warring States when he seized power and established the first centralized, unified, multinational feudal state in Chinese history. He fostered feudal landlordship, developed communications and standardized the written language, currency, and weights and measures.

Qin turned the stone barricades of individual states into the beginnings of the Great Wall, which in modern terms can be visualized as an elevated freeway traversing the countryside. It provided towers that linked village life at

Qin Shihuang and the Great Wall of China

China is the longest continuous civilization in the world, its culture going back 4,000 years. Standing as a paramount symbol of China's achievement is the Great Wall, known throughout the land as the Wall of 10,000 li (equivalent to 3,000 miles). The man credited with this colossal human feat, the longest man-made construction in the world stretching round one-twentieth of the earth's circumference, is Qin Shihuang.

There were walls before Qin's time. During the period of the Warring States, individual states built walls to keep out rival armies. It was only when Qin unified the whole of China - from the sea to the barbarian fringes, that the thought of constructing the Great Wall was mooted.

Why was the Great Wall of China built? Here, the personality of its creator is inevitably linked with his creation. In 246 BC, Prince Cheng, barely 13 years of age, assumed the throne of Qin. Already his tumultuous childhood and alleged charges of his illegitimacy had done much to affect his psychological well-being. Added to that, the Queen Mother's scandalous involvement with his Grand Counsellor during the first years of his reign had eroded his confidence in his family and advisors, so much so that he grew up suspicious of everybody, learning to rely entirely on his own judgment.

At age 38 he managed to unite the whole of China. Deciding he needed a grander title, King Cheng, ruler of Qin, named himself Shi Huang Ti, the First Sovereign Emperor. Already he had become obsessed with the idea of his own death (having narrowly escaped a few attempts on his life) and he had a morbid premonition that his work would be undone unless the most complicated accords were made in heaven. This fear of his mortality led to his tendency towards megalomania. He embarked on a policy of building monuments to his own glory whenever possible. The Great Wall remains his most awe-inspiring contribution to the world - a symbol of his own enormity as well as a useful defence against the northern "barbarians".

If the Great Wall became a symbol of greatness for Qin Shihuang, it also became a symbol of personal suffering endured by the hundreds of thousands who were forced to labor under barbarous conditions. The wall was built with the accumulated effort of men toiling in extreme seasonal heat and cold, lashed by rain or hail, ill-fed and housed in inadequate makeshift camps. They had to shape granite blocks, dig trenches and force the wall up hillsides so steep that historians believed the bricks must have been tied to the tails of mountain goats. Men dropped from malnutrition and exhaustion and their bodies were thrown into the trenches where the foundations were being laid as a form of impromptu burial, thus earning the wall the gruesome epithet of "The Longest Cemetery on Earth".

Today, as one climbs the ramparts, perhaps a quiet moment should be spent reflecting, not on one man's glory, but on the perseverance and suffering of a nation of men who gave the world one of its most enduring monuments, the Great Wall of China.

their base; these towers communicated via messengers, mirrors, and smoke signals. Military protection became feasible as troops could be rushed to trouble spots led by horse-cart drawn officers and combined military operations against rivals were carried out for the first time with great success.

When the first emperor Qin reigned, the name China was created and it was Qin who realized the early splendors of regal living. Remnants of palaces, artifacts of great curiosity, and beginnings of burial tombs reflected the life-style of those times.

Next following were 2 watershed periods of Chinese history, that is, the Western Han (206 BC-AD 9) and the

A section of the Great Wall at Mutianyu with 22 watchtowers.

Eastern Han (AD 25-220), both of the same period as the Roman Empire (27 BC-AD 395). In 206 BC, a petty official, Liu Bang, established the Western Han Dynasty and after a long interval developed a centralized landlord-class state government. Commerce flourished with the increasing number of cities linked along the waterways. Foreign trade opened up as traders from the Middle East found their way into the vast land of China, thus beginning the Silk Road through Central Asia.

In the year 25, Liu Xiu, an educated

Wu Guang in 209 BC led to the Lulin (Greenwood) Army uprising. The Chi Mei (Red Eyebrows) Army in AD 17-18 and the Huang Jin (Yellow Turbans) in AD 184 were the largest peasant mutinies in 700 years. They overthrew the 2 dynasties, swept away the hereditary landowners in power, and left chaos on the plains. Thus began the warlord era and a period of uncertainty and strife.

The Han Dynasty, over a span of 426 years, represented an era of enormous cultural, intellectual and scientific advancement during which discoveries, inventions and great thinking and traditions were to influence the lives of the Chinese, even 2,000 years later to the present times. A famous Han historian, Sima Qian wrote the first complete general history of China in his **Shi Ji** (Historical Records), while the distinguished thinker Wang Chong wrote **Lun Heng** (Discourses Weighed in the Balance). Han Dynasty scientist, Zhang Heng invented a seismograph and an astronomical instrument propelled by water power and Zhang Zhongjing wrote **Shang Han Lun** (A Treatise on Flowers), which had an important place in medicine.

Silk fabrics were distributed by the Silk Road traders and were already well known to the world during the Han Dynasty. The wife of Chen Baoguang of the Western Han invented a device to weave raised designs on fine silk, improving the technique of manufacturing exquisite fabrics. The invention of paper during Han times was a major

landed mandarin and a member of the Han royal house, established the Eastern Han Dynasty during which feudal economy continued to develop while various social contradictions formed. These began to grow and peasant uprisings eventually toppled the Western and Eastern Han Dynasties.

The revolts led by Chen Sheng and

contribution to world culture; primitive paper appeared to be in existence as early as the Western Han. Cai Lun of the Eastern Han, collating the experience of his forbears, used tree bark, bast fibre and pieces of cloth as material to make paper, thereby greatly improving previous methods. Buddhism entered China at this time and Confucian philosophy became the mainstream of education and politics.

China then divided again as the warlords of the **Three Kingdoms** battled for control and then reunited for a half century during the Western Jin (220-580). This era was a succession of dynasties north and south of the Changjiang (Yangtse), of which 24 were short-lived as the warlords perpetually raided each other, killing thousands, destroying cities and resurrecting the old feudal society of landlords with its incumbent labor service.

The prevailing disorder gave Buddhism scope and a wide appeal in China. Buddhist monks spread the teachings of *Sakyamuni* (historical Buddha) and carved images inside grottoes and on mountain sides. Temples spread on both sides of the Changjiang as the people were proselytized into the religion. At this time dynasties changed rapidly as warlords competed for the throne in China.

Progress of civilization again wound its way through the chaos of change. Again it was a watershed of advancement in discoveries and new scientific thinking. The Grand Canal was excavated by the Sui (581–618) stretching from Luoyang to Hangzhou, the northern and southern capitals. Zu Chongzhi computed the ratio between circumference and diameter, as Pi 3.1415926 and 3.1415927. His main technical equipment at this time was an abacus. Agriculture continued to thrive as methods, equipment, and irrigation improved. Metallurgy was sophisticated and advanced as Qiwu Huaiwen introduced the method of pouring molten pig iron on wrought iron to smelt it into steel.

Science, culture, medicine, pharmacology, and unfortunately for the world, the invention of gun powder continued to change the nation. Woodblock printing developed in the early Tang years, disseminating the works of literature, art, and poetry. China reached her peak in terms of cultural and scientific advancement during the Tang Dynasty (618–907) which was undoubtedly her Golden Age.

Peasant uprisings put an end to the Sui and Tang Dynasties while the undaunted merchants of trade goods were at the height of Silk Road traffic. Safaris of laden camels trekked across the Loess Plateau, the mighty Gobi Desert, the vast plains, through the mountains, and gathered at the trade centers in Central Asia and then dispersed again to destinations in India, Burma, and Persia. Such was the activity along this famed route.

From 907 to 960 China underwent again a period of fractional dispute among emerging warlords. The era of

Emperor Qianlong of the Qing Dynasty in his rightful place.

the **Five Dynasties** of the north and Ten Kingdoms of the south saw the Liao, Song, Western Xia, Jin and Yuan Dynasties in the north successively struggling for power while the south divided into Ten Kingdoms.

The **Songs** (960-1279) took over much of the land from their northern capital of Kaifeng from 960-1127 until the northern invasions by the Jin. For safety they moved to Hangzhou in the south for another 150 years during which culture bloomed. Military power declined during the Song period as refinement and the gentler arts prevailed. The compass was invented or introduced and navigation in the 11th century opened the seas to transportation and exploration. Agriculture, science and handicraft developed. Cotton was planted to produce a textile industry. A woman laborer by the name of Huang Daopo improved cotton spinning and weaving and, as a result, cheaper and more durable cloths were available for the masses. The movable type was reputed to be developed which helped to advance printing and literature by a gargantuan leap. It was a period where pottery and porcelains began to show refinement; Song dynasty ceramics are collected for its historical and aesthetic value today, at princely prices in the auction rooms of fine art.

It was at this time that China faced the restless and menacing Mongols in the north. It became increasingly difficult to put the Mongols down and after repeated attempts over decades they finally breached the Great Wall, descending from the north. Kublai Khan overcame the last remnants of resistance in 1279 and established the **Yuan** Dynasty (1279-1368) in China. The Venetian, Marco Polo, traversed China, mingled with the Mongols and informed an unbelieving world about the kingdom of Cathay. Prosperous industry and trade, more inventions, fascinating wealth, grandiose palaces, trained armies, and a sybaritic life style characterized this short era.

Peasants again rose in revolt to shrug off the yoke of foreign imperialism, and by 1368 the Mongols were defeated and the **Ming** Dynasty (1368-1644) was installed, bringing an era of peace, prosperity and further artistic developments such as in porcelains, painting, literature, furniture, to the capital at Chang'an, now called Xian. The Forbidden City was built to move the capital to Peking and the emperors devised elaborate tombs for their imperial descendants. Jesuits, among them Matteo Ricci, flooded the country and made their way into court life, advising the imperial families on western and Christian ways. They reported a remarkable civilization which later declined with the increasing power of the court eunuchs, at the expense of weak emperors, and also court abuses at the dire expense of the peasants.

Towards the end of Ming rule, famines ravaged the countryside and warlords again cropped up like snakes regrowing heads after being decapitated. Manchu tribesmen asserted themselves in the northeast and raided close to the capital. Imperial armies were weak, often unpaid and led by generals who themselves desired to be territorial emperors instead of pledging allegiance to the throne. The Ming downfall was actually brought about by rebel peasant armies led by leaders such as Li Zicheng, before the Manchurian armies forced through the Great Wall. The last Ming Emperor hanged himself in Coal Hill Park next to the Imperial Palace.

The Manchus, unlike the Mongols, integrated themselves with the Chinese while still in Manchuria. Having established the **Qing** Dynasty (1644-1911) in China, however, they kept political control firmly in their own hands while they adopted court and administrative systems.

The Manchus used defecting Ming generals to overcome the whole of the Chinese empire. Some, such as Wu Sangui eventually double-crossed the Qings, rebelled and then had to be suppressed. By 1683 the Qings had quelled the last uprising in Taiwan and unified the country once again.

In foreign relations, with the exception of the Emperor Kang Xi (1654-1722) who dealt extensively with the Europeans particularly the Jesuits, the Manchus on the whole were more restrained in their dealings with the West. They asserted control over the foreigners by restricting them to Canton and regulating the tea and silk trade. The English brought in opium from India and this became a lucrative trade for their merchants, draining the silver wealth of the country. Tension ensued when the Qing government tried to stop the opium trade. This led to open hostilities resulting in the Opium Wars (1839-42) which ended with unhappy consequences for China.

The Opium War ended in favor of the English with the signing of a treaty forcing 5 ports open. China continued to be further divided and weakened by the foreign powers, namely, the Russians, Germans, British, French and the Japanese, in the scramble for concessions. This meant that each power secured rights and concessions to certain territories and cities in China greatly in their favor but at China's expense. Fur-

Statue of Sun Yatsen, father of the Chinese republic, in front of the Sun Yatsen Memorial Hall in Guangzhou.

ther turmoil in the country was reflected in numerous uprisings like the Taiping Rebellion (1851-64), anti-Qing revolts and the Boxer Rebellion, a 55-day seige of the foreign embassies in 1900.

The failure of the latter gave the foreigners an opportunity to force their systems of government on the reluctant Qing. Pu Yi the last emperor, a mere boy at the time, resigned as Dr Sun Yatsen led the Nationalists (Kuomintang) in the revolution of 1911, also known as the "Double Ten" because it broke out on the tenth day of the month.

Enter a New Era

Sun Yatsen, the idealist rallied the people and the generals to overthrow the Qing government. He founded the Nationalist Party, designated the Kuomintang and on New Year's Day of 1912 declared the **Republic of China** (1911-49) a new democracy on the horizon.

Within 2 years Sun yielded to a former Qing Dynasty military leader, General Yuan Shikai who took over as a democratic proponent but soon turned into a classic dictator executing opponents and controlling supposed free election results. He put out a reward-bearing hit list on the Soong and Chiang clans who took refuge in Japan. Yuan died in 1916 leaving the country to the warlords once again with no forceful person to unify China.

The Soong Sisters

The modern history of China is interwoven with the fascinating family of Charlie Soong (Han Choshun) and "Mammy Soong" (Ni Kweitseng), their 3 daughters and 3 sons. Charlie was from Hainan Island who endeared himself to American missionaries while a student at the Methodist Universities of Vanderbilt and Trinity in southern United States before graduating as a Methodist minister.

Charlie gained his wealth as a publisher of bible China; he became an intimate friend of Sun Yatsen's and the banker for the revolution. Under the matriarch "Mammy" their 3 daughters went on to achieve individual fame and also became the wives of 3 of the most famous personalities in modern Chinese history. A famous Chinese saying can be applied to the Soong sisters: "Once upon a time there were 3 sisters, Ailing, Chingling and Meiling. One loved money, one loved power, and one loved China." The Soong sons became the financiers of the pre-revolution and the resultant contest between the Kuomintang (KMT) and the Communists.

Soong Ailing was reputed to be Charlie's favorite, opting for finance early in life. Her father took her to business meetings, rare in the days of closet-kept daughters and Ailing soon developed a financier's acumen. She was eventually sent to Weslayan College in Macon, Georgia, the first chartered college for women in America. The story of her education is a classic in the annals of Sino-American relations of the early 1900s.

After graduating Ailing returned to Shanghai and became the English language secretary for the energetic Sun Yatsen. She became the second wife of H H Kung, Finance Minister, and bore 4 children. Her daughter Rosamond married a KMT Officer, Jeannette became a New York heiress, her son David a New York financier and Louie a famous Dallas, Texas, oil man. Thus the Soongs continued the "dynasty".

Charlie being obsessed with American education, sent Meiling and Chingling to Clara Potwin's College Preparatory School in Summit, New Jersey. Letters reveal that Chingling, known as Rosamond was a serious quiet 15-year-old. Meiling, a "mischievous jolly little butter ball" 9-year-old, was curious about everything in the world. The girls developed lasting friendships which turned into future political alliances with the Americans.

Chingling spent the next 5 years in the United States, till the age of 20, in constant correspondence with her father and his friend Sun Yatsen. After her return to China, the family were in exile in Japan with other leaders, under a sentence of death imposed by the warlord Yuan. Sun Yatsen, a family friend and the "favored uncle" of the Soong children, became enamored of the young Chingling. Charlie in turn became angry and adamant, his Christian beliefs tortured – he refused to allow them to associate. On the family's return to China he arranged a marriage for his recalcitrant daughter.

Under such social disorder again and disappointment with the failure of the Chinese Revolution of 1911, the country was just ripe for the spirit and ideas introduced by the Russian Revolution of 1917. Mao Zedong, on the first of July, 1921 with others held the First National Congress in Shanghai and the Communist Party of China, vanguard of the Chinese proletariat was born. Marxism-Leninism spread over the immense areas of Russia and China into a third or more of the world's population.

By 1923 the Nationalists and the Communists decided to join forces to suppress the warlords of the north. On Sun Yatsen's death in 1925 Chiang Kaishek was appointed Commander-in-Chief of the National Revolutionary Army and leader of the Nationalists.

The aggressive stubborn young woman escaped, took passage on a ship to Kobe, Japan and became the second wife of Sun Yatsen and a strong supporter of his beliefs.

After his death the serious revolutionary widow of the country's idol Sun Yatsen, disparaged the warlord Chiang Kaishek and the communist Mao Zedong, and instrumented a short-lived third party in the embryonic new nation. Respected and honored, Madame Sun spent her life in the shadows of the turbulent People's Republic, in a garden home in Beijing, the pre-palace residence of the last emperor, Pu Yi. Today, it is a favorite museum for students of modern Chinese history and contains a lot of Sun Yatsen's memorabilia.

Meiling, relying on her effervescent personality completed school in the United States, weaving her way into American society as the "token Chinese", undoubtedly eased by the Soong's monetary influence. She attended Wellesley College in Massachusetts while her brother T V Soong, studied at Harvard. She graduated a graceful young woman armed with a southern accent. In 1917 she returned to Shanghai and energetically asserted herself in the international society.

A year later, Charlie died of a suspected stomach cancer. This marked the last time the Soong sisters would be together in their lifetime.

Chiang Kaishek and Soong Meiling met off and on over a period of years. Chiang was the father of the successor President of Taiwan, Chiang Chingkuo. He divorced, married again, begat a Japanese son, took a concubine, and was continually enamored with Soong's younger daughter. On 1 December 1927 the internationally celebrated marriage between the Generalissimo and Soong Meiling took place in the Soong home in Shanghai. It was reported that a thousand people were entertained at the reception in the ballroom of the Majestic Hotel on the Bund. Another thousand cheering friends gathered outside. In the evening they left the city with 200 bodyguards and headed for the Green Gang monastery on the mountain at Moganshan, Hangzhou.

The turbulent years of the civil war, exile in Taiwan, friendship in the highest offices of the United States including President Franklin Roosevelt's, and the notorious appellations of "Dragon Lady" and "woman behind the throne" gave Meiling a complete lifestyle opposing her sisters' – Chingling leading an austere life protecting the name and life work of Sun Yatsen and Ailing overshadowing her husband as a financier.

After the Generalissimo died in 1975 Meiling spent the rest of her life in seclusion at the David Kung estate in Lattingtown, Long Island, New York. Soong Chingling lived out her life on her estate in Beijing, finally succumbing to leukemia in May, 1981. Soong Ailing, the financier, lived out her life ensconced in the wealthy society of her Americanized family.

The joint effort of both the Nationalists and the Communists in putting down the warlords was highly successful. However, the efficiency of the Communists worried the Nationalists and by 1927 Chiang Kaishek began to eliminate competition by massacring thousands of the peasants and workers who supported the Communists. Here began the leadership of Mao Zedong, whose impact on China is not to be underestimated: 100,000 of Mao Zedong's army retreated in 1934 on the disastrous Long March; 20,000 survived, literally holing up in in the arid plateaus of the loess hills and valleys surrounding Yanan in Shaanxi Province. History repeats itself. This was the same area from where the Qin Dynasty began the unification of China 2000 years before.

Freize on the Memorial to the Martyrs of the 1927 Uprising, Guangzhou.

In 1936 the Nationalists and the Communists united again against a foreign aggressor, Japan. However, this truce fell through after the Japanese surrender and the Nationalists particularly the 4 big families, the Chiangs, Kungs, Chens and Soongs, began capitalizing on the fortunes of the war. Chief among these families was the family of Chiang Kaishek himself, the Soong clan, relatives of his wife Meiling Soong or Madame Chiang Kaishek, the Dragon Lady. In the final confrontation the Nationalists retreated to Taiwan, taking with them China's treasures and the businessmen of the time. The stage was set for the next 40 years of capitalism emerging on Taiwan and socialism on mainland China.

Mao Zedong on 1 October 1949 inaugurated the new nation, the People's Republic of China (1949-present) on the same platform of the Gate of Heavenly Peace, where emperors had been installed during the Ming and Qing Dynasties. The 2 Chinas of Taiwan and mainland China continued to fracture world opinion and cooperation for the next 30 years until President Nixon sent his secret emissary, Henry Kissinger, to breach the chasm. Events and plans lighted the torch of idealism sometimes enhancing, often destroying itself during this era.

First October 1949 began the kaleidoscope of turbulence under communism, an ideologically opposing system of ideas from the entrenched dynastic

The People's Republic of China : Principle Events

Hundred Flowers Movement of 1956–57 was intended to reassure the scientists, artists and academics that they had a place in the grand plans and were encouraged to speak out. However, their criticisms of the bureaucracy, nepotism and failures of the communist way were harsher and more destabilizing than the Party had expected and they were finally penalized with incarceration and death in an anti-rightist campaign.

The Great Leap Forward (1958–60) concentrated on renewing the resources of the country. Nationalization abolished foreign and private ownership. Communes were formed to provide food and industrial products. Reforestation, extension of railroads, construction of buildings such as the Great Hall of the People were undertaken to reorganize the country from the devastation of imperialism, warlordism, invasion, and civil war.

The Great Proletarian Cultural Revolution took place from its inception in 1966 to the mid-70s. Mao Zedong rallied the young overenthusiastics people of the Red Guard to eliminate revisionist tendencies. The result is sometimes seen as an attempt to destroy history, the intellectuals, the artists and respect for the institutions of learning.

Zhou Enlai was the restraining hand during this period of unleashed destruction : he saved some of the historic treasures, and worked hard on China's foreign relations. However, within China, universities were closed temporarily, the students sent to farms during the next 4 years to re-learn the basics of life and survival. City-bred youngsters were forced to do what farmers have done since time began. They stooped to plant rice seedlings, labored in thigh deep mud behind oxen, torturing muscles, tiring bodies to blot out thinking. Thus possibly grew a new generation of idealists, seeking democracy, though perhaps not realizing its impact or implication on the present structure.

Tiananmen Incident (June 1989). This became a vivid world news event of massive proportion. Tanks rumbled down Chang An Avenue while students in the great Tiananmen Square demanded democratic reform of their elders. Soon, an overwhelming sense of history replaying one of its more dramatic and tragic episodes filtered into the homes of people all over the world.

system. A red flag with a yellow crescent and stars waved over the communist land as Mao Zedong and his comrade Zhou Enlai created the idyllic land of the people. Slogans directed the Hundred Flowers Movement, Great Leap Forward and the 10-year Cultural Revolution. The infamous Gang of Four led by Jiang Qing, Mao's wife, however, subsequently subjected the nation to a series of regressive measures and it was a particularly unpleasant time. Deng Xiaoping, one of the many who suffered in their hands, emerged from home detention to lead China after Mao, with modernization and new political reassessments, blemished only somewhat by the Tiananmen incident which took place in front of the world's television revealing to the world, a rare occurence in China's political struggle from communist shackles.

China's present political structure remains communist, but the tentacles of capitalism appear to tempt away commitment to the Communist ideology. Predictions make out for China to head towards another great leap forward – perhaps out of the old ideologies to a freer and wealthier society.

A PEOPLE'S REPUBLIC

Government

Suspicion of foreigners began with the arrival of the Portuguese in Guangdong in 1517; the "Long Noses", with their deep set round eyes, fired a salute of cannons not knowing weapons were forbidden in the south. Apprehension filled the minds of the emperor's greeters and they instilled that feeling into the royal entourage.

Next came the Dutch and then the English. Fra Matteo Ricci founded the first Catholic mission and became a chronicler of history relating his adventures 200 years after Marco Polo. Like Polo he inveigled his way into the Imperial Court and became an adviser to the emperor. The Jesuits therefore became the inside contact for the Europeans to commercially invade the Middle Kingdom. Middle Kingdom refers to the middle of heaven from whence all royals received their eminence and around which the world revolved. One Ming emperor went to the extreme of destroying the entire Chinese fleet in order to achieve isolation, thus show-

A giant picture of Chairman Mao overlooks Tiananmen Square.

Mao Zedong, the Great Helmsman

"I was born in the village of Shao Shan, Hunan Province in 1893. My father's name was Mao Jensheng and my mother's Wen Ch'imei". So stated Mao Zedong to Edgar Snow, the American chronicler of the Long March in **Red Star Over China**. Mao related his autobiography to Snow over many evenings during the hiatus after the Long March. Mao's father was a moderately well-off peasant who was not particularly keen on studies but nonetheless young Mao was sent to school. When his father insisted that he worked on the farm, young Mao ran away from home to study in Changsha. It was here that he witnessed the execution of peasants who had come to the city to ask the officials for food during a period of famine.

During the turbulent years following 1911, Mao was actively involved in political movements with other students. In Beijing Mao came into contact with Marxist literature.

Mao told Snow that 3 books affected his life and belief in the people's struggle: The **Communist Manifesto, Class Struggle**, and a **History of Socialism**. The young radical in 1920 had become a Marxist destined to affect the lives of a billion people in his lifetime. He was one of the delegates at the first congress of Chinese communists held in Shanghai in 1921. Initially however, his views were not supported by other leaders of the Communist Party and it was not until 1935, in the course of the Long March, that his policy prevailed.

In that same momentous year 1920, he married another youth leader, Yang Kaihui, who was later killed by the Kuomintang. Yang was technically his second wife, the first marriage being an unconsummated child-marriage arranged by his parents. Mao's third wife was the notorious actress cum revolutionary, Jiang Qing who bore him two daughters. Madame Mao later gained fame as leader of the Gang of Four.

Mao was a writer throughout his career and was an epitome of the traditional Chinese "warrior poet". He never ceased writing generating poetry hand-in-hand with manifestos and lectures in political ideas and military concepts. An extract from the translated poem "Snow", one of Mao's best known poems :

This is the scene in that northern land;
A hundred leagues are sealed with ice,
A thousand leagues of whirling snow.
On either side of the Great Wall
One vastness is all you see.
From end to end of the great river
The rushing torrent is frozen and lost.
The mountains dance like silver snakes,
The highlands roll like waxen elephants,
As if they sought to vie with heaven in their
  height; and on a sunny day
You will see a red dress thrown over the
  white,
Enchantingly lovely!
Such great beauty like this in all our land
  scape
Has caused unnumbered heroes to bow in
  homage.

Mao, it must be said, was one of very few writers, who actually had the opportunity and attempted to realize the ideas that he put into his writing. During the 1939-49 civil war period, "On Coalition Government" attempted reconciliation with the Kuomintang. At the Seventh Congress of the Chinese Communist Party Mao was elected Chairman of the Central Committee and the Politburo, titles he held until his death.

The "People's Democratic Leadership" (1949) proclaimed the basic ideas of communist style socialism and Mao's "On the Correct Handling of Contradictions Among the People" (1957) launched the Hundred Flowers period of

ing the world they needed no outside assistance.

Envoys came bearing gifts to the palace at Beijing and returned taking gifts to their liege lords. They were treated well, and returned home excited by the adventure. Tales were rife with embellishment and ideas of how to trade with

free speech and free criticism. This effort was short-lived as it revealed the dissatisfaction underlying both the entire nation and within and outside the party. The so-called democratic dictatorship took advantage of its detractors' openness and carried out a drastic purge campaign.

Then came the "Great Leap Forward" from the mind and pen of Mao Zedong. The people were to take initiative to grow food and make steel in their own backyards, abandoning the communes in the cities. This led to the food crises and the disaster years attributed directly to Chairman Mao's little red book proclamations.

Lin Biao took over as Chairman and the ensuing struggle between the pragmatists (revisionists) and the party ideologues tore the country apart. At this time Kruschev was Premier of Russia and he parted from Mao, ridiculing his adventuristic flow of ideas. Conversely Mao became known as China's Kruschev with his dictatorial written manifestos. **Thought of Mao** produced an adoration of the venerable leader by 1965 and engendered a cult. However, a plot was brewing simultaneously within the Central Committee to get rid of the aging leader. The Great Proletarian Cultural Revolution was launched through a resolution at the eleventh Plenary Session of the Eighth Party Congress. It provided a means for Mao to get even with his opposition. Deng Xiaoping was relegated to jail-like retreat, other leaders destroyed. The resulting chaotic activities of the Red Guards almost destroyed the nation.

A summary of Chairman Mao Zedong: He rode to power on the back of the people, to lead the people from poverty, privation, starvation into a mighty nation with a nuclear bomb, modern industrialization, an army unsurpassed in number and equipment, technically trained and ideologically educated.

the 17th century, Europe was fascinated by the tales of the missionaries. The precious gifts of porcelain, cloisonne, intricate carvings and woven silk decorative panels became the rage in the sophisticated drawing rooms of the cognoscenti. Missionaries reported on the marvelous Confucian philosophies of the Chinese imperial courts. Education by examinations furthered the scholarly class and the emperors built munificent palaces. However, Qianlong (1735-96) decreed that there was no need for the European trade, that China was sufficient unto itself. Hence, Guangdong was the only port where a trickle of enticing goods could leave or enter. China traded its tea but only for silver, aggravating the British traders who preferred bartering with goods from their other colonies.

The Qings were continually concerned about the northern nomads and the rebellious groups within their own borders. The foreigners, believed under control, were tolerated for the silver they could bring. Marked points of history took over. The progressive reigns of

a population almost twice that of Europe. Ports were restricted however, frustrating the tempted marketeers.

When the Qings came to power in

Zhou Enlai - *The Small Mountain*

Zhou Enlai, the devoted follower of Mao Zedong, was born into a wealthy family in 1898 in Jiangsu Province. Thus, like Deng, he could afford to travel, first to Germany and then France in the 20's.

Zhou Enlai preceded Deng Xiaoping to France, organizing the roots of the future Chinese Communist Party (CCP) then called the China Socialist Youth Corps. A short stint in London and a year in Germany before returning to China via Russia in 1928, he met and began a long term friendship with Joseph Stalin, the guru of international communism. Soon after returning home he was elected to the Communist Party and the Politburo of the CCP's Sixth Congress. Like other embryo leaders of China, he attended the Sun Yatsen University to receive military instructions. Zhou Enlai was appointed political chief at Whampoa Academy, Guangdong, by Chiang Kaishek before the conflict in ideology kept the 2 men permanently apart. He gained the confidence of the young cadets destined to become the military and political leaders of the new era. Zhou was pre-eminent during the 30's, organizer of the Nanchang and Shanghai uprisings, Political Commissar and eventually General Commissar of the Army. Chiang was later to regret his training of Zhou and posted an $80,000 reward for his head during the civil war.

The appellation "Small Mountain" was applied because of his increasing assignments in diplomatic negotiations. In time Zhou became the chief diplomat in all world affairs of the CCP. The world came to know him better than Mao.

At one time he was the negotiator for Chiang Kaishek during the Sino-Japanese war but was unable to move Chiang in later peace negotiations as relations deteriorated.

Zhou was more modest than Mao Zedong and was considered the number two man in the party throughout the ascendancy of its era in China. There were those who thought he should precede Mao but loyalty to Mao was predominant through the agonizing formation of the party, the attempts at conciliation with the Kuomintang (KMT) under Chiang Kaishek, and the Long March.

As the chasm widened between the KMT and the CCP, Zhou tried to negotiate a coalition government. After World War II, 1945, the American Ambassador Patrick Hurley and General George Marshall attempted a reconciliation in Chongqing. It was Marshall's plan that eventually rehabilitated Germany and the war-torn countries of Europe. Neither could make progress with the adamant Chiang. His warlord background would accept no reconciliation, insubordination or disagreement. Eventually during the civil war, the people defeated the warlord and China became a socialist nation.

Zhou became premier and foreign minister from 1954 to 1958, working assiduously for peace. In 1954 he attended the Geneva Conference where he proposed the "Five Principles of Coexistence" for which he won recognition as the upholder of Asian nationalism against western imperialism. This was followed by subsequent missions such as the Sino-American ambassadorial talks. In 1957 he was the mediator

of Kangxi (1662-1722) and Qianlong (1735-96) deteriorated as less able emperors inherited the throne. The English forced their Indian opium into the land demanding silver in payment and thus denuding the Ming treasury. After the First Opium War (1839-42) the British military forced their way into Nanjing. Treaties were executed allowing further trade and territorial colonization. Shanghai and Guangdong were now open ports to foreigners. The people revolted in the Taiping uprising. During the Second Opium War (1857–60), the British and the French joined forces. Beijing was invaded and the summer palace burned in punishment.

Now many ports were forced open

between Russia and the European Communist parties of Poland, Hungary and Czechoslovakia. This was the period Kruschev reported to Russia and the world, the crimes and true nature of Stalin, denouncing previous policies and trying to break the Cold War. It was Zhou who tried to break the barriers of Taiwan and the United States.

In 1962, China's diplomacy took the opposite tack under the hardliners of the Politburo, demanding a choice between Russian or Chinese leadership of international communism. Zhou now had the task of fighting American imperialism or Soviet revisionism. These became trying times for the pacifist mountain of diplomacy as China became more isolated from the world. Only France, of the great powers, recognized the People's Republic of China while the Great Proletarian Cultural Revolution emerged racking the nation with a civil war.

It was a bitter period for the still eminent leader, torn between loyalty for Mao and the reality of his increasing senility. Zhou saved many of China's historic treasures from destruction by forcibly calling off the Red Guards in various instances. In 1971 Zhou led the country into the outer world when China gained membership into the United Nations and a diplomatic rapport with the United States was established. When Zhou died in 1976, he was mourned and revered far more among the Chinese people than even the Great Helmsman Mao Zedong. History recognizes *Shao Shan* (Small Mountain) as the rock foundation of modern China.

One of a group of revolutionary monuments on Tiananmen Square.

as the insidious invasion overcame all imperial control. Treaties were mere stamps of conquest, thousands of Chinese were forced into work-slavery; prostitution was rampant servicing the foreigners arriving without families and the infamous "Chinese and Dogs" prohibition was invoked in the foreign enclaves.

The Russians enlarged their railroad centers in Manchuria. The Germans entered the Bohai Sea and set up their headquarters at Qingdao. The Japanese easily conquered the Chinese, taking over Taiwan and Korea. The empire of the Qings was bleeding. The Boxer movement emerged in 1900 as the people revolted in the various enclaves of invasion. The "bloody" affair was predictably won by the foreigners combining their military might.

Sun Yatsen entered the political arena at this point fostering the overthrow of the empire and shaping the seething China into a new nation in 1911. A new era in history began with the establishment of the First Republic of China. Sun's followers were among

The People's Liberation Army.

the many Chinese forced into exile during the chaos of the deteriorating empire. They studied western ideology and the renditions of the mind of Karl Marx.

In World War I's peace treaty, the German territory in China was given to the Japanese, thus sowing further hatred of all foreigners, their entanglements, and their aggressive merchant-led governments. Russia assassinated their own imperials and the Communists formed Marxist-Leninist experiments of government for the people. They recognized China as an equal, took their leaders into their ideological schools and bred the Chinese Communist Party.

The end of World War II was the beginning of a new era for China, now having complete autonomy of her government, free of foreign interference. By aiding the Allies, they endeared themselves to the winners. Foreign enclaves dissolved, Japan departed and the puppet government of Manchuria dissolved. The civil war destroyed millions of Chinese. Mao Zedong (see History chapter), with his populace army defeated the warlord Chiang Kaishek, who retreated to Taiwan taking the merchant class and much of the nation's treasures and treasury with him.

The seeds of fear, sown by the Portuguese 4 centuries before, broke through the surface of the new government. Foreigners were now imperialist agents. Association with the elements of American democracy, adoration of God

Saga of the Gang of Four

1976 was a year of great significance in the history of the People's Republic. Zhou Enlai, the Small Mountain, died in January, Mao Zedong, the Great Helmsman, died in September and in October 1976 the Gang of Four were arrested as the Cultural Revolution came to an end.

The Gang of Four came into being at the beginning of the Cultural Revolution in 1966. Prior to this they were neither members nor even alternate members of the Central Committee (CC) of the Communist Party of China(CPC). At the time Jiang Qing, wife of Mao Zedong, did not hold any substantive position in the Party or government. Chang Chunchiao's position was higher: he was the Deputy Secretary of the Shanghai Municipal Committee and the head of its propaganda department. Yao Wenyuan was the editor-in-chief of Shanghai's Liberation Daily. Wang Hungwen was just an ordinary factory worker in Shanghai.

Although speculation and historians differ on the exact power source, Jiang Qing is credited as the Gang Leader, an eventuality of the time when Mao initiated the Cultural Revolution. The saga began with the writing of an article, "On the New Historical Drama, Hai Jui Dismissed from Office." Madame Mao was sent to Shanghai in 1964 to intervene in the cultural arena and produce plays (some examples being "The Raid on the White Tiger Regiment" and the famous ballet "The Red Detachment of Women") that exemplified the evil of imperialism and capitalism, while glorifying socialism. In 1965, the CC rejected Mao's intentions to distribute the tract in Beijing so he instructed Yao Wenyuan to write a new historical drama and to publish it in Shanghai. The Gang, then three, consorted to write, under Mao's editorial guidance, "On the New Historical Drama Hai Jui Dismissed from Office".

Thus began the Cultural Revolution, the formation of the Red Guards, an unmitigated disaster allowing gangs of errant students to lay waste the cultural and historical sites and the homes, schools, and lives of teachers, non-political dignitaries and whomever they chose to destroy. It also began the ascendancy of power of the Gang of Four and the shadow power behind the throne, Lin Biao. Lin Biao, a close friend of Mao since the days of the Long March, colluded and contested with Jiang. The Cultural Revolution called for the "overthrow of those in authority taking the capitalist road".

Lin Biao and Jiang Qing collaborated trading on Mao's prestige as the closest friend and current wife. The two directed their attack against the experienced cadres in order to improve their territorial conquest. Chang Chunchiao and Yao Wenyuan, centrally located in Shanghai, attacked people right and left in the mass media. Chang and Yao became members of the prestigious Politburo during the Ninth Congress of the CPC in 1969. Wang Huenwen, a mere worker, became the Vice-Chairman of the CPC shortly after. Deng Xiaoping returned to the fold in 1973 and Zhou Enlai literally wore himself to death combating the evils of the Cultural Revolution, saving hundreds of ancient historical sites from destruction.

On the sixth of October, 1976, Hua Kuofeng, Mao's successor, called an emergency meeting of the Politburo. The Gang of Four were arrested and their protégés rounded up. Lin Biao died in a mysterious plane crash. The **People's Daily**, Xinhua News Agency and the radio station were taken over. Troops were sent to the Gang of Four university strongholds in Beijing and Tianjin. The Nanjing Military Region assumed temporary control of Shanghai. Yao, Wang and their cohorts were removed from the CC. Shenyang, another control center, was temporarily placed under the command of the army. The whole affair resulted in an evidently well planned and well executed military coup against the invaders, called the Gang of Four. The gang leader, Jiang Qing, after lengthy court trials languished in custody for the rest of her life.

and the rule of the Pope was seen to endanger the innocent Chinese. By 1960 even the comrades of Russia withdrew from the country when the Chinese refused to submit their military to Kruschev. The Chinese Communist Party

Deng Xiaoping, the Survivor

Kan Tsekao was born in a small village 100 km from Chongqing (Chungking), Sichuan Province in 1904. He was the second child of the second wife of a Hakka landlord with 2 younger brothers and an older sister. His father had 3 other wives, part of the complex deteriorating feudal Chinese family system. Defeating the family lineage, he changed his name to Teng Hsaio-ping (Deng Xiaoping) on joining the Communist Party in 1925.

After leaving the Chinese equivalent of high school, he like other young students embroiled in the chaos of government of the 20's elected to go abroad in search of self-knowledge. Kan took courses for study in France in Chongqing (Chungking), graduating at the age of 16 among the top 10 students of his class. Young Kan who was made group leader of 92 students embarked for France in the summer of 1920. There he joined the Chinese Socialist Youth League which later became the Chinese Youth Communist League, the earliest Chinese Communist organization outside of China.

Zhou Enlai was the leader of the Party Branch at that time and he appointed Kan editor of a mimeographed fortnightly magazine, *Red Light*, where he proceeded to build his reputation as the editor. *Red Light* was distributed over Europe and in China. Deng eventually took over Zhou's post as leader of the European Chinese Communist Party and then returned to China. He spent some months studying at the Sun Yatsen University in Moscow, where the core of the future Chinese Communist Party (CCP) was forming.

In the early 30's, Mao Zedong's peasant-military strategy had lived through Chiang Kaishek's 4 annihilative operations. Deng a staunch supporter and organizer, was purged for the first of 3 times in his career, along with Mao's brothers and many others who criticized the Great Helmsman's plans.

In October 1934, Chiang Kaishek launched his fifth annihilation campaign to wipe out the Communists. Thus began the Long March as the remnants of the Communist forces fought their way out of encirclement at a high rate of attrition. Deng, returning from his banishment, became editor of the Red Army paper *Red-Star* *(Hung Hsing)* and eventually joined the Long March. The survivors of the event became the nucleus of the future leaders of China after the defeat of the Kuomintang in 1949.

Deng worked his way up through the party in the ensuing years, first as Mayor of Chongqing, Regional Commander of the Southwest territory, and by 1950 was a major economic manager and planner. In 1954-55 he became the Secretary of the Central Committee, Vice-Chairman of the National Defence Council, and Vice-Premier of the State Council. Inner party struggles ensued and the policy of purging those who disagreed, criticized or attempted power plays, was led by Deng. He was elected to the Politburo by the Fifth Plenum of the Seventh Party Congress held in April, 1955.

In August 1966, Deng was made Secretary-General and Standing Member of the Politburo. In October of that year, he made a self-critical speech at a meeting of the Central Committee and was denounced by the Red Guard as the second greatest capital-roader in the party. Deng retired until 1973. The Party had agreed not to expel him but to send him off to a cadre school to work and study. He became a worker serving rice and vegetables, and through a quirk of the bureaucratic system became head of the school, though he was still required to take part in physical labour.

By 1973 he emerged and appeared at state functions as Vice-Premier of the State Council and succeeded Zhou Enlai on his death 3 years later as Acting Premier. In the succeeding years he was accredited as the power mover, meeting foreign delegations and traveling as China's leader to other countries.

Deng Xiaoping is credited with the economic moves in modernizing all commercial aspects of China, urging the communes to take profit-oriented steps and lifting state subsidies from the factories so that they either sank or swam. Entrepreneurship is flourishing today, not only among the street merchants but also among those who undertook personal joint ventures with the outside world. Deng is considered the third most important person in the Communist movement, outliving both Zhou Enlai and Mao Zedong.

The Great Hall of the People, Beijing, the center of political activity and official functions.

GOVERNMENT

(CCP) elite, less than 10 per cent of the people, ruled the masses, promulgated 5-year plans to the public, built communes to feed the people and produced goods. They dressed the people uniformly, enlisted women as equal work force, attempted to control the swelling population with birth control regulations, and fostered their own period of discontent. 1966–76 saw the Cultural Revolution which was seen by Mao as part of the process of "continual rectification" of the party that it adhered to their ideology. These efforts, however, took a heavy toll on China's cultural heritage not to mention the lives of her intellectuals and artistes.

President Nixon broke the ice of international isolation of China and eventually opened direct trading with the most populated country in the world. Deng Xiaoping, the twice incarcerated dissident took over to introduce economic reforms to the extent of semi-capitalism and to buy tourist dollars with a country-wide joint venture program. Capital flowed into China, tourism provided quick cash and the 1997 takeover of Hong Kong was negotiated.

The aberration of the Tiananmen incident stunned the world as China seemed to step back in time but in the 1990's, unaffected by the world's fading angry opinions, modernization during Deng Xiaoping's era resumes its pace. Today China seems to be in a breathless pace to prepare for the 21st century, full of promise of progress and better times.

Economy

China is one of the earliest countries in the world to have engaged in agriculture, a fact archeologists have established from traces of a variety of crops and farm tools found at neolithic sites. In the remains of the Hemudu Culture in Zhejiang Province, for instance, large quantities of rice and tools for rice cultivation (primitive plows of bone and wood) were discovered. A large quantity of carbonized millet and sorghum grain were unearthed at the sites of Banpo Village (Xian) and Dahe Village (Zhengzhou) respectively. These finds confirm that, as far back as 4,000 to 7,000 years ago, ancestors of the Chinese had definitely cultivated rice, millet and sorghum in the Huanghe (Yellow River) and Changjiang (Yangtse River) basins.

China had from early times accumulated experience and innovated water conservancy, control and irrigation. Relics of farm implements and cultivation techniques show that the agricultural society was ad-

The small entrepreneur in the new climate of private enterprise.

A tea-leaf picker on the Hangzhou Dragon Well Tea plantation.

vanced. Processes and knowledge stagnated through the Ming Dynasty because of the constant turmoil of imperial changes, strife among the warlords and the devastation policies of the Mongols.

Emperors Kangxi and Qianlong of the Qing Dynasty promulgated advanced techniques, learning from the Jesuits and other foreigners allowed into the country. Then with the advent of the European invasion, the introduction of opium, the 2 world wars, and the emergence of the new republic, China's growth slowed down. Collective knowledge and advanced technology were stifled as the warring factions of the Nationalists and the Communists fought through the country for domination. Economics was reduced to survival of the individual.

Mao Zedong organized the farmers to fight alongside him against Chiang Kaishek's mandarin clique. Thus the winners emerged as an agrarian society again. Large farms were nationalized (confiscated) and redistributed to the people. Soon work forces were established as mutual aid teams, a collective socialist style of labor effort. By 1953 a new plan was developed by the Central Committee: Development of Agricultural Co-operatives, the pooling of land under centralized management. The co-ops enlisted 96 per cent of all peasant households by 1956.

Another resolution was promulgated by the Central Committee: Resolution on the Establishment of the People's Communes in the Rural Areas, August 1958. By the end of that year, all co-ops became communes. Ownership and operation is a 3-level system: the commune, the production brigade, and the production team. The commune comprises usually party members who saw to the execution of the federal plans and organization. The production brigade, the peasant mass, did the field work. The production team was the accountant, overseeing the land and equipment, certifying the yield and compensation of shares and marketing the crop. Goals were required of the commune to meet the grand plans of the central authority. Members were allowed to cultivate small plots and breed animals for their own use.

Farmer in a padi field tending to the Chinese staple.

By 1964 agro-scientific research institutes were spreading the knowledge of higher yields and better products. Specialized centers developed for studies in cotton, tea, fruit trees, tobacco, bee-keeping, sericulture (raising of silkworms and the production of silk), bast-fibre plants, forestry, aquatic products and meteorology. The basic plan to renew the devastated economy was first to feed and clothe the population.

Cash crops were introduced for export: the traditional bast fibres (bast is the inner layer of certain trees used for making ropes), tung oil (oil from the seeds of the tung tree used for a hardening agent for lacquers), tobacco, cotton, silk weaving and the famous Chinese teas (Hangzhou's Dragon Well Green Tea, Anhui Black Tea, Puerh and Black Tea, Jasmine and Oolong). Oil-bearing crops such as soya bean, groundnuts, and sesame; cottonseeds and sugar cane; and fresh, dried and canned fruit such as plums, persimmons and lychees were added to the export list. Cash crops provided the means for China to buy western technology.

In time many of the communes foundered and Deng Xiaoping changed the complexion of communist ideology to conform to the progressive ideas of the outer world. Farmers could now produce some crops out of the plots, even though they were communal, for their own marketing. The Catch-22 was, quotas had to be achieved first and the surplus could then be sold for personal

A hot strip mill in Shanghai which contributed to China's changing landscape.

incentive and profit.

For a while farmers were seen to have excess renminbi to spend for improving housing, buying television sets and appliances. It became common in rural cities to see the local gentry shopping in the foreigners' section of the Friendship Store. Like the factories, when the federal government ceased to subsidize non-profitable communes, the doors began to close.

Industrial Economic Transformation

Iron, copper, tin and other non-ferrous metals have enhanced the history of China's art and craft production for thousands of years. Bronze cooking vessels, copper-based cloisonne, tin-based pewter, cinnabar-based mercury for lacquer artware are found in the tombs of the Yuan, Ming and Qing Dynasties. Bronze musical bells, artware and weapons are some of the great finds dating back to the Xian tombs of Emperor Qin (221 BC).

Industrial production, however, is a modern development. When the Communists raised their flag in October 1949, China's factories were ill-equipped and the level of technology antiquated. By 1978 steel production reached over 30 million tons with 1,200 types of steel and 20,000 types of rolled steel products. Nanjing's bridge over the Changjiang was erected with domestic steel, begun with the Russians and finished by the Chinese when the Communist ideologies clashed and the relationship was severed. Ocean freighters were built, Shanghai's automobile factory produced thousands of cars a year. Changchun's and Shenyang's factories rolled out the railroad cars for passengers and freight. Technology also brought on the production of satellites and the atomic and hydrogen bombs requested by the military. Led by Shanghai and Wuhan, other cities in the northwest and southwest expanded the ferrous industry.

The vast expanse of China, aerial mapping combined with technical research, revealed further deposits of ferrous and non-ferrous metals. The rare group of thorium, uranium, lithium, beryllium, tantalum, niobium and germanium were a tremendous advantage to the economy and the burgeoning modern defense programs. Gold, silver, platinum, diamonds and semi-precious gemstones were by-products of the metal explorations. Their yields and locations were secretive, but contributed to the cash flow as factories produced and marketed the resultant jewelry and craft merchandise.

Machine building grew along with the development of industry. Whole plants and technology were purchased from the Germans, and other business-friendly nations. Tractor plants for the farmers' equipment flourished and machine-building plants further supplied production in the provinces.

The Industrial Revolution of the 19th century has now extended to the communist version of the Middle Kingdom, and this is now about to convert to a new economic revolution to take China into the 21st century.

Fuel and Power

Some of the largest coal deposits in the world are in China, the result of favorable geological factors. North China, during the Carboniferous Permian Period lay under a shallow sea which gave rise to the present large, thick layer of coal. The coalfields in the northeast were formed during the Mesozoic (205 million years ago, age of rock formation) and Cenozoic (60-70 million years ago, the age of mammals) eras. They are not deeply buried and are therefore easy to mine. The spread of coal deposits in most areas of the country accelerates industrial production and the growth of industrial cities.

History reports coal being used in 200 BC and by the time of the Tang and Song Dynasties (618-1279), coal was widely used in the smelting of ores. Within a 30-year period of the communist multi-plans, China had climbed to third place in the world in coal production producing over 600 million tons a year.

Oil and power developed as well. The Daqing fields in the northeast led in the production of oil as rich sources close to the industrial and agricultural centers were developed. Hydro-electric sources added to the needs of the factories and burgeoning population. With technology, nuclear facilities began to surface surreptitiously, alarming the potential enemies of China. Huge dams like the newest at Yichang on the Changjiang added megawatts of power to the greedy maws of industrial production and modernization plans.

Industrial Mores

China possesses a rich lode of mineral resources used in the chemical industry, such as salt, phosphorus, natural sodas, mirabilite and sulphur. The chemical industry embraces 3 branches: basic chemicals, chemical fertilizers and organic synthesis. Nitrogenous fertilizer is the largest product to augment agriculture. Synthetic materials swamped the country with plastic from shopping bags to home utility gadgets. Free market fairs abound with the cheap colorful products. Combined with low-cost labour, exporting factories turn out hundreds of thousands of container laden goods, shipped around the world with "Made in China" inexpensive commodities.

Building materials was a forced-need industry for the new emerging society. Jobs were required to organize the multi-millions of workers, who were guaranteed full employment. Construction required cement, glass, fibre board, asbestos, and other materials to provide manufacturing plants, administrative buildings and hotels for the tourist industry, and cheap housing for the populace.

Textiles were and are an important light industry. The country produces cotton, flax, jute, ramie (perennial herb, producing a fiber used in textiles), wool, silk and other raw materials. Cotton in particular was rationed in the early years because most of the material was imported. The markets of the world sought out cheap labor to produce their denim blue-jeans, printed tee-shirts through to designer silks.

Silk and linen, the ancient industries, were increased as the Silk Road became the silk sea and air highways. As early as 4,000 years ago, the people in China were already weaving and wearing silk. By 200 BC, silk began to be exported and earned China the name, "The Silk Country of the Orient". At that time, silk was transported from the upper reaches of the Huanghe to Central Asia and Europe through Xinjiang which

A textile factory in Harbin, Manchuria, an important light industry.

became the cross roads of the famous Silk Road.

The Chinese linen industry is divided into 3 groups: making of gunnysacks, ramie textiles and flax fabrics. Plastic has invaded this sector of industry as can be seen in the proliferation of the red, white, and blue travel and shopping bags seen at every point on the streets and transportation centers.

Wool spinning and weaving advanced as wool textile mills were built around the country. Tianjin led the cities in the production of small decorative carpets and hundreds of meters of covering for the floors of the hotels and administrative buildings. Woolen blankets and cashmere sweaters were great cash producers as the market hungry traders vied with each other to buy the artistic labor intensive products at bargain prices.

Foodstuffs, paper making, porcelain, cloisonne, craft-intensive factories grew in every province of the country. Clothing, once thought shoddy and cheap, improved in quality. Inferior products that overseas buyers refused could be foisted off on the domestic markets. As the dress and mores of the barbarian world invaded China, the Chinese people demanded color, quality and style for their own use. Joint ventures with the world's couturiers to produce fashionable goods slipped into the emerging entrepreneurship of street fairs. Easing of personal restrictions saw an increase in the production of cloth-

The porcelain factory in Wuxi straddles art and industry.

ing for domestic purchase.

Communications, Transport Money, Banking and Finance

Industry required the rapid advance of this important group of commerce. Threads of communications gradually revitalized contacts with the outside world. Shanghai, for example, has all the facilities of Hong Kong such as the international direct dialing telephones and the facsimile machines which replaced the antiquated telex facilities. Satellite television transmissions telecast world news in tourists' hotel rooms.

Railways are still the principal people and product movers followed by coastal and river steamers. The inland waterways are important especially along the Changjiang and the Zhujiang (Pearl) Rivers and the Grand Canal. CAAC, China's national airlines and many domestic regional airlines have computerized reservation systems and feeder lines which now operate fairly smoothly. The ancient Russian-made Antonevs and Tubelovs have been mostly retired in favor of Boeings and a small number of Europe's Airbus series. City streets are loaded with automobiles produced in China competing with Japan's imported passenger vehicles. Domestic production supplies the trucks of commerce, allowing very few of the Mercedes trucks, buses and cars, seen in other parts of Asia, to be sold in China.

Autonomous Economic Zones

Modern skyline of Shenzhen, one of the first territories assigned as a Special Economic Zone (SEZ).

Special Economic Zones (SEZs) were established in 1980 in recognition of the new open door policy. The area between Guangzhou and Hong Kong, known as Shenzhen, Zhuhai near Macao, Shantou in northeastern Guangdong Province, and Xiamen (Amoy), in Fujian Province were the first SEZs to be established. Hainan Island was added to the list in 1988. As you will note from the map, all are located within proximity to each other along the South coast of China and Hong Kong. This appears to be a big break with the Beijing bureaucrats who inevitably controlled all economic trade.

The experiment was to free regulations, already being surreptitiously ignored and offer tax and other incentives to attract foreign investors. Joint ventures could now be legally engaged by the individual SEZs and foreign capital was protected to some degree. Taxation negotiations were arranged whereby the rates were lower and tax-free periods granted during the start up years.

Reinvested profits were tax-free, import duties waived for goods to be brought in, labor-added, and re-shipped out. One major innovation was that after-tax profits could be repatriated. Investors could actually take some money out of China.

By 1984, another system was added to the apparent success of the SEZs. **Economic and Technical Development Zones** (ETDZs) were authorized in 14 cities: Dalien, Qinhuangdao, Tianjin, Yantai, Qingdao, Lianyungang, Nantong, Shanghai, Ningbo, Wenzhou, Fuzhou, Guangzhou, Zhanjiang and Beihai. These entities were allowed to negotiate contracts directly with foreign businesses and manage the resultant assets independent from the Beijing authority.

The key difference in the 2 systems is that SEZs had to be built from the ground up while the existing facilities in the ETDZs needed only modernization and capital influx. The cities had already been doing a certain amount of business with the outside world and were now recognized by Beijing.

By 1985, coastal zones were opened up in the southeast and northeast for accelerated economic development. The results, slowed down in 1989 and then heated up again as world opinion abated in the interest of business. The 1991/1992 statistics prove the point. Investment capital and technology flowed in as the world's producers took advantage of the new market and labor source. Capitalistic (profit-oriented) ideology invaded the state-run factories and enterprises, taking their lead from the SEZs and ETDZs' successes.

Bicycles are still the principal mode of transportation for the masses with motorcycles rapidly coming into prominence. Tricycle freight carts are still a common sight even in the big cities. Pony carts in the rural areas and massive construction sites perform the drudgery of moving piles of bricks and rocks in

The port of Shanghai moves into the 20th century.

ant-like long lines.

Emerging Changes on the Industrial Scene

In 1993, foreign journals report that China will open its post and telecommunications facilities to overseas joint-venture investors. This allows the import of technology at a cheaper price in the construction of factories to produce telecommunications and equipment for high-capacity digital telephone ex-

ucts from state control while the state still subsidized the factories producing the goods. Plant managers were faced with the difficult alternatives of increasing production and lowering costs to make a profit or close the factory.

Gross domestic product per capita in 1992 was 2,055 yuan (US$352), showing a 19 per cent increase from the previous year, a quantum leap in any statistical rendition. Along with this, industrial production increased 21 per cent, an obvious companion statistic. These basic figures were the most favorable since the red crescent flag was raised in Beijing 43 years ago. The switch to capitalistic goals in the factories took hold, as state-owned enterprises operating at a loss fell from 35 per cent to 25 per cent in 1991. Unemployment became a factor as more than one million workers were laid off. Some were given new jobs, others retrained and assigned new work. Retail sales climbed almost 10 per cent to 109 billion yuan (US$18.66 billion). Per capita income was reported at 1,826 yuan (US$304.00), farm income at 784 yuan (US$131.00), representing substantial increases over the previous year.

The country is back to business as usual, and tourists are again flocking to see the ancient wonders. World economics recognizes the potential of a billion-plus market potential and a monumental cheap labor source.

The 30 million phone lines in place in 1993 were estimated to grow to 100 million by the turn of the century.

changes, fiber-optic systems, mobile telecommunications and satellite equipment. The new policy of joint ventures is to guarantee investors a return and so encourage foreign investment.

China's 1992 inflation rate was published as 6.4 per cent but in reality the rate might have been double that. The cause was the release of many prod-

GORGES, GLENS & GREENERY

Geography, Flora & Fauna

China is the second largest unified territory in the world today, following only the vast lands of Canada in North America. A total of 9.6 million sq km stretches from the main navigation channel of the Heilongjiang near Mohe in the north (latitude 53 degrees north) to the Zengmu Reef of the Nansha Islands in the south (latitude 4 degrees north). Her breadth extends from the Pamirs in the west (longitude 73 degrees east) to the confluence of the Heilongjiang and the Wusuli River in the east (longitude 135 degrees east). The land boundary is more than 20,000 km long.

The Stone Forest in Lunan County, near Kunming is an example of China's geographical possibilities.

Korea shares a land border with China in the east and the People's Republic of Mongolia have a long line of mountainous country extending across the top of China. When the Commonwealth of Independent States (former USSR) settles down to the new territorial divisions, there will be more than one new

Yamdrok Tso Lake rests incongruously in the arid terrain of southern Tibet.

border companion emerging. Afghanistan, Pakistan, India, Nepal, Sikkim and Bhutan range along her western borders. In the south and southwest, Burma, Laos, and Vietnam crowd together in a pyramid. Bangladesh and Thailand are a political stone's throw from China's southwest and share many tribal minorities.

The coastline is an enormous 18,000 km to watch across. The South China Sea, East China Sea, Bohai, and Yellow Sea are contiguous to China and her sea neighbors of Japan, Philippines, Malaysia, Indonesia, and Brunei. Taiwan remains a national and political entity, although considered part of China by the Communists. There is a heritage connection but Chiang Kaishek's descendants do not agree. South China Sea and the other islands, numbering over 5,000, are also considered territorial China.

China is known for massive world geographical excesses. The tallest mountains on the earth, the Himalayas, border her domain on the Nepalese border, extending into the vast plateaus of Tibet. The highest point in the world, Mount Everest (8,848.13m) is the principal peak in this mountain range. Looking from a southwest to east profile, the staircase of China begins with the Qinghai Tibetan Plateau which average 4,500 m above sea level. This highest terrace in the world is also known as "the Roof of the World". On the plateau is Qinghai Lake (4,427 sq m) which

GEOGRAPHY, FLORA & FAUNA

The Gobi Desert, the uninhabitable part of China.

rank first among China's salt lakes. The Qaidam Basin, also on the Qinghai Tibetan Plateau is the highest basin in China.

The land then descends into the Inner Mongolian Plateau and thence to the shifting sands of the Loess Plateau. The immense expanse is realized when you fly from eastern cities to Urumqi over the Tarim Basin (the largest such formation in the world). Taklamakan is China's largest desert but you will not be able to see Lop Nor, the great salt lake, as nuclear testing is carried out in this area.

The land steps down into the Turpan Depression, 500 m below sea level, which according to Chinese geologists is the hottest place on earth. Changjiang (Yangtse River) is the next apparent geographical feature as the terrain drops to 1,000 m above sea level whilst sliding eastwards. This was the heart of the early dynasties when agriculture fed the populace. Thus the name Middle Kingdom came into being as succeeding conquerors shifted their capitals from Chang'an (Xian) to Kaifeng, to Luoyang and finally east to Beijing.

An aerial journey from Shanghai to Chongqing roughly follows the Changjiang, out-ranked in length by the mighty Amazon and Nile Rivers. At 6,300 km long, it traverses China from the Qinghai mountains, winding its way eastwards through Tibet until it empties into the China Sea near Shanghai.

Wang Wei, a Tang Dynasty poet

The Changjiang, a significant waterway which has sustained China's people and economy, in a romantic setting.

describes the riverscape, the physical world and alludes to a Middle Kingdom in the clouds :

Crossing the Yellow River to Ching-ho
Drift by boat upon the Great River
Massed waters touching the sky's very edge
Sky and waves suddenly split apart
The million houses of a district capital
And further on, see walls and market,
Then clearly appears mulberry, hemp
I look back towards my homeland
Vast floods stretching to the clouds

The second largest waterway is the Huanghe (Yellow River), which at 5,464 km is shorter than its southern parallel, the Changjiang. The Huanghe which also originates in Qinghai descends from a different mountain range before flowing eastward to create the heart of Chinese civilization and eventually reaching the sea east of Beijing.

Like the Great Wall, the Grand Canal ranks as the third greatest manmade waterway in China; at one time it stretched for 1,800 km from Hangzhou in the south to the capital of Beijing. First built in the 5th century BC, it was not completed until the Sui Dynasty (581-618). The Grand Canal is now only partially used because a lack of maintenance allowed a major portion of the canal to silt up.

Eleven per cent of the total land of China is arable for farming, this is included in the 40 per cent total land mass suitable for agriculture and forestry. The

The Mighty Shan - Mountains of China

Two-thirds of the land area in China are mountainous. Many of the world's famous mountains are found here: 9 out of the 14 in the world that are 8,000 m and above in height are located either inside China or on a Chinese border. From east to west range the Altay, Tianshan, Kunlun, Karakorum, Gandise, Himalayas, Ginling and Nanlin high altitudes of China.

Altay, translated as the Golden Mountains, run south eastward in the northern part of Xinjiang Ugyur Autonomous Region with an average height of 3000 m.

Tianshan cross the middle of Xinjiang rising from 3,000 m to 7,000 m, consisting of several parallel ranges with depressed basins in between. Aydingkol Lake in the center of the Turpan Depression is 154 m below sea level, "bottom of the world" so to speak.

Kunlun Mountains start from the Pamirs in the west and run 2,500 km to the northwest part of Sichuan. They are 5,000 m above sea level on average, some reaching to 7,000 m. Continually snow peaked, the Kunlun Mountains supply water to the Huanghe (Yellow River) and the Changjiang (Yangtse River) when the snows melt.

Qinling, 2,000 m to 3,000 m high, extend about 1,500 km across central China from southern Gansu to the lower reaches of the Huanghe and Changjiang.

Karakorum, the Purplish Black Kunlun, in Uygur start from the Xinjiang-Kashmir border in the northwest, stretching southwestward into Tibet. The main peak is Qogir, 8,611 m, ranking second to Mount Qomolongma (Mt Everest) in the Himalayas. Other peaks of the range rise to 6,000 m in elevation.

Nanling, the Five Mountains, is a general term for all the mountains in the central-south. They consist of the Yuecheng, Dupang, Mengzhu, Qitian, and the Dayu mountains.

Gandise, Master of All Mountains, tower 6,000 m above sea level over southern Tibet, forming the watershed between the continental plateau drainage system and the Indian Ocean. The Kangrinboqe Peak, meaning "Treasure of the Snow" is a holy land for Buddhist pilgrims.

Himalayas, granddaddy of them all, rise above the southern rim of the Qinghai-Tibet Plateau, along the Indian and Nepalese borders of China. They average 6,000 m above sea level, ranging 2,500 km. More than 40 precipitous snow-capped peaks are upwards of 7,000 m in elevation. The main peak, Mount Qomolongma, known to the world as **Everest**, "Goddess Peak" (Abode of Snow) to the Tibetans, soars 8,848.13 m on the Sino-Nepalese border, and is the highest in the world. Sir Edmund Hillary was the first mountaineer to conquer it from the south, now a mecca for the world's climbers to ascend its many faces.

The northeast-southwest ranges are mostly in the eastern part of China. **Changbai**, in the northeast average 2,700 m while others drop to 1,000 m across the Liadong and Shandong peninsulas, south to Zhejiang and Fujian provinces. These compose the **Greater Hinggan Range**, **Tiahang Mountains**, and the **Xuefeng Mountains**.

The north-south ranges consist mainly of the **Hengduan Mountains** in western Sichuan and Yunnan provinces. The former includes the **Daxue**, **Nushan** and **Gaoligong Mountains**, rising 4,500 m to 5,000 m, with the highest peak, the **Gongga**, soaring to 7,500 m.

Winding through the mountains are the rivers of China, dominated by the **Changjiang** (Yangtse), **Huanghe** (Yellow River), and the **Zhujiang**. The Changjiang has a total length of 6,300 km emptying into the East China Sea near Shanghai. Huanghe with the highest silt content, flows sluggishly 5,464 km finally emptying into Bohai Bay. Zhujiang is the largest river in the south, ending in the South China Sea near Guangzhou in Guangdong province.

other 60 per cent is barren land and mountains.

The happy side of China's geography includes hundreds of hot spring sites, used for thousands of years for health and recreation. Most of the more

Li Jiang River in Guangxi Province has also been dubbed the Green Silk Belt.

accessible mountains, those in the 1500 to 2500-m range, are equipped with stone steps and maneuverable people trails. Three of the most famous are Huangshan (Yellow Mountain) near Hangzhou, Emeishan in Sichuan Province near Chengdu, Wu Yi in the southern province of Fujian. Most have modest facilities for the domestic tourists.

Climate

Great differences of climate, dominated

east has a short cool summer and a severe winter where the people feature ice-sculpture as an art form.

River valleys of the Changjiang and Huanghe are warm and humid with distinct 4 season changes. Inner Mongolia and Xinjiang are known for extremities in weather. The saying "fur coats in the morning and gossamer at noon" typifies the changes within the same day. The Tibet Plateau is known for its inclement weather and bright sunshine.

Climate also runs the gamut of temperatures with snow storms in the north in winter and typhoons in the coastal areas of the South China Sea in summer. Visitors are treated to endless charts of weather variables for the area and period of the year when they intend to visit. Common sense will tell you that Beijing in the winter, like its latitudinal counterpart of Chicago in the US, is bone-chilling cold and hot, dusty and crowd-filled in the hot summer months.

Summer travelers head for Harbin

by monsoonal winds, are found in China due to the complex topography and extensive territory. Tropical and temperate year round areas called "Eternal Spring" range along the south. Hainan Island, Guangdong, Yunnan Province, and the South China Sea Islands are the most verdant with luxuriant vegetation. Heilongjiang Province in the north-

Nature's own ice sculpture in Harbin, Manchuria.

in the northern province of Heilongjiang and the seaside resort of Beidaihe near Beijing to escape the summer heat. Nearer the equator, the temperate weather of Yunnan to the west and Fujian along the eastern coast make these areas both pleasant and enjoyable almost all year long. Sailing up or down the Changjiang is one of the top destinations recommended. However, avoid the rainy season of July and August when floods are almost certainly assured. Spring and fall are the most delightful travel times in China.

Annual Temperature Differences of China's Major Cities

Cities	Average Jan	Average Jul
Beijing	-4.8 C	25.8 C
Shanghai	3.5 C	28.0 C
Qingdao	-1.1 C	23.7 C
Guangzhou	13.7 C	28.3 C
Wuhan	2.7 C	29.1 C
Urumqi	-15.8 C	23.9 C
Shenyang	-13.0 C	24.9 C

As shown in the brief chart, there is a vast difference in temperature between the north and south in the winter, but in summer the temperature is constant thus making China a popular summer tourist destination. The sharp seasonal contrast is due to the monsoons which govern the climate, as they do in the major part of Asia.

Starting in late spring through the warm half of the year, the wet monsoons blow landward from the Pacific

Rippling dunes outside Dunhuang, Gansu Province.

and the Indian Oceans. In the cold half of the year, prevailing winds blow towards the sea, marking the beginning of the dry period on land; cyclones, for instance, bring the winter rains to the Changjiang Basin.

For an experienced traveler, geography and the climate are common sense, relating to the traveling period selected. Beijing is hot in summer with the usual smog and blowing dust, but you need thermal underwear if you are going to see it in the winter. The south of Fujian, Guangdong and Yunnan are year-round delights, but watch for the typhoons if you are sailing your own yacht in the offshore waters between Hainan Island and Hong Kong.

The trekking steps of the mountains, installed over the past centuries by other nature lover dynasties, are delightful. They stretch across the smorgasbord of China, tempting the taste buds

Giant climber in the rainforest of Menglun Nature Reserve.

of the nature lover.

Flora and Fauna

The difference in climate and soils within China gives rise to a wide variety of natural vegetation ranging from luxuriant rain forests to vast grasslands and finally the barren deserts and inhabitable mountains. Hardwoods such as oak, birch, spruce, and pine are in the higher elevations. Further south, the sub-tropical evergreen broad-leaf forests predominate including the indomitable and forever useful bamboo. China has more than 32,000 species of higher plants, among which over 2,000 species are food plants. The lands support more than 2,800 species of trees, numerous species of herbal plants, and certain plants used for preparing valuable Chinese medicines.

1,100 different birds have been spotted in China (13.5 per cent of the world total) and these include rare birds such as the red-crowned cranes, golden pheasants and red-billed Teiothrix. Of the more than 420 kinds of animals, (11 per cent of the world total) some of the rarest wild animals like the giant pandas, the golden monkeys, takins and the white-lipped deer are also found here.

Mantis at prayer in the Menglun Botanical Garden.

Birding in China

Silver pheasant from the forests of south China.

During the Cultural Revolution and one of the many public campaigns of that era in the 1960's sparrows were suddenly proclaimed to be enemies of the people in China, presumably because they ate some grain, completely disregarding the fact that sparrows and most other perching birds are insectivorous during the summer months (i.e. the harvest time) as their young can only digest protein. Mainly in the non-breeding season do sparrows feed on seeds. Anyway, the Chinese obligingly went out and killed millions of all kinds of "harmful" birds around the villages during these years. Even today bird populations are reduced around populated areas, and although wildlife protection legislation has improved it is not always effectively enforced.

China today will not strike you as a treasure house of well preserved natural habitats as rich and confiding birdlife like India or Australia might for instance. It is a country in the midst of an explosive economic development, commercially and culturally it is evolving at a mindboggling pace year by year.

Now that the energies of 1.2 billion people have been released there is no telling how far this nation will go. Probably at some stage an interest in and concern for the wild birds will emerge. But so far today just a handful of the 1 billion even know how to recognize the different birds they see!

Beijing and the North

Nevertheless, try to look around and watch some new birds as you move around the countryside and the scenic spots. In Beijing the Summer Palaces to the northwest of the city center has some park and lake habitat that always attracts birds. This area is regarded as the best birding spot in the capital. The Kunming Lake especially is good for ducks, many species occur including the rare Baikal Teal and Mandarin Duck. In the surrounding reed beds herons and bitterns can be seen plus a variety of passerine birds like buntings and warblers so typical of this temperate climate environment. In the trees and the bushes nearby

The yellow bittern blending with nature.

The blue-winged pitta looking comfortable in its bright plumage.

....Birding in China

Mandarin duck.

look for thrushes, flycatchers, waxwings and tits. Around the edges of the park there are patches of denser scrub and woodlands where woodpeckers and the spectacularly beautiful azure-winged magpie occur. There are always especially many different bird species to watch around Beijing during the migration seasons in spring and autumn. And this is even more noticeable as you move out towards the coast.

In this part of China the winters are cold and bleak, the summers hot and dry until the typhoon-related rainstorms appear in late summer. So the best time to birdwatch is springtime when a combination of residents breeding and a huge influx of passage migrants create optimal conditions. Beidaihe is a well-known resort at the northern edge of Bohai Bay 280 km east of Beijing. It is also one of the finest locations in China (and in the world) to observe bird migration. Since 1985 regular observation teams comprising foreigners as well as local ornithologists have systematically surveyed the area. 345 different birds including 16 globally endangered species have been observed at this spot alone. Particularly the cranes provide stunning spectacles here as well as at many other wetland locations in China; 6 species occur, most numerously the

The crane, a symbol of longevity often found in Chinese art.

Common Crane which fly across by the thousands every year. But there are also exceptionally many raptors (birds of prey), storks, other waterbirds and passerines.

Parts of the best observation points and nearby resting areas for the many birds have recently been protected as nature reserves. There is fairly easy access to this part of China and ecotourism is encouraged. Visitors interested in seeing the wonders of bird migration at Beidaihe should contact Mr Xu Weishu, 1-1-302, Beijing Commission for Science and Technology Apartment, Ba-lizhuang, Haidien District, Beijing, PRC for more information.

East of Beidaihe along the Bohai Bay the Shuangtaizihekou National Nature Reserve is also newly established and can be visited. It covers some 80,000 ha, has 241 different birds and is especially important as a refuge for some rare Chinese species like Red-crowned Crane, Saunders's Gull and Reed Parrotbill.

Further South

Further south cities like Shanghai and Canton are the gateways to mainland China. During the last 10-12 years only these places have undergone astonishing modernization, a complete transformation happening quicker than anything witnessed in human history. But you can still take time out from admiring this develop-

ment wonder and enjoy the natural world and the different birds occuring here. In Shanghai the People's Park provide some habitat, note the appearance of some Oriental region birds like bulbuls and mynas - the Beijing area is part of the Eastern Palearctic region. Nearby the Changjiang estuary and adjacent islands are good migratory spots. There are especially many ducks and also swans like Whooper and Bewick's Swans.

Down south in the Guangdong Province you are firmly into the Oriental region. Look out for common birds like Spotted Dove, White-throated Kingfisher, Chinese Bulbul, Crested Myna, Olive-backed Pipit and others typical of this area. There is an important birding location at Bo Bao Shan with undisturbed primary forest, 125 species have been recorded here including many rarely seen forest birds. Generally the density of birds in this heavily populated and developed province is however not impressive. Traveling through you see no herons, no white egrets, no shorebirds, no gulls. In fact you are probably better off spending your time birding in nearby Hong Kong if you get the chance!

Remote Places

In China like most other places you have to go looking for birds if you want to see a lot. China has a large network of wildlife reserves and national parks in varying degrees of size and condition. Many are poorly surveyed and documented and in remote places traditionally closed to foreigners.

Increasingly these regions become more accessible, also to ecotourism. The American ornithologist Ben King has ventured into some of these sites, he also organizes public birding tours into China. He can be contacted at the Bird Department, American Museum of Natural History, Central Park West at 79th Street, New York, NY 10024-5192, USA.

The southern provinces of Sichuan, Yunnan and Guangxi especially have great potential. Out of the 1,195 birds occuring in China almost 100 are endemics, i.e. found nowhere else. And most of these occur in the south and the south-west where the climate is sub-tropical and the vegetation cover rich and tall. For example most of the many beautiful pheasant species which are so characteristic of the Oriental region birdlife are now very rarely seen. Woodpeckers, pittas, babblers and flycatchers are also well represented in these habitats.

Further to the west of here the birds have Himalayan affinities and in the massive and thinly populated Autonomous Region of Xinjiang most of the landscape is desert. But even here there are oases of fertile land along the rivers and lakes providing habitat for desert specialists like wheatears, sandgrouses and ground jays. The rare Relict Gull has been studied in detail at its remote breeding locations in Inner Mongolia.

Overseas ornithologists and amateur birders increasingly roam these remoter parts of China. Every year new discoveries are made and during just the last few years Collared Pratincole, Savi's Warbler, Wedge-billed Wren-Babbler, Short-tailed Shearwater, Rock Sandpiper and others have been added to the China bird checklist. Local awareness and appreciation of wild birds will follow, this is an exciting time for the birding pioneers in China.

More Information

Next to binoculars and notebook the birdwatcher's most important tool is his birdbook! The best field guide and introduction to Chinese birds is ***Birds of China*** by R M De Schauensee, Smithsonian Institution Press 1984. ***A Field Guide to the Birds of South-East Asia*** by B King et al, Collins 1975 covers most of the species found in southern China. Fieldguides available covering Hong Kong and Japan are also useful. For the connoisseur who wants access to all relevant information there is the recent "A Synopsis of the Avifauna of China" by Cheng Tso Hsin, Beijing Science Press, 1987. The Oriental Bird Club at The Lodge, Sandy, Bedfordshire SG19 2DL, England continuously publishes the latest news on birdwatching in China.

People

China's long history dating more than 4,000 years back has been recognized by the government's Commission of Tourism as cash-flow. Communism, the current system of government is of passing concern to the visitors who are irresistibly drawn to intriguing sights such as the Great Wall, the Three Gorges of the Changjiang and the ancient digs of Xian.

The scholar pores over the chronicles of the 4,000 years of recorded history while journalists and authors seek a tangent to acquaint the world about the anomalies of the Communist system. The most recent event of the Tiananmen incident shocked the world because of the media exposure more than the fact that the event was a repetition of history.

Travelers enjoy through their visits the re-creation of the marks of a grand civilization, as it was in its time. Unique cuisine and daily meals are of equal importance as is transportation and hotel accommodation. Of special interest is the variety of people, their culture and

Bright and beautiful a Hani ethnic.

A young girl of the Muslim Uygur minority.

lifestyle, in this vast land, hemmed in by the sea on one side and a dozen nations on the rest of her borders.

More than One Billion People

Within her borders China has 58 nationalities. The **Han** people constitute 94 per cent of the Chinese people among whom they share a common (ideographic) language and culture. The remaining 6 per cent comprise people of the other 56 nationalities. Minority nationalities whose population exceed one million each are the Mongolians, Huis, Tibetans, Uygurs, Miaos, Yis, Zhuangs, Bouyeis (Buyi), Koreans, Manchus, Tujias, Hanis, Dongs, Yaos and Bais. The Han live primarily in the river valleys of the Changjiang, the Huanghe and the Zhujiang (Pearl) rivers and the Song-Liao Plain in northeast China. The minority nationalities concentrate on the northern, western and southern borders of the central China heartland occupying vast areas of inaccessible land potentially rich in minerals. They either occupy an area exclusively or they can be found grouped with several other minority nationalities.

China is the most populated country on earth and has been since the recording of such facts. There were 51 million people estimated at the time of the Tang Dynasty, AD 742, living within the borders of unified China but 500 years later, the population had doubled to over 100 million. A census of households in 1662 revealed 111 million. It doubled again by the middle of the 18th century and by 1850 there was an estimated 400 million. In 1953 when censuses had become more accurate, 582,603,000 were tallied. Communism, the new wave of farming, proliferation and desire for more boys to work on the farms doubled the population again in the next 30 years. A new policy of one-child families was promulgated to halt the deluge now totaling over 20 per cent of the world's population at over 1.1 billion people. Demographers anticipate the population at the turn of the century will be 1,250,000,000.

Ninety per cent of this massive population live in the eastern and southern

Shanghai populace.

sections of China. The vast areas of the north and west contain the largest deserts of Asia, Taklamakan and Gobi, predominantly uninhabitable land. The Tibetan area is definitely hostile to human environment with the average altitude at 3,600 m. The steppes of southern Mongolia and Xinjiang offer living conditions comparable to the desert.

Experiments in the bowl of the Loess Plateau are the first significant success of turning floating soil into productive agriculture.

Ethnic Diversity

Until the communist takeover, the minorities lived their nomadic life of survival in the vast open spaces of the north and west with the few cities becoming trading centers for transient merchants. The new political system required communes to replace the village structure of the few urban areas. The fast growing population forced the new China to foster and urge migration to the less inhabited areas of the nation. Definition of settlements remained: it was a village if more than half of the population were engaged in agricultural activities; a town as soon as the pendulum swung opposite with mechanization of industry.

The Han people have a history of being technically and culturally advanced in comparison to the minorities. The government policy is to let the groups

Sex and Birth Control in the PRC

Kindergarten in the PRC.

The government, in order to control the swelling population, implemented a one child per family policy supported by counseling, education, a family planning officer in each community and punitive rules. The State Planning Commission admits to a 30 per cent unplanned birth average in the country, which is lower in the city.

Rural parents are rewarded at the birth of a child by a gift of a plot of land, the second child nothing, and if a third is born, the first child has to relinquish his gift of land. To a farmer, male children are his assured source of help to till the land and to turn to for security in his old age. They also ensure the continuance of the family line. Sex education is often limited to the grandmother's beliefs according to her own experiences and learning.

Urban parents are discouraged from multiple births under social and government pressure, forced to take counseling and often, fines are imposed at the whim of the local family planning official. Both father and mother can suffer reduced wages and be made to pay nursery school fees and doctor's charges, both services being free to single-child families.

The greatest pressure for urban families is living space. Large cities of Guangzhou, Beijing, Shanghai and Chengdu average 3.5 sq m of apartment area per person. Thus a family of 2 adults, 1 child and a pair of grandparents commonly live in less than 20 sq m of space. Cramped bedrooms, living rooms combined for sleeping, closet-like kitchens, toilet and bathing facilities, impossible by world standards, exert their own influence on birth control. New clusters of highrise apartments are constantly growing with need outweighing comfort. Retired grandparents often inherit the old quarters as the modern age younger people strive for privacy and modern amenities.

Pornography is avidly controlled by barring

keep their identity, spoken language, and live in their designated areas. Thus they grant them the right to live, according to the current doctrines. One glitch in the system, intentionally or not, is the sparsity of specific schools for each of the minorities. To date there is no university which teaches solely in a minority language.

Exceptions to the rule are the 5.5 million Uygurs belonging to the Islamic faith and Turkish culture. Bold and aggressive horsemen, born of nomadic independence, they refuse to knuckle under to the Han dictates of modern culture and science.

The large city of Kashgar is predominantly minority but Urumqi and

all semblances of sexually suggestive or explicit literature and possession of video tapes, magazines, or western sex novels bring harsh punishment for non-compliance. The Aids epidemic has yet to hit the nation in any admitted proportions, due to there being less promiscuous sex than government control. Prostitution rears its age-old livelihood in communities exposed to border traffic and businessmen.

Strangely, the history of ancient Chinese imperialism, mandarinism, literature and poetic romance is rife with sexual enjoyment. Concubines were an integral part of palace life, often glorified in monuments and burial sites. The Empress Dowager Ci Xi worked her way into the control of the last years of the Qing Dynasty through the passageways as number one ranking concubine.

Eroticism in literature is historic. Many Chinese read novels and the official who writes only of benevolence and righteousness in essays will be found, in private conversations, to be quite familiar with the heroes and heroines of *Chimp'inmei (Gold Vase Plum)*, a pornographic novel and *P'inhua Paochien*, an equally pornographic homosexual novel! Explicit textbooks on the thousand ways of making love have been reprinted, re-interpreted countless times, and exported all over the world. Hundreds of novels, plays and movies exist with themes of concubinal romance during the foreign business invasion of the 18th and 19th centuries.

Art memorabilia in the form of sexually explicit drawings and netsuke carvings of entwined lovers in ivory are valued collectibles.

the other major population centers have Han majorities. Military control is not viable in the vast area of the desert and steppes, except by elimination. A policy of cultural extinction is not possible or desirable with the current Politburo, obsessed with other far greater problems. The dissolution of the USSR was a frightening specter to the ancient leaders of the People's Republic.

The other more secretive, yet actively publicized by curious and adventurous journalists and world peace organizations is the enigma of Tibet. Unlike Xinjiang, Tibet (Xizang) is 98 per cent Tibetan. Two million extremely devout adherents to the Dalai Lama and the Buddhist Yellow Hat Sect live in Tibet. The Tibetans remember the devastation of the Cultural Revolution only too well as centuries old monasteries and temples were destroyed wantonly.

The current Dalai Lama, now living in India refuses to return on the invitation of the Chinese government unless the Han vacate his lands. The political environment has felt tentative for the past years. However, the particular culture and allure of this Himalayan country has growing appeal for tourists, whose value in terms of revenue cannot be underestimated, and despite its political volatility, tourism will be more relaxed.

Other peoples, like the Zhuang, second largest nationality in China, live in the autonomous region of Guangxi, located between Yunnan and Guangdong Provinces in the south. They have largely assimilated with the Han, their national characteristics being recognizable and distinct in the mountainous and remote areas only.

Difficulties arise when the minorities refuse to assimilate and are culturally similar to other groups across international borders. Refer to a map of greater China and note the nearness of

The Yellow Hat Sect monks of Tibet.

former Russian territories, Mongolia, Korea, Vietnam, Laos, Thailand, Nepal, India, Bhutan, Pakistan, and Afghanistan. The impossible task of protecting these borders against whatever designs the neighbor has in mind is the worst nightmare of the government.

Minority Nationalities

China recognizes 56 minority nationalities in the various regions of the mainland, Taiwan and Hainan Island apart from the predominant Han (estimated 900,000,000) and the Muslim Hui (6,500,000) nationalities. They are defined by the areas populated and the languages they speak.

South

The **Zhuang** people, are the largest of the minorities, numbering 12,000,000 in Yunnan, Guangxi and Guangdong Provinces. They have a common heritage with the **Dai** people of Yunnan. Both share the same language and basically a love for colorful clothing, singing and dancing.

The **Bai** people, more than 1,000,000 of whom are rice farmers in the high plains of Yunnan Province, are the original inhabitants of the region. The **Yao** people, 1,200,000 strong, also grew rice, maize, and sweet potatoes by slash-and-burn farming. Their habitat is spread over the entire south of

The Yi minority hill tribe in their traditional gear.

Guangxi, Hunan, Yunnan, Guangdong and Guizhou Provinces.

The **Yi** people, numbering almost 5,000,000, were the southern warriors who evolved an aristocratic society and a religion based on sacred writings. They spread north into Sichuan as well as Yunnan, Guizhou and Guangxi.

The **Miao** numbering 4,000,000 are spread over Guizhou, Hunan, Yunnan, Guangxi, Sichuan and Guangdong Provinces. They have also been identified in northern Vietnam, Laos and Thailand where the 4 nations converge. Sub groups are called the Black, White, Red, Blue, Flowery, and Cowrie Shell Miaos, generated from original tribes or families. As in many areas, the Han people during early times oppressed those minorities who refused to intermarry and integrate with their life style.

The Li people reside in Guangdong Province. Hainan Island is the refuge of the Li, well known for their constant rebellion against a succession of Han authority.

Other minority groups	**Population**	**Region**
Dai	760,000	Yunnan
Mulao	70,000	Guangxi Zhuang
Maonan	30,000	Guangxi Zhuang
Hani	nearly 1 million	Yunnan
Lisu	470,000	Yunnan

The Miao tribe in southern China.

			Other minority groups	Population	Region
Lahu	270,000	Yunnan			
Wa	260,000	Yunnan			
Naxi	230,000	Yunnan			
Jingpo	80,000	Yunnan			
Bulang	50,000	Yunnan			Guangxi
Pumi	20,000	Yunnan	Gelao	20,000	Guizhou, Hunan, Guangxi
Achang	10,000	Yunnan			
Benglong	10,000	Yunnan			
Jinuo	10,000	Yunnan	Jing	5,000	Guizhou, Hunan, Guangxi
Nu	10,000	Yunnan			
Dulong	10,000	Yunnan			
Buyi	1,700,000	South-central, Guizhou	Li	680,000	Hainan Island
Shui	230,000	South-central, Guizhou			
Dong	1 million	Guizhou, Hunan,			

West

The **Tibetans**, numbering 3,500,000, are well known to the outside world, their

Uygur women in traditional dress.

homeland being fabled, explored, and fantasized for centuries. Seventh century Buddhism led to the original formation of the state controlled by the pre-ordained succession of Dalai Lamas.

The Han took over again in 1959, abolished the feudal system, secularized the religion and attempted to convert Tibet (Xizang Province) into a modern agricultural integrated part of China. Intermittent revolutions and the flight of the living god, the Dalai Lama, continues to upset the plans of the Communist government. Basically the Tibetans are herders of yaks, sheep, and goats, farming barleys, peas, and tubers. Concentrated in the Tibet, some Tibetans have drifted north to Sichuan and Gansu and south to Yunnan. The **Luoba** and the **Menba** make up minority groups within the Tibetan influence.

The **Uygur** nationality, numbering 5,500,000 dominate the 12 minorities in Xinjiang Uygur Autonomous Region. Seven of these are Muslim, speaking Turkic languages and using Arabic script. Extensive irrigation helps the Uygurs produce some rice along with wheat, cotton, and fruit. Other minorities here include the **Kazaks**, known for their horsemanship and who have spread easterly from Xinjiang into Gansu and Qinghai; the **Kirgiz** (Kergez), are keepers of Bactrian camels who confine their lives mostly to communes now; the **Xibo** (Xibe) people who were border guards for the Manchus 300 years ago and are now living along the lengthy frontiers of the former Soviet Union and Mongolia, as far as Liaoning Province.

Other minority groups	Population (1 million or less)	Region
Luoba	200,000	Tibet
Menba	40,000	Tibet
Kazaks	500,000	Xinjiang, Gansu and Qinghai
Kirgiz	100,000	Xinjiang
Xibo	50,000	frontiers of the CIS & Mongolia
Dongxiang	200,000	Gansu
Sala	50,000	Gansu
Yugur	8,000	Gansu
Baoan	6,000	Gansu
Tartars	2,000	Xinjiang
Russians	less than 1,000	Xinjiang

Riding to the Sunday Market in Kashgar.

manship, stock trading, wrestling, shooting and archery. Some of the Muslim Huis also inhabit this area. A small minority called the **Tu** (Mongour) who once served the Qings as border guards, originated in Qinghai Province.

North-central

The **Mongolians** of the north-central area, are reduced from the hordes that once conquered China and established the Yuan Dynasty, to about 20 per cent of Inner Mongolia's population, estimated at 2,600,000. Many are still nomadic, living in *yurts*, the portable felt and hide tents. The annual Nadam Fair brings them together for feats of horse-

Northeast

The **Manchus** of the northeast estimated at more than 2,500,000 were once horse-mounted, warlike hunters and nomadic herders, who conquered the Mings in 1638 to begin the Qing Dynasty. They merged themselves with the Han combining ancient customs and identity. The Manchurians are concentrated in Liaoning, Jilin, Heilongjiang, Hebei,

A young Chinese woman from Hunan Province.

Beijing and Inner Mongolia. The smaller minority groups, the **Oroqen** and the **Ewenki** have just begun to give up their birch-bark and hide tents for a settled life in Inner Mongolia and Heilongjiang. Their deer breeding is now done in pens and communes. The **Daur** and the **Hezhe**, with a tradition of grain and vegetable farming and fishing during the summer, logging and hunting during the winters, also live in this area. Some 1,000,000 **Koreans** have infiltrated the Heilongjiang, Jilin and Liaoning Provinces for centuries.

Other minority groups	Population (1 million or less)	Region
Tu	120,000	Inner Mongolia
Oroqen	3,000	Inner Mongolia & Heilongjiang
Ewenki	10,000	Inner Mongolia & Heilongjiang
Daur	70,000	Inner Mongolia
Hezhe	less than 1,000	Inner Mongolia

Other Areas

The **Tujia** nationality are located inland from the east coast in Hunan and Hubei Provinces. They farm rice and corn, grow fruit and harvest lumber and are famous for an oil produced from tea leaves. Also on the east coast of Fujian, Zhejiang, Jiangxi and Guangdong Provinces are 330,000 people of the **She** nationality.

The **Qiang** nationality, a group of 80,000 are concentrated in the Han heartland of Sichuan.

Kaoshan (Gaoshan), 300,000 and **Han Kaoshan** are minorities of Taiwan and Fujian Province on the mainland. One time head-hunters, they are aboriginal mountain people whose languages have been identified as Malayo-Polynesian, signifying a possible immigration in the past from the equatorial and South Pacific islands. The Hans of the Kuomintang and their descendants, dating from the 1940 exodus make up the majority of Taiwan's population.

DEEPER MEANINGS

Religion

Pre-revolution writers talk of Chinese humanism as the Chinese ideal of life, "Doctrine of the Golden Mean", which may be called "the Religion of Common Sense". Current leaders of the People's Republic of China (PRC) are acutely aware of this thought, never to be completely expunged from the minds of the people.

During the transitional period and the civil wars with the Kuomintang, Vatican leaders took the side of the Nationalists and in fact, became anti-communist throughout the world. When Mao Zedong took over, the Chinese government ordered that the Chinese Catholic Church sever ties with the Vatican. Forty years later, they attempted reconciliation. Current policy of the CCP towards all religions is to bring socialism closer to the practice of all faiths to relieve the adversarial relationship existing between political ideology and religious belief. They insist, however, that people should place their nation first before religious teachings and performance.

Boddhisattva stands with pagoda in hands in the Sleeping Buddha Cave, Dazu.

Devotees at prayer in a Buddhist temple.

Confucianism

A dominant philosophy deeply entrenched in Chinese culture is Confucianism, which is unusual in that it does not offer a religion. There are no idolatry remembrances, such as Sakyamuni or Jesus Christ. Thoughts of the great humanist, Confucius, are the center of belief, not his person. So true was Confucianism to the human instinct that neither Confucius nor any of his disciples was ever made a god. Chinese military leaders, emperors, empresses, writers, artists, even concubines, were immortalized in tombs, and as local deities and there are hundreds of artistic mediums and styles of Guanyin, the Goddess of Mercy; Lao Shouxing, the longevity figure is in almost every Chinese home, yet representations of Confucius or Mencius, his principle follower, are mere sketches in books written about their philosophies.

The Red Guards during the destructive years of the Cultural Revolution had little to destroy in the Confucian temples. In the Confucian and ancestral temples, there are merely oblong wooden tablets inscribed with characters bearing the names of the spirits they represent, having as little resemblance to idols as a calendar block. These ancestral spirits are not gods, merely departed human beings, continuing to take an interest in their progeny as they did in their lifetime. It is essentially an agnostic system of worship.

Confucianism, common sense and realism are the bases of the down-to-earth quality of Chinese life. Even under the Communists' initial suppression of religious observance, the common sense was survival. For the individual, it was a matter of how to exist under the current circumstances. However, with the recent easing of the right to worship, Buddhist temples which have been renovated to attract the thousands of tourists, are now enjoying the daily adherence of the local Chinese. The small group of monks whose numbers were reduced during the early years of the PRC are swelling again to aid the people in their worship and beliefs.

Confucianism also propagated the Chinese classical education systems and cultivation of the reasonable man. The scholar, by dint of passing examinations was rewarded with administrative posts. Describing the theories listed in the **Analects** (sayings of Confucius), repeats the Golden Mean. Essentially it is the weighing of advice to solve problems and emperors, attuned to Confucianism would listen to both sides of the story and arrive at a mean or average, before making a common-sense decision.

Taoism

Taoism is defined as a pantheistic religion (belief that God and the universe are identical); the doctrine that God does not exist as a personality but is, rather, the expression of the physical forces of nature and theory, founded on the principles of the ancient philosopher Lao Tze. Taoism seeks to avoid complexity in life by conforming with nature.

Lao Tze, the proponent of Taoism said derisively about Confucianism, "No character, then benevolence; no benevolence, then righteousness". In other words, the great teacher Confucius always had an answer for behavior and no room for imagination or fantasy.

Taoists believe in the childish world of wonderment, romanticism, family, a return to nature, revolt against responsibilities, simplicity in life, art, and literature.

The departed are sent on their way with paper renditions of cars, houses, and money which are burned in their honor. Remains, after cremation, are

Confucius

Confucius, K'ung Futse, was a man of all time, born in 500 BC illegitimately, of a 15-year-old girl and a man old enough to be her grandfather. Ho Shuliang, a retired soldier was 70 years old when he sired the son who was destined to be one of the best known names in the history of mankind.

In his day, the father enjoyed a certain reputation as a military commander and probable descendant of the K'ungs of the Song royal family during the Zhou Dynasty (770-221 BC). Ho Shuliang endeared himself to the Duke of Lu in the struggle for a village, as the story goes. His troops had entered the compound on an offer of truce to the residents. The townspeople, however, closed the gate, set upon and almost destroyed them. Ho, a large, strong man, single-handedly forced open the gate and released his troops. The hero was given the military command of his village on retirement to mull upon the local problems and his own misfortune.

Ho, while taking many wives during his exceptionally long life, sired only daughters, thus had no one to carry on the family name. Having to dowry the nine daughters, the family was impoverished and it seemd that his own soul was doomed to wander without a son to perform ancestral rituals.

The tormented Ho hired a young woman to bear him a son, promising rewards if successful. In 551 BC she bore the retired general a son. The boy was named Ch'iu, a nickname meaning hill, the place the young mother went to pray before her conception; it was formalized into Chung Ni (mud's younger brother). The baby was reputed to be the ugliest ever seen in the town. His nose was twisted, there was a bulge on his skull and the huge bulk of a child was destined to be tall and heavy like his father. The general deserted the woman, died shortly after, and the family refused to recognize the illegitimate heir. The mother took the baby to the nearby larger city of Qu Fu, now considered the birthplace of Confucius in Jilin Province. She adopted the family name K'ung, as a rightful descendant of the royals.

K'ung Ch'iu, the scholar, studied hard, and at the age of 15 was giving advice. "At home respect your parents. Away from home, respect your elders. Be honest; love man; love what is good. If you have time afterwards, study." His passionate love of books and learning is reflected in another well-known saying: "Study as if you never could get enough of it, as if you were afraid something might get away from you." He lived in what is called the Spring and Autumn Period of the Zhou's, a feudal society, where warring was pre-eminent.

K'ung probed the classics **I Ching (Book of Changes)**, a strange collection of 64 different word patterns that required arrangement to study. **Shih Ching (Book of Odes)** is a collection of folk songs, which the scholar favored immensely. At 30 he began to travel the neighboring kingdoms, extolling his wisdom and being recognized by the various courts. He proposed peace, sometimes consolidation and acquired a mentor in the ruling families of the state of Lu. On his death bed, the Lord Meng proclaimed Ch'iu as the leading scholar of his time, directing that his descendants be taught by him. He thus became K'ung Futse (Master K'ung). K'ung Futse, long after his death be-

often kept in decorative urns, stored in altar-like cabinets, handed down to succeeding generations. This is called the cult of ancestor worship, in practice among Chinese to this day.

Confucianism and Taoism have long been a subject of scholastic dispute. Both respect family life, but while Confucians encourage participation, academic and work effort and contribution to the world, Taoist aims are much simpler, as an unknown poet wrote:

We go to work at sunrise.
And come back to rest at sunset.
We know nothing and learn nothing.

came Confucius during the era of the Jesuits who struggled to create the phonetics for the language (pinyun) to render spoken Chinese accessible to non-speakers of Chinese. Currently 75 generations of Confucius call themselves Kong.

One should imagine the figure of Confucius described as 2m tall, bumpy head, wide-set eyes, warts on a twisted nose, buck teeth, all making a shy youth conscious of his ugly appearance. He took friends among the blind, artists, and academicians of his time who valued his wisdom above all. He was known to have a catalogue memory, the curiosity of a monkey and the humor of a court jester.

Court circles adopted the ungainly scholar, but those circles changed with the military times. Various power struggles challenged K'ung Futse to bear with the ones that best suited his own philosophies. **The Analects** reveal one of his most famous sayings: "If you use laws to direct people and punishments to control them, they will only evade the laws and develop no conscience. But if you guide them by virtue and control them by customs, they will have a conscience and a sense of what is right."

In the year 501 BC, K'ung Futse was honored with an appointment as Governor of the Middle District of Lu, then subsequently appointed Minister of Public Works and finally as Minister of Justice, his most revered role. Many of the phrases, said to be repeated by him in the latter role still ring true today, 2500 years and 75 generations later, to wit:

"Among the ordinary people, the parents labor to sow and reap, but their sons do not understand hard work. They lounge in the streets vulgar in speech, disorderly in behavior."

"Another can judge a case as well as I. What I would like to do is correct the conditions that bring cases about."

K'ung Futse lived to an old age like his father. He had located him buried his mother next to him and performed the ancestral rituals of a son. He knew and advised most of the rulers of his day, philosophized with Lao Tze, the founder of Taoism, corrected the historical records of the era (Spring and Autumn Annals), wrote poems and bemoaned the loud rancorous music of his day as nothing but drums and bells. He died in 479 BC at the age of 72.

Disciples led by a brilliant grandson, K'ung Tze Sse recorded his fame in **Lun Yu, The Collected Sayings (Analects).** A century later, Mencius (371-289 BC) led the scholars of his time in his teachings and wisdom. Early Qin leaders destroyed Confucian scholars and their works in the interest of ritual posterity. The Hans resuscitated the Confucians, their philosophy and writings. Confucian ways persisted in government until the overthrow of the Qing Dynasty and the eventual takeover by the Communists, with their manifestos of Marx and Lenin.

Confucianism has been kept alive in Chinese culture over all these years. Indeed wherever pockets of Chinese are found outside of China, one may invariably detect Confucian appreciations, despite modern environments. An example of this is to be seen in the Chinese-majority nation of Singapore. Modern day Singapore is imbued with the Confucian philosophy, a shining light in the world today of a free, safe, and non-militaristic society.

What has the emperor's virtue to do with us?

Leave us alone to till our farms, enjoy our children and dream of dragons and romance, say the Taoists.

Confucians prefer to dwell on the past, the golden age of Emperors Yao and Shun. Life was elementary, and man needed little compared to today's complicated lifestyle. Worship of ancestors and the simplistic life were synonymous. The ideal family proposes that each member has a role such as "the man studied and tilled the ground while the woman helped in the harvest and

To light joss for prayers said, Xiyuan Garden, Suzhou.

spun and wove".

Taoism flowered during the Wei and Jin Dynasties (220-419), overshadowing Confucianism. Art and literature chided the formality of the decorous and ceremonial Confucians. It continued during the Tang Dynasty (618-907), became known as the "mystic religion", fomented by the Tang Imperial Court.

Blossoming of Taoism included the *Yin* (female) and *Yang* (male) principles, secret knowledge of herbs and medicines, magic, witchcraft, aphrodisiacs, incantations, astrology, a good hierarchy of gods, some beautiful legends and a priesthood. It took care, too, of Chinese athletics, by specializing in boxing. The combination of boxing and witchcraft produced the Huangchin Rebellion at the end of the Han Dynasty. Last of all, it offered a health formula. The application of the *ch'i*, deep-breathing, was practically universal, from the rays of a comet to boxing.

Sexual union was sedulously practiced as an art (with a preference for virgins), in the cause of prolongation of life. Therefore Taoism was, in short, the Chinese attempt to discover the mysteries of nature.

Buddhism

Buddha, "the Enlightened One", was a term applied to the great teacher Siddhartha Gautama, called Gautama Buddha by his followers. He was born around 563 BC and died in 483 BC. He was regarded by his disciples as a teacher possessing perfect enlightenment and wisdom.

Buddhism is a religion that developed in the 5th century BC in northern India and spread over central, southeastern, and eastern Asia. It teaches that right living will enable people to attain *nirvana*, the condition of a soul that does not have to live in a body and is free from all desire and pain.

Buddha's disciples journeyed to China during the Han Dynasty and was the only foreign influence that actually became part and parcel of everyday Chinese life. By the time of the last dynasty, children were called "little boddhisatvas" and the Empress Dowager herself was addressed as "The Old Buddha".

Guanyin, the Goddess of Mercy and Maitreya (Ho Ti), the laughing Buddha with the big belly and drooping ears were in every household. Guanyin was often depicted with many arms bearing gifts of love, healing, long life, good fortune and others. Maitreya usually had children playing at his feet and his fat tummy was rubbed each day for good fortune.

Buddhist monks became more popular than Taoist monks and increased their temples tenfold over the Taoist or Confucian followers; the Panchen Lamas from Tibet even journeyed to Peking (Beijing). Replicas of the Tibetan truncated pyramidal buildings were built in their honor. In one

A young monk in Yunnan working hard at writing scripture.

instance the Panchen Lama journeyed for a year to bring gifts to the imperial household in the Summer Palace at Chengde and a temple was built in Tibetan style in his honor, however, he sadly died of the pox a few days after his arrival.

In pre-Communist China, Buddhism invaded China as a philosophy and as a religion for the common people. Competing and often blending with Confucianism in the same household, Buddhism possessed a logical method, a metaphysics, and a theory of knowledge, while Confucianism was merely moral conduct. Scholars swung back and forth from the succinct and beautiful passages of Buddhist texts to the philosophical phrases of the **Analects**

Fertility god dressed up and holding a peach and lotus flower.

and **Book of Changes** of Confucianism. Blending occurred like the solving of moral problems using the philosophy of *hsing* (nature), *li* (reason), *ming* (predestination), *hsin* (mind), *wu* (matter), and *chih* (knowledge). There is a hanging temple carved in rock near the old capital of Datong, where Buddhist and Taoist monks worship with Confucianist followers performing their rites.

There is an aspect of Buddhism that is unique which largely restrains the eating of meats. Unlike the Hindus who consider cattle sacred, Buddhists are wary of killing a pig, dog, cow, or any animal for fear of retribution in reincarnation. One could return to this world as a member of the animal kingdom, therefore slaughter of such could be seen as killing an ancestor.

The true Sakyamuni follower is kindly, offering food and tea to the wanderer, as well as filling the daily bowl of local monks with rice and vegetables. This is considered an investment in future happiness when the state of *nirvana* is reached.

Travelers can understand the proliferation of Buddhist temples, the practice of vegetarian food habits, and idol worship when finding the temples and pavilions at various levels of mountains they climb.

The current crop of leaders, members of the ruling Communist Party have found it necessary to let the people worship openly again. Ancient temples are being rebuilt, reincarnated in some instances; monks are again allowed to fill out their ranks, as tension eases and sites are recreated to attract the cash crop of tourists.

Christianity

Christianity too, is being revived to some degree by the re-furbishing of existing churches and allowing foreigners to have places to worship. Pre-communist statistics estimated that there were over 3 million Catholics and 1 million Protestants in China. Catholicism remains in a weakened state without the priests and bishops recognized by Rome. Allowances were made in the late 17th century for Franciscans, Dominicans, Augustinians and the Jesuits because they took in the poor and the orphans, brought medical assistance, ran the Imperial Observatory and taught schools.

History relates that Nestor, founder of the Nestorian Sect, brought Christianity to China in the year 635. Nestorians refused the dogma of the Roman Catholics. Visitors will see the symbol of their religion, a cross with circles at the end of each arm, at the museum in Xian. Religious persecution was rampant but the missionaries spread far and wide over the land, until the time of the Mongols when it faded from the scene.

The stories of Marco Polo, his father and uncle, relate how their original quest was to take representatives of Rome to

Chinese style Catholic altar in Beijing.

China but they failed in that mission. Matteo Ricci, an Italian was welcomed at the Ming Court as was his successor Adam Schall Von Bell (1591-1666). Two to three thousand Christian missionaries were thought to be in China during this period. The Jesuits brought technical knowledge; Von Schall worked to improve the calendar. The fate of religious invasion curved from complete obliteration at times to enthusiasm and support by astute monarchs at other times.

Islam

Ten nationalities in China profess to be followers of Allah and the Koran. There

A mosque in Muslim Kashgar.

are approximately 14 million who enjoy special status under the Communists as a recognized minority rather than a religion.

Prophet Mohammed was born in the 6th century in Mecca. Evidently his teachings were not only confined to Asia Minor but brought into China by traders following the overland Silk Road and by sea to the ports of Amoy, Fuzhou and Ningbo on the southeastern coast. At one point in history, during the Qing Dynasty (1634-1911) there was pressure brought to bear against the Muslims.

20 thousand mosques existing today. Their right to worship is again respected, provided the other laws of the land and patriotism are observed.

Judaism

Jewish refugees from the Russian pogroms have a small place in history in China. They entered the Manchurian province of Heilongjiang and settled principally in the city of Harbin. Evidence of a synagogue still exist there though there is no overt practice of the Jewish faith at the present time. Like Catholicism, Judaism was forced underground during adverse periods of the communist reign.

Freedom of worship

In the final analysis, religion is re-asserting itself in the modernization program of Deng Xiaoping. Foreigners visiting China today can virtually attend services of their faith in the major cities of Beijing, Shanghai and Guangdong. The prevalence of embassies, trade agents, news media, and foreign workers hired for various reasons also require the opening of basic religious facilities in the major cities. This new perspective towards religion by the authorities has positive consequences in other ways. Religious sites are being re-discovered and restored. In the process other treasures are uncovered.

Intermarriage with people considered to be Chinese was forbidden and new mosques and migration were curtailed to contain them to the northwest regions.

The Cultural Revolution hysteria took its toll on the followers of Allah and their strange houses of worship. It is estimated that there are no more than

TREASURES & PLEASURES

Performing & Literary Arts

Rhythm of the fine arts of China is the proper relation of parts producing a harmonious whole, especially by repeating certain forms, colors and methods of composition. Dance is the movement of rhythm within the far reaches of the arts. The crafting of arts is a form of human activity which appeals to the imagination, especially drawing, painting, and sculpture, and it also includes architecture, literature, music, and dance.

The arts are civilization's storehouse of felt values, the rendering of what has seemed important to those of powerful imagination and profound feeling and great mastery of expression (Harper's).

China is probably the largest storehouse of arts in the world. Each of the 7 groups above has an enormous amount of literature on the library shelves. There is also an immense amount of Chinese art production existing all over the world. Sea captains loaded tons of cargo in the

Ancient Chinese scenery.

87

The art of Beijing opera, dramatised by make-up and costumes.

Ming and Qing Dynasties to fill the drawing rooms of the elite in Europe and the Americas. Safari traders trekked hundreds of thousands of camel loads of the same to Central Asia and Europe over the Silk Road. The world has more evidence of China than China has of the world.

Stage Center - Beijing Opera

All tours to China include at least one opera and one acrobatic performance as *de rigueur* of the schedule. Beijing Opera is the popular and traditional theater of China which visitors find exotic and fascinating. Half a century ago, describing his first experience in watching a Beijing Opera performance given by the great stage artist Mei Lanfang and his company, an American critic wrote:

"You will be puzzled all the way through, and a little bored once in a while; but in spite of knowing nothing of the dramatic background, in spite of hundreds of rigid conventions of staging and gesture, in spite of the musical accompaniment that often outrages your ears, you will be charmed and fascinated and now and then swept off your feet."

Encouraged by the tourist industry, China today has thousands of theatrical troupes, said to employ a quarter-million artists, set designers, make-up experts, and stage hands. Performances

Mei Lanfang - Master of the Opera

For over a half century, Mei Lanfang was the best known name in Beijing Opera both at home and abroad. He began his career at the age of 8 and made his debut on stage at 11 in a female role.

Men played the female roles for thousands of years because women were traditionally confined to the palace and their living quarters, harem style. Actresses first appeared after the downfall of the Qing Dynasty (1911). From the 1920's women took part on the stage acquiring great fame, but never more than Mei Lanfang in his female roles.

Mei Lanfang was born into an operatic family in 1894. Father, grandfather, and uncle made up 4 generations of what is considered the first family of modern opera. Mei Lanfang rose as a great master of Beijing Opera, first specializing in *qing yi* which is mainly a singing role. Later on he became skilled in playing the other types of female role, namely the *gui men dan*, an unmarried young girl and *hui dan*, women of the vivacious type and occasionally the *ma dan*, woman warrior.

Mei Lanfang was famous by the age of 20, his career extending for 50 years playing more than 100 different characters in the traditional Beijing Opera repertoire. He continued acting until his death in 1961. A study of his career, **Peking Opera and Mei Lanfang** (by New World Press) is the complete story of classical Chinese opera.

---

are regional in origin, such as the Beijing and Sichuan opera. The 56 minorities all have their specialized formats of theater and dance.

The costumes, representing court attire of the heyday of the arts date principally from the Tang and Ming Dynasties, featuring colorful silks with long hanging sleeves that are flung around in sequence to the dialogue. Makeup and masks are an art form by itself, each nuance of eye shadow, white paint, or black paint has a symbolic meaning, understandable only to the aficionado or student of opera. Papercuts of the masks are sold in all of the hotel kiosks and book stores, the best way (and inexpensive) to remember the more appealing characters.

Attendance is carefree, with none of the hushed audience of the western theater. Most often the dialogue is flashed on a side screen, and during the proceedings it would not be unusual to find that fruit is peeled and thrown on the floor, conversation and laughter carrying on in the audience, and patrons seemingly paying little attention to the performance. Constant repetition of the plots apparently make them as generic as the Little Red Riding Hood story.

Appreciating the instrumental side of the opera requires knowledge, patience, and tolerance (for the uninitiated) for the strident whining voices of the actors "outrage the ear" as reporter said. Even without your guide whispering the plot in your ear, it is easy to distinguish the good guys from the bad from their costumes and attitude. The poor little heroine about to be sacrificed as an unwilling bride to the household of the mandarin where other wives and concubines gather to tease, is an obvious plot.

Scene from a Chinese Opera : 2 generals in a serious discussion.

On the serious side, classical Chinese drama is a comprehensive performing art with a unique form of its own. It is an ingenious combination of elements from many sources: traditional Chinese music, poetry, singing, recitation, dancing, acrobatics and martial skills, all blended into one great theatrical art.

A performer must undergo 7 to 12 years of basic training in make-up, martial skills (whether or not acting such a role) to enhance the smooth ability to glide across the stage, pose as a piece of delicate sculpture, speak, and sing in the specialized manner of the stage. Every nuance of facial and body expression is a necessary element of the performance, indicating climbing a mountain or wading across a stream.

There is little scenery in Chinese opera, however there are certain dramatic codes. Instead, circling the stage, whip-in-hand suggests riding a horse, riding in a carriage is represented by an attendant holding flags painted with a wheel design; walking in a circle indicates a long journey; 4 soldiers and 4 generals flanking both sides of the stage represent a large army; and, on a stage bare of props, a performer holding an oar doing deep knee bends simulates a sea voyage with varying degrees of swells. The actor must be able to convey to the audience a mental scene of the background. Constant odd moments of music accompany and enhance a scene, as bits and dabs of song interjected at

Musical Instruments

The Lute. A deceptively simple instrument of the Chinese scholar.

The main stringed instrument used for operatic performances is the fiddle, known as the **jing bu** (Beijing fiddle) used for vocal accompaniment. Its sound box is bamboo, one end of which is covered with snake skin, while a bow is drawn across two strings. Supporting instruments are the **er bu** (second fiddle), slightly shorter strings with a lower tone and the **si bu** (4-stringed fiddle), all with the same bamboo and snake skin.

Plucked instruments are the **yue gin** (moon-mandolin) with a round body and short strings; the **pi pa** (4-stringed lute) with an elongated pear shape and refined mellow tone, a primary medium for instrumentalists. The **xian zi** is a 3-stringed lute of circular pieces of hardwood, over which the traditional snake skin is stretched, with a long neck and 3 strings, about a meter in length and rendering a slight overtone.

The **suo na** (Chinese clarinet) is made of a certain wood pierced with 8 holes, blown through a small tissue in the mouthpiece and a sound magnifier at the outer end. A flute-like instrument, **sheng** (reed organ) the only horn that produces harmony, is constructed of 10 pieces of bamboo, each containing a hole, all fastened to a frame. The suo na and sheng are often played in unison, giving the characteristic tonals of oriental music.

Percussion instruments are **luo**, gongs and drums of various sizes and shapes. This is what you will first hear when the actor steps on stage, for emphasis during pantomime and as an exit accompaniment. A 15 or 18-cm diameter **xiao luo** (small gong) is played for a female character's movements.

There are also clappers made of hard wood or bamboo. The **nao** (cymbals), usually brass, are the same as used in western orchestras. Bells of various sizes are used in synch, usually exclusively to keep time, while additional tappings on the bell are done to delight the ear.

The **jiu yin luo** (9-toned gong) is made of 9 circular pieces of brass, about 20 to 25 mm each, hung inside a wooden frame and hit with a small wooden stick. It is never played when an actor sings or talks for it is believed the tones will blur the voice. A really good drummer, usually the conductor, using an implement similar to a pair of chopsticks, is able to create a very powerful sound effect: sometimes loud, sometimes soft, sometimes strong and exciting, or sometimes faint and sentimental to bring out the emotions of the characters in coordination with the acting of the performers.

To the unaccustomed ear, the music often sounds strident and harsh to the ears until one realizes and understands that it is part of the dialogue of the performance.

propitious moments.

The music of wind, stringed and percussion instruments creates powerful sound effects to back up the performance of the cast. Men often play female roles, such as the famous Mei Lanfang, positively identified as *dan*.

The characters subdivide into the quiet and gentle, vivacious or dissolute, women with martial skills sword-and-horse-rider type, and old women (*lao dan*).

Male roles are the young man and the warrior type. The painted face styles indicate frank, open-minded, rough, crafty, dangerous, warrior or civilian; and clown, the court jester. Therefore Chinese opera offers more than the traditional concept of voice, costumes and movement.

Acrobatics

Acrobatics is the specialized theatrical form dating back 2,000 years when performances were held in the village or city square by nomadic groups of actors. Trained animals were often a part of the performances using monkeys, bears and, at one time, even pandas. Household goods and military paraphernalia are used for props linked to the everyday life of the people.

A stack of chairs and tables, balanced precariously with the artist stretching at the top, twirling plates from limbs, head and nose fascinate the locals. Leaping figures, themselves stacked a dozen or more high, are constantly bouncing around the stage, waving swords and cracking whips. An acrobatic show is generally a fast moving 2-hour performance that challenges the eye to view everything that is going on.

Literature

The pictograph, beginnings of recorded Chinese writings, evolved into characters that far exceeded the European and Arabic system of letters. Translators are perpetually challenged to convert the subtle meanings and beauty of a drawn

A deft plate-balancing performance from a Chinese circus.

series into an understanding by the mere equivalent of words for the English reader. Poetry was and is a form of writing desired and encouraged by the scholars and academics. They were songs written in a lyrical style, odes to record history, simple characters written on ancient oracle bones, or strips of wooden slats glued on a roll of material or parchment. These became the roll ups of scrolls and dictated the system of reading from right to left and top to bottom as the scroll unfolded.

Poets were venerated, especially

Tang Dynasty Poets

Early 7th-century poetry was primarily a stylized form of discourse practised mainly in court circles. During the 7th and 8th centuries, poetry was transformed from a minor diversion to an art that fully embodied private, social and cultural values.

The imperial court and the lesser courts of imperial princes and princesses had been the center of poetic composition. In 680, poetic composition was introduced into the *chin-shih* examination, an examination designed specifically to bring into the government candidates who were not scions of the great capital families. This was a strong inducement for the spread of interest in poetic craft. Hsuan-tsung's edict in 772 against the large entourages of the imperial princes dealt the final deathblow to the old social order of poetry. These 2 events sparked off an era of literary glory, unmatched in later dynasties, that produced great names like Wang Wei, Wang Chang-ling, Li Po and Du Fu, names that are revered even till today.

Wang Wei

In Wang Wei, exiled from the court to a low post in the east, is seen the controlled, austere style for which he is famous. The greatness of his poems is his interest in perception : how things are seen, how the physical world controls how things are seen, and how the forms of perception have inner significance.

Wang Wei's poem, by its simplicity of diction, challenges the reader to look more deeply into the significance implicit in the structure of representation. His major contribution to poetry was his distinctive style - he replaced the dense couplets of early Tang poetry with a purity and simplicity of style that definitely compels.

Wang Changling

The serious intellectual concerns that characterize Wang Wei's poetry is absent in Wang Changling. He sought a style that in a few quick strokes could evoke a mood, a figure, an emotionally fraught situation. Most of his poems are true mood pieces, like the following :

As sky's frost falls then, filling hearts
A lean horse galloping, eyes on the north,
And exiles grieving for songs of the South east.
Oh, when shall the border grasses turn white,

In Wang Changling can be seen the craft of the master of the evocative image, the dramatic gesture, and the suggestive scene.

Li Po

Li Po was a poet par excellence, but the one great legacy he left behind to future poets was an interest in personal and poetic identity. To him mere excellence was no longer sufficient - he had to be both excellent and unique. Li Po was a poet who suprised his readers and violated their sense of poetic order and decorum.

Li Po hailed from Sichuan, and anecdotes suggest that as Sichuan was a less stable region than central China, violent behavior or the boasting menace of violent, unpredictable behavior was an asset there. Whatever the reason, Li Po found a concept of poetry that could comfortably accommodate his Sichuanese persona - he possessed a divine nature that legitimized wild eccentricity in both poetry and behavior. Out of this heady liberation from everyday humanity came his multiple guises : Li Po the wild drinker, the womanizer, the man who cheerfully disregards authority and social decorum, the poet who dashes off verses without thinking, the spontaneous genius.

Ho Chih-cheung, the director of the Imperial Library, commended on his "Song of the Roosting Crows" as being able to "make gods and ghosts weep". He possessed a capability that very few Chinese poets before him had - a fictional imagination. Li Po's talent distinguishes itself in this respect - he was more convincing describing an encounter with an immortal or a fight through the heavens than when he described some social occasion at which he was actually present.

A pervasive theme in 8th-century poetry was rejection of public life. It is an important and nearly universal attribute of high civilization that those who have attained wealth and power are fascinated by the prospect of renouncing what they have coveted so greatly. But all the various roles that Li Po assumed in his poetry were outside the twin roles of scholar-official and serene recluse - the immortal, the drinker, the eccentric. Through these roles, Li Po was saying that he was different from other poets, in fact, "better than". As the poet without legitimate social background, he had to "invent" himself. Through this concern with "inventing" himself, Li Po was able to liberate himself from some of the more restrictive aspects of the poetic tradition : the passivity of the perceiving subject, the repression of human will, and the tyranny of the external world. Li Po's manner, which he perfected, came virtually to define genius in poetry.

Du Fu

To the literary world, Du Fu is the greatest Chinese poet. He is almost beyond judgment, like Shakespeare, his literary accomplishment has itself become a major component in the historical formation of literary values.

Du Fu's poetry is an experience in several dimensions. He was also one of the first Chinese poets to discover the energy of tragi-comedy - his inclination was to "complicate", to draw in opposing dimensions and then to "complete" this knowledge. His "Facing the Snow" is a classic example.

> Weeping over battle, many new ghosts,
> In sorrow reciting poems, an old man all alone.
> A tumult of clouds sinks downward in sun set,
> Hard-pressed, the snow dances in whirl winds.
> Ladle cast down, no green lees in the cup,
> The brazier lingers on, fire seems crimson.
> From several provinces now news have

Li Po, the often inebriated, but celebrated poet.

> ceased
> I sit here in sorrow tracing words in air.

Here, the correspondences between the political world, the cosmic cycles manifest in the seasons, and the scene before his eyes all come together in Du Fu's vision of the snow scene. The reader can visualize the conflicting elements : in the battlefields, many "new" ghosts, the young dead slain unnaturally before their time; within is the solitary "survivor", the old man for whom death would be appropriate. Gradually the world faced grows closer, first in clouds on the horizon, then in the snow whirling before the window. These are nature's correlatives of disorder and rebellion. The poet faces a world of disorder, white in the growing darkness of night and these echo the interplay of cosmic forces.

Du Fu then "balances" what is faced with the one who faces - the poet and the world inside. The antithesis of the winter world is warmth, light, and color - the wine that is gone and the fire that is dying, growing redder as it burns down to the embers.

In form and style, "Facing The Snow" is an example of the `classic' Du Fu - poetry that is a configuration of fragments, insistently symbolic.

East meets west in contemporary China painting.

during the artistic era of the Tang Dynasty (618-907). **Quang Tangshi**, a prolific collection of poetry contains almost 50,000 poems rendered by over 2,000 poets of that period. Confucian ideas prompted the writings of **Du Fu** (712-770) whose cottage in Chengdu is heavily touristed. Most paintings were completed with a few characters of poetry written in a corner, followed by the artist's seal, a character representing his name.

The range of fiction in Chinese literature follows history. The modern classics revolve around **Lu Xun**, who managed to placate the Communists, more or less, with unprecedented freedom inside China. The collected works of Lu Xun are published in a 4-volume series, the writings notable because of the exceedingly rich and varied scope. He researched, studied, wrote and taught during his lifetime and was an early supporter of the Sun Yatsen directed revolution in 1911.

A brief list of the classics include:

A Journey to the West. The king of the monkeys, Sun Wokong, travels to the West (India) with a pig and a monk, to collect a copy of the holy scriptures.

The Bandits of Liangshan Moor is a novel from the Ming period about robbers. Song Jiang is a Robin Hood character operating in the northeast province of Shandong.

The Plum Blossom in a Golden Year, describes Ximen, a Casanova character of the Ming period confronting

Lu Xun the Writer

Lu Xun (nee Zhou Shuren) was born the 25th of September, 1881 in Shaoxing, province of Zhejiang (see Hangzhou section), of a scholarly official family. The traumas of the times deprived the family of the grandfather and father, leaving Lu Xun in the hands of a dedicated, self-educated mother. He took her name, Lu, as his own in her memory.

He was an avid reader, beginning the study of the ancient classics at the age of six. Said to have a photographic memory, the range of his studies covered the Chinese classics, mythology, unofficial histories, miscellaneous essays, anecdotes, painting, picture albums, woodcuts, romances and cartoons.

From the official government line of reviewing his life, he was greatly influenced by the encroachment upon the country by foreign powers and the bankruptcy of Chinese feudalism. Growing up in a family, impoverished by the imprisonment of his grandfather and death of his father, Lu Xun's early writings reflect the hardships of the times. Most notable is the famous novella, *The True Story of Ah Q*, the tale of a most unfortunate character. Ah Q suffered all the indignities of man including a scalp scarred with ringworm that glowed when he became angry.

At 18, Lu Xun, as his biographers write, took off for Nanjing with the silver equivalent of 8 dollars to take the entrance examinations for the Naval Academy. Though he passed and entered the academy, he transferred a year later to the School of Railways and Mines. This too did not satisfy him and indicative of his nature, always seeking a new medium, a fresh outlook on life. It was in Nanjing that he became enamored and involved in the Reform Movement of 1888, the seeds of revolution that eventually toppled the Qing Dynasty.

Lu Xun graduated from the school and was awarded a government scholarship to study in Japan, where he became further involved with the student group fomenting the revolution known as Guang Fu Hui, the anti-Qing revolutionary party. He entered a Medical College, and, as before, immediately became disenchanted.

In 1909, he returned to China to teach physiology and chemistry in Zhejiang Normal School and Shaoxing Middle School. In 1912 he was appointed a member of the Ministry of Education overseeing studies of Chinese culture and studies of the Indian Buddhist classics, as the country became further embroiled in the chaos of changes. His first short story, *A Madman's Diary*, appeared in *New Youth*, a magazine which guided the cultural and democratic revolution in 1918. It was also the first magazine to introduce the ideas of the October Revolution and of Marxism-Leninism. At this time the budding author began to write penetrating, militant essays dealing with social problems. In 1923, the publication of his first volume of short stories, *Call to Arms*, which included such immortal works as "My Old Home" and "The True Story of Ah Q" established Lu Xun as father of new literature.

bureaucrats, schemers and the evil underpinnings of the fading Mongols.

Dream of the Red Chambers is published in 3 volumes, literally the soap opera of lifestyle in the Qing Dynasty. There is a main character, Jia Baoyu, a son of a Manchu mandarin, and his affairs with a dozen women of the household. Over 400 characters complicate the reading, a compliment to the work of a lifetime for the author Cao Zhan.

Water Margins is introduced by its 13th century author with the following: "A man should not marry after 30 years of age; should not enter the government service after the age of 40; should not have any more children after the age of 50; and should not travel after the age of 60." The compilation of stories involves 108 heros driven to isolation for various

Han Suyin - the Romanticist

Han Suyin, the daughter of a Belgian mother and a Chinese father, chose to travel to Europe on a medical scholarship at the age of 19. After completing a pre-med education at Yengcheng University, she continued medical courses at the University of Brussels.

Destination Chungking was written in 1940, while she was married to an ex-Sandhurst Chinese general officer in Chiang Kaishek's army. The Sino-Japanese war at the time provided a multitude of experiences in mid-wifery and trauma medicine in the interior.

Her husband was appointed military attache in London in 1942. The general returned to China in 1945 leaving Han Suyin in London to complete her medical studies. In 1947, war-widowed, she accepted a post as a doctor in Hong Kong.

A Many Splendoured Thing, a Eurasian love story, said to be her own, won plaudits around the world. ***Crippled Tree***, part of her China autobiographical series tells in historical sequence the marriage of an English woman to a Chinese man. ***The Mountain is Young*** resulted from the author being invited to attend the coronation of the King of Nepal in 1956. The event took place in Kathmandu, land of the gods, land of snow peaks and temples, tigers and roses, palaces and Ranas. ***My House Has Two Doors***, part of the autobiographical series took place during the chaotic years of the Cultural Revolution. ***Till Morning Comes*** is another novel of a love affair between a western foreign correspondent and a Chinese doctor. The literature renders a remarkable insight into the lives of people caught in the fringe.

---

crimes to the mountain Liang Shan Bo. They venture out to cure the evil events which overcome people.

The prologue contains the following poem written in the reign of Emperor Shan Tsung of the Song Dynasty by a famous scholar named **Shao Yaofu**. The milieu is the chaos of the Five Dynasties (907-960) following the glorious Tang period.

> *Amid chaos of dynasties five,*
> *Peaceful days at last revive;*
> *Mountains and rivers are of yore,*
> *Benevolence of hundred years and*
>   *more.*
> *Orioles sang in forest trees.*
> *Entrancing music filled the air;*
> *The people dressed in gorgeous silks,*
> *Contentment reigned everywhere.*

Among the many expatriate Chinese writers is the fascinating and memorable **Han Suyin**, most remembered for ***A Many-Splendored Thing***, described by ***The London Times*** as "an astounding love story...brilliantly topical, but far more than that, for Han Suyin handles an eternal theme with power, insight and unfailing artistry." Those visitors to China who choose to view the country through the lives and loves of people during the past half-century will enjoy the range of biography, history and fiction in the many books written by Han Suyin.

Literature is the thread of history of China. There is no brief way of comprehending the cloth it weaves without an academic lifetime study. The casual traveler will, however, by reading some of the above before entering the Middle Kingdom better understand and enjoy this strange and esoteric world.

Traditional Chinese painting in the Government Arts and Crafts Factory, Foshan.

Contemporary Chinese Painting

Wu Zuoren wrote, "The culture of a nation is like a long turbulent river, whose eternal currents surge forward despite the many bends along its course". During the Ming and Qing Dynasties (1368-1911) painters had the habit of copying ancient works of art using the basic rules of line drawing, shading and textural brush strokes, applying dots and using natural objects for composi-

The Folk Artist - Qi Baishi

Flowers, birds, insects and fish were the main subjects of Qi Baishi (alias Qi Huang, Qi Weiqing, and Qi Pingsheng) (1863-1917). Born to a peasant family in Hunan Province, Qi received his early art education as apprentice to a woodcarver. He studied painting, poetry, calligraphy, and seal-engraving, eventually maturing as a traveling artist of great reputation and fame.

Qi was a great admirer of many earlier masters, his initial works showing their influence. He altered his style of painting several times until a mature style of his own emerged, characterized by a vigorous and elegant simplicity. He ingeniously fused traditional freehand brushwork with folk art techniques.

The works of Qi Baishi have a fresh lyrical quality, reflecting the extent to which he derived his inspiration from nature. His painting combines direct observation of nature with feelings and sentiments that sought to achieve a likeness both in shape and spirit of the subjects he portrayed.

He was able to suggest the essence of a subject with a few strokes. One can perceive in his art a high sense of reality. Everything he painted bubbled with life, joy, optimism and often humour, thus reflecting his view of the world.

tion. They disdained the western methods of perspective, shadow and light. Qing Emperor Qianlong (1736-96) is reputed to have created over 2500 paintings and ten times that of poems. The Imperial Academy in Beijing was the center of the art world in that age of renaissance of art and architecture and led in the new style and perspective to art that were to follow.

Traditional paintings can be classified by subject matter into figure paintings, landscapes and flower-and-bird renditions. Student Chinese artists, since the era of the Silk Road and the opening of China to foreign education, traveled to the European centers of art.

Budding masters assimilated the characteristics of foreign art into traditional Chinese paintings. More important they realized the importance of free expression, innovation in style and subject. Galleries, such as the one in Shenyang, display bold communist theology in workers' subjects, classic renditions of the "Three Friends" of winter, the pine tree, bamboo and prunus tree, and distinctive nudes, in addition to more mundane subjects of flowers and birds.

Among the many contemporary artists of note is **Qi Baishi**, Honorary Professor at the Central Academy of Fine Arts, Chairman of the Chinese Artists' Association and a deputy to the National People's Congress during his lifetime. Another is **Xu Beihong** who acquired the distinction of being elected Chairman of the Chinese Artists' Association and President of the Central Academy of Fine Arts.

Today visitors will find an enormous amount of street art, generally considered souvenirs, in the free markets of the cities. Book and art stores in the major centers have a limited amount of original art for sale. Good examples of the older forms are found in the

The Painter of Horses - Xu Beihong

Xu Beihong (1891-1953) learned painting from his father, a village art teacher while working on the farm, gaining an early respect for his future talent in painting horses. In 1916, he entered Fudan University in Shanghai to study French and went to France to study western painting in the Ecole Nationale Superieure des Beaux-Arts. Like other art students of the period, Xu visited Berlin, Milan, Rome and other famous art centers to study the legacy of classical European art. This exposure forms the basis of his works.

Xu Beihong was a master of both oils and Chinese ink. His early works included large historical oil paintings, impressing the public with their striking themes and exquisite, realistic techniques. In his efforts to create a new form of national art, he combined Chinese brush and ink techniques with western perspective and composition. Firm and bold brush strokes blended with precise delineation of form and defined a new approach to the art. As an art teacher, he advocated the subordination of technique to artistic conception and emphasized the artist's experiences in life.

An acknowledged master at painting horses, Xu Beihong captured their spirited movements vividly and accurately with a great economy of line. With simple bold brush strokes the animals give a sense of freedom and vitality, literally leaping off the medium. Visitors will see Xu's horses reproduced in carpets, embroidery and a myriad craft and art forms.

antique and curio shops, newly matted. Of special interest to collectors are the silk-paper paintings removed from old fans, mounted and matted on silk brocade paper. Treasure hunting can yield fascinating results.

Architecture

Dagoba - A dome-shaped monument containing relics of Buddha or a Buddhist saint.

Pagoda - A temple or other sacred building with many storeys forming a tower.

Pavilion - A light building, usually somewhat open, used for shelter or pleasure, meditation or social communication.

Stupa - A Buddhist dome-shaped structure erected to commemorate a certain person or sacred spot.

Then, there are the fabulous and legendary palace enclaves and tombs, memorials of the good life enjoyed by the imperial dynasties.

Chinese architecture is an amazement to the casual visitor, a reflection of the culture to the more discerning. Pagodas with their umbrella-like tiers and turned-up eaves seem to occur wherever the eye roams in every corner of China. Buddhist in origin, the pagodas were initially burial places which later developed into temples of worship. Often, dominating the skyline from hilltops, they were used as lookouts during periods of warring. Usually 13 storeys, they represent the 13 ways to achieve *nirvana*. Non-Buddhist Chinese pagodas, following the same general design, were constructed with larger areas on each tier which were used for viewing and worship.

Wood was always the major con-

Qing Empress Cixi's passion for the Summer Palace led to immeasurable works being carried out.

struction material because of local supply and the general method of artistic construction. The builders enjoyed the structural challenge of merging beams to carry the weight of decorative domes. Often built without nails or raffia binding, the wood poles were so marvelously interconnected that they lasted for centuries. Wood also provided a medium for carving decorative motifs, brightly painted with the symbols of religious belief.

Historical records prove the beginning of pagoda construction with the growing advent of Buddhism through the Three Kingdoms and Jin periods (220-420), though none of the wood structures actually survive today. In the travel section the reader will encounter the oldest example, **Songyue Pagoda**, built 1400 years ago. It bore a charmed life, surviving the early destructive periods of the Mongols and the latest of the Red Guards' during the Cultural Revolution. Nearby is another survivor, the **Pagoda Forest** next to the Shaolin Monastery. Over 200 burial pagodas of modest height exist in this cemetery for deceased monks.

More famous examples can be found in the **White Dagoba** in Behai Park, Beijing and the series of pagodas surrounding Hangzhou. Xian, the favorite travel destination of most visitors boasts pagodas with the unlikely name of **Great Wild Goose** and **Little Wild Goose**, originating from fanciful tales written in the early novel ***A Journey to the West***.

China's early builders copied from the architecture of the Buddhists and then embellished the designs with greater structures using their favorite building material, wood. The imperial palace enclave in Beijing, the **Forbidden City**, tells it all. Great poles of hardwood were somehow transported from the forests in the south. Massive ceilings and roofs were balanced and interwoven, the more wondrous when you consider the lack of modern construction cranes and mechanical equipment. Paintings and sketches show construction scaffolding of bamboo woven inside and outside the building sites, rising dozens of meters high. Heavy timbers had to be precisely fitted without the benefit of nails and metal strapping and then leveraged into place. Artists followed ant-like up the scaffolding to sculpt the surfaces like they do the Coramandel variety of paneled room screens. Hard enamels of cinnabar base were used to finish the designs, still vividly copied today.

Superstition followed by placing figures on the ridges and eaves of the buildings. Strange animals were created like dragons carved into the ends of the beams, caricatur faces reaching skyward to plead for rain or fame. The Qilin, a combination of dragon, deer, eagle, and unicorn, is often used on the upturned corners, to ward off any manner of potential danger.

However, spoiling the dreams of seeing Old Cathay through the eyes of Marco Polo, are the modern buildings of

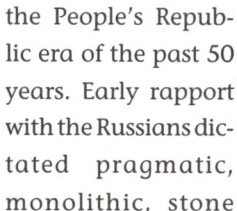

Intricate carvings on the roof of the Forbidden City.

the People's Republic era of the past 50 years. Early rapport with the Russians dictated pragmatic, monolithic, stone buildings for official use. Then utility-grade apartments rose in fields of vertical brick sticks with no beauty and minimal basic comforts. Architectural genes of the ancients with their ingenious methods of construction for durability and appearance lay dormant during this period. Remnants of construction material is strewn around like garbage near buildings long ago finished. Planting of trees and floral decoration can be seen to have run in fits and spurts of Politburo edicts.

20th Century Contribution

In the earlier days of tourist cash-flow (70's) when hotel accommodations were in demand, pre-fabricated packaged units of construction were imported and assembled on site like children's toys on Christmas Eve. Joint ventures (80's) brought in the 5-star version of Hong Kong's 10 and 20-storey edifices with atrium centers, electronic room gadgets and western television blaring CNN news from roof dishes collecting satellite transmissions.

Restaurants served ordinary Lipton tea and had munificent Sunday brunches with imported Danish, Italian, or French cuisine flown in daily. A new hotel advertises itself as "Once an Imperial Palace...Now a Luxury Hotel. Uniquely different from other hotels, the deluxe Grand Hotel Beijing is proudly situated on the grounds of the former Imperial Forbidden City." The accompanying photograph showed an atrium lobby with glass elevators rising to open-tiered room floors–modern day tourist architecture.

Thus the modern day Marco Polo must use his imagination to satisfy yearnings to visualize the architecture of ancient days and seek out those rare locations where there are enough remnants of China's more beautiful and unique style.

TRADES & TRADITIONS

The Crafts

For the traveler, the immeasurable variety of crafted objects are representations of China's history, past and present. The acquisition of an antique bowl, a collector's netsuke, a strand of cloisonne beads or bracelet are the memorabilia of a visit. The prized souvenir recalls an experience or a story: the exquisite meaning of a pine tree, the intriguing sinuous dragon, or the mystery of 5 bats depicted on a gemstone sculpture.

Some traditional crafts take the form of wood block prints and others like paper cutting are the folk form of artistry. Painters were the coveted artists of the old courts, their art being mainly elaborate and scholarly renditions of landscapes, animals, flowers, and calligraphy. At much less courtly level were art and crafts drawing on more accessible materials and common subjects.

The art of bronze casting dates back to the Shang and Zhou Dynasties in the millennium before Christ when the

The crane and the turtle, symbols of longevity, stand in front of the Imperial Palace.

Chinese ladies used to sit on porcelain stools and embroider with the help of a bamboo frame.

kings were presented with huge metal cauldrons and tripods from the labor of indentured artisans. These cauldrons were used for rituals to communicate with ancestors and were buried with their imperial owners to facilitate the next life. Unearthed tombs reveal a myriad of bronze objects along with the other trappings of jade, porcelain, silk woven adornment, ivory, shell, coral, turquoise and other cherished riches.

The craftsmen were coveted by the imperials and mandarins of each dynastic period. Each family of artisans handed down the special secrets of their art from generation to generation. Factories employed thousands of workers but the handful of knowledgeable masters were the celebrated idols of their generation. As the dynasties became more sophisticated, they organized more bureaucracy to oversee the production of crafts in each area of the realm. This was the forerunner of today's world of extensive production lines of labor in every form of factory produced goods. The laborers were classed in order of their experience and talent: to form a clay mould; apply the basic glazes; draw the background of continuous design; until finally the supreme artist would do the intricate shape of the dragon or phoenix to finish the imperial vase.

Guilds were formed as professionalism accelerated and the crafts moved into commercialism. Wealthy mandarins desired the fine porcelain dinnerware, bronze cooking vessels, covered

Bronze incense burner with a Fu lion on top, the guardian of the hearth.

stoneware pots to store pickled and dried foods. Elaborate urns were required to contain the ashes of their ancestors.

The Silk Road and opening of southeastern ports demanded enormous quantities of goods for trade. Itinerant stone sculpting artisans were hired in the extensive periods of Buddhist religious fervor to fill caves with enormous reproductions of Buddha, his disciples and protectors, and endless thousands of small renditions of boddhisattvas.

For the modern traveler, the ultimate experience is the visit to the partially uncovered army at Xian. Imagine the multitude of artisans sculpting each figure of soldier, horse, military vehicle and other objects. Over a half century was required to complete the task as the young emperor, at the age of 16, provided for his future after death.

Fathers would teach sons who would take over on their death to complete a task such as cave sculpting and tomb decoration. Daughters were never taught as it was believed that they would move to new households on marriage and reveal craft secrets. Women were seldom allowed to work outside the house but could teach each other the more feminine arts of weaving, embroidery, and ceremonial clothes making.

A major change occurred at the onset of the new republic as women were released into the workplace on an equal status as men. Visiting a cloisonne factory today reveals long tables of women doing the basic tedious work of applying the hundreds cloisons to each item. At other tables the largely female workers are painting various colors of enamel into the tiny metal forms and carrying racks of the product to the ovens for baking. However, the intricate detail of mirror-matching the design of an elaborate dragon is applied and finished by a venerable group of male artists, 2 or 3 generations sitting side by side.

China's arts and crafts reached a plateau of pragmatism during the Han Dynasty (206 BC-AD 220), revealed in the elaborate tombs invaded by commercial robbers and curious archeologists. The dragon was emphasized because his powers extended to controlling nature, inhabiting the sky and the sea. Emperors adopted this emblem as

Thousands Buddhas Cave, Fubo Hill. Buddhism was the inspiration behind much of Chinese sculpture in the early days.

the symbol of power. The marvelous properties of jade, symbol of purity, longevity and toughness of character were displayed in whole burial suits, amulets, impervious drinking cups and all manner of symbolic treasures.

The art of silk production represented by elaborate brocade designs on clothing, woven bolts of cloth, charmed the Middle East and Europe, thus the development of the Silk Road. The Golden Age of Tang followed by the Song sophistication saw the emergence of painters and the great age of porcelain during which time art grew in untold significance. Mongol invaders of the Yuan Dynasty (1271-1368) were enthralled with the European art of cloisonne and imported hundreds of craftsmen to teach and produce the lovely decorative works. The durability of metal and enamel leads to the proliferation of this craft from modest bracelets and table accessories to meters high vases appearing in hotel lobbies around the world.

Emperors Kangxi (1662-1722) and Qianlong (1736–95) of the Qing Dynasty are credited for the remarkable abundance of what we call antiques today. They established imperial complexes as their forbears of the Qin did to produce elaborate art treasures in ivory, jade, glass, porcelain, gold, enamel, and the relatively new art of carved lacquer. Artists were free to innovate and present the court with the finest objects. The term "imperial jade" originated when

Wuxi Silk Factory, a modern development of her silk history which goes back 1500 years.

only the purest, translucent, emerald green material was transformed into works of jewelry and ornamental art for the emperor.

Advent of the turmoil of the early 20th century slowed down the pace as trade was limited to survival. Communist ideology deplored the use of personal treasures culminating in the tragic destructive period of the Cultural Revolution. However, the need for cash-production, new emergence of China in the family of nations, and desire for technical knowledge have led to the resurgence of the arts. Foreign merchants roaming the country and attending the bi-annual massive trade fairs in Guangzhou, are willing to buy the new production of cloisonne, porcelain, lac-quer, wood, straw, paintings, pearls, jade, gold, and gilded silver products. The canny traders have found warehouses filled with the older products in dust-covered bins and rooms. Origin was seldom discussed as much of the antiques were items pillaged in the early Communist endeavors to stamp out all evidence of capitalistic thought and western intrusion. The new tourist boom required filling hotel kiosks, friendship stores, and antique curio shops with everything from valuable antiques to colorful kites.

Motifs and Symbols

The intrigue of mysterious meanings to

Mighty Dragon, Creature of Good

The dragon has always been associated with omnipotence and good in Chinese culture.

Unlike the fierce dragons of European lore fought by St George to save princesses, the Chinese dragons are friendly characters bent on doing good for humanity. A classic depiction is a pair sculpted in *blanc-de-Chine* from the famous De Hua kilns of Fujian Province. They face each other playing with a ball of fire, which is supposed to represent the sun. The long scaly sinuous bodies float among the clouds or play in the waves of the sea. Their fierce heads with flaming hair and beard, breathe fire and the 5 claws (Qing style) reach in all directions to ward off evil.

Artists through their knowledge of history depict 9 varieties, thus the advent of 9 Dragon Screens, often seen before buildings such as The Forbidden City in Beijing, created in green tile. Guanyin, the Goddess of Mercy is depicted riding a dragon out of the clouds to bring compassion to her people. Cast bronzes recovered from tombs depicted unicorn-like horned dragons with 1 or 2 legs, some more reptilian in style. The gemstones were a medium for carving fantasized versions. The dragon provided the ultimate motif because its very nature was adaptable to change in personality and environment.

The phoenix, representing the Empress, is often paired with the dragon. The combination of pheasant and peacock is elaborately depicted in wild colors, in ceramic, paintings and posters. It is a favorite of embroiderers and artists of all mediums. Jade carvers are masters of sculpting the 2 figures out of a single piece of twin-colour jade. Each figure is carved of a single color, merged cleverly into the whole sculpture.

all of art decoration is the most important factor to historians and purchasers. In the beginning of language there were symbols drawn to indicate a fish, the sun and moon, and the 5 elements of nature: wood, fire, earth, metal and water. The dragon, qilin, phoenix and other fantasized animals joined the decorative features as civilization advanced and craftsmen became innovative and expert in the execution.

The homophone (like sounds) use of symbols like the Red Bat (*hung fu*) whose sound-alike "abundant good fortune" (*hung fu*) is in common usage. Gold fish (*jin yu*) is a very popular carving symbol in jade and subject for expensive paintings and cheap wall posters. Its sound-alike *jin yu*, "gold in abundance", is a wish for prosperity.

Characters and events in the tales and sagas of thousands of years of history are often the themes used by the sculptor, artist, or folk crafters and portrayed in symbols. Depiction of Chang E (Moon Goddess) is a favorite. According

Dragons are often used as symbols of good. Dragon Wall, Beijing.

to the tale, she stole the drug of immortality and flew off to the moon to escape her husband's ire. Depictions show a lovely woman in flowing gown ascending at an angle from the earth to the sky. Another similar rendition is the reverse as Chang E occasionally descends to the earth for a look-see. The **White Snake and Black Snake** saga is the story of a beautiful maiden evolving from a white snake out to protect her family from the evil forces. It is most often told in a series of hand-painted wood block pictorial with elaborate scenes of sword play and marvelous characterizations.

"Plum blossom" (prunus) is pictured as a 5-petaled flower on twisted knotted branches symbolizing the resurgence of spring. The "pine tree" represents endurance and longevity, while "bamboo" means vigor and durability. The 3 together mean "3 friends of winter", representing happiness and endurance in old age as all 3 bloom in the winter of life.

"Lotus" symbolizes purity and is the sacred emblem of Buddhism. Guanyin, the Goddess of Mercy is almost always standing or sitting in a field of lotus. More complex meanings emerge because of a play on words. *Lian sheng gui zi* means lotus, mouth organ, and cassia with a child carrying them. The play on words is translated as "For successive generations, may you give birth to sons who attain high rank".

The "peach", bursting with juice is an often used symbol for a long and

Jade, Virtuous and Valuable

Chinese ancient custom defines jade in the following colors: red as a coxcomb, yellow as a steamed chestnut, white as congealed fat, and black as lacquer.

For the gemologist, jade divides into 2 classes. The shiny vitreous variety occurring in a rainbow of colors is the regal and more valuable **jadeite**, its principal source being the Kachin Mountains of Burma. It occurs in boulders with a "skin covering" which conceals the contents until sliced open. **Nephrite**, the greasy, wax-like cousin is found in larger quantities all over the world tending more to the dull green and white shades. North America has provided huge blocks of the opaque green variety. Others in the mutton fat colour have provided big blocks to carve larger-than-life size Buddhas, carved reclining and sitting. Both varieties have the character of extreme toughness, translucency and transparency transmitting beauty with the passage of light. Value increases as world supply is depleted. Endurance of the stone guarantees its antiquity in the execution of the art of carving.

Nephrite jade is accredited a place in Chinese history from the Shang to Zhou Dynasties (1523-256 BC). Because of the remarkable durability of the stone, evidences turn up in all the tombs, some handed down from previous generations. Pure white was considered the finest until the advent of the Burmese Jadeite. Such material began to be traded in the Yuan Dynasty (from 1271). The finer translucent emerald green variety of the jadeite became the most desirable, and was thus designated as imperial, literally belonging to the emperor.

The range of the art of jade carving can best be seen in the museums and include small mountains for the mind to wander over. Pocket jade was common for the mandarins to conceal up the long flowing sleeves, to be rubbed before reaching a decision. These forms were often in the shape of tentacles as in the octopus, described as the fingers of Confucius, a constant consultant of the sages. Animals, using the natural shape of the stone with bits of colour for adornment were common. Fancy wine cups and bowls for food, cleverly decorated, were desired by the palaces, and considered a time honored gift to be exchanged for a favor requested.

The Europeans brought the habit of snuff to China and the small capped bottles were ideal for the material. Amateur carvers wonder at how the bottles could be hollowed out so perfectly, adorned with relief objects on the outside. Early drills were bamboo, impregnated with corundum or steel tipped, and revolved with small bows.

Old Chinese sculptors were known to study a piece of jade for years before realizing what figure was concealed inside. The theory was that jade carving was releasing the potential artform from its skin. Well-to-do artists and calligraphers would have a water container in the form of a lotus for mixing ink on an ink stone, and a paper weight to hold down the long sheets of rice paper, also in jade. Highly decorated brush holders were carved and decorated. Belt hooks and belt buckles were common, decorated with dragon heads, and the intricate symbols and motifs listed in this chapter. Ladies had collections of jade hair pins to insert in the coils of long hair piled on top of the healthy life. Lao Shouxing, the bald, stooping bearded figure of longevity carries a peach in one hand, his dragon headed crook in the other. A classic wedding gift is 3 children holding a peach larger than they are, wishing a long life and many sons. "Pomegranate", with its many seeds indicates fertility and prosperity. A wedding gift of a pillow case, box, vase or scroll with this symbol on is a wish for many sons.

In the realm of flowers, "chrysanthemum" means longevity and tranquility; "orchid" symbolizes virtue and morality; "narcissus" (water fairy) is often used to represent the new year as

head. Tone sounding plaques were carved, pierced for a cord and hung to swing free when tapped with a hard instrument.

Jewelry jade is predominantly the Burmese jadeite jade, cut en-cabochon (domed top) from the rare slices of fine material. The colors of the green jadeite range over the following expert classifications:

Western Terminology	Chinese Terminology
Imperial/Emerald	Old Mine
Glassy	Canary
Apple Green	New Mine
Spinach	Oily
Moss-in-snow	Pea Green
Apple Green	Flower Green
None	Melon

Other desirable colors range from gray to pale blue, brown to red, and various shades of lavender. Certain merchants and traders have been known to soak the stones in colored dyes to enhance the color. This can usually be identified under magnification as the edges of the stone absorb the agent.

When the jade boulders are opened, the fine material is usually in thin veins, thus most fine jadeite jade jewelry is formed of thin stones and carved designs. Bangle bracelets, carved in a single solid circular piece, are rarely the same color all around, their value being determined by the amount of fine green coloring. Multi-color jade sculptures are the result of the use of layers of veins carved through to release a particularly reluctant dragon or turtle.

bulbs were often cultivated to flower at that time. "Peony" is a favorite of artists. It means good fortune and is the flower of wealth and honor.

Artists will often use the "willow tree" as a symbol for feminine beauty because of its long branches of leaves and its sensual swaying in the wind. Ladies of the night and courtesans were often said to live in the Willow Quarters. The willow pattern produced in English porcelain was called willowware and thought at first to have come from China.

Colors have precise meanings and symbolism from their use over the centuries. The Qing imperials used yellow as the principal color in their robes, ceramics and other artware. Blue was the color of the Mings and their memorabilia reflect the lovely blue and white vases, urns, wine vessels and elaborate incense burners. Lacquerware earned the color of red due to the use of the mercury-based lac of cinnabar, *dan*, the ingredient of immortality. Red is also the most important color in nature, as noted by red banners and flags used during holiday and festive periods. Green is an important color of jade, itself meaning virtue and toughness of character. White jade was also honored in its purest shade, snow jade, and associated with religious and spiritual mystery. Black represents the dormant part of nature, used in winter scenes but not funereal. White was the funeral color.

Animals were even more deeply involved in symbolism, fantasy, and the crafts of artistic depiction on rice paper or carved in gemstones. The Chinese love of gold is expressed in the jewelry store windows of the streets of Hong Kong. High karat gold content is cast or formed in the dragons, horses, qilins, in addition to the bunches of bangle bracelets and chains sold by the gram plus a small percentage for labor.

The intricate dragon design embellished in gold on the roof of the Temple of Heaven.

The rat, ox, tiger, rabbit, dragon, snake, horse, goat, monkey, cock, dog and pig represent the 12 animals of the zodiac. Each represents the strange habits and nature of persons born under their sign.

Fairy-like renditions of the "goldfish", emphasizing the large eyes and filmy tails are seen throughout the gamut of craft forms such as papercuts, woodblock prints, gemstone carving, and others. They present wishes of good fortune because the name, *jin yu* sounds like "gold in abundance" (*jin yu*). To give a replica of a "carp" to a student is to wish him success on his examinations or career ambitions. Paper carps are used at weddings to wish fertility.

The "peacock" was associated with official rank in the imperial courts. Peacock feathers containing 1, 2, or 3 eyes were worn extending from the hats of ministerial officers to denote their rank in the hierarchy. Live peacocks were favorites in the gardens of the palaces, paintings and embroidery replicate the resplendent finery of the plumage.

"Mandarin ducks", depicted in pairs represented marital fidelity and happiness. The noisy "cicada" carved in jade were often found in tombs because of the nature of the insect to shed its skin and regenerate itself. The burial symbol represented the wish for reincarnation. "Rabbits" the symbol of intelligence and longevity, often shone with the halo of a moon, representing immortality.

"Horses" were a special favorite of

the artist Xu Beihong, connoting intelligence, swiftness and persistence. Often depicted in groups of 8, said to be the steeds of the Eight Immortals, they run, play, roll and gambol in the many craft forms.

The wispy "butterfly" represents the sound-alike *hu die* and the octogenarian *die*, therefore a symbol of longevity. "Bats", also because of the play on words *hong fu* and *wu fu* are associated with good fortune, tranquility, wealth, longevity and virtue.

"Fu dogs" or "fu lions" are a common tourist acquisition, used to guard buildings and homes as a pair on either side of the gate. From tiny jade carvings to massive stone sculptures they are seen throughout the world as Chinese symbols of guardians of the hearth. Originally they were Buddhist symbols of fierce animals, later they resembled the snub-nosed Pekinese, one with a ball underfoot, the other of the pair holding down a baby. Debate has gone on for centuries as to whether the father is playing with the ball and the mother watching the baby or vice-versa.

The strange animal, "qilin" has the spike of the unicorn atop the head of a dragon, the body of a deer, the legs of a horse and often the wings of the eagle. It is a special favorite of gemstone carvers and comes often in pairs symbolizing longevity because of the unicorn's fantasized life expectancy of a thousand years.

The crane, spotted deer, pine tree, and turtle are all symbols of longevity,

A forbidding sculpture to keep'em out. Forbidden City, Beijing.

often depicted together. The bald stooped figure of Lao Shouxing, usually has 2 or more of the above depicted with him and his luscious peach. The rare fungus of immortality, *ling shi* is part of the longevity circle, said to be found only by the sensitive nose of the spotted deer.

Mountains are a constant symbol of sacristy. Strength, durability and toughness were often related to the male force of *yang* in nature. Natural stones in the yellow Huangshan jade that resemble mountains are prized more than the valuable imperial green jade. Turquoise and other crystallization are kept in a natural state if they resemble a mountain. Artists often render the mountain with paths, bridges, pavilions, boats on nearby water, all to tempt

Cloisonne

Mongol Emperor Kublai Khan was so taken with gifts of cloisonne from Europe that he imported craftsmen to teach the Chinese artisans the art. In Mandarin the art is called *Jingtai Lan*, after the Emperor Jingtai (1450-57) of the Ming Dynasty who set up large workshops to pursue the craft.

In the pure form, copper is used to make the base of the desired object, such as a bracelet, mounted Fu lion, ewer, shaped boxes, snuff bottles, incense burners, elephants and other elaborate objects from charms to tall urns. Gilded wire forms are applied with solder or flux to create the patterns following the classic motifs or wild imagination of the artist. Different colored enamels are then applied in the cloisons and fired to its vitreous state. Hollows often occur requiring repeated processes to render a smooth finish. Polishing, additional gilding, the setting of stones, carving out to give a sculptured effect are advanced finishing for the more unique objects.

For the collector, older cloisonne objects are found in the antique curio stores, new products at the Friendship Stores and the factory showrooms. The range of products today include orders from international merchants with their own ideas of the product, including such mundane items as ballpoint pens, cigarette lighters, pocket measuring tapes, picture frames, tissue boxes, and the like.

A simple method of identifying the newer cloisonne products is the series of tiny cloud wires used for fillers in less intricate designs. *Mille-fleur* (thousand flower) paired vases for instance are much more beautiful than the commoner hibiscus centering in a maze of the clouds. Bordering patterns indicate a higher art form, as well as the rarer inside-outside designs of bowls and boxes. The less important pieces are simply enameled on the inside. Gilding around the lips of vases gives a more finished effect. The art of mirror-imaging paired units can be identified by facing the design toward you and rolling the 2 objects together inwardly.

The cloisonne factories in Beijing are extensions of the former imperial shops, employing hundreds of artisans and trainees. It is a favorite on the list of places to visit on tourist itineraries. Travelers should endeavor an independent visit to a factory to watch the intricate but intriguing work on cloisonne. Look carefully over the items in the factory showroom.

the viewer to mentally enter the picture and participate. A method of self-hypnosis to note is to imagine yourself wandering up the path, meditating in the pavilion, gossiping with old friends or having tea in a roadside temple.

Tao-tie is an often used decoration on ceramics, usually seen in series. Details by the artist can make 2 zoomorphic patterns coming together look like a fierce dragon mask. Swirling clouds and waves of the sea, spirals or key-shaped motifs symbolizing thunder are constant edge-and-filler designs for all manner of arts and craft. The sun is frequently depicted with a 3-legged crow and the moon with a rabbit inside. *Yin* and *yang*, the pairing of forces is represented in hundreds of ways, the most common a black and white swirl-divided circle. The swastika, dishonored by the Nazis taking it as their symbol, is a symbol of antiquity.

One hundred sons (modern version 100 children) expresses the wish for longevity of the family line. Eight precious things, that is a painting, coin, lozenge, mirror, stone chime, pair of books, pair of rhinoceros horns, and a leaf are associated with happiness and the good

Again the dragon on an equally outstanding pot, is a hint of imperial presence in Huaqing Hot Spring.

things in life. They are depicted on ceramics and embroidery as good wishes for brides. Eight Buddhist symbols are used throughout the Buddhist world, each with a separate meaning: wheel, conch, umbrella, canopy, lotus, vase, pair of fish and the endless knot.

Twelve symbols of authority are grouped together as palace decorations and embroidery on robes to be kept near to the person of power. They represent the essence of the universe: sun, moon, three-star constellation (pyramid), mountain, ax, dragon, pheasant (the phoenix), sacrificial goblets, waterweed, grain, fire and the Fu sign. The three most common characters seen on craft works are *shuang xi* (marital bliss), *shou* (longevity) and *fu* (good fortune).

The Fine Art of Chinese Ceramics

Earthenware. Dishes or containers made from unrefined white, red or buff clay mixed with sand for extra strength fired to a lower temperature than other ceramics (800-1000°C). When glazed, earthenware is suitable for containing food and liquids.

Porcelain. A very fine earthenware having a translucent white body and a transparent glaze made from a refined white clay called *kaolin* mixed with another clay of partially decomposed granite (petunze). Porcelain is normally fired at 1300°C or more, after applying a liquid surface of the petunze, fusing the

Blue and white Ming porcelain.

shiny black with the proper proportions.

The Tang (618-907) sophisticated age produced multi-color ceramics such as the horse and camel figures widely sold at the Xian digs. Potters were encouraged to experiment with ceramic research to produce finer products. Porcelain came of age during this period although kilns and earthenware were known 2,000 years earlier. Drinking of tea in an elegant and sociable manner required the proper porcelain cups and tea pots, often carried in straw-fitted baskets.

The Ming (1368-1644) porcelains perfected the under-glaze painting, using cobalt blue. Jingdezhen in Jiangxi Province became the center for produc-

whole into a smooth semi-translucent vitrified surface.

Bisquit (Bisque) is the firing without a glaze, giving a matte surface.

Stoneware. A hard dense vitreous kind of pottery ware made from siliceous clay, or a mixture of clay with a considerable amount of flint, sand, prefired clay, or the like, to give it greater strength. It is fired higher (1,000-1,250°C) than earthenware and often glazed with salt.

Colors are produced in the higher temperature glazes by using metallic substances. Cobalt produces the blue; iron was the ingredient for the celadon gray and green; and copper provided the red and peach shades. Mixtures produced unusual shades; iron and cobalt performed together and could yield a

A court lady wearing an elaborate dress of satin and silk decorated with symbols befitting her station.

A snuff bottle painted painstakingly inside to depict a small gathering.

tion and innovation. The potters were given royal decrees for specialized designs of the blue and white swirling dragons, floras, mountains and gardens. Experimentation produced underglaze painting, over-glaze enameling, and designs in between called the slip.

The Qing (1644-1911) court was famous for its brilliant yellows featuring the Emperor's dragon symbol and the Empress's phoenix. Court scenes were painted in panels around 4 and 6-sided vases. Beautiful ladies in regal dress, flaunting fans or mirrors, said to personify the concubines of the age, decorated the porcelains. Europe demanded more and more of the celebrated celadons, elaborate sets of dinnerware, decorative artware, tea pots and matching cups, rice bowls, and sculptures of famous religious deities, filling the harbors of Amoy and Canton with trading vessels.

During these periods, artistry flowered with international commerce until the Europeans began producing porcelains of equally good quality. The Americans were able to make shiploads of cheaper dinnerware with much shorter distances to the markets. Wars upset commerce around the world in the first half of the 20th century. The PRC, looking for export-cash reopened the great porcelain centers. Jingdezhen re-fired their kilns some 2,000 years old. Research centers were established to rediscover the ancient methods and to apply new techniques. Contests, prizes, and artistic competition raised the art forms to a higher level.

Travelers today are invited to visit these factories wherever their itinerary takes them. Managers proudly show the modern production methods, lines of workers busy at the wheel, the kiln, the decoration and design tables. The tour culminates in an inevitable showroom with articles offered for sale; prize-winning pieces standing proudly behind glass doors, not for sale.

Centers, such as Jingdezhen in Jianxi Province and the *blanc-de-Chine* artware at De Hua in Fujian Province can now be visited by tourists and merchants alike. Cash payment in foreign currency is accepted and the eager trade representatives arrange door-to-door delivery to almost anywhere in the world.

GRANDEUR & SPLENDOR

Beijing

Beijing can trace its history back as early as 500,000 years ago. Here, some 50 km away is Zhoukoudian, where Peking Man (*Homo erectus Pekinensis*) lived in the caves of Dragon Bone Hill. Beijing became a prosperous market town during the Zhou Dynasty (1100 BC - 476 BC). Since then it has been made the capital city by various dynasties, each time gaining in grandeur and splendor. Marco Polo, the Venetian traveler, who visited the city during the Yuan Dynasty, was so deeply impressed with the grandeur of the city that he claimed no other city in the world could rival it. The name Beijing (Northern Capital) was first given to the city by the Ming emperor, Yongle.

Qianmen was the Front Gate of the walled city of Beijing in ancient times.

The May 4th Movement of 1919, in protest against the verdict of the Versailles Peace Conference, started in Beijing, and was also the focal point from where revolutionary martyr Li Dazhao first disseminated Marxism and where Lu Xun, the great writer and thinker, fought the corruption and

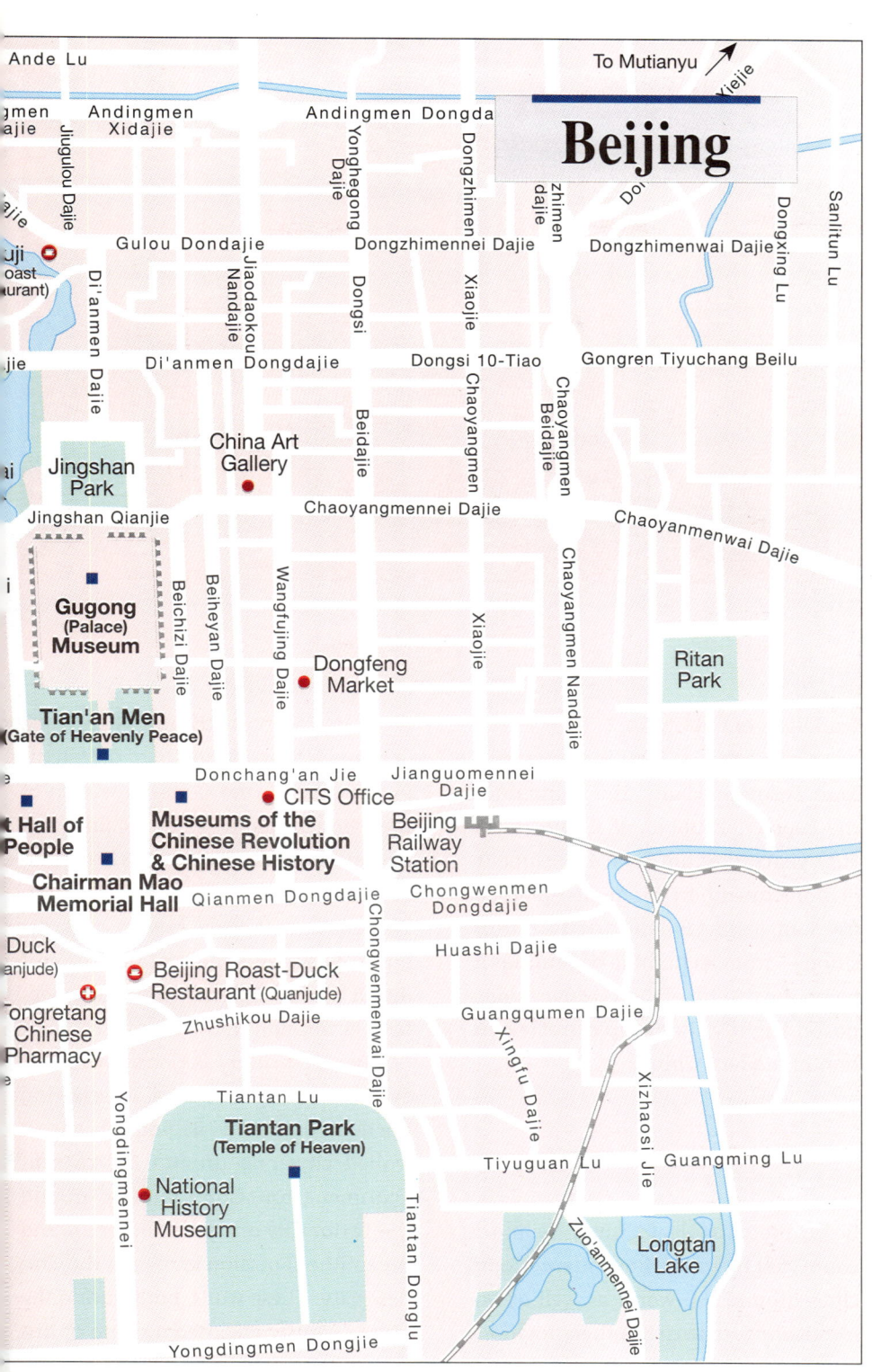

Mass bikers in Beijing.

feudalism of old China.

On October 1st 1949, in Tiananmen, Mao Zedong declared the founding of the People's Republic of China (PRC). Fifty years later, on June 4th, students demonstrated here for greater political freedom. Beijing is indeed a city in transition — from its humble beginnings to being the capital of 3 successive dynasties and rightly, the birthplace of revolution in modern China.

Orientation

Being the capital of China, Beijing is connected by air to most international cities around the world as well as domestically to at least 35 other provinces. If you decide to use the rail, there are 2 options — from Hong Kong, a 36-hour journey, or via the Commonwealth of Independent States (CIS). Beijing, has seasons corresponding to cities like Philadelphia, Indianapolis and Denver. Though each season has its own delights, autumn is the best time to visit and it usually extends from early September through mid-November.

Beijing's artery is Chang An Boulevard, running east-west intersecting the heart of the city. Beijing was once a walled city: one around the present Qianmen (Front Gate), another around the Tartar City and yet another around the southern portion known as the Chinese City. These walls, built during the Ming Dynasty enclosed a string of historically significant buildings. Most of the walls do not stand now but as you travel throughout this ancient city, a glimpse of a part of the wall would remind you of the past splendor of the Forbidden City, which was the center of imperial power in the Middle Kingdom for more than 500 years. Beijing is not a city that can be explored in a few days. The treasures of the Forbidden Palace demands your attention; the monuments the emperors built bear mute testimony to the reverence paid by the common people to their ruler.

To really immerse yourself in Beijing, do it the way the locals do. Hire a bicycle and a whole world of adventure will literally open its door to you. From the resplendence of ancient buildings, you can cycle into narrow *hutongs* (lanes), peek into Chinese courtyards and see the Beijing most visitors miss. And of course, a visit to Beijing should not be restricted to just sightseeing. Indulge yourself in its cuisine renowned throughout the world, or attune your audio-visual senses to the art of Beijing Opera or appreciate the exquisite workmanship of its handicrafts.

The Heart of the City

Tiananmen (Gate of Heavenly Peace) stands in front of the entrance to the former Imperial Palace, now called Gugong, the Palace Museum. Between this gate and Tiananmen Square is Chang An Avenue.

To the east, south and west are the city's busiest commercial districts — Wangfujing, Dazhalan and Xidan. From all directions, pedestrian and other traffic converge here. If you stand here, with your back to Tiananmen, the Great Hall of the People is to your right, the Museum of Chinese Revolution and Museum of Chinese History on the left, the Monument to the People's Heroes straight ahead and behind it, Mao Zedong Memorial Hall.

Tiananmen was first erected in 1420 during the Ming Dynasty and was first known as Chengtianmen (Gate for Receiving Orders from Heaven). Seriously damaged towards the end of the dynasty, it was rebuilt by the Qing in 1651 and given its present name. During both dynasties, Tiananmen was the main gate to the Imperial City and the residential and administrative quarters of those who served the Imperial Palace. Tiananmen was also known as the State Portal. During solstices, when the Ming and Qing emperors ventured out of the Forbidden City, the main gates were thrown open: Wumen, Duanmen, Tiananmen

The Peoples Liberation Army exercising in Tiananmen Square, Beijing.

and Zhonghuamen (Central Flowery Gate, no longer extant). The emperor, in full imperial regalia, passed through the gate at the head of a grand procession of civil and military officials. When the emperor personally led his troops into battle, he made a sacrifice for the journey in front of the Tiananmen.

Tiananmen itself consists of a red platform with 5 vaulted gateways, surmounted by a wooden gate-tower. The top of the platform provides a rostrum for viewing the square in front. Before and behind the gateways are 2 pairs of *huabiao* (carved ornamental columns). The *huabiao* have a long history in China. According to ancient records, King Yao, one of the sage kings, set up a wooden pillar on which the people could carve their criticisms of officials. This wooden pillar was the predecessor of *huabiao*. Each of the white marble *huabiao* at Tiananmen weighs more than 10,000 kg.

Tiananmen acquired a new glory and came to symbolise both Beijing and China when Mao Zedong proclaimed the founding of the PRC from here. The national emblem has Tiananmen as its central motif, and the emblem, floodlit at night, is now suspended from the upper roof.

Looking south is the impressively vast 50-hectare **Tiananmen Square**. It is the site of grand assemblies on occasions like the International Labour Day on May 1st and China's National Day on October 1st.

Mao Zedong Memorial Hall, Tiananmen Square.

The **Great Hall of the People** is the center of political activity in the country. It is where the National People's Congress convenes and where Chinese and foreign guests are entertained at banquets, receptions and memorial meetings. The Great Hall occupies 171,800 sq m — even larger than the effective construction area of the whole Imperial Palace. However, where it took altogether 36 years to construct the Imperial Palace, the Great Hall was erected in only 10 months in 1959.

To the east of Tiananmen Square stands a cream building with green and yellow eaves. It houses 2 **museums** — the north wing chronicles the Chinese Revolution and the south wing, Chinese history. Revolutionary documents dating from the May 4th Movement in 1919 are exhibited in the 2-storey hall of the Museum of Chinese Revolution. Venture into the south wing and a permanent exhibition of 9,000 historical relics plunges you into the development of Chinese society: from primitive man 600,000 years ago, through slave society, and feudalism culminating in the period of the old Democratic Revolution (1840-1919). Both museums are open daily, until 5 pm.

Dominating the center of Tiananmen Square is the **Monument to the People's Heroes**, the biggest monument in the country, rising 37.4 m high. The granite obelisk has an inscription in gold, drafted by the late Mao Zedong and written by the late Premier Zhou

It took 36 years to construct the Imperial Palace.

Enlai. Pay special attention to the reliefs carved on the lower plinth at the top of the granite stairs. These depict scenes from Chinese history since 1840. It took China's leading sculptors and stonemasons more than 5 years to complete the 170 figures in the reliefs.

Mao Zedong Memorial Hall, standing between Tiananmen and Qianmen, contains the embalmed body of the late chairman of the Chinese Communist Party (CCP). If you pass through the carved *nanmu* (fine hardwood) side-doors and enter the central

regions in China. The mausoleum is open daily from 8.30 to 11.30 am and closed throughout winter (December to March).

The Forbidden City

China was known as the Middle Kingdom and the Forbidden City was where the Son of Heaven wielded his almost awesome powers. This collection of palaces was strictly out of bounds to the commoners, hence its name. Twenty-four emperors lived here over a span of 491 years, from the Ming emperor Yongle to Puyi, the last of the Qing emperors.

The **Forbidden City** served the emperor as both living quarters and head-

hall, you will see Chairman Mao's body lying in state draped with the flag of the CCP. His body is in a crystal coffin on a black marble base surrounded by banks of flowers. Outside the southern entrance of the Memorial Hall, running from east to west, are 30 bright red flags, representing all the provinces (including Taiwan), municipalities and autonomous

Picture posing at the Forbidden City.

quarters for the administration of the empire. In Ming and Qing times, Beijing consisted of 4 parts: the outer city to the south, the inner city to the north, the Imperial City within the inner city and the Forbidden City within the imperial city.

Within the Forbidden City are 9,999 buildings, a number symbolizing long life and reign for the emperor. The first and main hall in the Forbidden City is the **Taihedian** (Hall of Supreme Harmony). Because this is where the emperor's throne was, it is the most striking building in the entire palace. The vast hall is propped by 72 pillars standing in 6 rows. Note the 6 gold-lacquered pillars in the middle which are carved with coiled dragons. In front of the Taihedian is a courtyard covering more than 30,000 sq m, which means about 25,000 officials could be assembled at any one time when the emperor holds court. Two other outer buildings, the **Zhonghedian** (Hall of Middle Harmony) and the **Baohedian** (Hall of Preserved Harmony) served the emperor on less formal occasions.

South of the Taihedian, you will find a series of halls which served as the study premises for the Crown Prince during the Ming Dynasty and also housed the imperial printing press.

Enter through the **Qianqungmen** (Gate of Celestial Purity) and you will step into the realm which in the days of the Ming and Qing Dynasties, only the emperor had access to. This is the inner court and it served as living quarters for the empress, concubines, maids and eunuchs. The **Qianqinggong** (Palace of Celestial Purity) was the emperor's bedroom; the empress had hers housed in the **Kunninggong** (Palace of Terrestrial Tranquility). During the Qing period, the Kunninggong was used as the emperor's bridal chamber. Outside the east wall, you will spot a sedan chair covered with red and yellow satin — this was used to carry the empress around the palace grounds.

Between the 2 palaces, you will find the smaller **Jiaotaidian** (Hall of Celestial and Terrestrial Union), used for ceremonies such as the empress's birthday. In spring, the empress would raise silkworms here to show her industry and capability and to set an example for her women subjects. During the Qing Dynasty, the Jiaotaidian was used to store the official seals of the emperor and empress; today there are still 25 imperial seals on exhibit here, together with traditional Chinese clepsydra (water-clocks) and a western clock.

The Qianqinggong represents the heavens, the Kunninggong earth and the Jiaotaidian their union. The Rijingmen and Yuehuamen, 2 gates in front of the Qianqinggong, represent the sun and the moon. These symbolized the emperor's reign to be as eternal and glorious as the universe.

Around the 3 central palaces are numerous courtyards and minor palaces. Most of these are now exhibition halls on Qing palace life and traditional Chinese arts. Opening hours are irregu-

Grand View Garden

Grand View Garden, or Daguanyuan was the famous garden in Cao Xuepin's classic, *A Dream of the Red Chambers*. The novel, sometimes known as "The Tale of the Stone", is indisputably one of the world's best known works. The red chambers where the dream took place, is actually the abode of the Chia family who was related to the feudal court through kinship with the royal family.

Grand View Garden is a miniature reproduction made by Ye Qilong and his family of artisans in Zhejiang Province. It took the 17 artisans 10 years to complete the 'Red Chambers', based on the Grand View Garden drawn in the novel. On a scale of 1:13, the garden totals an area of 42 sq m. Not only is every stone and brick made to proportion, but plants, paths and streams are made to harmonize with the buildings, as Chinese architecture is essentially a garden-art that sets structures in natural scenes.

Attendants dressed in Qing costumes, representing the characters in the novel, lend the garden an authentic feel of 18th century aristocracy. You can view the Grand View Garden at Liu Yin Street, near the Shishahai Lake.

---

lar, check the *China Daily* for details. If you proceed north of the Kunninggong, you will be heading into the Yuehuayuan, will the pleasure gardens of the imperial family. Ancient cypresses, roads, springs, flowers, shrubs and pavilions with names like Crimson Snow, Myriad Springs and Thousand Autumns add to the calm and tranquility of the garden. In the gardens is an imposing temple named the **Hall of Imperial Peace** which has the distinctive features of the architecture of the Yuan Dynasty. It is sacred to the Great God of Black Heaven; legend has it that he actually showed his saintly appearance and helped put out a great fire in the palace. Look carefully at the stone steps leading to the temple — the footprints there were believed to be his!

Imperial Parks & Gardens

Besides its magnificent collection of buildings, several famous imperial parks and gardens greatly enrich the beauty of the city and its outskirts. Most famous of all is **Yiheyuan** which means "Park of Nurtured Harmony" but it is known to

From the gardens of the Imperial Palace, Beijing.

Oldest Observatory in China

Beijing's ancient observatory is an often missed sight by busy visitors. Built during the Yuan Dynasty in 1279, it is fascinating even to the non-technical observer. The precision of the cast bronze instruments impresses you with the advanced civilization and innovative scientific ability of the age.

The Bronze Globe is the largest of the instruments, and looks like any modern globe that can be moved at the touch of a hand. The delicately balanced instrument indicates the relative positions of the sun, moon, stars in motion and the hours of the day. Studs are impressed on the globe to indicate the 1800 stars precisely located.

For time keeping, the Bronze Dripper was devised before the advent of clocks and watches. Five bronze tanks, filled once a day are enough to keep it precise and running, more reliable than a sun dial. A bronze figure holds an arrow, which falls with the water levels indicating the time. The observatory is centrally located near the Jianguomen Flyover. Have your taxi stop there on the way to the Friendship Store.

the world as the **Summer Palace**, just as Beihai Park was known as the Winter Palace. Yiheyuan is in the northwestern outskirts of Beijing and especially noteworthy is the ingenuity of the park's architects in adapting the buildings to blend in and accentuate its natural surroundings, abandoning the formal courtyard style of the Forbidden City.

Yiheyuan was plundered by colonial forces, restored, then damaged again in 1900. Cixi, the Empress Dowa-

Empress Dowager Cixi's whim, the Marble Boat in the Summer Palace.

ger, who was the power behind the throne then, had the palace restored and it became her summer resort.

The Empress Dowager's life at the Yiheyuan exemplified the excesses of the imperial court. When she visited, the attendant eunuchs on horseback and members of her entourage numbered more than 1,200 and more than 40 carriages formed the procession. The kitchens occupied 8 big courtyards and more than 128 kitchen eunuchs prepared food just for her.

On the day after her arrival at the Yiheyuan, she would attend an opera in the Deheyuan (Garden of Moral Harmony). Once over 500,000 taels of silver were spent on stage props alone. To prepare for her 60th birthday, 5,400,000 taels of silver was drawn from the state treasury. Just the marquee alone set up before the **Renshoudian** (Hall of Benevolent Longevity) used 227 km of colored silks.

Yiheyuan has many scenic spots. Three quarters of its 660 acres is occupied by **Kunming Lake**. The broad expanse of the lake is embellished with an island on the southeast, which is connected to the east bank by the **Seventeen-Arch Bridge**, hanging like a rainbow across the water. To the west you will see a long causeway — among its 6 bridges is the graceful full-bowed **Yudaiqiao** (Jade Belt Bridge) which looks like a jade belt from a distance.

Equally exquisite and a must-see is the famous **Long Gallery**, a covered way with 4 octagonal pavilions along

The White Dagoba, in Beihai Park built by the first Qing emperor.

the north bank of the lake. Its beams are painted with historical and fictional events and landscapes taken from the West Lake at Hangzhou. So vivid and mesmerizing is each detail that you will feel as if you are walking through an art gallery. This leads to the **Tinglinguan** (Hall for Listening to the Orioles), a former theater, converted into a restaurant. Further on, is Cixi's **Marble Boat**, built with funds earmarked for expansion of the navy. The boat acquired an infamous reputation but it is an outstanding creation — 2 decks built from large stone blocks, with stained glass windows and elaborately carved marble facings.

Beihai (North Lake) **Park**'s history goes way back to the Liao Dynasty, even

The Bell King

Dazhong, the Great Bell Temple is a quick stop-and-look on your way to the Summer Palace. The temple has an orchestra of old bronze bells varying in size and age. Emperor Qianlong wrote a commemorative sign in his own hand, now slightly faded, about the grandest of them all,

The Great Bell is over 7 m tall weighing at almost 50 tons. It now hangs in the hall, subject to visitors making it ring with coins or other metal objects. It is remarkably cast, if you can imagine the equipment available during the Ming Dynasty. The amazing uniqueness is that the casting included an entire surface decorated with 17 Buddhist scriptures totalling 227,000 Chinese characters.

Archeologists suggest that a huge pit was dug deep in the ground to accommodate a matching set of earthen molds containing the calligraphy appearing on the outer shell. They estimate the casting was done in one throw of the molten bronze. It is in perfect condition to this day. Its peals are said to carry over 50 miles.

longer than the Yiheyuan. In the 10th century, its emperor built a pleasure palace on an island in Beihai named **Yaoyu** (Jade Islet). In 1264, the Mongols rebuilt the park and Kublai Khan decided to live on the island. The big jade bowl in the **Tuancheng** (Round City) and the **Tieyingbi** (Iron Shadow Screen) on the north bank of Beihai are all legacies of the Yuan Dynasty. The emperors of the Ming added other treasures: the **Wulongting** (Five Dragon Pavilion) and the **Jiulongbi** (Nine-Dragon Screen). Also on the north bank, are exquisitely carved writhing dragons. The Jiulongbi, with its vivid colors and vigorous style, is considered one of Beijing's finest artworks of the last 500 years. If time allows, walk up to the **Baita** (White Dagoba), built in 1651 by Shunzhi, the first emperor of the Qing Dynasty. The view of the surrounding lake and Beijing from here is memorable.

Tiantan Park (Altar of Heaven), located in the southern district of Beijing, is a must-see in your itinerary. Tiantan is the largest group of temple buildings in China, dating back to 1420. The main temple buildings are clustered at the northern and southern ends of a long central causeway in Tiantan, known as the **Danbiqiao** (Cinnabar Stairway Bridge) or **Shendao** (Sacred Way). The most important temple is the **Qiniandian** (Hall of Prayer for Good Harvest). If you step inside Qiniandian, take a moment to observe its interior. This 38-meter high structure still stands today, making it as old as 500 years but what is outstanding is the absence of iron nails or reinforcing rods in its construction. The whole structure is supported by wooden mortise and tenon joints — a fine example of traditional Chinese architecture. The 28 red-lacquered pillars are of *nanmu*, symbolizing the 28 constellations.

The **Echo Wall**, towards the southern end of the causeway, is another marvel. It is built according to the principle that a sound wave bounces off a curved wall many times in succession. If

Qing Emperor Qianlong took a special interest in Jinshan Park and had the ground stocked with trees, animals and birds.

you whisper at one point of the wall, this can be heard clearly on the opposite point. Further south is the **Huanqiu** (Circular Mound). This was where the emperor would offer sacrifices to Heaven. The Huanqiu was built in 1530. Despite several earthquakes since then, its marble terrace has remained extremely even, with not a stone out of place — a splendid tribute to the craftsmen and stonemasons of old China.

Another park worth visiting, just north of the Forbidden City, is **Jingshan Park** (Prospect Hill). The park takes its name from Jingshan Hill, an artificial mound covered with pines and cypresses which was originally part of the Imperial City during the Yuan Dynasty. When the Ming Dynasty rebuilt the city, earth excavated to make the moat around the Forbidden City was piled onto the mound, forming the 5 peaks which can be seen today. Jingshan was also called Meishan (Coal Hill) because coal was once heaped around the foot of the hill. Jingshan was a park favored by the Qing emperor Qianlong, who had fruit trees planted and the grounds stocked with birds and animals. But Jingshan goes down in historical annals as the site where the last Ming emperor took his own life. On March 19, 1644, a peasant army led by Li Zicheng stoned the Imperial Palace. Emperor Chongzhen reportedly had his entire family killed, then climbed the eastern slope and hanged himself from an old locust tree. A new tree has been planted

Giant panda sunbathing in Beijing Zoo.

to mark the site.

If you walk northwest from Jingshan Hill, you'll soon come to the site of an imperial park which houses the oldest zoo in Chinese history. The **Beijing Zoo** had been an experimental farm formed under orders from Empress Dowager Cixi. Known as Wanshengyuan (Garden of Ten Thousand Beasts), it was opened to the public in 1908. Occupying over 50 hectares, Beijing Zoo contains more than 6,000 animals of over 550 species. Perhaps the major attraction of the zoo is the giant panda. Originally a carnivore, it now subsists mainly on bamboo. Zoologists have labelled the giant panda a "living fossil" as it possesses certain structural characteristics of ancient mammals.

Beijing Environs

Notable among the places worth visiting, outside Beijing are the Imperial Tombs, the magnificent Great Wall, the archeological finds in Zhoukoudian and Loguoqiao, known to the west as Marco Polo Bridge. In addition the environs of Beijing include Tianjin the carpet center, Beidaihe, the summer capital and Chengde, the site of the summer palace.

The Imperial Tombs

Most of the emperors of the last 2 feudal dynasties chose the mountains around Beijing as auspicious sites for their burial grounds. Using the age-old divination method of geomancy, each site was carefully selected and when you visit the area, the beauty and tranquility of the location will impress you. The Ming tombs are concentrated on the northwest of Beijing, the Qing tombs to the east and west.

The **Ming Tombs** lie at the foot of the Tianshou Mountains, 50 km northwest of Beijing. Because 13 of the 16 Ming emperors were buried here, the necropolis is known as Shisanling (Thirteen Tombs). Its construction continued over 200 years, almost as long as the dynasty lasted. The "Sacred Way", along which the bodies of the deceased emperors were carried, stretches 7 km from north to south through the center of the site. The Sacred Way leads first to the main gate, the Dagongmen (Great Palace Gate), with 3 passageways, the central reserved for the deceased emperor. Further in, you will see a stele pavilion, and beyond that an impressive array of 24 stone animals followed by 12 stone human figures, each carved from a single piece of white marble. At the end is the Longfengmen (Dragon and Phoenix Gate) and paths leading to the separate tombs, each ending with a Minglou (Visible Tower), the tallest building in the area. Further on are the tumuli and beneath them the stone "underground palaces", where the emperors' coffins lie. The largest and most interesting are the Changling and Dingling, which are also the only 2 open to the public.

The **Changling** contains the re-

The Ming Tombs and its surroundings.

mains of Yongle, the third Ming emperor, and his empress. Entry to the sacred area is through 3 huge courtyards, the second of which leads to the imposing Ling'endian (Hall of Prominent Favor) where sacrifices were made to the deceased emperor. Note the 32 huge gilded pillars of *nanmu* that support the coffered ceiling, each made from a single trunk. This fine hardwood came from southwest China and took more than 5 years to transport to Beijing.

Dingling is the tomb of the 13th emperor, Wanli and of his 2 empresses Xiaoduan and Xiaojing. Wanli ascended the throne at the age of 10 and became the longest reigning Ming emperor, occupying the throne for 48 years. Wanli began building his own tomb in 1585 when he was only 22. Dingling took 6 years to complete, costing 8 million taels of silver — 2 years' land taxes for the whole country! In 1956, Chinese archeologists excavated the underground palace, the first excavation carried out on the Ming tombs.

The underground palace is 27 m below the surface. To enter, go down 3 flights of stairs set into the tumulus. A series of halls leads to the burial chambers. If the floors of these halls look especially shiny, note that these are specially made 'golden' bricks. Each brick was fired in a kiln for 100 days, then soaked in tung oil. Making the 50,000 bricks took 3 years, but the bricks are smooth and shiny and hard wear only makes them more polished. The rear hall, the largest chamber, contains a dais on which the coffins are placed surrounded by pieces of jade, thought to preserve the bodies from decay. Also buried with the emperor were many precious objects, including a gold crown and 4 phoenix crowns. The phoenix crowns were worn by the empresses at grand ceremonies. Decorated with various combinations of dragons and phoenixes, each crown is inlaid with 5,000 pearls and precious stones.

The Qing Tombs

The Qing emperors were buried in two sites in Hebei, known as the Eastern and Western Qing Tombs. Though beautiful, they attract fewer visitors than the Ming Tombs because of their greater distance from Beijing. **Dongling** (Eastern Tombs) is located in the Zunhua County, about 125 km east of Beijing. It contains 15 tombs of 5 Qing emperors and their empresses, concubines and daughters, including that of the infamous Empress Dowager Cixi.

Construction of the first tomb began in 1663, based on a similar arrangement as the Ming Tombs. This tomb, the Xiaoling, houses the remains of Shunzhi, the first Qing emperor. West of the Xiaoling is Yuling, where the Qianling emperor lies buried. The second imperial tomb to be excavated, Yuling is open to the public and is particularly famous for its fine marble carvings which cover the walls and ceilings. The most notable features are the 8 boddhisattvas, 4 devaraja and thousands of Buddhist sutras carved in Sanskrit and Tibetan.

Further west is the tomb of the controversial Empress Dowager Cixi. Technically and artistically, its construction is the most advanced of all Qing tombs. Cixi is best remembered as the wily concubine who seized power after Emperor Hsien Feng's death and together with the docile Empress Ci'an, maneuvered the strings of the empire behind the "curtain". Pay special attention to the carving on the central ramp on the flight of stairs leading up to the main hall : it shows a dragon and phoenix playing with a pearl in the clouds but in complete reversal to other tombs — the phoenix (symbolizing the empress) is above the dragon (symbolizing the emperor). The Empress Dowager's underground palace is the first such burial site of an empress to be excavated and is open to the public.

Xiling (Western Tombs) is situated in Yixian county and is 100 km southwest of Beijing. The first tomb built here was the Tailing, for the third Qing emperor, Yongzheng. It is believed that Yongzheng chose this site as he felt uneasy at the thought of lying in the same necropolis as his father, Emperor Kangxi.

Rumors were rife that Kangxi had willed the throne to his 14th son but Yongzheng had the will altered to name the successor as the 4th son, himself. The Western Tombs, as well as the other Qing and Ming Tombs, are under government protection. Xiling is particularly tranquil, with acres upon acres of pines and cypresses providing shade. In spring, peaches and plums blossom around the golden and vermilion halls and in autumn, apples and persimmons add their color to the scenery.

The Great Wall

Fifty kilometers northwest of Beijing is a stretch of the famous **Great Wall**. The road leads past the ancient **Juyongguan** (Dwelling-in-Harmony Pass) and up to the fort of **Badaling** (Eight Prominent Peaks), where you can catch a magnificent view of the Wall.

The Great Wall is a gigantic defensive project which starts from Linzhao (in Gansu), and passes through modern Inner Mongolia, Shaanxi, Shanxi and Hebei to the eastern part of Liaoning. This is only about 2,000 km, but the wall winds over high mountain ranges and valleys, and at some strategic passes, doubles back and redoubles, so that its total length is more than 5,000 km — equivalent to more than 10,000 Chinese *li*, thus it became known to the Chinese as Wanli Changchen (Ten Thousand Li Long Wall). Qin Shihuang, the first emperor who united the whole of China in 221 BC, linked up the existing fortifications and extended it. He employed a workforce of almost a million, representing one-fifth of the total labor force of the country at that time. Many of the laborers succumbed to the severe hardships and there are many tragic stories which have become widely-known folk tales and legends.

During the Qing Dynasty, the wall was abandoned and fell into ruin. It has been restored at various places and now you may visit Badaling or Mutianyu, 2 passes nearest Beijing. Badaling is 64 km away from the capital and if you travel by train, you will see the bronze statue of the celebrated engineer Zhan Tianyou (1860-1919) at the Badaling station.

Zhan Tianyou is credited with taking on the impossible task of building a railway through extremely hazardous terrain of steep cliffs and deep valleys between Nankou and Badaling in 1909. Pass south of the statue and the Great

Legends of the Great Wall

It was inevitable that storytellers of old China would seize upon the Great Wall as a fount of source material for their art. Popular tales speak of the miraculous tools that Qin Shihuang possessed, which enabled him to build the wall in such a short time.

One of the treasures the emperor had was his 'Drive the Mountains Whip'. It was believed that a flick of the whip would move a whole range of mountains or cause the flood waters of the Yellow River to ebb to enable his workmen to get on with their work. Another of his treasures was a shovel that could throw up a mile of earth with 3 scoops.

But there was one legend that survived the ravages of time, told of the personal suffering caused by this giant undertaking. The story of Meng Chiang-nu is a moving account that has been passed down in numerous versions. It tells of a beautiful and talented girl, Meng Chiang-nu, who married a brilliant scholar. Soon after, Meng Chiang-nu's husband was conscripted into the labor force to construct the Great Wall and because years of poring over the classics did not prepare him for harshness of manual labour, he perished soon after and his body was at once buried in the wall.

Meng Chiang-nu waited in vain for news of her husband and finally decided to look for him. When she arrived at the work camp, she learnt that he had perished and she fell to the ground and wailed to the heavens.

The tale goes on to describe how the heavenly deities heard her and moved with pity and compassion, caused lightning to strike the wall. Suddenly, there was a loud rumble and a gaping hole appeared in the wall. The bones of thousands of dead workmen lay exposed. How was she to find the remains of her beloved, to take them back to their hometown to give them a proper burial, without which his soul would know no rest?

The gods told her to make a cut in her finger. Unhesitatingly, she drew a knife across her index finger, then walked among the skeletons and let her blood drip over the bones until she reached a spot where her blood sank into one of the skeletons and she knew these must be the remains of her husband. Gathering them all up, she trudged away from the site to prepare for her long journey home. Qin Shihuang was, at this time, passing by on an inspection tour and he spotted the lone beauty. Captivated, he proposed to make her part of his harem. Meng Chiang-nu could hardly refuse as the alternative would be a sentence of death for having caused part of the Great Wall to collapse. So, she agreed on condition that her husband be given an immediate state funeral on the shores of the Eastern Sea.

On that day, after prayers were offered, the faithful widow leapt into the sea to join her husband's released soul. With the coming of western technology to China, local legend insists that the hole in the wall caused by Meng Chiang-nu was never closed up and remained to provide the gap through which the Peking-Kalgan railway passes.

Wall appears along the crest of the mountains. Beyond a narrow valley is the entrance to the fort at Badaling. Built of white marble, the gate's interior are bas-relief carvings of Buddhist themes thought to date from the 14th century.

The Great Wall at Mutianyu is 81 km from Beijing but you would have to hire a car or rough it on the local bus to get there. This section of the wall, steeper in certain parts than at Badaling, is 2 km long and has 22 watchtowers.

Remember always to wear comfortable shoes with non-slip soles when attempting to climb either section of the Great Wall. It is a difficult ascent at certain parts, but when you finally get to the top tower and gaze at the wall snaking its way across the mountains,

One of the lions on the 800-year-old Logouqiao (Reed Gully Bridge).

you will understand why it is one of the wonders of the world.

Logouqiao and Zhoukoudian

Fifteen kilometers southwest of Beijing is one of the longest ancient stone arch bridges still existing in North China. **Logouqiao** (Reed Gully Bridge) is named after the river which it spans, once known as Logou, now the Yongding. Since ancient times, this area had been vital to communications between the north and south. In 1153, when the Jin Dynasty set up capital around what is now the southwestern district of Beijing, it decided the small wooden bridge was inadequate to meet its needs so a new bridge was laid in 1193.

Though Logouqiao is already 800 years old, its load-bearing capacity is still substantial — a 400-ton flatbed truck passed through it safely in a test carried out recently. At each end of the bridge are 2 *huabiao* (carved ornamental columns), similar to the ones in Tiananmen. Beside them, you will see a white marble stele pavilion — the northern stele has an inscription by Kangxi, the southern by Qianlong.

There is a saying in Beijing: "The lions on Logouqiao are impossible to count," yet visitors to the bridge seem to delight in counting them. Counting the big ones are easy but the smaller ones, only a few centimeters tall are easily

Zhoukoudian, 50 km from Beijing, is known as the home of Peking Man.

missed. There are actually 485 lions on the bridge, 287 big and 198 small. Most of them have been restored since the 14th century.

Besides its historic value, Logouqiao is also remembered as the site of the "July 7 Logouqiao Incident." Here, in 1937, the Japanese fired the first shot that began the invasion of China. Under the leadership of the CCP, China resisted Japanese in a war which lasted till 1945. You can still see the marks left by the Japanese bullets and artillery bombardments on the bridge.

Thirty-five kilometers from Logouqiao is an enormous natural cave in **Zhoukoudian**, known throughout the world as the home of the Peking Man *(Homo erectus Pekinensis)*. It was here that a team of international scientists discovered the first complete Peking Man skullcap. On the eve of the Pacific War in 1941, the skull was put under the care of the American-run Peking Union Medical College. It disappeared during the wartime evacuation and has never been recovered.

There is a fossil exhibition hall at the site, open from 9 am to 4 pm, Wednesday to Sunday, but check before you go.

Chengde - Hebei Province

In 1703, Emperor Kangxi of the Manchus in the Qing Dyansty decided to have a summer home away from the heat of

The Summer Palace in Chengde of both Qing Emperors Kangxi and Qianlong.

Beijing. He selected the cool mountain air of **Chengde** in the north of **Hebei Province**. Grandson Qianlong, also a lover of the good things in life, carried on the project.

In the 18th century going to the cottage for the summer was an expedition that involved elephants, camels, horses, sedan chairs and walkers to accommodate the entourage. The trip would take a week or more to get everyone there. Now you can hop on a nice comfortable soft seat train and be there in 5 hours on the honeymoon express or 7 hours on the shuttle.

The interest in Chengde is to follow the paths of the emperors, visualize the enormous volume of the life sytle. A 600-hectare (1500 acres) **Summer Palace** enclave is surrounded by a 10-kilometer of wall similar to the style of the Great Wall, not too far away. The main reception hall, **Hall of Simplicity and Sincerity** is now a museum but still reeks of the aromatic hardwoods used. Gardens attempted to duplicate the elegance and intricacy of Suzhou's beautiful creations.

The Kangxi period was one of trying to accommodate and encompass the Tibetans. **Putuozongsheng Temple** imitates the Potala Palace built to honor the 60th birthday of Qianlong. **Xumifushou Temple** was completed in 1781 in time for the 6th Panchen Lama's visit.

According to legend, the Panchen Lama traveled from Lhasa to Chengde with his large entourage on elephants, loaded with gifts for the emperor. The trip took 9 months but the unfortunate Panchen Lama died of the small pox soon after he arrived.

It is said that the Qings deserted Chengde after a run of imperial bad joss. Emperor Jia Qing died when lightning struck during a thunderstorm (1820). Forty years later his descendant Emperor Xian Feng died trying to escape the foreign invasion of Beijing. The Dowager Empress Cixi took over soon after that and stuck to her marble boat in Beijing's Summer Palace.

For a change of hotel venue, ask to be put up in the hotels within the palace compound. They are relatively new, the Qiwanglou fashioned after the Red Mansions and the Dujia Village designed in the Mongolian *yurt* style. Airconditioning and television detract considerably from the ambience but the linen is clean and a thermos of boiled water is supplied. A *yurt*-shaped restaurant is part of the ambience serving local specialties. The *yurt* dwellers of Mongolia never had it so good.

Beidaihe the Summer Capital - Hebei Province

Beijing and Tianjin diplomats, escaping from the summer heat in their ghetto-like residences made a summer resort out of **Beidaihe** in the last of the 19th century. They built villas along the seafront and once had a golf course. The hierarchy of communist China discovered the pleasure of bathing in the Bohai Sea and erected their own guesthouses with private villas for the leaders. They let the golf course go to seed but graciously reopened the village to foreigners again in 1979.

Arrange the 5-hour train trip CITS style: a guide greets you at the depot, has a car ready, exchanges business cards and begins to describe all the wonders of this vacation resort. With luck Villa #2 at the Central Beach Hotel is waiting to serve its distinguished guests.

A VIP villa (2 units in a building) consists of a foyer, entertaining and lounge area, bedroom and bath. The cocktail table has pretty porcelain tea service, a caddie of green tea and the ever-present thermos of hot water. A small refrigerator sits proudly in the corner, significant of modern conveniences. The bath tub on ancient clawed legs is rust-stained but deep and the houseboy promises hot water every day between 4 and 6 pm.

The travel program begins with the guide pouring tea and offering the menu of local interest. Closely structured meal hours are explained, served in the main and only dining room. A tentative itinerary is planned, including an auto trip to the Great Wall where it begins at the Bohai Sea.

Beidaihe offers pleasant walks by the sea and swim if you like in the sand-murky shallows of the beach. Fresh steamed crab and seafood are regular items on the lunch and dinner menus. Music blares constantly and the attendants will delightedly play your tapes if you have them with you. Walking through the village is pleasant with a stop at the original Keissling's German Bakery for ice cream and a torte.

A day trip with your guide leads north paralleling the train tracks through the **Qinhuangdao** an industrial smog-filled no-need-to-stop port city to **Shanhaiguan**, where the Great Wall ends at the sea. The First Gate, so described as the entrance to the Heaven of China is completely opposite the rebuilt, crowded mass of confusion at the Badaling sections of the wall near Beijing.

A handful of visitors, the earthen ramparts, a pleasant tower house of pictorials and souvenirs present an ambience of *deja vu*. You walk out on the wall's wide earthen surface and imagine a team of horses, 5 abreast, racing towards you pulling a military cart. Spear-carrying soldiers man the vehicle protecting a famous general commanding the area. A pictorial story is on the wall of the tower house explaining a local saga.

Tianjin, Centrally Administered Municipality

World famous Tianjin carpets are reason enough to visit **Tianjin**. Somewhat off the tourist route, the free Economic Zone of Tianjin is easy to get to with a 2-hour train ride from Beijing. Pleasant hotels, an incomparable Food Street, the sea port of **Tanggu (Xingang)**, 50 km away and the fascinating art center of **Yanglinqing** offer an interesting 4 or 5-day visit.

Hotels abound but the Tianjin Garden Hotel set in a garden and river ambience will let you walk the paths of its famous international predecessors. Try calling direct for a reservation before leaving Beijing. The rooms are diverse, ranging from simple quarters to large suites amply furnished. The dining menu is designed for dignitaries and high ranking government officials. Other major hotels, Sheraton Tianjin, Victory Hotel, Hyatt Tianjin and the Crystal Palace are listed in the Directory.

Tianjin was forcibly opened by the foreigners at the end of the 19th century for trade. The English and French started the occupation and were followed by the Japanese, Germans, Austro-Hungarians, Italians and Belgians. Touring the trading city is a lesson in international architecture. Parts of these concessions still exist to challenge the historians.

Shopping streets in the town center also remind you of the European influence with Kiesslings Bakery producing chocolate cakes to eat with ice cream. **Goubuli** on Shandong Lu in the heart of the city is the dumpling gourmet center of the nation. The dumplings, pork or chicken filled with spices and gravy and served in bamboo steamers, are a memorable delight. **Commercial Street** claims

Making merit in Tianjin, a city known for its carpets and architecture left over from the European occupation.

Beijing (Peking) Duck

It is a dish famed the world over. Beijing Duck has a history of 600 years, going way back to the Ming Dynasty. Its method of preparation is unique. Ducks about 2 to 3 months old are used. Their skins are coated with syrup which accounts for the rich, red color and its crispness when roasted.

Roasting the ducks calls for a specially-designed wall oven with parallel horizontal bars from which the ducks suspend. Hardwood fuel (usually jujube, peach or pear wood, which produces the least smoke) is burned in a firepit in front of the oven. The heat of the pit is reflected to the roof of the oven, then to the suspended ducks. This cooks the ducks evenly, as well as impart a special aroma.

Serving Beijing Duck calls for skill in carving too. Usually the duck is sliced into 120 thin pieces within 5 to 6 minutes after being taken out. The slices are then either wrapped by each diner in a thin pancake or stuffed into a hollow sesame seed bun with shredded green onions and minced garlic in a sweet bean sauce, and with thinly-sliced cucumber or turnip in season.

---

to be the busiest in China with over 500 shops attracting a half-million shoppers a day.

Over 100 restaurants make up **Food Street** in the southern part of the city. The 3-storey arcade has snack shops on the main floor, European style on the second floor and the top floor is for banquets. You can sample both Kiesslings and the Goubuli at Food Street branches. Concentrated shopping areas of the Quanyechang Department Store, Yiling Art Gallery and the International Market show more easily purchased retail wares than the whole of the Guangzhou Trade Fair.

The art gallery at **Yangliuqing**, in the western suburbs dates from the early 17th century. The woodblock hand-painted prints are an art form, featuring happy children, called New Year's paintings.

Sometimes whole book fables in picture are available. Other colorful woodblock style paintings, inexpensive prints, papercuts, book marks and note paper are impossible to resist. If you purchase enough they can be encouraged to package the whole lot and ship it home for you.

Several of the finest wool and silk carpet factories are in Tianjin. They are open for visits and shopping. Their method of weaving and hand-embossing is elegant. Price them at home before leaving so you won't be shocked at the high value of the superb treasures. Shopping addicts liken Tianjin to a treasure trove.

Shopping in Beijing

Beijing has everything you want, if you know where to look. **Friendship Store** at 17 Jianguomen Wai Street has daily necessities and luxury items not available elsewhere. But more fun and cheaper is to rummage around with the locals. Shopping streets abound in Wangfujing, around the corner from Beijing International Hotel, Qianmen and Liulichang (for antiques).

Wangfujing is the principal venue for an afternoon's wandering after you have done the morning's serious tours. The first major store on the right hand side is the **Xinhua Book Store**. The third floor has a foreign language print section. The classics like ***A Dream of Red Mansions***, ***Water Margin***, ***Lu Xun's Selected Works*** or ***The Scholars***, are available in English. Dozens of colorful children's books fill the shelves tempting grandparent shoppers. Many are blatantly ideological, others interesting tales written hundreds of years ago. The works of Lu Xun, one of their more prolific writers of the 20th century is a favorite. His short tale, ***The True Story of Ah Q*** is an international classic. Xu Beihong, the painter of leaping horses is evident on the walls of poster prints. There is a papercut and a bookmark section, nice for light weight souvenir collections. Packets of scenic prints are inexpensive, printed with dual bilingual explanations. An hour later you realize this is only the first stop.

Everything you ever wanted is available at the multitude of stores on Wangfujing. The remarkable thing is the level of business. Many of the shopping malls would be in the seventh heaven with this amount of spending public traffic.

Xidan Avenue runs parallel to Wangfujing, a few long blocks down Chang An Avenue, a replica on a smaller scale. Both shopping avenues have a plethora of snack and eating shops.

Taxi stands are at the Minzu Hotel near Xidan and the Beijing International Hotel at Wangfujing.

From Qianmen, head west and you will come to the **Dazhalan** *hutong* with a definite medieval flavor. Dazhalan was a hangover from imperial days when shops and theaters were not permitted in the city's center, so you will find many of the city's oldest shops along this area. Shops that still preserve the tradition and qualify include **Liubiju**, a 400-year-old pickle-and-sauce emporium; **Zhimielou Restaurant**, serving imperial snacks; and **Liufuxiang**, a material and silk store which goes back a century ago. Or if you are seeking a cure for that persistent ailment, wander into the **Tonrengtang**, which has been around since 1669 and used to be a royal dispensary during the Qing Dynasty.

Liulichang, in the southwest section, is the antique collector's nirvana. Book stores and galleries combined with seal carving shops have fascinating inventories of odd stones for carving and antique seals. For instance **Rongbaoshai** (Glorious Treasures Studio) dating from the 17th century, still produces woodblock prints and will accept commissions. A taxi will take you there and wait to take you back.

Dining in Beijing

Restaurants in Beijing are so numerous, you will wonder how you will be able to sample the many different dishes that Beijing is famed for. But most of the city's restaurants are located within walking distance from places of interest or hotels, so finding them should not pose a problem.

A few are in the landmark itself. It includes the **Fangshan Restaurant** in Beihai Park, well-known for its carefully prepared and beautifully served dishes, set off with a taste that is subtle yet with crisp and tender textures. A notable example is the 'goldfish duck webs' — the dish is arranged in perfect symmetry of a goldfish. The **Tinglinguan** in the Summer Palace was a theater in imperial days before being converted into a restaurant in 1949. The menu here is based on imperial recipes of the Qing and Ming Dynasties.

Of course, a visit to Beijing is incomplete without tasting Beijing Duck, found in many top restaurants in Beijing. Most famous is **Beijing Kao Ya Dian**, known to locals as Sick Duck as the restaurant is located off Wangfujing in a lane leading to the Capital Hospital. Its sister restaurant, the **Big Duck**, is located in Qianmen.

Another well-known restaurant is the **Super Duck**, the world's largest Beijing Duck restaurant. It is in Xinhua Nan Street, in a 7-storey building with a seating capacity of 2,500.

Another celebrated dish is "rinsed mutton", also known as mutton hot-pot. This dish has a history of over a 1,000 years and was part of the winter menu in the Qing court in the mid-17th century. Today, the best known restaurant serving this hot-pot is **Donglaishun** on Wangfujing Street, a Muslim restaurant which opened for business in 1903.

Another Manchu dish which has become a Beijing specialty is barbecued meat. In the Qing Dynasty, during the Double Ninth Festival, officials who picnicked in the hills around the capital would bring with them boiled beef and mutton, seasonings and garnishes and an iron-pan for recooking the meat. At their chosen venue, they would light up a fire, sear the cold boiled meat and dip it in their concoction of sauces. This dish was gradually introduced into restaurants. Most famous is the **Kaorouji**, a restaurant picturesquely situated just north of Beihai Park.

A roast duck dish à la Kunming.

NORTHERN HINTERLANDS

Manchuria

Aubkai, the Mongol, descendant of Nurhachi, leader of the Manchus came down from Shenyang to conquer the Mings and found the Qing Dynasty in 1634. It lasted until the reign of Pu Yi, the last emperor in 1911. The name **Manchuria** evolved from the Manchus, then designated Manchukuo by the Japanese when they controlled Pu Yi. Dongbei is simply Mandarin for East North.

The Russians and Japanese bounced the northeast around like a rubber ball between them over the centuries. The attraction for Japan was a land area 3 times the size of their whole island nation loaded with timber, oil and possible agriculture. In between the

The frozen river, a winter scene in Harbin.

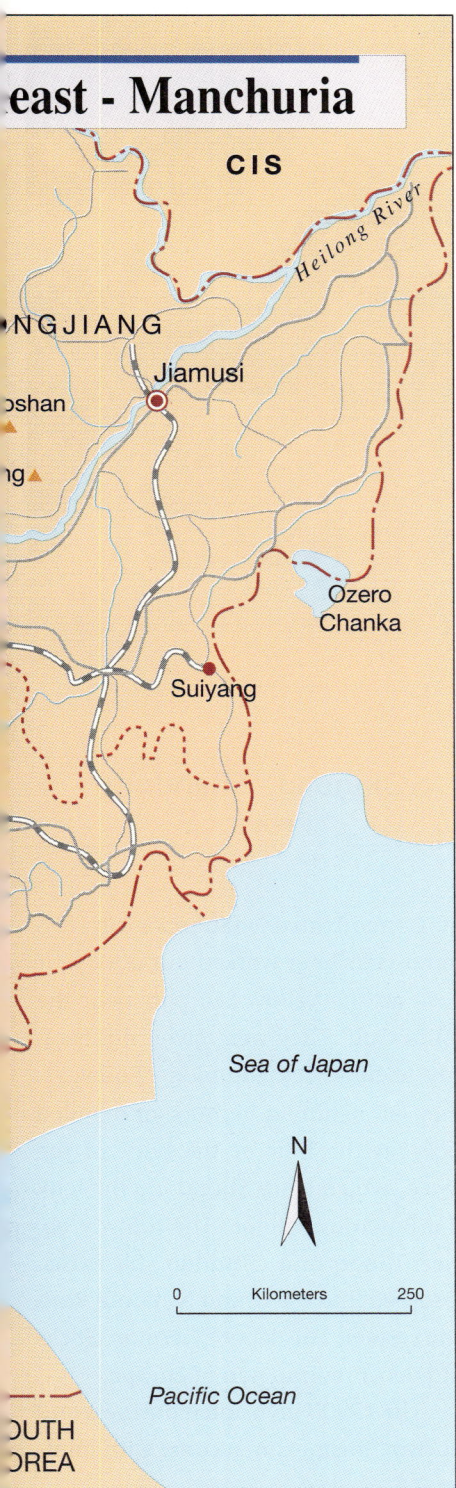

2 conquerors, warlords took over to subjugate the people. Forces of Mao Zedong and Chiang Kaishek continually tried to assimilate the local armies rather than attempt direct invasion after the Japanese surrendered and finally left.

Manchuria represents an offbeat path with little of the temple-museum historical sights. It is a fascinating part of the emerging dragon offering a variety of travel opportunities to explore the hinterlands. We suggest a coastal steamer from Shanghai to the port of **Qingdao** (Tsingtao), available on a daily schedule.

The port of **Qingdao**, known for its beer production left over from the German occupation, will help you get your land-legs back and allow you to go for a swim in the Yellow Sea. From Qingdao, consider a side trip to Qu Fu, the birthplace of Confucius to wander in the halls dedicated to his philosophy and that of his disciple Mencius.

Go north from Qingdao to **Yantai** (Chefoo) by rail to the Bohai sea, spend a night and cross over to **Dalian**. Dalian is also known as Luda or Dairen, sometimes confused with its neighbor Port Arthur, also known as **Lushun**. The multiplicity of names comes from the constant changing of ownership. Dally in Dalian for a few days and enjoy the beaches and wonderful seafood. Port Arthur was a valuable treaty port of Russia, the rail head of its Manchurian line to the sea. The Russian port of Vladivostock is closed many months of the year because of ice and cold.

Confucius Temple in Qu Fu, Shandong Province, was said to have been the birthplace of the sage.

Shenyang is next on the rail route north. It is from here that the Manchus set forth to oust the Mings. There is history to revel in and a wonderful art museum-gallery here and then on to Changchun the northeast odyssey, to enjoy a VIP villa, real Mongolian hot pot and maybe get a walk-on as an extra in a Chinese movie drama. **Harbin**, almost the top spot on the northeast adventure reveals the history of the Russo-Sino attempts at being allies. When the snows are blowing and if you enjoy sub-zero weather, visit during winter, see the magnificent massive ice-carvings and watch the brave swim in the freezing waters. In summer side trips into the mountains and rural villages are fascinating.

Qingdao - Shandong Province

The Germans invaded Shandong in 1898 and a year later worked out a 99-year lease on the Yellow Sea port near the Bohai Gulf. They were given rights-of-way to build the Shandong Railways. They left behind a heritage of red-tiled roofs on the hills at the back of the beach, which lends Shandong the look of a Bavarian village. The railway between Jinan and **Qingdao** still exists, absorbed into the China National Railway system. The depot's German clocks and decor remind you of Europe.

The 1990's invasion is business and tourism. Businessmen came with joint-

Qu Fu, Shandong Province

Confucius, the sage whose teachings are pursued to this day.

Confucius (K'ung Futze) was born here in 551 BC, then the State of Lu. Confucius advocated familial respect, respect for authority, respect for education and continually preached peace and arbitration to the rulers of his day.

Relics uncovered in the area date the settlement over 6,000 years ago. From 205 BC Confucianism was the official religion of China and the prodigious descendants of Confucius became the Yuan Dynasty.

Qu Fu is west of Qingdao in Shandong Province with access from Beijing by rail to Jinan, thence to Yanzhou for auto transport to the city. Air flights are available twice weekly to **Jiaxing** nearby. From Qingdao, it is possible the CITS could arrange a cross country trip by auto. Modest accommodations are available in the **Confucius Mansions** for ambience of classical architecture or a newer Queli Hotel in town. **Yanzhou** or **Jiaxing** are more sophisticated for overnights, so make Qu Fu a day trip only.

Confucius Temple, in the center of town, is a group of interlocking courtyards around a massive central hall. Like many historic sights, there is a history of deterioration, rebuilding and the devastation of the Cultural Revolution. **Kong Family Mansion** (Kong being the family name of the sage) is over 900 years old, the former center of Confucian rule. Occupants claiming to be the 75th and 76th generation direct descendants live in and take care of the premises. Most of the town residents profess to be part of the family also. They tell the story that during the Cultural Revolution, the citizens removed most of the steles and other memorabilia from the temple and mansions to bury in the Forest Cemetery. Thus much of the original works have been restored.

Confucius Forest, cemetery of the Kong family outside the city, contains the bodies of the many generations. **Temple of the Duke of Zhou**, Confucius' mentor, lies east of the City. **Yanhui Temple**, is dedicated to Mencius, Confucius' most famous disciple. **Ni Mountain (Nishan)** is reputed to be the actual birthplace of Confucius.

Traveling to an offbeat spot like Qu Fu takes determination, the reward being to sit in the ambience of a great thinker with modern ideas that are relevant and in great need today.

venture projects in heavy industry of steel products, locomotives, tractors and automobiles. Light industries in electronics, textiles and straw products make the city port important with the ease of overseas shipping. The tourists come because of the temperate climate most of the year, sunny beaches and the ambience left over from the Europeans a century ago.

Hotel rates are very modest, with the glitzy Sea-and-Sky Hotel on the beach

Polar swimmers waiting for a dip in the winter waters of Harbin.

charging half of Beijing and Shanghai prices. The Badaguan Guesthouse is a secret of the cognoscenti with its villas, Old Stone House and the former Governor's Mansion, at prices still moderate for a standard room in a big city.

Shandong cooking style has the most flavor of northern cuisine. The Chunhelou Restaurant on Zongshan Road is the center of business-oriented banquets and gourmet visitors.

The Old German Quarter contains 2 fine department stores, a curio-antique store, beautiful cotton and silk cloth at a dry-goods store and handicraft shops featuring the local shellwork, framed montages and massive soapstone sculptures. Pick a pretty piece of pink and gray stone and the artist will carve your seal while you wait.

Qingdao Brewery and Huadong Winery welcome thirsty visitors and they offer tasting privileges. The winery produces a vintage, which has won prizes in international competition. *Tsingtao* (market name) boards ships at the nearby docks stowed in the largest containers, bound for worldwide destinations.

The beaches are numbered like department stores. #1 is the longest at about 600 m, with a changing hall and toilet facilities. #2 beach is quieter, fronting the villas, once the summer cottages for dignitaries. A former German governor's palace-like residence is at the end of #2, said to have cost two and a half million taels of silver and his job as governor according to local lore.

In the winter the crowds come to watch the **winter swimmers**, polar bear enthusiasts who deign the warm waters of the summer. The prevalence of male business travelers encourages the capitalistic entrepreneurship of black market money and other nocturnal activities.

After you have had a sip at the brewery and winery, **Zhaqiao Pavilion**, **Qingdao Art Museum**, **Qinghai Pier** and the aquarium at **Lu Xun Park** will take up a full afternoon. Stay an extra day and visit the lighthouse and gardens on **Little Qingdao**, a small island offshore. **Yellow Island**, a new Special Economic and Development Zone for joint ventures offers access by ferry to **Xuejia Island** where you can picnic and spend the day on beautiful sandy beaches away from the crowds.

Thirteen kilometers away is the source of **Laoshan Mineral Water** which is served throughout China and exported. The mountain provides fine marble for major edifices owing its origin to geological explosions a billion or more years ago. The Song Dynasty **Taiqing Palace** (Toaist Monastery), houses the monks in charge of the mineral water production. Mountain walking is in order on the numerous paths of the 1,133-meter high Laoshan. Temples, waterfalls, rock formations, all aptly named by the locals, pepper the area. **Beijiushui** (Nine Northern Waters) is a health resort featuring mineral pools and spas for those desiring long life.

Travelers can reach Qingdao by coastal steamer from Shanghai, air flights or train from Beijing or Shanghai. Many of the cruise boats stop for a day or two at this port of call.

Yantai - Shandong Province

Yantai is a relaxing 5-hour train ride from Qingdao. The pleasant Yantai Hill Hotel sits atop the **Yantaishan Park** above the harbor. We suggest taking the morning train from Qingdao to Yantai, lunch and rest at the hotel. Enjoy the fresh air and a short walk in the park for exercise after siesta. Tour the city in the afternoon and then take the night boat across the straits to Dalian.

Yantai, at the northern tip of Shandong, was once the naval lookout point for the Bohai Sea. Translated the name means "Smoke Terrace" for the fires that were lit to warn fishing boats of pirates before the wars and to spot naval vessels during the various occupation periods. The beacon tower is long gone from the hill. However, a 15-minute climb from the road below is rewarded by a magnificent view of the Bohai Sea.

The **Yuhuangding** is a complex of pavilions and other buildings on the tip of another hill in the center of the city. The Yuan Dynasty started it and the Mings completed the meditation area. **Fujian Guild Hall** is the other most important place to visit in Yantai. Historical sagas and fairy tales are represented in the colorful carvings in the roof beams and supporting columns, a

Colorfully illuminated ice sculpture at the Harbin Ice Festival.

pair of dragons carved into the entrance pillars guard the entrance.

Yantai is surrounded on 3 sides by the sea creating a temperate climate suitable for grape growing. Many of the famous Chinese wineries use the produce from this area to make their wines.

Cruise boats occasionally dock for the day to add another exotic port to their advertised itinerary, disgorging passengers for a day's shopping on their way down the coast. Yantai produces wines and liquors found in great abundance in the shops at modest prices in case you want to stock up for the rest of your trip.

If you have a few days to spare, there is more to see in the Yantai Peninsula. Coastal roads make car travel comfortable. Small villages, rural life style and historic sights offer an interesting adventure. There are many medicinal spas with mineral rich hot springs and sunny beaches in summer. West of the city is **Penglai**, the fabled residence of the immortals. The remnants of a naval base can be seen. The government, in the interest of tourism is now reconstructing the ancient city of **Dengzhou** nearby. Offshore are the Fairy Islands of the **Changshan Archipelago**. Twenty islands make up the group over a hundred mile stretch of sea. There is access to the important islands by boat. Each has interesting buildings and a local culture unfettered by tourist commercialism. **Cape Chengshan (Tianjintou-End of the World)** is a must for those travelers who enjoy reaching far points of land, the ends of the road.

The night ferry across the straits from Yantai to Dalian is a real change of pace. The boat is as crowded as a Japanese subway car during rush hour. Your assigned berth in the cabin for 8 or 16 persons is useless due to the conglomeration of people, goods and children. Join the young college crowd heading for the university in **Jilin**; they gather on the fan tail (rear) of the main deck and discuss politics the whole night. Most of them speak English and welcome a foreign visitor to discuss democratic ideology.

Dalian - Liaoning Province

Emperor Wu Di in 108BC declared the port open to traffic with Korea, across the straits. **Dalian**, Dairen or Luda as it has been called at various times, was fought over and occupied by many conquerors. The latest was the Japanese invasion in 1935 giving territory-hungry Japan a foothold in Manchuria and an operating naval base during the ensuing war. The various names indicate the succession of occupiers, each seeking to take a bite out of the empire.

Dalian is a strategic port on the Bohai Sea, complementing Yantai as the northern observation point. Sino-Russian and Russo-Japanese naval battles were fought until the Japanese took over in 1930. Their defeat in 1945 opened up the pressures again and the Russians stayed for another 10 years. Today Dalian has prospered as a free economic zone, allowed to operate on its own without the heavy hand of Beijing interference. The ice-free port is one of the largest in China with modern container ship facilities. Travelers can enjoy it as a relatively tourist-free city with good business-hotel accommodations, excellent seafood restaurants and a chance to mingle with the everyday Chinese. Access to Dalian is by overnight ferry from Yantai or air flights from Beijing or Qingdao.

The central city square yet retains the name of Stalin from the post war Russian influence achieved from the infamous post World War II Yalta Agreements. Downtown shopping is intriguing because it is not tourist oriented. You can buy local products, cloths, shell arts and crafts and maybe a new cowboy-style straw hat at local prices. Friendship stores are available; an older one on Sidalin Lu and the newer shop in the Furama Hotel. There are modern hotels (see Directory) like the Holiday Inn. Our choice would be the Bangchuidao Guesthouse, out of town on a beach spit of land. The beach is a strange one of small stones and fields of kale in the shallow waters. Japanese visitors can be seen harvesting the fresh seaweed to dry and send home. Crab and fresh fish are plentiful and go well with the local *Dynasty* wine (white semi-dry), plentiful because Dalian is an export point for the product.

You can also visit the **Natural His-**

tory Museum and the beaches. A tour of the dock facilities is interesting. You might try bobbing for apples because Dalian is noted for the finest apples in the north. Evening entertainment is at the hotels or the Seaman's Club with imported video movies and a theater for operas.

Golden Pebble Beach (Jinshitan) is an hour's drive along the coast from Dalian City. A small quaint hotel is available for overnight stay. The West Beach is a mile-long, sandy stretch for swimming and sun-bathing in the summer. Pebbles and odd rock formation is the scenery on the East Beach. Pillars of rocks extend for a long vista, angling out of the sea like a herd of dragons sunning themselves. The golden hue at sunset reflecting off the rocks created the name for this unique area.

Prowl the rock formations at low tide to view the curious formations of ancient sea beds, twisted and turned, eroded and sculpted into strange forms. Off a small island resembling a turtle is **Turtle Beach (Aotan)** where the receding tide reveals shells for the visiting collectors and sea urchins, sea cucumbers and starfish for the locals.

An overnight camping experience is offered at **Ice Valley (Bingyu)** in the mountains northeast of Dalian. Trekking the trails up the mountain and clear-water streams amid the virgin forest make up for the sparsity of the cottages and backpack food.

Dalian is a leisure stop for travelers, so relax on the beach for a couple of days and then take a 6-hour train ride north to Shenyang.

Shenyang - Liaoning Province

Shenyang, the original home of the Manchus is the industrial center of the north, rivaling Shanghai in importance. The rail lines bring in coal and steel to manufacture machinery, aircraft and city buses. Textiles, pharmaceuticals and even condoms for the birth conscious nation are important local products.

Ask to stay in the commodious villas of the Friendship Hotel as a change of pace from sparse hotel rooms. There is much to see in Shenyang and you will linger a little longer. In the morning, order in advance a true Mongolian hot pot for dinner that night.

The **Imperial Palace** is a mini-model of the Forbidden City. Recorded history tells of Emperor Shunzhi being crowned in the great **Dazheng Hall** before setting off in 1644 to storm the Great Wall and conquer the Mings. The palace is actually a museum with an impressive collection of 17th and 18th century armor. Emperor Qianlong of the 18th-century Qings added a courtyard and residential wing, now housing the anthology describing his travels and accomplishments. Other exhibitions of paintings, calligraphy, jade and porcelain artifacts, musical instruments and furniture help to visualize the high-living Manchus.

Stalwart and sturdy the horse is still a form of transport in Harbin.

The **East Tomb** has the remains and memory of Nurachi and the **North Tomb** is similar to the Ming Tombs near Beijing. It is the burial place of Huang Taiji (1592-1643), founder of the Qing Dynasty with large animal statues on the approach.

Qianshan is the local mountain about 50 km away with the **Tanggangzi Hot Springs** at its foot. Emperor Pu Yi is reputed to have bathed here with his various concubines when he was in nearby Changchun during the Japanese occupation. Now it is the site of mineral baths and a hotel.

Zhongshan Park has the world's largest collection of the fabled red-headed cranes. This is the delicate long-limbed bird often depicted in traditional Chinese paintings as a symbol of grace and longevity. The Shenyang Acrobatic Troupe is one of the best in China, traveling to the United States, Australia and other countries as a goodwill ambassador. Don't miss a performance if they happen to be in residence at the time you are there.

Liaoning Exhibition Center is a large Russian style building with one section housing an art gallery with a marvelous collection of modern and classical paintings. Many works of the tenets of communist and socialist philosophy, and strength of the people are on display there. Bold calligraphy, flowers, mountains, horses and the beautiful ladies of history are the classic subjects. The expressionist paintings are of particular interest because of the divergence from classic subjects. The curator will advise that you cannot purchase the work but the artist would be delighted to render a copy given time to produce and ship.

Qianlianshan (Thousand Lotuses Mountain) is an hour's drive from Shenyang for a day in the park or an overnight side trip. The park entrance has tee shirts for those who collect them, and steep hill paths to climb for the energetic. The tee shirt concession is new but the stairs and assorted temples are from the Tang, Ming and Qing Dynasties.

Six hours by train west of Shenyang is a cradle of history, rivaling Xian in importance. The digs of **Jinzhou** on the **Liaodong Gulf** have revealed a civilization more than 30,000 years old. Northern conquerors like Khitan of the Liao Dynasty (916-1125), around the year 1000, took over the whole northeast including Inner Mongolia. The Liaos left their name imprinted on the province, Liaoning, and scattered in the bays and edifices of the region. This regime was destroyed by Kublai Khan when he established the Yuan Dynasty.

A 57-meter pagoda dominates the center of the city, said to have been erected in 1057 to contain a relic of the Buddha Sakyamuni given to the Liao Empress Dowager . The **Guangji Universal Relief Monastery** dates from the same period and has been renovated in the subsequent Ming and Qing eras. Outside of the city is the **Guanyin (Goddess of Mercy) Cave** sheltering a pavilion dedicated to the goddess. The scenery is magnificent in the mountainous area of Beizhen County. Time permitting, a car tour to the northeast reveals pagodas of Chongxing Monastery, Yuwulu Mountains, Beizhen Temple and old palaces of the Qing and Ming emperors. Further west is the **Chaoyang** area and more archeological digs of a 5000-year-old civilization.

Other excursions can be made in the South of Liaoning to the historic towns of **Xingcheng**, site of many battles between the Manchus and the Mings. This area is especially unique for sinologists and tourists delving into the constant struggles of the dynasties to best each other.

Shenyang is an air and train hub of Dongbei. You can fly as far south as Xiamen, north to Harbin and as far west as Urumqi. The train trip to Changchun is about 5 hours.

Changchun - Jilin Province

Nanhu Guesthouse in the South Lake Hotel area is luxurious by Chinese tourist standards and you can ask for one of their villas. In the interest of time and space most guide books and tours pass up **Changchun**, known as Xinjing during the Japanese occupation (1932). Thus the limited tourist commercialism creates an interesting stop of true travelers. The city was the capital of

Vegetable wholesalers on the way to the market.

Manchukuo (Manchuria) then.

The guide will show you a local brochure listing 40 places of interest in the environs and ask how many weeks you are staying. Unless you have several weeks or a special interest, we suggest you pass up the #1 Tractor Factory, the Railway Carriage Factory, Jilin University and Medical College as well as the Provincial Athletic School.

Instead, arrange a visit to the film studios where all sound is dubbed in after the filming. You can ask as many questions as you like while watching the strange contortions of film makers. The stars are delighted to talk to the few visitors that come their way. If there happens to be a filming session in one of the many parks, it is possible you will be enlisted as an extra, without pay of course.

The **Changchun Arts and Crafts Export Company, Inc** is a wonderful stone and wood carving factory to occupy a morning. You can purchase some of their treasures to be packed and shipped home. A native medium is Changbai stone, a green marbleized material from the Changbaishan mountain. The factory also produces a unique form of wood carving from the odd twists of azalea roots.

The Last Emperor, film of the life of Pu Yi, was created in part here. Pu Yi was exiled to Tianjin after the 1911 revolution and then sent to Changchun in 1935 as the puppet emperor of Manchukuo. The **Pu Yi Palace and Exhibi-**

Yalu River Border with North Korea

The Yalu's claim to international notoriety came about during the Korean War. A 1940 steel bridge transported the thousands of Chinese soldiers and supplies to aid the North Koreans fighting the United States Armed Forces led by the famous General MacArthur.

The 800-kilometer river originates in Jilin Province in the Changbai Mountains, flowing eventually to the Yellow Sea. Most of its length becomes the border between China and North Korea.

At **Dandong** on the China side and **Sinuiju** on the North Korea side, tourist ferries ply close to the opposite shore. The city ports are freight junctions for important rail transport used in the exchange of goods between the 2 countries. The old steel bridge was finally bombed during the war and replaced by a new open girder bridge. The exact center is the border crossing for foot or vehicle travelers, who must have a proper visa to enter either side.

North up the river is **Tiger Hill (Hushan)**, a low mountain. Historians claim this is the western end of the Great Wall rebuilt by the Mings (1368-1644). Coach tours by land and boat tours on the river provide glimpses into Korea. Cross-border socializing is difficult because both countries are fierce defenders of their territories and cultures. As always the people wave to each other, manage clandestine trade and ignore much of the 2 governments' rulings to suit their own convenience.

tion Hall is available for those followers of movies documenting history.

The capital of Jilin Province is **Jilin City** a couple of train hours from Changchun. The Spring Festival at the end of January brings overseas tourists for the unique icicle show, caused by the warm waters of the hydroelectric system steaming the Songhua River. Nearby is the **Songhuahu Ski-Grounds** at **Daqingshan** (945 m) with lifts and ski equipment.

The **Meteorite Exhibition Hall** will give you a glimpse of a 1,700-kg piece of the sky that fell in the area, large enough to remind you of the Apocalypse. A day trip is sufficient to see Jilin City. Ask your guide to make it by car instead of train to better see the countryside.

Harbin - Heilongjiang Province

The International Hotel may appear a little seedy to you but it has a small VIP suite available and the dining room serves the local delicacies of bear paw, moose nose and frog soup. The Mongolian hot pot is almost as good as the one in Shenyang. The Swan Hotel is newer and Friendship Palace Hotel is the scenic spot on the **Songhua River**. There are

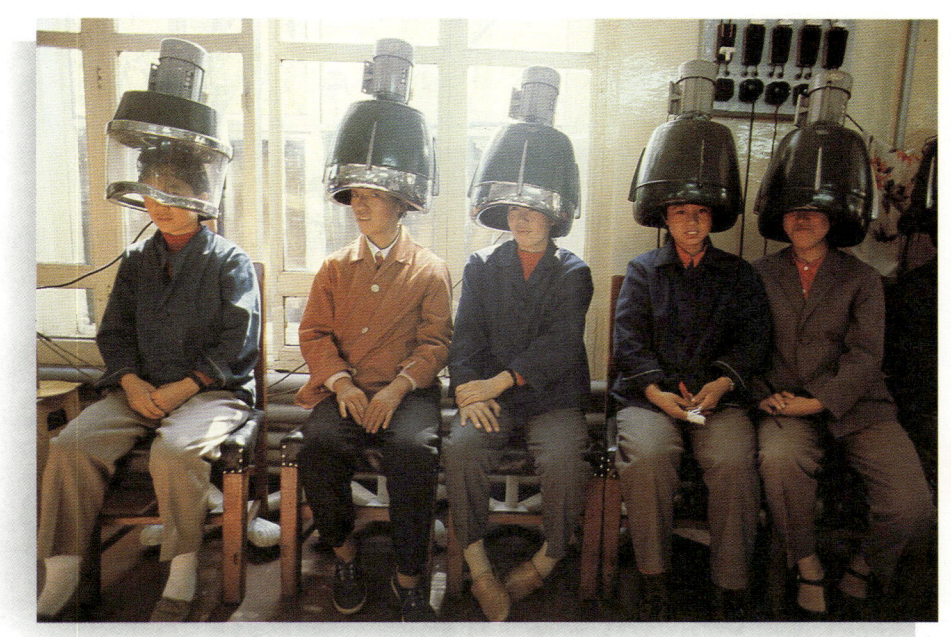

'Getting set' in a Manchurian beauty parlor.

many fine restaurants, the Regency Gourmet Center across from the International is reputed to be the top. **Harbin** is a relatively modern city. Restaurant dining outside the hotels is reasonably hygienic, so the traveling gourmet can dine in physical comfort.

The newest innovation in dining, reported by the international news media, is a result of Russian labor influx, who came on the invitation of the Chinese. There are Russian cuisine restaurants, entertainers in the karaoke vein, bar girls and some entrepreneurial joint ventures primarily in the restaurant and service industries.

As noted in the Dalian section, the Russians negotiated the Trans-Siberian railroad concession in 1896 with Harbin, the switching center for Valdivostock their own port. Dalian became the ice-free port south.

In 1917 the White Russians flocked to Harbin to escape the revolution and before that the Tsar's Cossack depredations on the Jews forced a migration of thousands of refugees to Harbin. Seventeen Russian Orthodox churches exist with onion spires and cupulae. Two synagogues remain as testament to the Jewish community, forced again to go underground during the communist anti-religious manifestos.

Russian influence remains dominant in the buildings, Stalin Square in the city center and a Stalin Park down by the Songhua River. In the same area as the churches, **Daoliqu**, has an inter-

Ice Carving Capital of the World

An ice sculpture in the Ice Festival in Harbin.

Sculptors from a dozen countries gather for an annual competition held in **Zhaolin Park**. Huge pagodas are built with colored lights assembled inside the carvings. Whole castles are designed complete with furnishings inside. There are thousands of carvings, houses, bridges and pavilions, many replicas of world-famous buildings, all carved from ice.

The Ice Carving Capital of the World is the tourist promotion line of Harbin's Chamber of Commerce. The only problem of seeing the building size sculptures of ice is that you must visit in the winter. It is very cold up there in the winter time. The Songhua River freezes and supplies the building materials for this rare art form.

The waters are transparent due to the fast-flowing river carrying very little silt. Blocks, 1 m thick and 2 m long are sawn out of the ice and transported to the various building sites. To carve a 10-meter dragon, the blocks are assembled and sprayed with water to meld together.

World famous chefs often congregate during the festival to learn and take a hand in the proceedings by entering the competition. All chefs who think they are adept at table ice carvings make a point to visit Harbin during the festival.

During Harbin's Ice and Snow Festival, a mass wedding is held each year on **Xiaonan Island** in Zhaolin Park. Couples gather from all over China for the traditional ceremony. They marry in an ice castle, then slide down a long chute to the ground to the fanfare of music and drums beating.

esting variety of shops that deserve wandering time. **Dazhi Dajie** is another shopping area not far from the International Hotel.

The downtown business section is composed of onion-shaped domes, pointed roofs and European style shop buildings. The neo-classical facade of the Education Bookstore has an intricately carved figure of a bare-breasted female, rarely seen in today's China.

There is a great deal of Russian architecture in Harbin. A thin web of French design occurred because of the Russian tsarist court's love for the language and culture.

A shopping mall exists under the **Qiulin Department Store**, inculcated in a maze of tunnels. The air raid shelter built during the wars was converted into stalls and small shops selling all manner of goods for the populace. It is warmer in the winter and cooler in the summer, making all day shopping and eating in

Heilongjiang Steam Locomotives

The province of Heilongjiang, northeasternmost in China is internationally noted for its collection of steam locomotives, many of which are still in use. The Chinese Railway Bureaucracy has decreed that all rolling stock of steam engines be taken off the tracks and sent to the province. At the last count there were over 1,000 of the glamorous relics consigned to and still puffing along the tracks of Heilongjiang.

Fierce winters block the local roadbeds in the outlying areas of the province, leaving the nostalgic trains the only means of transportation for the people. Frost covers the windows, the aisles, closed in with benches, allow only one person at a time to pass. Snow plows clear the tracks ahead and everyone wears the quilted clothing necessary in the minus zero temperature. Heating in cars cannot be depended on, so bundle up.

Summer is an entirely different story for the international tourist and steam engine aficionado. Day trips are engaged on the narrow gauge rail lines in areas outside of Harbin. The classic engines puff and huff their way through the forests, whistling to the natives as they pass. The antique stations have ancient red phones, signaling equipment consisting of red and green flags, and other relics of the century-old system. International collectors continually shop for period memorabilia.

the food stalls comfortable.

The early twenties and Russian cuisine is represented by the Huamei Restaurant on Zhongyang Street. Reputed to resemble the Kremlin, the interior is decorated in marble columns and carved statuary suitable for a palace. The menu includes the famous borscht (beet soup), goulash, roast meats and many dishes no longer even found within Russia.

Two kilometers of track in the **Children's Park** are used by a miniature railroad. The engineer and conductor are children taking care of 100 or more passengers on each 20-minute run.

The enmity and fear of Russia has abated with the de-clawing of the Russian bear. Cross-border trade is developing and tourism, the magic cash-temptation of all nations, plans great things to augment the Trans-Siberian Railway. New hotels are cropping up and the modernization of creeping capitalism is uplifting the ambience.

Across from Stalin Park at the river is **Sun Island**, intended as the largest tourist attraction in Harbin. A lake, hunting range, parks, gardens and picnics among the trees are all in the works. In the winter you can skate and in summer swim if you don't mind chilly waters.

An arts and crafts factory, division of the national chain Chinese Arts and Crafts Import and Export Corporation, produces a variety of interesting goods including straw figures, egg-shaped boxes, shell pictures and gemstone carvings.

For sports buffs, **Shangzhi Ski Resort** is near Harbin and in the winter there is ice-sailing on the Songhua. For 12 days of July the **Harbin Music Festival** attracts national and international performers and visitors. International competition of massive ice carving is an important festival of the winter.

Winter sports abound beginning with the first freeze and snow in October. Water is poured around official buildings, schools and factory for ice-skating rinks. Lunch hours provide time for skating. On the lake ice yachting on skis and runners can generate high speeds when the fierce winds blow.

Winter swimming for the hardy is provided by cutting the large blocks of ice out for the ice carving festivals leaving a gaping 100 sq m of open water. Sports enthusiasts dive and swim in the 4°C waters, claiming great health benefits. Naturally, agree, for a mere germ could hardly exist in this climate.

watchers may spend days chronicling the 250 species of birds at the **Zhalong Nature Reserve**. It is in the west of the province in the **Wuyur River Valley**. Many come to see the some 500 red headed cranes, a rare species almost extinct in the world today. **Dailing** in the Lesser Hinggan Range, is a secondary spot usually included in a special tour.

Fisherman's Delight is a tour arranged in the northern part of the province during the fishing seasons of summer and fall. Sturgeon, pike and trout are some of the fish caught in the near freezing waters. Outdoor camping is *de rigueur* for those enthusiasts who like to tent-down by the edge of the river and dine on their catch.

Cycling tours are arranged in the summer months in the mountain and forest areas traveling from 30 to 50 miles a day. **Trekking** is scaled for the A,B,C's of ability for those hardy hikers who desire 2 to 7-day walking tours over hill and dale.

River trips down the Heilong River are the newest tourist attraction on the border of what was once the Soviet Union. All of these specialized tours in-

Other Activities in Heilongjiang

Binocular and notebook equipped bird

Live chicken destined to reappear in hot broth.

clude the magnificent wonders of China's northeast, the minority groups living in the area, and the rare wildlife still extant in this part of the world.

Fortunately the **hunting season** is in the fall after the summer tourists have left. Guides, lodges, hunting dogs and even released prey are provided in the **Taoshan Game Reserve. Yuquan** is another area within 50 km of Harbin. Fifty species of animals and over 250 species of birds are hunted in the virgin forests of these reserves. Big game hunters journey here from all over the world as one of the few places trophy expeditions are permitted.

Splurge, take an extra 3 or 4 days and entrain north in the summer to the hunting and skiing mountain ranges. A hunting village near **Yichun** is 5 or 6 hours train ride into a forest preserve, a glimpse into the rural life of a northern community. Walking the dirt streets past the homes surrounded by stacks of firewood will remind you of expected snow-filled cold winters. Hike on the wooded trails and have no fear of the bears. Your guide will inform you that the big browns know it's against the law to eat a tourist.

With the proper visas you can venture into Russia or return to the world outside China via flights into Beijing, Shanghai or Guangzhou. Travel tip: make your return reservation on arrival in Harbin. Computerized reservations are in their infancy in remote parts of the country.

PARIS OF THE EAST

Shanghai

Shanghai is often suggested for your first visit to China. Five-star hotels, a modern airport, taxi service and prevalent English speaking people, familiar of all cities, help the foreign visitor ease into a markedly different culture. With a proper visa, you can fly into Shanghai confidently, without having to be met by a guide. Immigration hassles are minimal, and shouting taxi drivers vie for your business. International hotels accept and honor a reservation. Subsequent visits to Shanghai are inevitable, so don't fret if you don't cover the entire **Huangpu** waterfront the first time.

Like Beijing, look for a centrally located hotel for easy foot and taxi access. The Jin Jiang Hotel is in the middle of the what was once the **French Quar-**

The Bund in Shanghai reveals European presence in its architecture.

Shanghai

ter, close to Nanjing's shopping mecca and within walking distance of the Shanghai Arts and Crafts Exposition Center. The central area and waterfront is an interesting 5-kilometer walk or a short, wild taxi ride away.

The Jin Jiang is inside a compound with a north wing for FIT (Foreign Independent Travelers), a south wing for tour groups and a new modern tower for amenity conscious guests. If you care to splurge ask for the South Tower Nixon Suite that Bob Hope slept in.

A taxi queue at the main gate is accustomed to foreigners asking for a ride anywhere from downtown to **Huangshan Mountain**, about 12 hours away. The compound contains boutiques, an arts and crafts shop, a bookshop, a communications office including facsimile service and a mini-mart grocery to alleviate your nervous-hunger symptoms. The *International Herald Tribune, Asian Wall Street Journal, Time* and *Newsweek* are in the book store only one day late. Sheraton, Shangri-La, Hyatt, Hilton and Nikko are among a large number of hotels, short-listed in the Directory, up-market and available for advance reservations.

Shanghai is for eating, shopping, some city touring and a hub for traveling to the nearby cities of **Hangzhou, Wuxi, Suzhou**. Access by ship to the northeast, southeast and up the **Changjiang** (Yangtse) is excellent with a variety of schedules. Subsequent visits to China will usually mean more return visits to Shanghai, as a port of entry, than Beijing

A typical side-street scene in Shanghai.

or Guangzhou.

Shanghai is credited and discredited as a literary and thought center for various events such as the founding of the Communist Party in July 1921. Mao Zedong launched the hordes of Red Guards on the nation during the Cultural Revolution by publishing the fomenting articles in Shanghai in the 70s. The Green Shirts (Green Tong) was founded by the opium boss Du Yuesheng in Shanghai who supposedly funded and controlled Chiang Kaishek and the Kuomintang.

Shanghai began as China's capitalist center and whenever the leashes loosen slightly the latent instincts sprout again, no matter the style of government. The first Chinese Stock Exchange, since the communist takeover in 1949, opened recently. The demand is so great that the purchaser must stand in line for hours to buy a queue position for buying a lottery chit entitling only the lucky winners to buy stock.

The Communists changed Shanghai from the wild, frenetic, sensual world created by and for the foreigners but this is again emerging from its underworld domain. Business flourishes in the hands of the neo-entrepreneurs; night clubs and dancing are emerging. The press, with its new license of limited freedom, reports arrests of prostitutes and their clients.

Joint-venture companies are excited about the new business area being developed to ease the strain on Guangzhou and Shenzhen. The Shangri-La Hotel group has completed their "city within a city" complex of hotels, apartments, business offices, communications center and trade service offices. If you have a yen to stay for 3 months and study the language, there are about 200 research institutes, colleges and universities in Shanghai running the gamut of sciences, including atomic energy. The list has no end because each month, more are added to the roster. With the lifting of certain economic constraints and the government actively promoting economic growth, Shanghai is bursting with renewed energy.

A footnote to the above. New gleaming modern architecture sprout all over the still-growing Shanghai. Towering Hong Kong style hotels are scattered about the city. Imposing commercial buildings depict capitalism in the massive new Shanghai but the romance of the Paris of China is still there to seek out.

Shanghai Architecture

The Treaty of Nanjing in 1842, following China's defeat in the Opium War forced the opening of 5 ports as foreign concessions. The trading invaders moved in along the waterfront and a foreign population eventually grew by 1930 to an estimated 30,000. The British and Americans eventually merged their territories into the International Settlement; the French kept to their own farther inland where the Jin Jiang Hotel is.

Inevitably evidence of this near 100-year spree of foreign influence appear in the varied architecture. You can take a stroll down tree-lined streets in a little corner in the French Quarter, northwest of the Jin Jiang Hotel, amid squat 2-storey houses with backyards and old estates with spacious gardens. The French Quarter centers around **Huaihai Lu** and the Jin Jiang Hotel. Stop off at a cafe and pick up a pastry at some of the excellent bakeries.

Step across **Yan'an Lu**, the unspoken dividing line between the French Quarter and the International Settlement, and you will be walking down a lane of townhouses, or you will be looking up at Victorian mansions through iron gates.

Along the **Bund** are the 1930s edifices of Chicago and New York comprising mainly commercial building, trading houses and banks. They are decorated uniquely with clock towers, marble and bronze-decorated entrances, wrought iron accouterments, carved guardian lions and leaded windows. The 7-storey Hongkong and Shanghai Bank building has an Ionic facade of polished marble and a magnificent dome. It is now occupied by the People's Municipal Government.

A 3-storey mansion at Guandong Road is now an electronic games entertainment center. The extraordinary stained glass windows, if you are fortunate to view them on a sunny day, stream light through European themes.

The Bund, the main promenade of Shanghai.

Vaulted ceilings are covered with glittering mosaics in Byzantine style, portraying Grecian women, cherubs and pillars. Red Chinese lanterns detract from the European villa ambience. It is said the building once belonged to a nefarious Shanghai character who had a harem of concubines, ensconced within for his personal use and service to business clientele.

Less imposing but very interesting buildings, gardens and former domiciles of the rich, line and pepper the parallel and intersecting streets to

Taking taiqi exercises in the Renmin Park.

Zongshan Dong Lu. It is a fascinating array of the early 20th century world, well worth a few hours walking tour.

The Neo-Gothic **St Ignatius Catholic Church** and **Bai Chongxi's Islamic residence** in **Xuhui** district are evidences of imported religion. An hour's drive out of Shanghai to **Sheshan Hill** is the imposing 1873 Catholic Church, "Our Lady of China." A famous pilgrimage takes place there every May if you are fortunate to be there at the time. History relates that the Chinese Catholic church became independent of Rome in 1957 but still does the liturgy in Latin.

Finally, the plethora of skyscrapers comprising hotels and commerical buildings adds the last touch to Shanghai's architectural landscape as they continue to rise among the historical buildings to make their statement in the modern city.

Shanghai Circuit

Walking **Zhongshan, Dong Lu (the Bund)**, which stretches along the river

Wuxing Teahouse in the 400-year-old Yuyuan with its zig-zagging bridges to disorientate the devils.

and was once the Wall Street of China in the Concession Days, is a favorite pastime.

Try the promenade early in the morning and join the *taijiquan* group or relax in the afternoon siesta period on a bench and if you nod a bit, no one will notice; others are doing the same. When having dinner out one night, have the taxi drop you off at the Bund (tell them Peace Hotel, it's easier).

In the evening the pier and harbour glitter by the lighted ships, and after dark, lovers appear holding hands. Ven-

For an introduction into the educational life in Shanghai, guided tours will usually include the **Children's Palace** and a typical commune. The Children's Palace offers extra-curricular courses in manual trades and the arts; classes are held in electronics, computers and crafts of all kinds, including drawing, sculpture, music, song and dance. You are often invited to visit the apartment of a typical commune resident. Though it is stilted and obviously pre-set with paid volunteers, the visit would be interesting.

The **Old Town**, **Yu Gardens (Yuyuan)** and **Wuxing Teahouse**, are together in the circular area bounded by Remin Zhonghua roads. If you are wandering without a guide, have the hotel concierge write out the places you are going to, in Mandarin. Most young people speak a little English and with the cue card, will be delighted to direct you from one area to another. The **Old Town** exudes an ambience of Shanghai as it was in the last century, that is, with bazaars, the red light district and luxury enjoyed by wealthy mandarins.

The delightful Yu Gardens were said to have been designed 400 years ago by a city official (they were rich in those days) for his father's old age. Stone dragons undulate over garden walls, zig-zag bridges discourage devils who can only walk a straight path. Goldfish ponds abound, and knolls to ponder life on are equipped with benches.

There are pavilions and tea houses in which you may discuss Confucian

dors set up stalls displaying Levi pants, sandals, tee shirts, food and whatever the clever free market entrepreneur can think of to make a buck on the side. Artists display their watercolors, pinned to clothes lines, for souvenir prices. The Bund is symbolic of the people of China, reflecting history and the struggle to emerge into the modern world.

Jade Buddha Temple is known for its two Buddha carvings of solid white jade.

thought with a friend or stranger, scattered throughout. It is amazing how many English-speaking school teachers aggressively approach foreign visitors for the sheer pleasure of exchanging knowledge and learning about the outer world, for the average citizen seldom gets the opportunity to travel.

Wuxing Tea House is nearby in the middle of a pond reached by a series of zig-zag bridges. Have tea and a sweet cake to finish the tour and summon a taxi to return from the past to the present.

Jade Buddha Temple, along Anyuan Lu, is famous for 2 Buddha carvings of solid blocks of white jade brought from Burma in 1882. The reclining figure is to celebrate departure from life into *nirvana* while the sitting figure depicts the peace of prayer.

Intrinsic in Shanghai is its more unique aspect as the intellectual and radical seat of China. **Lu Xun** (1881-1936), China's greatest contemporary literary figure and noted thinker is particularly remembered for ***The True Story of Ah Q***, the forerunner of what we call Murphy's Law. Everything that could happen to an individual fell on that poor soul Ah Q. **Lu Xun's Tomb** and a museum devoted to his life and works, housing a collection of manuscripts, books and articles of daily use, is found in **Hongkong Park**.

Number 7 Xiangshan Lu is the home of **Dr Sun Yat Sen** now converted into a museum. The leader of the 1911 revolution that overthrew the Qing Dynasty

Chinese Freshwater Pearls

Cultured, sea water pearls, the Mikimoto system of Japan, are achieved by implanting a round bead of pearl shell into the mollusk. Freshwater, lake or pond grown pearls are developed by implanting several pieces into the mantle (outer muscle) of the oyster. In each case the irritant is gently covered by secretions of *nacre* (tears of the oyster) over a period of time. Thus several pearls are produced in the freshwater process as against a single pearl in the cultured system.

The beauty of the odd shaped freshwater pearls is in the unique self-imposed forms and in their lustre, translucency and varied colors, the result of temperature changes in the water. The whole pearl is pure nacre, the flesh-irritant having disappeared.

Pearls derived from this system are harvested from 1 - 3 years after implantation. During the nuturing period the mollusks are constantly cleaned by lifting the cages containing them and scrubbing them to remove algae. Normally the hardy fellows can sustain 3 seeding and harvesting periods before reaching the ripe old age of 10 years and retirement to Mother-of-Pearl heaven.

The pearls are then sorted for shape, size and color. Elongated ovals are termed "rice-shaped", flat-round ones are "buttons" and usually cross-drilled through the flat side. Almost round are "baroque." Length of growth determine the size; turbulence of the waters affect the odd shapes that sometimes occur. The occasional very large one is sometimes hidden deep in the flesh of the mollusk and is only found when the growth period is over.

Shanghai Pearl Branch of the Arts and Crafts Import and Export Corporation purchases the harvest. The staff sort the huge piles of pearls on long tables in a swift hard-to-follow maneuver. Entirely feminine crews using a pair of tweezers and daylight filtered through dirty windows, sort the first batch into 3 piles by shape and a 4th pile for any other non-conformers. Each pile is then sorted out again into groups by their size. Individual rare color and unusual size pearls are put aside for special marketing treatment. They are sent to the Jewelry Manufacturing Branch to be set in rings, brooches and earrings.

Drilling is the next process. The ancient and presently-used way is to secure the pearl in a bamboo basket, shaped like a dumpling tray. The pearl is wedged into cross braces with another bamboo stick. A small bow is then applied, using a vertical pointed arrow embedded with corundum paste. Quick sure strokes are applied before the pearl is turned over to the other side. In seconds the drilled pearl joins the pile of finished material. Japanese drilling lathes are now introduced to do part of the drilling.

The final operation is to sort out by color and string the lovely matched pearls in 16" lengths, tied in tens into bundles of 10, thus each bundle being 100 strands. The bundles are graded according to quality and size, and then sold at auctions during the various trade fairs around the country. Finished strands and jewelry are offered for retail sale at the Friendship Stores.

has been keenly memorialized for having brought China out of her firmly entrenched non-progressive monarchical system and initiating her transformation into a republic. The museum displays the house as it was during Sun's lifetime and his library of 27,000 books.

Sun's wife herself, **Soong Qingling**, created quite a stir though she led a quiet life. Her communist sympathies brought enough discord during this turbulent period, in her relationship with her sister, who was married to the KMT Chiang Kaishek. Her garden-like house at 1843 Central Huaihuai Lu has been left just as it was during her lifetime.

Shanghai was also the site of the First National Congress of the Chinese

The Arts and Crafts Center, designed in European style architecture, exhibits and sells crafts from all over China.

Communist Party (CCP). The CCP was officially founded in the home of one of the founders at 76 Xingye Lu. The scene re-enacted for visitors sounds uncannily like the Last Supper : "12 stools surround the table which is set with tea bowls and ashtrays for Mao Zedong and his 11 comrades." The historic meeting was terminated by betrayal and flight. The episode ended on a happier note, however, as the meeting resumed on a pleasure boat in Zhejiang Province.

Finally, **Zhou Enlai**, one of the more favored Chinese Communist leaders

Scene from A Dream of the Red Mansions, a Chinese classic.

lived in 73 Sinan Lu. Initially this was the office of the CCP and it was here that Zhou met his wife when they were organising the communist underground movement. During the later part of his life Zhou stayed here during his frequent visits to Shanghai. The house is now open to the public.

For professional interest like medicine, Shanghai boasts 380 hospitals and training centers for divergent diseases including cancer. Archeologists and artists can take in the **Museum of Natural History** and the **Shanghai Museum of Art**. Merchants should visit the various trade offices along the Bund, purveying the production of pearl, gold, jade and precious stone jewelry, clothing and the myriad of arts and craft.

The Arts and Crafts Industry Factories are often suggested by your CITS guide. The one in Shanghai is one of the finest jade-carving factories in China supporting 150 of the world's best gemstone sculpture artists in the suburbs. Next door to it is a famous carpet factory rivaling Tianjin for honors.

The **Shanghai Arts and Crafts Export and Import Corporation** has under its auspices the freshwater pearl industry in Lake Dianshan and the Shanghai environs. The sorting and drilling of thousands of kilos of the lovely mollusks' output is fun to see.

There is a substantial diamond cutting industry, a branch of the same organization. Visits there are not common but can be arranged if you show personal interest. It is necessary for CITS to arrange an invitation and guide to take you there. Neither the pearl nor diamond factories have showrooms in which you can purchase the products. The portion kept for domestic use is sold through the Friendship Stores.

In 1956, the **Arts and Crafts Institute** along Fenyang Road was founded. It was set up to study the traditional arts and crafts throughout the country, such as woolen and silk embroidery, jade and ivory carving and paper-cutting. They also create prototypes for the small factories and workshops around China and provide technical advice for the specialist factories in Shanghai. Presently well-known artists and craftsmen gather here.

Shanghai Environs

On another day, buy a ticket for the daily cruise up the **Huangpu** to the **Changjiang Delta**. Board early so you can get a good deck chair on the shady rail-side if it is a hot day. Tea and refreshments are served while you watch the kaleidoscope of water traffic: rusty old freighters, bright new cruise ships, ferries and small boats scooting like water bugs, barges hoisting the Lego-like container boxes from the ships that cannot get to the pier. The shoreline is smoky with spewing factories and littered with hundreds of years' of dock debris.

Grand View Garden

Grand View Garden as described in ***A Dream of Red Mansions*** is located in the Changjiang Valley 65 km southwest of Shanghai in the watery valley of Lake Dianshan. The detailed replica of Daguanyuan (Grand View Garden), home of Jia Bayou and his fictional prosperous mandarin family of the 18th century, is a splendid insight into the lifestyle of that period.

Several buildings of the enclave are secreted behind a stone arch as well as a marble screen carved with characters from the famous novel. Once inside, the buildings are exposed in a southern style of black and white. There are gates, small bridges, moss covered rocks and ponds and paths around the various lodges and cottages depicting the story.

Furniture of the southern style is complete including parlor, bedroom and kitchen. Porcelain, cloisonne, cinnabar, wood and ivory furnishings are real antiques of the period. Scrolls, flower and plant pots and pickle jars for storing foods adorn the shelves and walls. The earthenware pot for preparing herbal medicines sits beside the bed of heroine Lin Daiyu. Her story is that of frail health and a deep love for her cousin Jia Baoyu, frustrated by the household staff and family.

The most important building in the garden is the **Grand View Pavilion** with a facade of white jade and a pond in front. The white marble archway is inscribed with the characters "House of Reunion". The lovely edifice was built in honor of the family's most famous member, Yuanchun, an imperial concubine. In the story, Yuanchun is to return home to celebrate the Lantern Festival.

The author Cao Xuegin describes the event thus: "It was wreathed with the perfumed smoke of incense, splendid with flowers, brilliant with countless lanterns, melodious with strains of soft music. Words fail to describe the scene of peaceful magnificence and noble refinement."

Each afternoon a local theatrical group re-enact the celebrated concubine's arrival which is greeted with song and dance by the family and friends. Guests stand at various places in the gardens, while the presentation takes place on the portico of the pavilion. The costumes, characteristic period music and lilting high-pitched voices of the actors are enchanting.

Restaurants and food stands provide snacks and if you have brought lunch, there are places to picnic in the area. While there, time permitting, ask your guide to take you to the pearl farms nearby.

Lake Dianshan

Lake Dianshan is the largest freshwater pearl producer in China. Ponds are scattered like rice fields with buoys supporting long lines of baskets immersed in the rich waters of the Changjiang Delta. A small museum gives an account of pearl farming to visitors.

Having Fun in the Big City

Start a typical day in Shanghai by going out into **Mao Ming**, the adjacent street, for *taijiquan* stretching exercises with the locals. Also stretch your legs by walking around the whole block (15 minutes) during which you could buy a fried twisted doughnut but pass up the rice gruel.

After breakfast take a stroll down **Nanjing Road** to the Huangpu River. It takes less than an hour at a brisk pace or 3 hours if you are going to dawdle in some 500 stores and boutiques on the way. The array of antique-curios, art supplies, hardware and the prevailing abundance of Chinese arts and crafts test a shopper's endurance. It would be wise to take your luggage trolley, in anticipation of the shopping that you cannot resist.

Shanghai teems with people.

Shopping

Number 1 Department Store at #830, corner of Xizang Road is reputed to be the largest in all of China, carrying a wide assortment of items. The daily traffic is often in excess of 100,000, not excessive if you consider Shanghai has upwards of 12 million residents.

Of special interest is the **Duo Yunxuan Art Store** at #422 Nanjing Road which deals in art supplies and on the second floor are small paintings, prints, cards and note papers. #345 is the famous **Xinhua** book store. The third floor has an English section with the prettiest children's books, cards and book marks you have ever seen. Another favorite if you are into inexpensive gifts is the agglomeration of colorful scenic posters and packages.

Shanghai Arts and Crafts Service Department Store is at #190. The third floor, reserved for foreigners, has antiques, semi-antiques and almost-antiques among some rare items. Except for buses there is no room on Nanjing Road for motorized vehicles during the day. Masses of people vie with the bicycles for space. It is easier to walk in the street than on the sidewalk. The massive circular overpass at Tibet and Nanjing Roads is for the thousands of people passing the intersection hourly. Entrance and exits are in the stores, at the corners.

About half-way down Nanjing Road, you can stop at the Park Hotel for tea and taxi service is available there if you are beat.

The landmark greenish blue roof of the Peace Hotel eventually comes into view as you approach the end of Nanjing Road at **Zhongshan Dong Lu**, otherwise known as the **Bund**. Get an early lunch at the hotel and sit at a window table on the 8th floor of the **Dragon and Phoenix Restaurant**. The view is the fascinating Huangpu River traffic, an endless array of bug-like small craft skittering from side to side. Tugs maneuver the larger craft into dock positions, many of which have to anchor in the middle of the river for lack of space and are unloaded by barges.

Anything you ever wanted in Shanghai cuisine is on the menu, printed in English and Mandarin, from noodle soup to steamed pomfret. Rice is steamed or stir fried in a dozen different ways. Noodle dishes take up a whole page; they are prepared in soups, fried with vegetables, meats or seafood. Sometimes, if in doubt, watch what is being brought to the next table and point to that delectable looking dish. The most difficult order to obtain is vegetables "steamed, no oil please." Chinese chefs have an abiding addiction to using the basic cooking oils for everything.

The **Peace Hotel** was once the Cathay House, considered on par with the Oriental in Bangkok, Raffles in Singapore and Peninsula in Hong Kong and as the "in" place for deluxe business residence on the Bund. Remnants of the former glory can be seen in the marble floors and the high chandelier ceilings. The tiny elevators are fearsome, especially when the luncheon crowd head for the 8th floor at noon. Overstuffed and worn out leather lounge chairs may still be there, scattered around the lobby for a 10-minute nap after lunch. The CITS desk for independent travelers is in the lobby if you need to make travel arrangements and a taxi desk has drivers at your disposal if you have had enough for the day.

Friendship Stores are China's gift to the foreign shopper. The 3-storey Shanghai model is 2 blocks from the Peace Hotel, complete with modern escalators and supermarket check-out counters. Because Shanghai is a distribution center for clothing, furniture and arts and crafts, the store has a grand selection of goods. Prices are about the same or slightly higher than Hong Kong as a general rule. Shipping facilities are available if you intend buying 2-meter tall cloisonne vases or large items.

The best antique-curio shops are: the Shanghai Antique and Curio Store, 194-226 Guandong Road; antiques and curios branch of Shanghai Friendship Store at 694 Nanjing Road; antique section of Shanghai Friendship Store, 33 Zongshan North at Suzhou Creek. Weixin Antique Store at Jinling Road East specializes in clocks and watches. The **flea markets** are at Kuaji Road, Zhongua Xin Road and Dongtai Antique Market. It is customary and not expensive to have the taxi wait for you or take you on a tour of the shops or open markets. Your guide and the taxi dispatchers know them by that name. See the Shopping section for suggestions on buying antiques.

On a lazy half-day, the **Shanghai Arts and Crafts Exhibition Center** is about a 20-minute walk from the Jin Jiang. It is a 3-unit, U-shaped, large Russian style enclave. Tour buses line up bumper to bumper but don't worry, the crowds dissipate in the cavernous buildings. The exhibitions of crafts from the various provinces are well worth inspection. The center sells everything from carpets to fine jewelry. They offer shipping services and take credit cards. Don't let them charge you the 4 per cent commission they have to pay the credit card companies. Scream foul or pay cash instead.

In an afternoon or evening, prowl **Huaihai Zhong Lu**, the next street from the Jin Jiang. Huaihai has always been the shopping area for the diplomats, housed in apartments and complexes down the avenue. It still boasts modern boutiques and department stores. There is an excellent store which sells tea on the corner of Mao Ming Lu and Huaihai next to the bakery.

The tea is displayed in bulk, weighed and packaged to suit the orders and are contained in pretty tea caddies. Hangzhou Dragon Well Tea is considered the best green tea; black teas can be bought by the numerical grading and Pu Erh is the fine red tea from Yunnan Province. Don't be surprised by the high prices on the better teas; you are paying the same price as the Shanghai elite.

Delightful Dining in Shanghai

Shanghai cuisine is described as one of China's most distinctive enjoyment of food. The districts make a difference: Hangzhou Carp in the West Lake area and the delta of the Chiangjiang (Yangtse) provides fresh shellfish. *Shaoxing* wine, the yellow nectar of rice served warm like Japanese sake is produced in nearby Zhejiang Province. Red cooking, the method of braising in soy, wine, sugar and beef or chicken stock is exported all over the world.

Irrigated by the delta waters, farms grow freshly available produce for the restaurants. Steamed freshwater crab (October through December), shrimp served over sizzling rice and eel in a heavy garlic sauce are favorites. Some say Beggar's Chicken originated here and that the vegetarian chefs compete with each other to disguise their concoctions to look like mock Beijing Duck.

Shanghai is credited with over 600 restaurants and a National Chefs School. The tourist is best served in the hotels because touring is tiring and the weary often want to eat and retire early. However adventure in eating is a spice of life and a few of the better known restaurants are listed in the Directory, like the Xinya Cantonese Restaurant at #719 Nanjing Dong Lu with private booths on the third floor. It is close enough to the Jin Jiang to stroll home after dinner. Unlike many other major cities in the world, there is no street danger after dark. In fact you will find many couples taking the night air, holding hands and greeting foreign strangers affably.

Culture and Entertainment

The list of things to do and places to visit in Shanghai goes on and on. Shanghai has no less than 6 internationally respected professional performing arts traveling groups among the dozens in operation. The list includes ballet, opera, symphonies, puppet troupes, acrobats and a circus. **Shanghai Acrobatic Theater** at #400 Nanjing Lu has shows 6 days a week. You can stop on your shopping trek and buy tickets for the performance that evening. A mite old-fashioned with china plates twirling and spinning from every arm and leg, teams of acrobats fling themselves around like rubber balls, but the acts vary and the evening is satisfying.

A movie theater on the Huaihai Lu corner next to the Jin Jiang Hotel may have an old Charlie Chaplin for nostalgia. The performance theater, the next corner in the opposite direction often has a stage performance. Writers are in the brave "chance it" mode now and you may witness a political parody. Try asking a friendly waiter or waitress in the hotel restaurant to meet you there. Government protocol makes them shy at social contacts but buying their ticket casually at the entrance breaks the ice and guarantees a translation.

VENETIAN TRIANGLE

Suzhou, Wuxi & Hangzhou

An hour and a half pleasant train ride from Shanghai is the 2500-year-old beautiful city of Suzhou, with its almost unique and picturesque Venice-like waterways, arched bridges and cobbled stone streets. They were impressive even to Marco Polo who described the city of "thousands of stone bridges, below which some would pass a galley". Known as the "Venice of the East" the city used to be crisscrossed with canals and is encircled by the historic Grand Canal and the city's outer moat.

Chinese gondolas in a Suzhou canal.

Some of the stone bridges and cobbled streets are original, with keystone wedges expertly placed for perfect arches and foundation. The explanation of Suzhou's longevity is evident when looking at a map. It is one of the keys to the Changjiang (Yangtse) Basin before it empties into the sea. In addition the **Grand Canal**, completed during the Sui Dynasty (589-618 AD) ensured Suzhou's location on the major trading route.

Suzhou's success also came from being a leading producer of silk.

Marco Polo observed "the inhabitants being occupied with stripping the cocoons of the fine threads and wearing garments of silk."

Sericulture, the growing of silkworms fed on mulberry trees is still its main industry; the sweatshops and paltry wages continue to exist. Visits can be made to the silk factory in CITS organized tours.

Machines now replace much of the hand work and computers dictate to the machines to enhance production. Industry has come to the area to produce electronics, machine building, ferro-concrete products for boat construction and chemical products. Fortunately they are relegated to the outskirts and do not marr the city's old-world ambience.

In the 16th century travelers reported that there were over a hundred gardens. Today, innumerable parks remain as vibrant with nature as with history. Hence, Suzhou's alternative fame as "the Garden City".

Suzhou Museum is near the Garden of the Humble Administrator, and exhibits a history of sericulture, many relics of past dynasties and an especially good collection of old maps. The **Garden of the Humble Administrator** is an example of the intricacies of Suzhou garden artistry, copied around the world. There is a water park consisting of streams, ponds and bridges.

Many of the private gardens still

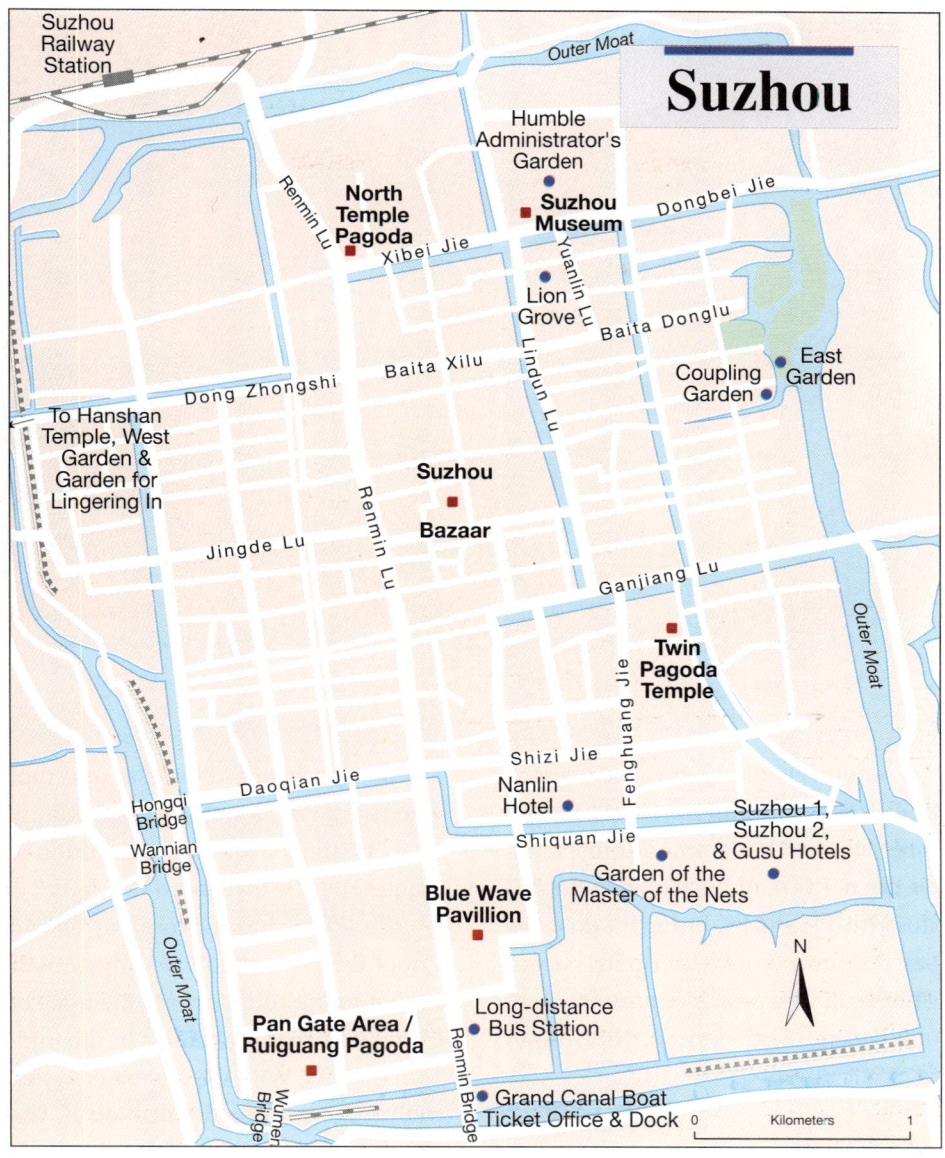

exist, created primarily with rockeries and ponds. Like the Japanese Zen gardens there are few flowers, the foliage consisting mostly of bonzai trees. Intricate secret niches for contemplation surprise you when you bend low to pass through an arch of lava rock. Add the **Blue Wave Pavilion**, **Garden of the Master of Nets** and the **Garden for Lingering** to your visiting list, even if you have to stay another day.

Finding your way among the maze of canals and bridges is an adventure outside the tourist trek. Little markets pop up and Suzhou's inhabitants busy themselves with their daily activities.

Known as "Venice of the East", Suzhou used to be a maze of canals.

Another walking spree includes the bazaar in **Guanqian Jie**. Shops, restaurants, silk merchants among others clutter the network of back alleys which is closed to all vehicles during the day. The best restaurants are found in the bazaar where eating is an adventure. Food not only depends on the season, it also comes in exotic dishes.

Wuxi - Jiangsu Province

Less than an hour's pleasant train ride from Suzhou is the town named for its lack of tin. The name came about when the local tin mine was exhausted during the Han Dynasty (206 BC - AD 220). Recorded history takes it back another 1,000 years before that. It is said that when the tin mining stopped, tranquility set in, giving the town the reputation of a quiet spot on the Grand Canal.

However, located on the Grand Canal **Wuxi** inevitably became a cloth harbor in the 16th century, then one of China's 4 rice trade centers in the mid-18th century. With the advent of industrialization and modernization in the late 19th century, the city began to be called "little Shanghai". It is now one of China's top 15 economic centers. Its oldest activity is the silk industry which dates back to ancient times when Wuxi was the prime producer of silkworms which fed on mulberry leaves.

Wuxi produced silk yarn for weaving 1500 years ago by tediously un-

A boy playing with his grandfather.

into the region's pride.

However, the town is now being promoted as a resort area offering a variety of activities like courses and programs to retain the visitor over a longer period of time. Like **Suzhou**, the city has its alluring features. The Grand Canal crosses Wuxi in a north-south direction and is the town's main thoroughfare with innumerable waterways deviating from it.

Wuxi's Environs

Just south of the city is **Lake Taihu**, China's third largest freshwater lake. The lake straddles Jiangsu and Zhejiang Provinces and is hence linked to Hangzhou's West Lake. Visiting both lakes is supposed to be good luck as they're said to represent the *"yin* and *yang"* of Taoist philosophy.

A number of mid-lake hills known as **72 peak**s gives Lake Taihu its unusual scenery. The lake also supports a fish farming industry which provides more than 30 varieties of fish. On its shores are rice paddies and tea plantations; mulberry and citrus trees abound. Hence the locality has been nicknamed "the country of rice and fish".

Nearby is **Meiyuan** (Plum Garden) where the famous Wuxi peaches are grown. Thousands of plum and peach trees blossom in the spring. Peaches are a historical symbol of good health. Porcelains of Lao Shouxing usually proffer a luscious dripping peach. A tradi-

winding the barely visible thread from vats of hot water. Today Wuxi's **Number 1 Silk Factory** boasts machinery systems that allow one person to monitor 60 filaments at one time. Machines then take over twisting them together into a weaving thickness. A visit to this factory can be arranged through CITS. In summer visits to farms rearing silkworms are also organized.

Another intrinsic trait of the region is its lifelike clay figurines. This special art of Wuxi has a history of over 400 years. Some traditional themes include "Lao Shouxing" (Old Man of Longevity) and the "Da A Fu", a plump little boy holding a fish or a peach indicating prosperity. A visit to the **Huishan Clay Workshop** will give you a good insight

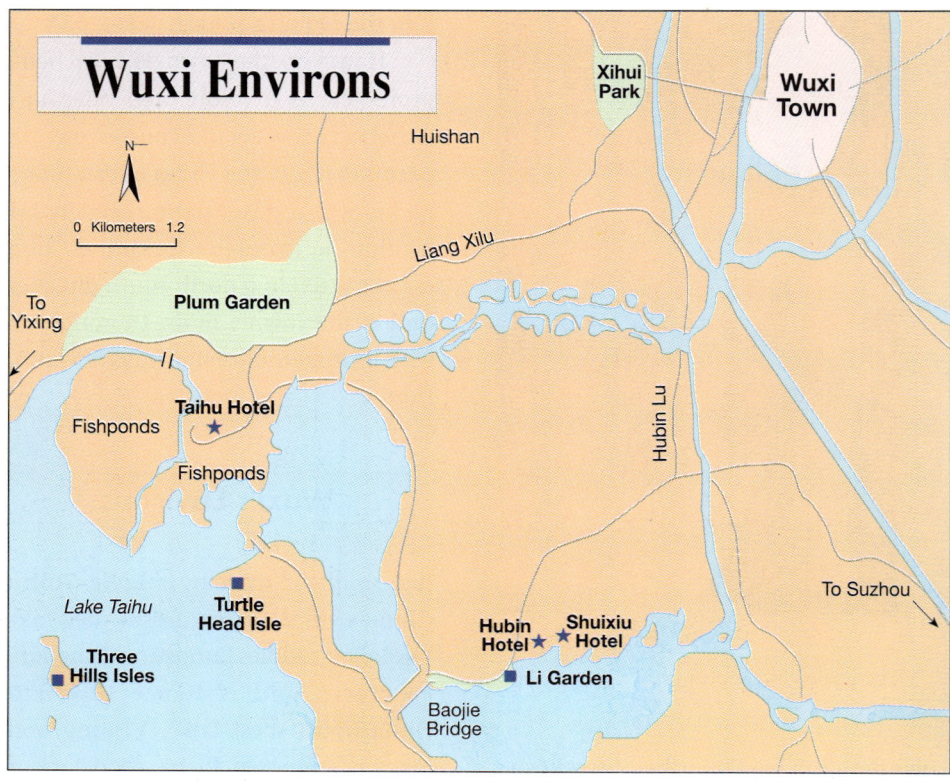

tional wedding gift you will see often in the shops is a large peach being supported by 3 young boys. A symbolic wedding gift, it wishes the couple good health and boy children.

A beautiful scenic spot which provides a good view of Lake Taihu is **Yuantouzhu** (Turtle Head Isle). The peninsula is so named because it resembles the head of a turtle. The area is "walkable": it has more than its fair share of hill-lake scenery and historical sites. For another view of Lake Taihu, you can take a ferry to the island **Sanshan** (Three Hills Isles), 3 km southwest of Yuantouzhu.

Lying west of Wuxi is **Xihui Park**, so named because it is caught between **Xishan** and **Huishan Hills**. Huishan Hill has a number of historical sites and abounds in natural springs. On the top of the hill you have a view of Lake Taihu and the city of Wuxi. On the eastern foothills is **Jichang Garden**, a Ming garden renowned for the ingenious incorporation of the landscape within its garden design.

Your guide will suggest an afternoon's boat trip around Lake Taihu, over 2,000 sq km containing 100 or more islands. Turtle Head Isle boasts a restaurant and viewing gallery on its peak.

Li Garden Island has a marvelous example of Suzhou garden design, complete with rockeries, twisting paths,

Numerous waterways cut into the Grand Canal, the main thoroughfare in Wuxi.

arched bridges, pavilions and a 5-storey pagoda. An interesting feature is a wooden covered gallery faced with 90 flower-shaped windows, each looking into a pretty garden.

The Taihu Hotel blends into the shore of Lake Taihu with older style commodious rooms overlooking the lake. Three other joint-venture modern hotels are listed in the Directory. Local eating specialties are spare ribs in bean sauce and crispy fried eel along with a variety of fish, crab and shrimp dishes.

Wuxi boasts a 2-storey shopping adventure, the **Dongfanghong** bazaar and a good department store. Like all small towns, check the local antique-curio shops, which often have items not seen in the heavily touristed cities.

Hangzhou – Zhejiang Province

Hangzhou, otherwise known as Paradise on Earth, was described by a Franciscan friar, Odoric, in the 14th century, as having "Twelve storey buildings…eleven thousand bridges …twelve gates, eight miles apart…etc." In 1127, Emperor Gaozong of the Song Dynasty was so impressed with its beauty that he moved his capital from Kaifeng to the shores of West Lake. Travelers today visit Hangzhou for its beauty and tranquility, one of the great pleasure stopovers of China.

Travelers today can take a comfortable 2-hour train ride from Shanghai to

Yangzhou - Jiangsu Province

An often missed travel treasure is the small town of **Yangzhou** at the junction of the Grand Canal and the Changjiang (Yangtse). Stops like this in a travel schedule is a break from people, temples and museums. A railroad stop less than 2 hours from Wuxi to Zhenjiang, then a ferry crossing the Changjiang is the easiest way to Yangzhou. CITS will arrange for a car to meet you at Zhenjiang.

Yangzhou's history dates back 2,400 years. The town was at its height during the Sui and the Tang Dynasties. During the Qing Dynasty, Yangzhou was a rather unusual artistic town. Story tellers would recite stories from the classics from platforms which were lined along the streets leading to town. Yangzhou was also known to have set the stage for a new art form in painting.

Today, the town is known for its arts and crafts although not readily evident in the street shops. Arrange a visit to the lacquerware factory which produces magnificent screens of lacquer, cinnabar and intricate designs of stone-carved pictorials. The papercutting of Yangzhou is world-famous, and created in story sets, applied to note cards, and the larger ones for framed pictures. The trick to framing papercuts is to use double-glass with no backing. The ensemble is then hung so as to allow light from the window to pass through. Papercutting is a delightful, inexpensive folkart recounting the stories and tales of ancient China and are often the work of women peasants. Colorful opera masks, playful lions and pandas are favorite themes among hundreds of others. A collection album of papercuts and book marks is a charming way to remember your visit to China.

Red Mansions Feast at Yangzhou

The classical novel, ***A Dream of Red Mansions***, is a 3-volume tale of mandarin life during the heyday of the Qing Dynasty. The Yangzhou Hotel's Red Mansion Dining Room is decorated with blackwood furniture, lacquer accessories and silver tableware. On certain holidays there is a special Red Mansions Feast prepared by the master chefs of Yangzhou who duplicate the names and components of the foods described

the metropolis. Joint-venture hotels abound, the preferred being the Shangri-la Hangzhou, a classic older hotel next to the **Yue Fei Temple** on the lake.

West Lake, surrounded by gardened hills dotted with pavilions and pagodas, is Hangzhou's main claim to fame in the tourist annals. It is favorably compared to Guilin and Suzhou as beauty spots of heavenly grace. Wuxi's Lake Taihu is often referred to as East Lake, the *yin* counterpart of the *yang* of West Lake.

The people of Hangzhou are as handsome as the area they come from. Women are fair-complexioned, they dress in the latest fashions and are lithe and graceful. Their tall escorts, as you see them hand-in-hand romantically walking the pathways of the lake, have impressively bold features.

The shops show modern style clothing for the ladies, and western suits for the men. You may have the good fortune to see a wedding couple at the hotel, the bride in a white-veiled gown, the groom in a dark suit, white shirt and red tie.

Mahjong is played in the back rooms, while beauty parlors give perms

in the novel.

Five parts of the feast are: "A Grand View of Three Dishes", "Cold Dishes of the Jia Family", "Dishes of the Ningquo andRungguo Mansions", "Refreshments of Happy Red Court and Famous Guangling Wine". There are more than 30 courses, whose names translate to poetic medleys: "Peacock spreading its Tail", "Butterfly and Flower", "a Landscape of Water and Mountain", "Duck Tongues and Webs Pickled in Wine", "Golden Pins and Silvery Ribbons", "Emerald Green Feathered Clothes" and "Crystal-like Stewed Pig Trotters.

Main courses feature "A Pearl in an Oyster Shell" made with mandarin fish balls and egg whites. "Linked Ducks Pickled in Rice Wine" consist of a domestic duck, a wild duck and pigeon stewed in rice wine the 3 heads placed decoratively on the serving platter as the centerpiece of the dinnner.

Waiters and waitreses dressed in Qing Dynasty costume and the music of the period completes the ambience. Be sure to inquire before going to Yangzhou if there will be a Dream of Red Mansions dinner available for dreamers of the good old Qing-a-ling days.

Cultural Hangzhou

Qing Dynasty (1634-1911) Emperor Qianlong is credited with the reconstruction of major buildings during his reign including the principal edifice, **Lingyin Temple** (Temple of Inspired Seclusion). Zhou Enlai is credited with saving the temple during the Cultural Revolution by a personal order countermanding the Red Guards' attempt to destroy it. A 9-meter tall figure of Maitreya sits in the Hall of the Four Heavenly Guardians flanked by protective dragons. The Great Hall behind displays a 25-meter tall statue of Sakyamuni carved from 24 exquisite pieces of gilded sandalwood.

and show the women how to apply modern cosmetics. Gold-plated jewelry is affordable and worn boldly by the women though pierced earrings are still a no no.

Each morning before 7, at the Wulin Gate, *taijiquan* seems to have metamorphosed into disco exercises for the young and old, a mark of how times have changed.

Selecting where to go during a short sojourn in Hangzhou is difficult, especially if you want to enjoy the romance as well as the history of "Paradise on Earth."

The Lake Taihu area just outside Wuxi is known as "the country of rice and fish".

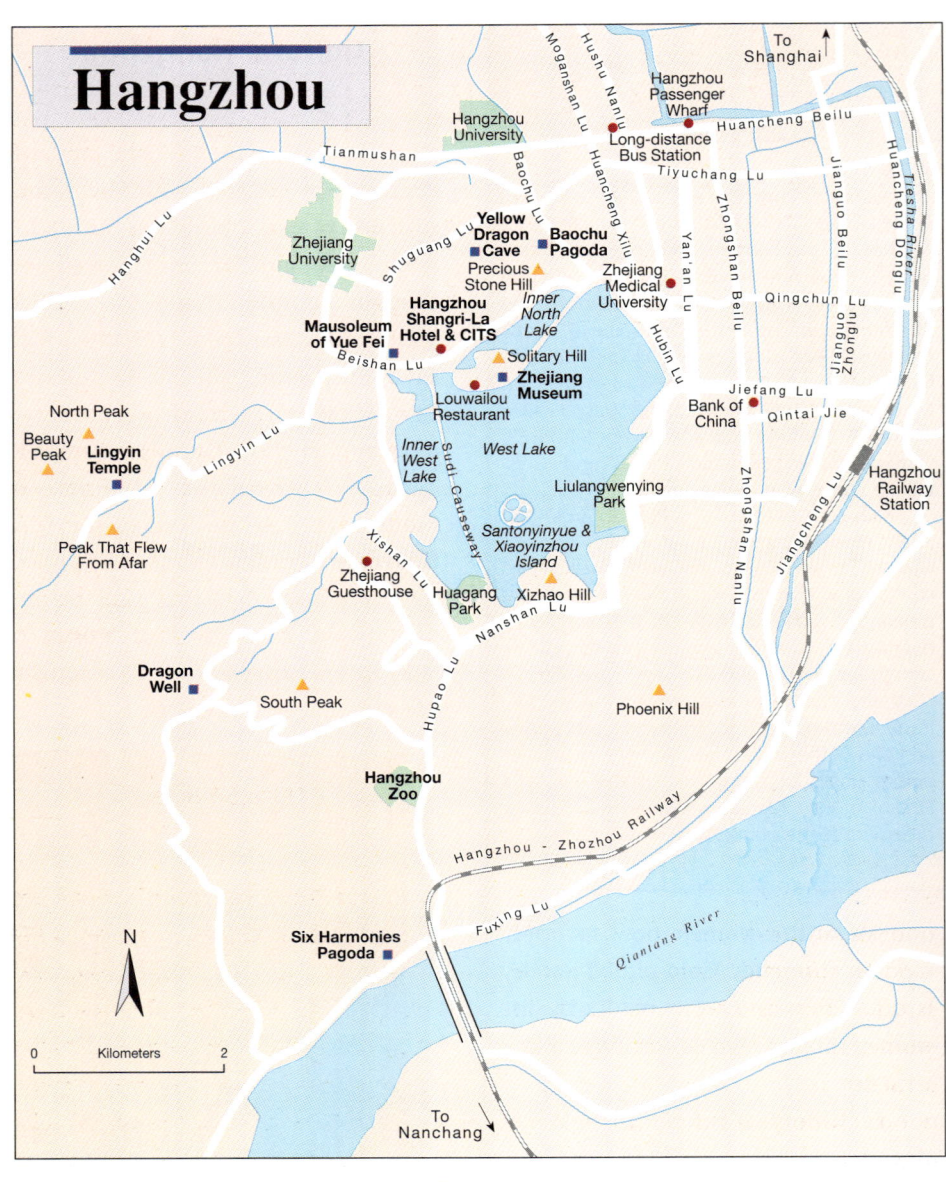

Feilai Peak (Peak that Flew from Afar) is a hill facing the temple, fabled as being a mountain from India, discovered by a traveling Indian monk in the 3rd century. About 400 statues have been found in the cliffside caves here and on the rockface outside dating between the 10th and the 14th centuries.

Visit **Yellow Dragon Cave**, where a well provides the clearest water for Dragon Well Tea. **Baochu Pagoda** (Protect Chu Tower) and the **Six Harmonies Pagoda** make an interesting tour. Because there is so much to see in these

Maitreya, the laughing Buddha, ensconced in Feilai Park.

exhibits, the various pagodas and pavilions on the **Six Hills**, it is best to hire a CITS guide and car for a minimum 3-day tour of exploration.

Not far from the Shangri-La Hotel is the **Zhenjiang Provincial Museum**, part of Emperor Qianlong's residence during his reign. It differs from the usual museum because it features relics of natural history such as a whale and a dinosaur.

Fine gourmet restaurants are available outside the hotel. Do try an opera if there is one available during your stay and the local movie house often has a classic Shaolin martial arts film. Don't worry about understanding the Mandarin dialogue, the action tells the story adequately.

West Lake

At the **Bai Causeway**, colorful boats are available for charter. They resemble dragons or phoenixes, richly decorated replicas of Song Dynasty pleasure craft. Many have a voluble English-speaking gondolier, who delights in regaling you with the fairy tales of the picturesque points. Be sure to bring the local map of the lake to mark down the various buildings seen from the boat, as there are over 50 scenic spots, each with an enticing name and scene, "Listening to Orioles Singing in the Waving Willows", "Last Snow on the Broken Bridge", "Autumn Moon over the Calm Lake", "Three Pools Mirroring the Moon", "Watching

West Lake is Hangzhou's pride and principal attraction.

Goldfish at Flower Harbour" and "Lotus Flowers Swaying in Quyuan Garden" to name a few.

From the middle of the lake you can see the islets close by, their pavilions and pagodas and the shore. The light green mountains provide a background as beautiful as the artists have depicted in traditional paintings for a thousand or more years. It is a romantic ambience that imbues you with a relaxed feeling of being in another world.

Autumn Moon over the Calm Lake is the islet called **Solitary Hill** in the

lived in the State of Qi of the Southern and Northern Dynasties (479-502), is remembered.

Poor Su, a ravishing 16-year old beauty, raised in a prominent brothel of the time, had a great love affair with Yuan Yu, son of the Prime Minister. He departed and Su, spurned, spent her life yearning for her lost lover, eventually succumbing to a broken heart. Her tomb can be seen near **Xiling Bridge** properly inscribed with the sad tale.

Su Causeway, is actually a 3-km paved road built parallel to the lake. Su Dongpo, no direct relation to the spurned beauty Su Xiaoxiao, built the road during a prefectural governor's reign. The particular features are the several arched bridges breaking the long straight road. Stone benches are scattered among flower beds where dreamers can rest and contemplate the tranquil lake and their lives.

Three Pools Mirroring the Moon is reached by boat from the islet called Little Yangzhou. Three stone pagodas built by Su Dongpo have 5 round holes in which lights are placed during each full moon. The reflecting light complements the moon's reflection on the water, a sight that lovers traditionally come especially to see.

Broken Bridge offers another classic tale. The saga is called "Romance of the White Snake". Known to all, it is often performed in opera as a tragic love story of a young scholar, Xu Xian and his sweetheart, White Snake, a beautiful woman.

middle of the lake. The best of Chinese architecture is seen here in the classic pavilions, towers and terraces decorated in bright red with contrasting orange and yellow.

Black and white are used effectively on the tiles and eaves of some buildings. It is on this island that the sad tale of a famous courtesan, Su Xiaoxiao, who

Hangzhou After Hours

After dark West Lake has a different personality. **Ruandu Huanbi**, an evening performance, is open to the public from April to October recreating the style of yesteryear. Sedan chairs meet the visitor at the boat dock where red lanterns reflect waving banners. Attendants beat drums as if for an imperial parade. Tea is served in the village while classical dancers perform traditional routines.

The night garden at **Listening to Orioles Singing in the Waving Willows** has Shaoxing Opera, stand up comedy and a magnificent view of the lake. Lights reflecting on the waters are spectacular. Performances are presented during the summer on a special show boat.

For the nightclub set, the Yikoule Restaurant on the ground floor of the Hangzhou Hotel and the Jingu (Mirror Lake) Hall at the east entrance of **Xiling Bridge** have romantic candlelit tables, tea and cakes with soft music enhancing the ambience. The big hotels, Hangzhou Shangri-La, Huanglong and others generally have dance floors in the lobby or ballrooms open to the guests. Tea and coffee shops throughout the main business sections are alive and busy during the evening. In Hangzhou you need not retire early.

The Arts and Crafts

Hangzhou, Jiaxing and Huzhou were known for the manufacture of silk woven fabrics 4,000 years ago, a reputation that expanded during the Tang Dynasty (618-907). Hangzhou was a source of silk, satin and brocade when the emperor demanded tribute of silk. Then, as today, reputation gave prominence. The reputation continued as "The best under heaven" during the Ming (1368-1644) and Qing (1644-1911) Dynasties. Over 30 different kinds of silk are woven here. Ask for a tour of the **Hangzhou United Silk Printing and Dyeing Factory**.

The **China Silk Museum** was recently opened in the scenic area south of West Lake. Displays of the products date from the Jin (265-42 BC) and the Tang (618-907) Dynasties. The process of sericulture is fully explained and displayed from the growth of the silkworm to the spinning, weaving and dyeing of silk.

The **China Tea Museum**, glorifying another of Hangzhou's finest products displays the various teas and the history of tea service. The **Southern Song Guan Kiln Museum** traces the history of porcelain during the Song dynasty (1127-1279). The **Traditional Chinese Medicine Museum** the only one in China, displays the Chinese pharmaceutical business called the *Huqingyutang*. It is small but the scope is large and includes the display of herbs, minerals and animal parts used in Chinese medicine.

Environs of Hangzhou

At **Yellow Dragon Cave**, visitors are greeted by sedan chair carriers in traditional dress who solicit fares in the swaying ancient human taxis from the bus stop to the gate. Large bamboos and ancient trees decorate the hillside and a small lake. A pavilion provides costumed singers, dancers and music played on ancestral instruments. A wineshop and a tea house are pleasant to stop at for a brief snack and rest. You must have a cup of the famous Longjing (Dragon Well) tea. In another pavilion an orchestra plays and acrobats perform. The sport of archery is demonstrated and a local opera group perform "The Lion Playing with a Silk Ball."

Lingyin Temple (Temple of Soul's Retreat) is in a small forest near the shores of West Lake. The temple was constructed in 326 AD engineered by an Indian monk who appreciated the beauty of the unusual mountains. A 24-meter tall statue of Sakyamuni dominates the main building. At **Felai Peak**, the Peak that Flew from Afar, the gross belly on Maitreya, the laughing Buddha, bulges in stone among other statues from the Song Dynasty (960-1279).

During the Tang Dynasty (618-907) **Fuxing** (Star God of Happiness) **Taoist Temple** was built on **Jade Emperor Hill**, which overlooks the lake. A nearby pavilion provides a picturesque view of West Lake. The surrounding area below the hill is divided into 8 parts depicting the Eight Trigrams of the Taoist belief. It is a favorite prayer spot for people of the surrounding villages, who are different from the urban Hangzhou population.

Liuha (Six Harmonies) **Pagoda** is on **Yuelin Hill** and appears to have 13-storeys although in reality there are only 7 floors; the pagoda exterior is built with 2 tiers on each floor. Various sculptures of Buddha, flowers, human figures, fish and other animals are portrayed around the interior circular stairway.

Dragon Well is between **Nine Creeks** and **Eighteen Gullies**, a beautiful park area suitable for an afternoon's stroll. This area has soil and weather conditions suitable for growing the famous Longjing Dragon Well Tea. **Tiger Spring** is the destination along a flagstone path, which took its name from a fable: a monk dreamt that 2 tigers would provide water in the drought stricken area. It is said that the next morning 2 tigers were seen digging the ground which produced the necessary water, thus the name. Mineral spring water is

Palace of the Prince of Shi Jinhua, Zhejiang Province

The charismatic Prince of Shi of the Taiping Heavenly Kingdom (1851-64) lived in the Heavenly Palace in Jinhua, then the capital of the Taipings.

The Taiping Rebellion, at the height of their conquest of Zhejiang and most of the southern provinces consisted of peasants and artisans disgruntled with the Qing emperors. Li Shixian, the leading general of the rebellion, made Jinhua the capital and took over the Qing Court buildings.

The palace has survived for more than a century and is one of the best examples of imperial residences built of wood and highly decorated during the Qing period. Especially interesting is the collection of artifacts and memorabilia of the period which survived even the Cultural Revolution.

A drum tower and archway precede the customary Dragon Wall Screen that protects the complex from devils not able to negotiate the turns. The Gate of Protocol guards the main hall where much of the planning of the Taiping Revolution was said to be evolved. That planning came close to toppling the Qing Dynasty until the rebellion was quelled in 1865. Halls pass into wings and wings into rooms, where the artifacts are displayed.

A lifelike model of the young general and prince stands behind a desk in the central hall of the west wing. Behind him is a ceiling high impressive mural of a dragon. Even more impressive are the huge murals on the east and west walls. The east wall mural is of a battle scene with the Taiping Army assaulting a city. The opposite wall is a complete picture of the palace itself. Every large wall in the palace is decorated with an extensive mural, favored by the Taipings. After capturing Nanjing, they elected to move the capital there and continued to decorate the government buildings with murals awarded to a central artisans administration. They used flowers, trees, animals and birds to render folk tales into picture stories and historic events.

The Prince of Shi died at the age of 31, at the hands of his own courtiers at the defeat of the Taiping's Army.

---

sold as a health drink and is the finest water to make Dragon Well Tea with.

An unusual but very interesting side trip is to the **Hu Qingyu Tang Pharmacy**, which has a 700-year history of dispensing medicines. The traditional arched entrance gives an impression of a temple guarded by gargoyles and dragons with hanging large lanterns. The dispensing area is filled with drawer cabinets called "Hundred Eye", shelves of bottles and show cases containing modern packaged medicines. A sign in the background advertises imports of rhinoceros horn, bezoar (stomach concretion used as on antidote for poisons), round cardamon (herb of ginger family) and pitchuck (unknown to Western world). Hu Xueyan, remodeled the pharmacy in 1874 with the assistance of doctors and medical experts. They concocted 400 known recipes of the time and manufactured medicines, most of which are still in use today.

Farther afield is **Qiandao** (Thousand Island) **Lake**, infinitely larger than West Lake, containing over a thousand islets of various sizes. It is a man-made lake resulting from the massive Xinanjiang Hydroelectric Power Station. The water is clear, reported to be 33 m deep in the central islet free area.

Day trips can be arranged for visits to the most important islets. It would be

The 24-meter Sakyamuni resides in Lingyin Temple located in a forest near West Lake.

more fun to allocate 3 days, venturing out each day in a different direction from the town of **Pailing**. Villages populate the larger islands, otherwise on most of the islands on the whole, you will find historic pavilions, caves, a stone forest and natural formations generating a thousand tales of the thousand islands.

The deep clear waters generate large fish, caught and served the same day in the Fish Flavour Restaurant. Delicious local fresh fruit such as plums pears, oranges and others with unfamiliar

Hangzhou Dragon Well Tea

The **Book of Tea** (Lu Yu 738-804) lauded tea cultivation in 2 Hangzhou temples, the Tianzhu and Lingyin. Longjing (Dragon Well) is the name of a spring, a temple and a village. Fine spring water was discovered nearby in the Song Dynasty (238-250). The farming area is on hills rolling under southerly winds giving it the constant moisture needed for the tender tea plants and mulberry trees used in sericulture.

The written record of daily tea drinking in China is 4,000 years old, verified by the discovery of brewing and drinking paraphernalia recovered from tombs. Dragon Well's fame and fortune grew through the efforts of Bian Cai, a Song Dynasty monk and Su Dongpo a writer of the 11th century. Qianlong (1736-95), the great builder of the Qing Dynasty, favored Hangzhou and described the special tea, "Though the tea seems tasteless, it imparts a comfortable feeling that lingers in the mouth believing that tastelessness was the best taste of all." He designated 18 tea plants in the garden as imperial tea plants, the yield sent to the palace as tribute. Decrees such as these so enhanced the reputation, that Dragon Well became the supreme tea of China.

A 5-kilometer area in the Lion Peak Hills, Dragon Well Village is the epicenter of the noblest of all teas. The leaves are picked in early April called the Qingming Festival, within 2 or 3 days of the new spring sprouting. The tender leaves are picked by hand requiring 10 tea-leaf pickers to produce a half-kilogram of yield in 1 day's toil.

The processing is labor intensive : the tea leaves are dried on long tables for several hours and they are turned and agitated constantly. Then 200 g at a time are baked in a pot, also rotated and shaken to give equal heat access to each leaf. One kilogram of special Dragon Well tea consists of 60,000 to 70,000 leaves. The final appearance of each leaf is likened to the sparrow's tongue pressed between the leaves of a book.

Pou Yul tcha tea culture in the old days.

Hangzhou locals brew their tea in a more mundane manner than normal tea making. They use a glass instead of the traditional pots, water poured only half-full over the leaves allowing them to expand, uncovered. After a few minutes they fill the glass diluting the brew, continuing to add boiled water as they drink several glasses from the same leaves. The more serious drinkers also get their water only from Tiger Springs in the Dinghui Buddhist Temple on Daci Hill.

The **Chinese Tea Museum** in Twin Peaks Village comprises several buildings. Building One houses the halls of history, production, tea customs and samples of outstanding teas with a tea ceremony coming last.

names are a treat. As visitors are rare, the local villagers often invite them home and offer them food and hospital-

ity. With good fortune you will see a team of fishermen in their black raincoats and white hats completing an

Hangzhou Cuisine

The Cordon Bleu of China is reported to be Hangzhou. International chefs come here to learn, gourmets to feast on the Zhejiang cuisine. There are 2 categories: one for the refined taste and the other for popular eating.

Southern Song imperial dishes (try the Bagualou Restaurant which has a lovely classic ambience) are in the refined class. A dinner might start with steamed softshell turtle soup with mutton, which is a thick broth, the meat falling-off-the-bone tender, strong tastes and aromas disappearing in the meld. Mince with asparagus and fish shreds prepared in 2 ways could follow. Bean curd and crab meat are served in a porcelain replica of a crab. The more popular dishes are West Lake Water Shield Soup said to be good for health and a cancer preventive. Dongpo braised pork is served in a pot and Aunt Song's fish potage (Hangzhou Restaurant overlooking the Su Causeway) is an imperial dish brought from Kaifeng. The potage consists of West Lake carp cooked with ham, bamboo shoots and mushrooms in a chicken broth.

Shaoxing wines are served with the meals and a special treat is Beggar's Chicken, if you find it on the menu, its anecdotal link lying in the tale of a young beggar who found a chicken and lacking cooking utensils, wrapped it with clay abandoned by a wine shop. Cooked in the embers of the fire, he then broke open the baked clay covering to find the meat so tender, it fell off the bones. The aroma attracted neighbors who copied the recipe in their homes thence in grand restaurants which add spices and herbs to enhance the flavor further.

Beggar's Chicken is served in the covering, sometimes a baked bread, ceremoniously broken apart and eaten family style. The tender morsels are easily handled with chopsticks and loud bone sucking noises. Try the Louwailou Restaurant, a 140-year-old pleasure boat at the foot of Solitary Hill. The boat sails on the lake while you are having dinner a pleasant and romantic evening for honeymooners.

involved netting process. The large fish reminds you of sea-going trawlers fishing the huge tuna, flipped overhead from a side boat onto the mother craft.

Further adventure involves taking a boat trip on the **Xinanjiang River** in Anhui Province, part of the complex of **Qiandao Lake**, and staying at the Floating Hotel. The river trip is an eating paradise with a continual supply of fresh mussels, fried clams and fresh fish served steamed, Mandarin style.

Hangzhou is also the expedition take off point for **Huangshan** (Yellow Mountain) and **Moganshan**. Spend an extra couple of days in Hangzhou when you take on these expeditions.

An interesting way to see more of Zhejiang Province is to hire a car and driver from CITS and venture south to **Shaoxing** and Jinhua and thence to Wenzhou.

Shaoxing - Zhejiang Province

Shaoxing is a delightful small town, with tree-lined streets, few mechanical vehicles and a Mandarin country inn that is very unusual in developing China. The one and only accommodation for foreign tourists is a dormitory-like building with adequate, small comfortable rooms. In the compound is an old mandarin's home, built around a courtyard

Huangshan - Anhui Province

Huangshan (Yellow Mountain) is the name of a range of mountains in the south of the province, one of the 5 famed mountains. It is an interesting side trip for class B-trekkers and stair climbing mountaineers. Huangshan is now accessible by air : you may take the flight from Shanghai to Tunxi (an hour and a half from the mountain), then the train to Hangzhou or a private car (5 hour trip) or bus from either.

The area is now open to foreign tourists and there are hotels at the base of the mountain. For the quick-tripper or those unable to hike, a cable car has been newly installed to take you to the top. There are adequate facilities to stay for a night or 2, to take in the magnificent sunset and sunrise vistas. For those who are more adventurous and who desire to join the hundreds of climbers, it is a hefty 8-kilometer steep hike up and another solid 11 km down the other side.

Tourist mountain climbing in China is the sport of ascending thousands of stone steps, hour after hour around switch-backs, hairpin curves and sometimes fearsome bridges with frequent rest stops in between. You will be shamed by the old hikers who pass you, hardly puffing or sweating. Stare at the bulging leg and thigh muscles of young men and women porters carrying 50 kg backpacks of food and supplies for the hotels at the top. Snicker at the occasional sedan chair carried by a pair of stalwarts for those poor souls not in as good condition as yourself. Your guide will relate many stories about the royal entourages ascending these same steps a thousand years ago carried in similar sedan chairs.

The view points have names but it is more fun to apply your own for your own identification. The stone formations have tales of love and sorrow and you can invent your own when stopping for a breather. When the body gradually acclimatizes to the exertion and the altitude, the surrounding views come into focus.

It is a fairy tale world, the scenic wonders obliterating the physical woes. Suddenly you turn another corner for a panorama of incomparable views. Clumps of clouds appear to float on peaks of mountains. Trails of stone steps curve endlessly ahead and behind, covered with the ant-like hordes of fellow climbers. The trail above and below, enhance the satisfaction of accomplishment.

Eventually you top out to the aerie-like fairyland with a pleasant guesthouse, claiming to give you the same small suite Deng Xiaoping stayed in on his last visit. The attendants supply quilted jackets and feather bedcovers for use while there. Temperatures drop to near zero as the sun sets in a view that even a camera can't capture in the same way as the mind.

In the dining hall, mentally thank the muscular porters who hauled up the vegetables, fish with a few rooms still fitted in Qing Dynasty furniture. Heavy mahogany-like blackwood beds, armoires, tables, chairs and decorative art ware, take you back into the 17th and 18th century lifestyle of the upper-class. The dining room is at the base of the classic "U" shaped patio, the wings converted into rooms for the visitors. An adjacent, more modern hotel accommodates those visitors wishing more amenities.

The fun of finding a small village like Shaoxing is a change from visiting temples and museums. Walking in the afternoon or evening is a pleasure. The railway station is the center of town. Local people are delighted to see foreign visitors and greet you with pleasant smiles.

The CITS office in the hotel compound has a total personnel of 2, elated to have a client to break the monotony. The room has a bottle of Laoshan water and a good sized sample of the famous

and other food stuffs. Noodle soup and steamed rice taste like nectar of the gods to the starved body strained beyond its logical endurance by the climb. Rubberized leg muscles begin to contract and stiffen in the cool night air. As you begin to relax, realization suddenly sets in that there will be another part to the story, the 11 km walk down the other side of Huangshan. Experienced trekkers are aware of the fallacy that going down is easier than climbing.

Two days at the top for partial recovery of muscle control and then the trip down will be a good idea. The Jade Screen Tower Hotel (minimum service) half way down can accommodate an overnight stay if you wish to break the journey. It is true that the longer downside trail is more beautiful and adventurous, with hazardous tunnels to inch through, rail guards protecting you from cliff hanging trails and the ever present hordes of travelers laughing and joking their way down.

Knowing the nature of foreign hikers' weakness, the ancient designers provided stone benches at view points. Enterprising vendors have somehow hauled watermelons and orange crush to the various sites. Don't worry, you'll make it. Your legs will eventually resolidify, toe nails may blacken and drop off later. Back pains will disappear after a month or two. The memory of Huangshan, Yellow Mountain, will forever remain.

yellow wine. A tour of the factory is appreciated by the manager and his staff, welcoming a chance to describe their wares and the history.

Shaoxing's Pride

Zhao Shuren, pen name **Lu Xun** (1881-1936) is China's most celebrated and prolific 20th century author. His father was an impoverished scholar, who died early in his life. His aggressive mother, Mother Lu, from whom he took his pen name, taught herself and her son to read and write. Lu Xun wrote during the turmoil of the fading Qing Dynasty, the new Republic, the repulsive warlords and the rising communist threat to independent thought. The challenges are reflected in his works which survive today as major insights into the turbulent years of China's traumatic birth into the modern world.

The short stories tell of the hardships of daily life endured by the author, friends and family in the small town of Shaoxing where he spent the first 18 years of his life. His austere birthplace and home is memorialized and the **Lu Xun Museum** gives an insight into existence, particularly the social and emotional turmoil, at the turn of the century.

A short distance out of town is **Dong Hu Lake** where a pleasant relaxing day is spent cruising through the grottoes, surrounded by limestone mountains and lush greenery. The artificial lake is exceptional because of the deep clear and very cold underground lakes inside the caves.

Shaoxing wine is another claim to fame for the town which has been producing the yellow nectar for 2,300 years and winning international awards. There are 6 varieties of the wine produced from glutinous rice and wheat leaven, and served warm as the Japanese sake. With an alcoholic content varying from 15 to 20 per cent, *Shaoxing*

Moganshan - Zhejiang Province

For a lighter trip, try **Moganshan Mountain Resort** about 60 km north of Hangzhou by car to the villa door. You can do your climbing after arrival. There is a relatively modern hotel but the older villas are far more interesting. Ask for the one where Madam Chiang Kaishek stayed. With good fortune you might get the very room the famous Dragon Lady had for several weeks during the grueling period of the Nationalist retreat. The ancient clawed, rust-stained bath tub could easily have bathed the famous body, all according to local lore.

The bamboo and fir forest is paved with pleasant walks, mild climbs, overhanging-gorge bridges and an adequate restaurant in the hotel. Local specialty is frog legs. The chicken-like tender bones are a delicacy not to be passed up. They grow a fine **Cloud Tea** in the area, sold in bulk at a very modest price, well worth taking a few hundred grams back with you.

Moganshan resort is known for waking its guests minutes before sunrise to view a rare panorama rising through the clouds and miles of vista. Imperial and rich mandarins came here centuries ago to escape the summer heat, as rock wall graffiti attest. Poems were etched and painted to memorialize the visitors. Waterfalls, bridges and distant vistas attract artists and student artists to replicate the scenes.

A morning walk to the **Sword Pool Waterfall**, when bamboo is in full expression of myriad shades of green is a delight. This strange plant is suitable for building light scaffolding, walls of homes, tubes of food and water, and a hundred or more other uses. Delicious bamboo shoots, are often used in cooking. The forest is lush, springs of clear pure water trickle and spout, birds are as plentiful as the artists trying to capture their beauty.

Moganshan is an off-the-beaten-track treasure, seldom touted by the travel industry. Sneak it in on the itinerary.

wines are known as an excellent aperitif. Likewise the medicinal qualities are said to aid digestion and relieve fatigue.

The most interesting part of the factory is the production of fancy porcelain containers for the wine. Decorated with hand-painted scenes from history, sizes to contain from 1 - 25 liters, straw-stuffed wooden shipping cartons, the art-decorated bottles are shipped all over the world.

Access to Shaoxing is by train or car from Ningbo or Hangzhou. An interesting on-going trip is to hire a CITS automobile for a long day's drive to Wenzhou on the coast. The scenic countryside, small out of the way villages and roadside picnicking are memorable asides in China traveling.

Children standing in front of Kai Yuan Monastery.

Jolly lady selling Dragon Well Tea.

SOUTHEASTERN COAST

Zhejiang & Fujian

The southeastern coast of China, which encompasses the Zhejiang and Fujian Provinces, is a treasure trove. It is modern enough to be reached in several ways: coastal steamers, train service, airlines and best of all, by hired car. (No, you can't drive-it-yourself yet in suburban China and maybe you don't want to either.) Road signs, when they have them, are in Chinese. Detours by ferry across rivers are routine and the little-old-lady road builders still break rock to lay many of them. CITS can be persuaded to provide a car, driver and guide if you wish.

The highlight of the trip is the rural countryside where one may empathize with the women stooping over to plant rice seedlings, strain with the men following a big, gray, horned ox through knee-deep mud, steering a wooden plow. It is a common sight in 'rice country' to watch rice and wheat pounded on the pavement to break the grain, or the more modern application of hand-turning a metal barrel in the field. Massive stacks of straw can be sighted rolling down the road burying whatever transportation is steering it underneath.

The remarkable lotus has a history of religious symbolism.

Southeastern Coast

Shanghai simply because taking a slow boat in China is more fun and less expensive than any other mode of travel even though the Chinese tourist moguls and travel agents do not promote this method of travel.

Get a car for a long and interesting day's drive to Wenzhou (8 to 10 hours from Shaoxing), the Hong Kong of the coast, which faces Taiwan across the straits. Then another auto-cruise (8 to 10 hours) south to the ancient province of Fujian (Fukien to the thousands of emigrants who left these shores to settle around the world). Fuzhou, Xiamen and the Wu Yi Mountain will leave you with a yen to go back and explore the nooks you didn't have time to see on this trip.

The deep south, Guangdong Province, Canton, Shenzhen and Hainan Island are a separate world tied tightly in commerce to Hong Kong and Macao.

It is friendly in the small villages and one can have a cup of tea with the locals and engage in small talk with the aid of a conversational handbook, finger pointing with a ray of smiles. Picnics can be had by a wooded stream or a scenic point overlooking a mountain vista. Work is often done to the sweet voice of Chinese singer Zhu Xiaomein lilting traditional and pop songs on tape.

Marco Polo traveled and wrote extensively about this area. Hangzhou, the capital of Zhejiang, forms a separate section. Use either Shanghai or Hangzhou as a starting point for the southeastern coast. We suggest an overnight coastal steamer to Ningbo from

Ningbo - Zhejiang Province

The coastal steamer leaves Shanghai on the Huangpu Jiang at dusk with that splendiferous feeling of being on an ancient trade ship pulling out to the beckoning seas beyond. It is dank and dark by the time the ship tosses into the East China Sea (Dong Hai) and you settle in a spacious cabin on the foredeck or in the lounge depending on the ship's accommodations. The best dish to order from the galley is noodle soup with 3 treasures. You may not recognize

A sailing junk in Xiamen, an island just off the coast of Fujian Province.

the treasures but the soup will be piping-hot and the noodles filling. That and your swagbag will help you plod through the night. If the moon is up, saunter around the deck before turning in. The gentle roll of the ship will lull you to sleep.

At dawn the ship sails into Ningbo harbor where the **Yongjiang**, **Yuyao** and **Fenghua Rivers** converge to empty into the sea. Neolithic artifacts date Ningbo back to the 5th and 4th millennia BC. The remains of decorated pottery, wood buildings, remnants of rice paddies hint at an advanced age of urban life 5,000 or 6,000 years ago.

The Yongjiang River divides the old and new city and its banks are busy naval and commercial port sites because of the ease of loading and close access to the sea. Records of the Song Dynasty (960-1279) and the Tang Dynasty (618-907) reveal that the chief exports were the products of silk, pottery, porcelain, wooden handicrafts, pharmaceuticals and tea. Japan, Korea and Southeast Asia absorbed the prolific carvings of Buddha and the copies of Buddhist scriptures crafted in Zhejiang Province.

Ningbo is one of the free economic zones established by Beijing to draw capitalistic cash into the country, thus the harbor teems with ships, the docks heavy with products ready to be loaded. Ningbo's Hong Kong sons, like many overseas Chinese have contributed prodigiously to the field of education, notable being the Ningbo University and the Ningbo Teacher's College. There are 18 major Ningbo Foreign Trade Organizations if you so desire to tarry and do some business.

Among the sights to see, the Tang Dynasty (618-907) **Drum Tower** can be seen standing, with an ancient 3-storey building perched on top of it. An incongruous occidental **Bell Tower** stands next to it. There is also a traditional Gothic style Catholic church which gives added testimony to the foreign influence and world commerce done in this area.

Tianyi Ge Library is reputed to be the oldest existing library in China, dating from 1561. Whether scholarly or otherwise, the estimated 300,000-volume collection provides a handsome

The Free Economic Zone of Ningbo

Foreign investors are given preferential treatment under the rules of a Free Economic Zone. In Ningbo for instance, the Federal Government presides over the Ningbo Economic and Technical Development Zone (NETDZ). That mouthful is under the supervision of the NETDZ United Development Company, Ltd consisting of the NETDZ Administrative Committee and the China National Metals and Minerals Export and Import Corporation. This organization encourages foreign investment and breaks down the mountains of red tape that strap and strangle capital trying to operate a company.

The tax rules are complicated but favor the investor in that they pay tax on only 15 per cent of the profits, watered down by a free initial 2 years and then half of the 15 per cent for the next 3 years. In addition, labor is organized authorizing wage scales and the unusual privilege of dismissing non-productive workers. Special imported building equipment, machinery, even personal goods for the foreigners are not charged any inbound customs duties. Decisions are made on the spot by the committee to expedite construction and production.

More than 7,000 factories stud the cityscape of Ningbo with 18 major trading companies of China engaging in contracts with foreigners.

---

view, albeit through glass windows and cases; among these over 80,000 volumes are considered rare. The water trough in the forecourt is original, intended for fire control and large stone lions guard the gate to ward off evil.

Tianfeng Ta Pagoda, the highest structure towering over Ningbo, was first built in the 5th century and further building took place again in the 14th century. Architectural enthusiasts will be interested in the 18-storey structure with only 7 storeys clearly visible. Another 7 are hidden and 4 are underground. If you have been in China long enough to be step-conditioned, clamber to the top of the pagoda for the best view of the city. The Chinese have a saying: "Those who wish to command a view of a thousand miles must first be prepared to climb an extra flight."

Sprawling east of the hotels is **Moon Lake** which was eulogized a thousand years ago by poets of that era. A children's park offers an interesting backdrop for those who wish to capture them on film.

Lull away a few hours at the park. **Zhongshan Park** houses a small zoo and **Riverside Park** has pleasant walks which unravel the river scene. You will have to be discerning, given the many temples that beckon a visit. The heavy Buddhist influence can be seen on many fascinating examples of historic architecture. The **Baoquo Temple Complex** was built entirely with wood in the 11th century. According to folklore, the birds, the vermin and wood-eating bugs have never ventured in. Experts claim that the yellow Chinese juniper wood has an aromatic oil which is apparently offensive to the normal pests. **Xuedo Mountain**, **Dongqian Lake** and **Xiku Town** offer scenic beauty.

Putuoshan, a nearby mountainous coastal island, is for those travelers who have a yen for lumbering beyond the gates. However, it is open to special guests only, because of a military installation on the island. A friendly CITS guide may be able to arrange a visit if you can give him a sound reason. A circa 9th century, Guanyin (Goddess of Mercy) is on Putuoshan to protect the temples and scenic wonders on the island.

Ningbo is famous for the juicy honey peaches and a special variety of bamboo shoots from Fenghua, oranges of Zhenhai and red bayberries from Yuyao. The Zhuangyuan Restaurant is renowned for its classic 10 dishes and the stuffed dumplings of Gang Ya Gou (Vat Duck Dog). A tale recounts how an imperial emissary in the Qing Dynasty passing through Ningbo feasted on a dish of soft-shelled turtle with crystal sugar. It so impressed him that he labeled the dish and the restaurant Zhuangyuan, "Unequaled in the World". Lightly fried river eel, yellow croaker dressed in dried bean-milk cream and fried finless eel are some of the celebrated dishes in Ningbo.

From the culinary arts Ningbo also offers other forms of art. The Ningbo Arts & Crafts Import & Export Corporation specializes in wood, stone and oxhorn raw materials and at the Embroidery Factory it is fascinating to watch the deft fingers fashion this lovely art form. The Friendship Store houses an arresting assortment of handicraft. As Ningbo is off the beaten tourist track, unusual treasures can be found hibernating on the dusty shelves. Pore over the display for showpieces which are tucked in the corners. Major hotels are listed in the directory, the most recent is the Golden Dragon opposite the southern railway station. The building is tall, modern and crowned with restaurants dressed in inviting Chinese decor.

Ningbo is adequately serviced by air, bus and train from Beijing, Shanghai, Guangzhou and a direct flight from Hong Kong twice a week. Few tourists and tour agencies think about highway touring in China. This is a wonderful opportunity to drive from Ningbo to Wenzhou and possibly divert via Shaoxing.

Wenzhou - Zhejiang Province

Wenzhou is some 8 to 11 hours by car from Ningbo, depending upon road and ferry-crossing conditions. Ships from Ningbo, Shanghai or Fuzhou steam into its port. This is a splendid opportunity for land cruising through the green countryside, stopping at villages, kibitzing with the populace, an experience you will enjoy immensely. One travel option is to travel by car or train from Ningbo to Shaoxing (see Hangzhou Section), a charming dainty town renowned for its special rice wine.

There is hardly any language barrier. Your driver may speak only a smattering of English, but don't worry, even in the smallest of towns you can get something to drink and fruit, dump-

The styling of old and new fashions in Xiamen.

lings or noodles to eat with your conversational Chinese manual. Invariably the person you are talking to will want to read the book and bandy English words with you. The local folks have a burning interest to learn English.

Wenzhou, the commercial hub of the coast, is like Guangzhou, laden with goods that are branded as "forbidden fruits". The street outside the hotel teems with free-market vendors selling blue jeans, sunglasses, cigarette lighters and other made-in-Taiwan products. Of great interest is the local produce, fresh farm fruit and vegetables. Alleys around the city hotels thrive and throb with more freemarkets and when night closes in, the main streets come abuzz with part-time entrepreneurs trying to make a buck. Wenzhou is small enough for a stroll on its city streets. Shell pictures and creative shell novelties are the major local products. Some ceramic activity keeps the place humming. Outside of town, **Qiatou Village** is the button capital of China.

Seafood and decorative platters are characteristic features of Wenzhou dining. At a normal hotel dinner, you are likely to be served an entree of assorted vegetables and shrimp presented in the form of a brilliant peacock or golden carp swimming in a lake of green grass.

Jiangxin (Island at the Heart of the River), is a pleasant day's excursion. Pagodas stand on the peak of 2 major hills. Temples dating back to the 10th and 15th centuries and the **Wenzhou Museum** provide a peek into its arresting history. Wander the gardens and hills, stroll along the beaches and snack at the tea-shops.

Yandang Mountains provide a cool relaxing side-trip in the pine forests with fairy-tale scenery up on the rock formations. Resort hotels are at Lingfeng and Xianglingtou. The most enjoyable way up there is to engage a friendly guide, car and driver from CITS for a 3-day trip. The system requires you to pay for meals and lodging for your guide and driver at a modest cost. It is a delectable adjunct to have a good guide as a companion.

Nanxi River meanders sinuously down from the mountains to the delta entrance of Wenzhou. A white-sail boat trip from Shatou is leisurely, skimming through clear waters fed by crystal streams and brooks. The peaceful shoreline, mountains in the backdrop and smoke curling from villages enliven the picture. **Lord Tao Cave**, **Lion Rock** and a Song Dynasty monastery lend visiting interest to the side trip.

The Jinghan Hotel is considered Wenzhou luxury in a scenic location at the fringe of town. The Overseas Chinese Hotel and the Wenzhou Hotel are in the city center. Facilities are modest. You will see more foreign business persons than tourists.

Wenzhou can be reached by train via Hangzhou, or by ship from Ningbo or Shanghai. The planned airport will make access easier from these cities.

For an ongoing trip down the southeast coast, try an auto-trip to Fuzhou in Fujian Province. Road and ferry conditions are improving every year. You can expect to spend 8 to 10 hours on the road breezing through some beautiful forests and agricultural areas, occasionally kissing the coastline for a glimpse of the South China Sea. CITS will arrange a car and driver, there is no need for a guide. The hotel will pack a picnic lunch and don't forget your swagbag.

Fuzhou and Fujian Province

Fuzhou is the capital of Fujian Province, a free economic zone which is bursting at the seams with new commercial projects, hotels, marketing centers and bustling streets. The first emperor of the Qin Dynasty established the city more than 2,000 years ago. Its history is colored with trade and commerce. Marco Polo mentions it with fondness and affection as an arrival port.

Fuzhou has good air, train and bus access from other major cities in addition to the automobile ride suggested in the Wenzhou section. There is also an inexpensive boat service from Shanghai.

Modern accommodations include the Hot Spring Hotel, located centrally and with mineral spring waters piped directly into your bathroom. The Foreign Trade Center has its own hotel in the new business complex. Outside the central area, the new 1,000-room Xihu (West Lake) Guesthouse is on the fringe of the lake. The 12-storey, 900-room Hong Kong joint-venture Haishan Guesthouse is another. Fuzhou is hankering after business and tourism in a big way.

Nantai Island is in the middle of the Min River and it suspends 2 stone-arched bridges to the north and south sections of the city.

The peony bushes and chrysanthemums in the thousand-year old **West Lake Park** have been sites depicted by artists since the Tang Dynasty (618-907). Flying Rainbow Bridge and Garden in the Hall are scenic sights in addition to a zoo with pandas and the Fujian Province Exhibition Center. West Lake Hotel with VIP suites is located in the park.

Twin Pagodas at the foot of **Yushan** and **Wushan** are symbols of Fuzhou. Yushan is a large hill and the hub of town with many scenic spots overlooking Fuzhou. A library, memorial hall and exhibition hall stand guard on the hill. It is on this hill that the 1911 Revolution began signifying the downfall of the Qing Dynasty (1634-1911).

Drum Hills, sprawling about 20 km out of town is a trove of Buddhist history for the Fujians and tourists. In **Yongguansi** (Bubbling Springs Temple) there is a treasured relic reputed to be the actual tooth of Sakyamuni. The temple is over a thousand years old and has been rebuilt and refurbished many times during its history. You can see, by special request, the archives which showcase 30,000 volumes of Buddhist sutras and another special collection of 650 volumes written in blood over the lifetime of a devoted monk.

The surroundings are clustered with caves, halls, winding streams and a hot springs spa. Tea stops are scattered in pleasant glades. Plan to spend a full day. The Songtao Restaurant will assuage your hunger and provide a breathtaking view near the top of Drum Hill.

The Seaman's Club with its fine location overlooking the port is a scenic lookout. You may find some goodies for your swagbag and the snack bar has great ice cream in cones to give you that extra edge while lumbering up the hilltop park.

The calm and tranquility of Xihu Park Pavilion on West Lake, Fuzhou.

The most famous artistic products are the bodiless or weightless artware, tediously formed from hundreds of layers of lacquer. After setting, the interior forms are removed, leaving the very light, extremely durable product. It is highly resistant to surface damage and is decorated in modern and traditional styles. Vases standing 2 m high are common and a pair of temple lions 3 m tall guard the factory door. Despite their height, they can be lifted easily. Lovely boxes, trays, nesting objects, vases and urns in graduated sizes fill the shelves of the major production factory.

Nearby is the ancient village of **De Hua** (see box), source of the *blanc de chine* porcelain wares which are made of fine white clays and fired in kilns that are thousands of years old. There is a showroom in the Fuzhou business center and a day trip to the factory provides a pleasant drive and a memorable experience. One of their most beautiful products is the rendition of Guanyin (Goddess of Mercy) depicted with multiple arms (as many as 100), each hand holding an object of religious meaning or gift. For shipping, an ingenious packaging has been devised to ensure safe passage.

A modern commercial complex is busy with international buyers, more than half from nearby Hong Kong. Many of these are hometown boys returning to do business with old friends and relatives. They consider Fuzhou a central source of supply for contracted manu-

Lacquerware of Fujian

Archeologists date lacquerware in tomb excavations as early as the 4th century BC. The variety of the art form is seemingly endless. Various Fujian factories specialize in metal inlays of gold and silver. Sea shells are a common motif for design or handles. Delicate chips of egg shells are colored and inlaid in a mosaic of traditional patterns.

Lacquer is a resin from the varnish tree, found mostly in southern Asian countries. On contact with the air, the sap or resin hardens forming a durable coating resistant to moisture, rust, acids and insects. The raw lacquer is collected and purified forming a transparent liquid. Mineral pigments of iron and mercury are added to produce the black and red material before they are sealed in airtight containers. The lacquerware is then produced by adding multiple layers of the material, drying in a moist-free environment, then polished.

Carving through layers of the material called cinnabar, often referred to as the red product, is an art form. It may have as many as 100 coats. Special effects are evolved by carving through crowning layers of red to expose black designs underneath.

The production of the special bodiless lacquer of Fuzhou is fairly uncomplicated but tedious. It involves applying gauze material onto wooden molds which are then swathed with layers of lacquer before the molds are removed. Thus vases, urns, serving dishes are churned out in multicolor etched artware. A 2-meter vase weighs but a trifle and is extremely durable. The reputed inventor, Shen Shao'an worked for the famous Emperor Qianlong of the Qing Dynasty who was said to have pioneered the process when he discovered signs where the lacquer-coated wood endured and where the untreated wood rotted away. Thus the idea emerged to form artware of solely the lacquer material.

The modern procedure is to create a mold of plaster, swathe it with gauze material of hemp and then apply many coats of lacquer. When the lacquer hardens, water immersion melts the plaster away leaving the lightweight product. Two to three-meter tall temple lion figures and massive vases are not uncommon lacquerware. The surface is resistant to alkalis and acids and is suitable for decorative designs resembling the finest porcelain.

---

factured products.

The city is small enough to explore after dinner in the hot humid summer. As in most of the tourist cities where regulations are more relaxed, the night air brings out a raft of entrepreneurs who set up stalls on the main thoroughfares, dangling paintings from lines strung up. Sellers of watermelon or pineapple slices do a dripping business and a shoe display may parade a hundred pairs of simulated Nikes on the sidewalk.

A pearl industry is burgeoning, rivaling the extensive fresh water products of Shanghai and the cultured sea water farms of Japan. Hong Kong-trained jewelry artists now produce up-market fine jewelry in gold and precious stones for export. Showrooms dazzle visitors with an array of samples, many of which are unique prize-winning jewels.

Mount Wu Yi, one of the 5 famous mountains, is within a day's journey. Wu Yi is so renowned that special charters run air transport tour trips out of Hong Kong.

Seafood is a specialty of Fuzhou with a quirky mouth-watering dish called Buddha Jumping Over the Wall. Fried conch, fish balls, pickled chicken and scallops are also specialties. Juchunyun and Huafulou Restaurants

Porcelain Cities

De Hua is a small city 3 hours' drive from Fuzhou. It was a bursting export center during the Ming and Qing periods of the *blanc de chine* or ivory porcelain molded and carved into small sculptures under a thick creamy translucent glaze. These were usually pure white or cream in color, untouched by any other color. De Hua produced pieces have been found in museums throughout Europe; the production system has been replicated for centuries.

Today the market calls for more variations of decoration and artware and industrial porcelains are produced. The showroom at the factory has exquisite examples of prize-winning porcelains. Sometimes the manager can be induced to part with a particular favorite of yours. Prices are negotiable.

The more popular figures of Guanyin, the Buddha Ho-Ti (Maitreya) and the immortals can be purchased in the showrooms of Fuzhou. A visit to the countryside stopping at Dehua's ancient factories can be easily arranged with the local CITS.

Longquan in southern Zhejiang Province is another example of an ancient kiln. It was dormant for centuries before its reopening in 1950. This factory produces fine celadons, stoneware and porcelain covered with a thick, smooth, shiny glaze in shades of soft gray-green, with carved or relief decor under the glaze or a crackle glaze.

Jingdezhen (Jianxi Province) kilns date from 1369 and were set aside by the first Ming Emperor. (See Changjiang section). This city is the largest producer of all the fine porcelains such as egg shell, stone ware, Qing imperial yellow dragon glaze dinnerware and accessories. One factory produces only Ming imperial blue and white porcelains, wine jugs, vases and dinnerware. Various other art-porcelain factories reproduce the classic figures of the immortals and gods.

Imperial banquets called for mass production of the fine porcelains with one court in 1546 reputed to have used over 100,000 pieces. Every time a new palace was built by the Ming and Qing royal courts, decorative and functional porcelains were produced.

Collectors' items of the egg shell are so thin that a finger's shadow can easily be seen through the glaze. Carved flower pots, incised pickle jars, fish bowls from table sizes to those over a meter in diameter are available to the traveler. Jingdezhen's trade group will amass selections from the various factories for shipment in a 1 m square crate. This packaging is less costly and is easily shipped to any destination.

Guangdong Province has its **Shiwan**, Foshan art studios. **Liling** in Hunan Province is renowned for bowls and vases with bird and flower paintings of scenes from the local countryside. **Cixhou** pottery from Handan and Pengcheng in Hebei Province, stoneware teapots of **Yixing**, Jiangsu Province and many others have notable re-activated ancient kilns, thus a visit to them is mandatory.

are famous for Fujian cuisine, Qingzhen for Muslim and vegetarian dishes.

Fujian Tourist Souvenirs Production and Supply Corporation have the best selection of local products at prices less than the Guangzhou Friendship Store and Hong Kong Arts and Crafts Store. They pack and ship your purchases. Fuzhou Friendship Store, Fuzhou Arts and Crafts Store and Bailing Department Store are all on Bayiqi Road.

For shopping fun, take an afternoon to browse around in the people's stores, on Bayiqi, Dongjiekou and Wuyi Roads. The stone-carving factory and the bodiless lacquer factories are open to visitors.

Quanzhou, Fujian Province

When you are sated with Fuzhou, hire a

Xichan Buddhist Temple, Fuzhou, with symbolic dragons on the roof and guarded by the Fu lions at the entrance.

Village of Xunpu

Eight miles south of Guangzhou, where the River Jinjiang meanders into the sea, is the tiny fishing village of **Xunpu**. Merchants ride their bicycles laden with baskets of oysters slung almost to the ground as they peddle in the light of dawn to the morning market.

Xunpu is an insight into the past for the lifestyle has been left unmolested by the modernization of its neighbors, Guangzhou and Xiamen. The women still dress their hair in buns, decorated with dewy-fresh chrysanthemums, and wear gingham or floral blouses and skirts. Faces and profiles seem strikingly different as they are scrawled by centuries of commerce with Persians, Indians, Europeans and Americans who called at the port.

The neighboring village of **Yuanlu** grows abundant crops of flowers delivered daily to the markets. The women immediately purchase their daily floral accouterments to adorn their hair giving a lively ambience to the ancient hamlet. Yuanlu was once the private garden of a rich Guangzhou mandarin during the heyday of international commerce.

Trade waned when the delta silted up, forcing the commerce down to Xiamen and leaving Yuanlu in a flux of suspension. The silted marshes brought new business to the small village. Oysters thrived in the environment, propagated by the millions to feed the larger cities nearby. The people found the shells a perfect building material for their homes providing insulation, durability and decoration.

Winding through the twisted streets resembling the convoluted *hutongs* of Beijing are cheerful women sitting on doorsteps repairing nets, shelling oysters and singing. The children are drilled at an early age to help with the chores and they sit alongside their mother to join in the blithe clatter and chatter of noise.

Weddings are common and with good fortune you will arrive when the local matchmaker has arranged a suitable marriage in the settled practices of tradition. As a leading light in the affair, she will often ride with the yellow-garbed bride in a horse-drawn cart or jeep to the home of her future husband. Bridesmaids carry the dowry with them in a colorful procession. Terms negotiated by the matchmaker usually take several weeks of shuttling between the families. Brides are more liberated today but still must live with the grooms' parents under the iron clutch of the mother-in-law. The processions are colorful, filling the narrow streets with riotous music and celebrations. Because the townsfolk are said to have descended from a single stock, the wedding is a family affair celebrated by the whole town.

car and driver from CITS, journey down south and lunch at Quanzhou on your auto-trek from Fuzhou to Xiamen, a serene coastal city with a population of 1.2 million friendly people. Marco Polo stopped there during his journey, calling it Zaton, which was then a busy city port and the hub of commerce with the Arabs, hosting a bustling Muslim population. Gradually the port silted up and economic activity drifted north to Fuzhou or south to Xiamen. The half-million population crossed the straits to Taiwan or moved down to Guangdong Province. Try either the Mantang or Furenyi Restaurants on Zongshan Road. They have a delectable cuisine and a separate room to entertain foreign visitors. Slender rice noodles, in soup or fried, are the famed local delicacy.

There are city streets to explore after lunch. The shops exude an aura of the Ming and Qing Dynasties. A tour around the many temples, mosques, pagodas and nearby mountains requires a guide. One of the most interesting

View of Xiamen from Gulangyu Island, a quaint little island a short boat-ride away.

sights on the way out of town is **Laojunyan**, the Old Man. It is a large statue of a Taoist sage carved out of the rock sometime in the 11th century. You are allowed to climb up, sit on his knee for a picture and rub his capacious tummy for good luck.

Ask your guide to stop at the nearby artistic marble-carving factory on the outskirts of town, a huge indoor-outdoor enclave. The management is usually amenable to the rare visitor. Two and three-meter stone temple lions lie about with the various carved cornices and classic decorations used in major building construction ready for shipment. In the showroom are unusual decorative art carvings with variegated colors of pink, black, gray and pure white marble. You might find a treasure in a rendition of Lao Shouxing (the god of longevity) or the Laughing Buddha, Maitreya, carved in a marble never seen before in your hometown. You will have to carry it on to Fuzhou or Xiamen but there are shipping facilities in those ports.

Xiamen in Fujian Province

Xiamen, an island just south of Fuzhou, formerly known as Amoy, is the closest point to Taiwan. It is linked to the mainland by a very long causeway. It is a pleasant day's drive down the picturesque Fujian coast packing a lunch stop at Quanzhou.

Old European houses on Gulangyu Island revealing a strong European presence in the late 19th century.

Xiamen is destined to be the next boom city of China. Lying just 3,700 m away from the Taiwanese island of Jinmen, its paradisiacal beach, dressed in Mediterranean climate, was the target of artillery shelling in the 1950s. But today, Taiwanese cash is flushing, a reversal of fortune when one recalls that it was from Xiamen in the 17th century that a Chinese national hero, General Cheng Ch'eng-kung launched an amphibious attack which liberated Taiwan from the clutch of the Dutch. Today, Taiwanese investment is seen as the key to free Xiamen from the fetters of communism, considering that the coastal port now enjoys one of the highest wages and living standards in China.

Xiamen has been singled out as the hottest target of Taiwanese investment not only because of its proximity and the emotional bondage but also because the Taiwanese have found it more economical and discreet to maintain a mistress in Xiamen. So whether it is business or mistress, the funds that have cascaded into Xiamen have been estimated at US$6 billion in 1992 alone, despite the lack of official ties.

Besides its reputation as a booming town, Xiamen has much to offer: colonial mansions, a labyrinth of twisting streets, turn-of-the-century Latin quarters, balmy breezes that sweep across its palm-fringed beaches. All these and more have prompted former US President Richard Nixon to rank it as one of the most beautiful enclaves in his dec-

Boat folk on Gulang Yu Island.

ades of globetrotting.

Foreign influence dates back to the Portuguese and Spanish attempts to trade with the Mings in the 16th century. The town center wears the past in the Spanish-style business streets with sun-shading arcades, apartments above, shops below, twisting down to the waterfront. A small pretty park with a jetty for ferries heading for the intriguing island of **Gulang Yu**, is at the end of the street.

Stay at the Xiamen Guesthouse up on the hill instead of one of the new modern hotels. It is charming, with gardens and pools and personalized food service. The chef will ask what you would like for lunch and dinner and do his marketing accordingly. The VIP guesthouses were designed to accommodate special foreign guests and high-ranking members of the Communist Party. The centrally located Xin Xiao Hotel has been refurbished. The newest joint-venture East Coast Hotel is on Zongshan Dong Lu, the waterfront. The downtown area is compact, even the Xiamen Guesthouse is within easy walking distance downhill. You can also arrange for a taxi to take you back to the hilltop at dinner time.

Gulang Yu Island

A visit to the island of **Gulang Yu**, once or twice is a must while in Xiamen. Crossing the straits is a 5-minute ride on

Nanputuo Temple, Xiamen, a Tang Dynasty complex housing among other things a library of scriptures, calligraphy rolls and engraved ivory.

a spine-tingling boat, so crowded and low in the water, you fear the gunwales will awash with the next cresting wave from a passing freighter.

The island of Gulang Yu has a colorful history. During the late 19th century, foreign embassies and all foreign residents who lived on the island were forced to return home before nightfall. Two versions for this have survived. One is that the trading houses of the foreigners feared the uncertain temperament of the Qings and a repeat of previous annihilation edicts. They retired to

Whatever the case, the foreigners are gone but the winding streets of European-style homes survive. The shops are reminiscent of small Swiss towns like Zermatt. A motorized vehicle blithely takes you through the town teeming with wondrous delights. A small mountain overlooks the straits to another island called Quemoy (Chinmen) occupied by the Nationalists. A sidenote about Gulang Yu. The colonial houses once contained pianos, bringing out a latent talent for music when the foreigners departed. A physical reminder is the ferry landing which has been shaped like a piano.

You must climb the hill of Gulang Yu to **Sunlight Rock** at the peak to have good fortune for the rest of your days. Take your time and enjoy the breathtaking view. The lower part cuts through the shopping streets and former residences of the foreign enclave. **Koxinga Memorial Hall** is at the base of the rock, a place to stop and have a cuppa and watch the stream of people antclimbing to the peak.

Stop at the **Lotus Nunnery** halfway up, a rare enclave in China. An antique-curio shop is tucked in a nook for the curiosity seeker. Along the way are evidences of gun-emplacements of the once fortress-hill overlooking Quemoy, the 20th century foe. At one time mainland China bombarded Taiwan from this island which threatened to re-open the battle between the 2 enemies.

The crown of Sunlight Rock is heav-

the island for safety and garrisoned it with 2,000 Sikh soldiers.

Another version is that the Qings wanted to save face and retaliated against Shanghai for barring the Chinese from certain areas of that city by passing a decree that all foreigners return and remain on the island from dusk to daybreak.

ily buttressed with iron railings for safety. The good fortune seekers revolve, in a steady stream, making it to the top for a 360-degree view.

The city behind you undulates with the hills like a miniature Hong Kong. The harbor is colored with freighters and ferries such as the local Love Boat Cruise steaming towards the glitter of Hong Kong.

Overseas Chinese Contribution

The Jimei cruises on Friday and the Gulang Yu sets sail every Wednesday to ferry overseas Fujians back and forth to their old homeland. They bring television and video cassette recorder sets, appliances, fancy liquor and money for their relatives. Occasionally, they bear greater gifts such as the Jimei School Complex, joint-venture hotels, factories and other trade ventures in the area because of their emotional ties with their homeland.

On the other side of Gulang Yu are beaches for you to get a bit of sun tan and take a dip in the sea. Lanes of free enterprise entrepreneurs crowd the trails including a paper-cutting wizard who cuts silhouettes of you at the drop of a 5-yuan note.

Jimei School Village is a seaside campus wedged between the causeways. It is a cluster of small colleges built by a Singaporean, born in Xiamen. Tan Kah Kee emigrated when he was young, became very successful in industry and like other overseas Chinese invested some of his wealth in his birthplace for philanthropic reasons.

Xiamen University in the city is also a gift from overseas Chinese and houses the **Museum of Anthropology** covering the Malay States, China and Taiwan.

The Buddhist temple, **Nanputuo** which lies south of town was built during the Golden Age of the Tang Dynasty (618-907). There are 3 Great Halls, a Drum Tower, Bell Tower in a courtyard and a pavilion at the rear of the compound which is a treasure house of recorded paraphernalia of history. The scriptures, calligraphy rolls and engraved ivory make a handsome library.

Unfortunately it is normally closed to visitors except on special occasions. Ask your guide to wangle you a quick private tour. The halls have assortments of statues including the favorite Maitreya, the laughing Buddha with the capacious stomach and large drooping ears. If you care to study the culture intimately, each of the ferocious guardians, the many boddhisattvas have ex-

Wu Yi Mountain

Several hours' train and bus ride from Fuzhou or a special tourist's flight to Chong'an in Fujian will take you to another of China's 5 famous mountains. Unlike the masses of people climbing Huangshan or Emeishan, **Wu Yi Shan** is more remote, and consequently foreign tourists seldom take the time to visit it. You have the opportunity of scaling the 2,900 steps of the Great King Peak with a certain degree of solitude to behold the magnificent landscape and wandering waterways rumbling far below.

The tourist industry has generated the government's interest in providing accommodations, guides and easier transportation and designating safer climbing areas. The fun of Wu Yi Shan is to spend time climbing, viewing the strange peaks and listening to the endless fairy tales describing their origin. The waterways below provide the scenery which has inspired artists for centuries. Hopefully the various teastands have not been replaced by canned soda.

There are several varieties of local teas, some piquant in taste because of the hardy tea bushes growing in the few areas of non-rock land on the slopes of the mountains. Disdaining the fancy tea containers of the big cities, roadside vendors hawk the product in plastic bags. You have to make your own labels to remember the names.

Ancient structures and relatively modern pavilions and mansions dot the terraces. Getaway homes for the famous are noted, such as Chiang Kaishek's near the Miaogao Shanshuang Resort, your probable hotel accommodation.

The 8-kilometer Jiqui Shi (Nine Curves Stream) wends round most of the peaks in the range. Bamboo rafts are fitted with chairs for comfort, the stream is mild as it is sheltered from winds by the rocky shores.

The **Celestial Caves** is near the massive and frightening Dazang Peak towering above the **Wolong Tan** (Lying Dragon Pool), reputed to have a depth of 20 m. The caves are used as burial grounds giving a spooky air to the area.

Small villages are pleasant places to stop along the stream. Caves above gape invitingly for exploration but call for the expertise of spelunkers. **Shuilian Dong** (Water Curtain Cavern) is accessible and can accommodate the London Philharmonic Orchestra with an audience. **Xuyun Dong** (Clouds-Breathing Cavern) has a constant temperature, **Feng Dong** is a windy city and **Ling Dong** is populated with bats, variety enough for all personalities.

A rare frog called *Gudong* breeds in the area. It is large enough to gobble snakes, unless the snake gets it first. Patients afflicted with the disease Osteomalacia (softening of the bones) come to take tonic from the Gudong.

Mount Huanggang and the **Wuyi Conservation Zone** are nearby if you have a longing to stay and explore further.

---

plicit meanings and purposes.

Xiamen is a town appreciative of art. There are studios scattered along the way from the Xiamen Guesthouse on the hill down to the main center of town. Trundle down on a shopping trip and hail a taxi back to the hotel to save the uphill struggle with packages and heart-strain. Enjoy the tranquility of this small town in the southeast of China and linger for a few days.

Xiamen Botanical Gardens is a leisurely morning stroll for the casual visitor and a special haunt requiring days for the aficionados of botany. Over 4,000 tropical and sub-tropical plants are cultivated in a traditional Chinese architectural setting. It is a living showcase of gardens-within-gardens, each with a specialty. A hothouse incubates the new babies, medicinal plants, succulents, orchids, rose and pine and fir gardens delineate the varieties.

Thousands of Rocks Reservoir, an

Wanshi Shan Botanical Gardens, Xiamen, in its magnificent setting, is a haven for botanists.

artificial lake, is the centerpiece fringed with bamboos and garden paths. The very rare Metasequoia and Gingko are name teasers for the serious botanist, said to be existing 20 million years ago. US President Nixon bore gifts of California's famous Redwood Sequoia trees during his inaugural visit in 1972.

Cactus is a common sight, but Xiamen has a long history in cultivating the 2000 varieties. Some have food value, others medicinal. One has a poisonous protein now being used to research cures for cancer.

Purple Cloud Rock draws wanderers to the most delightful spot in the park. Tall Magnolias provide a shade for plants and visitors. Piled granite rocks are built to resemble natural formations with pavilions, bridges, pools and shaded areas for the 200 varieties of plants that blossom in the sunlight.

Near the Botanical Gardens is **Thousands of Rock Lotuses Temple** which is another enclave on the botanical tour of Xiamen. Bougainvillea and other flowers adorn the path leading up the stone steps to the temple. The variety appears endless and when you get to the Small Peach Source brook, there is a gigantic rock on which two characters are etched. They are liberally translated as "Clouds and Mists Float amongst the Rocks" or "Thousands of Rocks Lock the Clouds."

Scenic wandering is endless in Xiamen, Gulang Yu Island and the university on Jimei. Xiamen will probably be a major seaside resort one day if the government's plans to encourage more tourist dollars come to fruition. Resort hotels could spread down the miles of white-sand beaches. The best swimming beach is littered with concrete block houses, reminders of the military confrontation with nearby Quemoy.

Xiamen now has air transportation to Hong Kong and other major domestic destinations. The 2 cruise boats run weekly. Return to Fuzhou by car and loop through De Hua, the internationally known center for *blanc de chine* white porcelain sculptures. Guangzhou and Hong Kong are an hour's flight away.

South China is next. It can be another trip or an extension of this one. Guangdong Province featuring Guangzhou (Canton) is a story in itself and Shenzhen, an explosion of modern links to Hong Kong. Hainan Island is virtually a world unto itself.

JADE-CLASP MOUNTAINS

Guilin & Environs

"A turquoise gauze belt, the mountains like a jade-clasp," eulogized Han Yu, a Tang Dynasty poet (768-824). The limestone peaks scattered around the region are like unwrapped Hershey Kisses, challenging China's artists for centuries to replicate their ethereal beauty. The peaks and the famous River Li (Li Jiang) have become a picturesque symbol of China around the world.

Guilin is a mecca for tourists, spurred by the government to such a degree that the beauty must be enjoyed by blotting out all the littering accouterments of the tourist trade. Ignore the rows of tour buses, mini vans, crowded hotel lobbies, queues of foreigners and enjoy the characteristic charm of the area.

Special charter flights are available from Hong Kong, regular daily flights connects Guilin with Beijing, Shanghai, Guangzhou and even Kunming and Chongqing in the west. Many new hotels are sprouting and supplying creature comfort, restaurants

Perfect view of Elephant Trunk Rock sitting in the Li River.

Cave carving of Sakyamuni found in the Thousand Buddhas Cave on Mount Fubo.

and evening entertainment. Banyan Lake Hotel is the VIP place for foreign diplomats being hosted by the Politburo.

Lijiang is the most convenient downtown facility. Holiday Inn and Sheraton are both on the Li River slightly out of the city bustle. The hotels are not too far off within walking distance of the central area.

For a short 2 or 3-day stay, touring is wearying and hotel dining is easier and more comfortable. Restaurants abound as in all tourist centers if you have the time to stay and explore the culinary splendor. There are tales about eating rat in Guilin, true to a degree. It is actually the bamboo rat, an armadillo-like creature now becoming extinct because of the eating habits of the select clientele.

Some travelers are just becoming accustomed to eating eel in various places in China, the bamboo rat and the snake dishes will be a long way down the preference list.

There are several small hill climbs to enjoy on your own within the town environs. **Elephant Trunk Hill** has a fanciful tale of its origin. Cresting the hill is a dainty pagoda which symbolizes the hilt of a dagger wielded by a jealous god. **Diecai Shan** (Folded Brocade Hill), provides a leisurely climb which offers a stop at a pavilion for tea, a visit to a memorial hall, threading through the Windy Cave to see the Breeze Greeting Tower.

A girl in Guilin performing the ribbon dance adroitly and gracefully.

Duxiufeng (the Peak of Unique Beauty) offers a spectacular view of the city atop the 300 steps to its peak. **Mount Fubo** has the Returned Pearl Grotto on one side and the Thousand Buddha Rock on the other, the thousand having been reduced to 300 sculptures over the centuries. **Flying Phoenix Hill** and **Fighting Cocks Hill** are among the others; the names alone evoke the poetic ambience of Guilin.

A 225-meter **Mountains of Colored Layers** gives an excellent overview of the city and the River Li. Across the bridge is **Seven Star Park** with peaks stretching out like the Big Dipper. Seven Star Cave is illuminated among other caves in the park. A bonsai tree section and a zoo add to the scenic wonders.

Guilin Environs

Ludiyan (Reed Flute Cave), 6 km from the city is the most beautiful and impressive site in the region. It displays a magnificent subterranean water and landscape. The centrally featured chamber called Crystal Palace of the Dragon King is dramatically lighted. Stalactites and stalagmites form eerie imaginary figures.

A large slab of white rock hangs from a ledge opposite a large stalactite resembling a Confucius-like figure. As in all such areas, fables have evolved over the centuries to fantasize such formations. One such saga explains the figure as a scholar who visited the cave

Yangshou

Tour group escapists choose to bypass the famous Guilin for the small village of **Yangshuo**. The River Li boats dock here at the end of the magical trip, hordes of tourists debark, thread through the gauntlet of sidewalk stands, the market place and then clamber onto the buses to return to Guilin.

The pretty town is then left to the travel treasure hunters who revel in the same limestone peaks that charm the throng of international visitors to Guilin. The peaks have been named and are low enough to climb for a view of the unfettered river and town. Jealous Guilin has forced the closure of several guesthouses but modest accommodations are available or you can take a late bus back to Guilin.

Yangshuo's surroundings has inspired much poetry. The peaks around Yangshuo have been described as "steep and delicate, looking like piled up petals. Their inverted images mirrored in the river resemble green lotuses sprouting out of the water, elegant and graceful."

Yangshuo itself, however, is a tourist town, screaming and screeching with restaurant signs like "Today's special yoghurt - muesli - banana - fresh squeezed orange juice - coldest beer". Sidewalk cafes line the streets along with the curio-shops selling postcards, colorful masks, wickerwork, chopsticks and everything a visitor could possibly want to take home.

A few kilometers away is the small village of **Gaotian**, a simple farming settlement. Wooden ferries pole on by, the limestone peaks delineate a backdrop for the fields of green produce and rice paddies. Ancient banyan trees shade the resting old one watching the rural scene and occasional passerby. You take a space capsule back in time a hundred years or more.

wishing to write a poem of the cave's beauty. He took so long to craft the words that the water dripped over him and solidified before he could finish. Another story is that the cave is the home of the legendary Dragon King and the various imaginary figures are his entourage of snails, jellyfish and weapons bested from his traditional foe the Monkey King. Details are in the classical novel, *A Journey to the West*.

Travel note: bring a light jacket and walking shoes with substantial treads. The cave is damp, the rock paths wet and slippery.

The River Li, the "Green Silk Belt"

The River Li trip ranks with the Great Wall as the crowning glory of a memorable holiday in China. Cruise boats leave from the bridge or Elephant Trunk Rock farther down, for the 5 to 6-hour trip down the winding river. Don't worry that the water is a silty brown, stand firmly on the tiny rear platform of your scow and shove off.

Lotus Flower Crag looks out at you. Wave to **Old Man Mountain** in passing. Enjoy **Nine Horse Hill** (Mural Hill) with the veins resembling prancing and playing horses. The interesting vegetation on **Folded Brocade Hill** causes you to pole to the edge and examine the variety of flora. **Crescent Moon Hill** has a cave resembling a quarter-moon, supposedly hiding evil deities until nightfall.

Cormorant fishermen, with their pets tied with long strings at the neck to

The more prosaic aspect of Guilin with the mountains relegated to the background.

keep them from swallowing the catch, wave, as do the women on the bank rubbing the washing against the rocks. Running children try to follow the boat laughing and shouting greetings. **Yangdi** village is about halfway, fortunately the water level is high enough and you can plod on to **Yangshuo**.

Yangshuo, the cruise destination is 80 km from Guilin and transportation awaits the passengers. They must run the gauntlet of souvenir hawkers by the landing and are given a few minutes to browse through the town's open market. The return trip by road is 2 hours offering a view of the countryside, following the river.

Some veteran travelers choose a different trip, preferring to take a bus or car to Yangshuo and then hiring a small boat to drift farther down the River Li, said to be rural and uncluttered with tourist debris.

Guangxi Province has more to offer after seeing Guilin and Yangshuo. The climate and ambience are similar to Kunming and Yunnan Province, temperate most of the year.

Xingping and **Wuzhou** are downriver from Guilin, accessible by river boat, automobile or biking if you like to take your own time. Accommodations do not match those in the big cities but they are adequate and inexpensive. Check your luggage in Guilin, take a swagbag backpack, rent a bicycle and wheel off, free as a breeze.

The minorities of southern China

Houseboats on the Li River in Guilin.

adorn the countryside and enhance its beauty. Twelve minorities inhabit Guangxi including the Miaos, Yaos, Dongs and the Zhuangs, one of the largest groups in China. Throughout the area are relics and memorabilia of the Buddhist life of the Zhuang people.

The minorities dress in bright colors, embroidered vests and collars, bright shirts, skirts and trousers. Women embellish their hair and some headpieces are designed with a platform to carry food and supplies on. The change from the austere Han People in other parts of China are drastic and demonstrates the independence of the minorities and their sense of identity.

Xingping was once a trading town, the river being the highway to Hong Kong. Today the narrow streets, choked with buildings and shops, are still in evidence. At the wharf you will see the cormorant fishermen gather at dusk to take their trained slaves out to fish for them. An offer of a few yuan will get you a trip out to watch the crafty birds fill the baskets with the catch.

Wuzhou is reputed to be the oldest city in the province of Guangxi graced with the same ethereal beauty of the more famous Guilin. The **Wuzhou Museum** and **Xizhu Garden Nunnery** provide interesting tours.

The cuisine of Wuzhou is world famous because of its game exports of tortoise, civet and thousands of snakes.

Representative of the Miao tribe, one of twelve minorities living in Guangxi.

With good fortune you will be able to devour the valuable tonics of snake gall, snake's blood and three-snake wine. More palatable to the western visitor is papilote chicken. Small birds are boned, wrapped in bamboo paper with spices and ginger and then fried.

Little boat congee is a famous local dish served in the night market, a small boat partitioned and filled with condiments to add to your bowl of rice congee. Fill your bowl and then choose from the selection of delectable additives: peanuts, dried fish, pickled vegetables, noodles, eggs new and old, meats and poultry—everything you have ever dreamed about tasting.

You can reach **Liuzhou** and **Nanning** by boat heading west along the Xunjiang River. **Liuzhou** is the geographical center of Guangxi appearing as an island surrounded by the River Li on 3 sides. **Marquise Liu Park** memorializes a poet and writer from the 7th century. The most profitable product of this community is coffins and souvenir miniature models are available if you are looking for unusual souvenirs.

The **Geological Museum** (White Grotto) in Liuzhou is unique. The back caves of the grotto are used to display geological phenomena and its bearing to human life. Outside an ancient jungle is replicated containing prehistoric monsters, giant pandas and other Paleolithic animals.

Fishing with the cormorant in Guilin.

Nanning is the capital of the province, with a small population of 500,000. The city is proud of its age and heritage, displaying avenues adorned with a variety of fruit trees and homes with private gardens.

Explore **Yiling Cave**, once a subterranean river. **Xishan** (West Hill), in nearby Guiping, is known to be a quiet contemplative retreat for poets and sages.

An enormous night market provides the evening's meal, entertainment and shopping for locals and visitors

The Three Treasures of Guangxi

In and around Guilin the tropical fruit **Shatian pomelo** is an agricultural treasure. The pear-shaped grapefruit tastes succulent, has a pleasant aroma and is reputed to have 100 mg of Vitamin C in each 100 g of the juice, 10 times that of apple juice. The fruit is reputed to be a health booster and from rind to pits is used for food, medicine and candy.

Lingxiang grass is a perennial legume, used as a perfume, bug repellent and an ancient medicine. It is cured over a charcoal fire and is used for headaches, common colds, fever and dysentery. The essence is a favorite export item to other Asian countries that use it for soaps and perfumes because of its lingering fragrance.

The third treasure unique to Guangxi is the **Luohan fruit**, vine-grown like the gooseberry. A tale is told of a bee-stung farmer in Longjiang Village, Yongfu County who picked a fruit and rubbed it against his injured hand and the pain and swelling disappeared. The fruit was also discovered to have a pleasant aroma and flesh sweet to the taste.

A local doctor, Luohan, who gave his name to the fruit, further discovered the fruit had other medicinal properties. It could cure the cough and other alimentary illnesses. Rich in glucose and fructose, 300 times sweeter than refined sugar, it is used to pep up soft drinks as well as a cure for the common cold.

---

alike. Streets are shut off at dusk and the stalls roll in to replace the vehicles. Food is one of the stellar attractions offering an interesting variety that would at least arouse your curiosity. The bohemian crowd mixes with many of the colorfully clad minorities and the pervasive atmosphere is one of a carnival.

Turtle preparations are popular and considered a tonic. Chicken and duck, stewed, fried or boiled are prevalent as local dishes. Visitors have a natural reticence to eating out of the oft-used and doubtfully rinsed bowls.

Most locals carry their own chopsticks as do seasoned travelers.

The Dragon Boats gather for an annual festival, a glorious spectacle if you are fortunate enough to be there at the time. Caves dot the entire part of the province and are fascinating to explore offering unexpected experiences of nature undisturbed. Like other famous tourist traps, the touted feature leads you there but there are many other unexpected and delightful experiences awaiting you.

Man on a Dragon Float during the Dragon Boat Festival.

SIMMERING SOUTH

Guangzhou, Guangdong & Hainan

As 1997 approaches, 60 per cent of China's commerce will revolve around Guangzhou (Canton), Shenzhen and Hong Kong. China's official policy on Taiwan, Macao and Hong Kong is that they are provinces of the People's Republic of China (PRC). With Macao returning to the fold of the PRC in 1999 and Hong Kong in 1997, the world awaits with bated breath, the future of the boiling cauldron. Hainan Island is included because of its proximity and share of embryonic capitalists. Ancient history though prevalent is buried in the burgeoning capitalism. The fun is in seeing and comparing both.

The statue of the Five Rams symbolizes Guangzhou.

Nanning, capital of Guangxi Province (see Guilin section) is an interesting side trip with the possibilities of an esoteric adventure across the border of Vietnam. Trade and economics have forced militaristic fears onto the sidelines.

Guangzhou (Canton) like all large busi-

ness cities in the world is worth a short visit for enjoyment of luxury hotel life, shopping, eating and planning travel adventures. China is vast and will overhelm anyone with its temples, parks, tombs and history. Travelers are sometimes sated by the time they arrive in Guangzhou, tending to forgo the travel itch in the modern ambience. Nearby are pleasant hot spring and hill resorts to laze and lounge in for a couple of days. **Shenzhen**, besides being on the road to Hong Kong, has luxury resort hotels of some interest if you want to loll around a swimming pool at less than Hong Kong prices with a little more space to breathe in.

Shenzhen and Guangzhou are often used as a paradigm for Hong Kong tourists who have not the time or inclination to travel extensively in China. A day trip or overnight stay will give an impression and perhaps a yen to come again and stay longer.

For an off-beat way to wind up a China odyssey from Guangzhou, drive to **Zhuhai**, across from Macao. Spend a few days in the luxury resort there and in Macao before returning by hovercraft or jetfoil to Hong Kong.

Hainan Island, however, is a different story. It is idyllic. Once more you can get on the road with a car and circle the island and enjoy small towns and

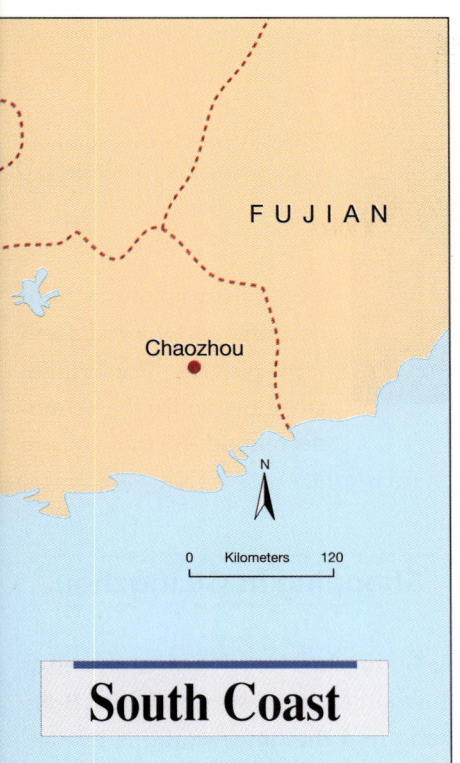

the Dutch, the British and the French. The early contact with foreigners fashioned its theological bias, architecture, culture and culinary splendor and fired its people with a revolutionary zeal. Among the prominent Cantonese revolutionaries who have colored China's checkered history are : Hung Hsiu-chuan (leader of the Taiping Rebellion), Liang Chichao and Kang Yuwei of the 1898 Reform Movement and Sun Yatsen, the father of modern China who spearheaded the 1911 revolution which broke the dynasty order.

Guangzhou is probably the most familiar Chinese place to the outside world because of the hundreds of thousands of Cantonese and Hakka who emigrated to other parts of Asia, United States, Canada, Australia and in some degree, to every corner of the world. They share a style of cuisine, a work-effort philosophy, a family and ethnic cohesion.

Shamian Island was once called island of the former concessions, the exclusive enclave of the British and the French. The infamous sign "No Chinese or dogs allowed" is always noted by historians who recorded the era of the barbarians. Less than a kilometer in length, 2 bridges and the private road of the White Swan Hotel join it to the mainland. Apartment blocks loom amid the vestiges of the foreign buildings, historically important banks, trading houses and consulates.

You might as well stay at a modern hotel like the White Swan on Shamian

coastal resorts. The tropical ambience ensures a plenitude of fresh fruit, vegetables and bountiful yields of the sea.

Both Guangdong Province and Hainan Island can easily be added at the last minute to your travel itinerary.

Guangzhou - Guangdong Province

Sprawling on the delta of the Zhujiang (Pearl River), the city of **Guangzhou** (Canton) has been in contact with the outside world for more than 2,000 years. The Arab seafarers were there. So were the Portuguese Jesuits, the Spaniards,

The city port of Guangzhou once known as Canton.

Island because there is little charisma of ancient China in the Dong Feng or glamorous China Hotel. Because of the White Swan's slight isolation on Shamian Island, it is possible to peek at Guangzhou through a window.

Transportation is no problem, taxis stack up waiting for you. Walking at night, out of the back door of the hotel into the *hutongs* of the island is like wending through a secret garden gate. The crass materialism of modern capitalism contrasts starkly with the real world of the locals.

On a warm evening, the apartment windows and doors are open, fans whir in the air, porches are filled with the old ones, lovers walk in the park looking in vain for a bit of privacy. Raucous western music grates from dozens of portable radio and tape players. The bridges crossing a soiled river channel remind you that you are on an island.

Shopping in Guangzhou

As Guangzhou is so heavily endowed as the vaunted gatepost to capitalistic Hong Kong and the outer world, it is often forgotten as a tourist stop. Non-business visitors have an infinite variety of shopping at their disposal. **Beijing Road**, though not as long as Nanjing Road in Shanghai, is qualified as one of the most complete shopping areas in China.

Zhongshan Wulu Department

Mother and child on a street in Guangzhou.

Eating Cantonese

Cantonese cuisine is exported all over the world and that of Guangzhou is credited with being the finest in China, challenging the gourmet's ambitions to seek them out and sample the rare dishes.

The Banxi (Friendship) Restaurant, along Longjin Xilu, overlooks a lake and sprawling gardens and is famous for its dumplings, chicken in tea leaves, roast pork and Beijing Duck. It is large and accommodates over a thousand guests in various pavilions.

The Snake Restaurant serves snake breast stuffed with shelled shrimp, stir fried assorted snake shreds, cat or dog meat. If you know the chef you might be able to get something cooked with snake bile guaranteed to promote blood circulation and release wind.

On the less adventurous side, the 80-year-old 8-storey **Datong Restaurant** is just off Remin Lu overlooking the river. Ask for a table on the rail for a romantic candlelight dinner of crisp fried suckling pig, duck or chicken.

The Guangzhou Restaurant, known as "the first house in Canton", is a 4-storey affair offering a garden ambience. Dating from the 30's, it is reputed to have the finest chefs in China, entertaining royalty, officials and dignitaries. It is located along Wencheng Nanlu.

For a taste of Cantonese, western, eastern, northern and southern cuisine, heaps of marvelous food is on the China Hotel's buffet luncheon. Come early, stay late and have a sedan chair ready to ferry you to your hotel. You won't need much more than an apple and a Tums/Rolaid for dinner.

Don't worry about addresses and phone numbers, they are well known at your hotel concierge's desk. Let him book a table for you and write an instruction note for the taxi driver. Keep a card from the hotel for the return trip. The nice sophisticated daytime taxi drivers go home to their families at dinner time. Night drivers are a different breed with tourist communication skills of -.05 to 1 on a scale of l-10.

Shamian Island was once a European enclave.

Poster on Beijing Road, a shopping area.

Guangzhou Trade Fair

The trade fair, largest in China, is held in the spring (15 April to 15 May) and in the fall (15 October to 15 November), drawing 50,000 to 100,000 buyers annually. Technically you need an invitation to attend the fair, obtained by requesting it directly or aided by a Chinese business organization. You can have the CITS intercede on your behalf as a happenstance business person wanting to attend or go directly to the registration desk with a business or professional card.

The official and more time consuming way is to apply directly to Guangzhou Trade Fair, Guangdong Province, China, at least 6 months before your trip. Your letter should include an outline of your business inclination, volume and scope of merchandise. You will receive either an invitation or a more involved application requesting further details.

International buyers flood the halls, rooms and exhibit areas seeking products without having to travel into the interior. Almost every province in China sends a trade delegation to Guangzhou to participate in the fairs with samples of their products. In between the major fairs, mini-fairs are held in the hotels with specific invitations to listed buyers.

Travel note: Despite the thousands of hotel rooms in Guangzhou the "Fully Booked" sign is always out during these periods. Even Hong Kong gets overbooked as the world's merchants beat a hasty path to the doors of China. The trick is to come later in the trade fair periods and fax the hotel a credit card guarantee. The best times are the last 2 weeks when the masses of merchants have drained their money and left the city.

Retail stands with special prices are opened on the fair grounds, especially for the foreign buyers and tourists who wish to make small personal purchases. Wholesale purchasing works on a different level and is more complicated. Payment can be made by obtaining a cash advance at the Bank of China office in the complex on your credit card. Most business firms use Letters of Credit or electronically transfer funds from their bank to the Bank of China. Foreign currency is acceptable to exchange for yuan at the bank. In rare instances the selling organization will ask for US Dollars in cash because they get a special premium from the government in some way. So, if you want to buy something, they will figure out a way to take your money.

Shipment of goods is arranged on the spot with insurance and transportation costs padded to the price. Wholesale prices are considerably lower than retail and there are minimum dollar quantities in most cases of US$10,000.

Always project yourself as a business buyer with great potential for future purchases to ensure an automatic invitation the following fair date. The invitation itself gives you an automatic visa on presentation at any of the international Chinese Consulates, Embassies or CITS offices. They give you 2 months as a rule. After the fair you are free to travel independently or on arranged CITS tours.

Store is at the intersection of Zhongshan and Beijing. A large music store to purchase traditional Chinese instruments and martial arts paraphernalia is next and then a medicine and fascinating aquarium shop. Clothing, arts and crafts, books and hardware, games and sporting goods, art supplies and cookware totter on the crossroads of the major intersection. A full afternoon will fray the most avid shop-o-holic.

Remin Road is another shopping strip extending from the Zhujiang up to Zhongshan. A modern 3-storey **Friendship Store** is next to the Dongfang Hotel selling everything from groceries to the general arts and crafts produced in China. Across the street from the Dongfang is the **Guangzhou Trade Fair Complex** open in the spring and fall,

drawing a hundred thousand or more buyers from around the world.

Three major antique-curio shops are in Guangzhou for the connoisseur willing to spend the time and money to acquire treasures no more than 120 years old (any item older is restricted from export).

They are Guangzhou Antiques Shop on Wende Road, Antiques Shop on Honshu Road and Guangzhou Antiques Export Company on Honshu Road. Be sure to have the hotel concierge give full instructions to the taxi. It is common practice to have the taxi wait (small charge) until you have finished shopping and are ready to return.

Sightseeing in Guangzhou

For scenery touring in the immediate area, **Yuexiu Park** about does it all. Sprawling over 250 acres it is more for the people than the visitor, except those interested in the history of the revolution. The **Sculpture of the Five Goats** symbolizes the city's mythical origin. The original tale says that 5 immortals descended from heaven on goats to found the city. Goat Brand still symbolizes some of Guangdong's products and the name Yangchen (Goat City) is often referred to by elder Chinese.

Zhenhailou (Tower Overlooking

The extensive Yuexiu Park.

the Sea) is a 5-storey pagoda on top of the highest hill dating back to 1380, surviving wars and countless renovations. It houses the **Guangdong Historical Museum** displaying an interesting succession of Chinese artifacts as you ascend.

The **Sun Yatsen Monument and Memorial Hall** was built soon after the famous leader died. His last will and testament for China is inscribed at the base. Sun Yatsen, born in Guangzhou, fathered the 1911 Revolution that ended the 5,000 years of dynastic rule in China.

Home of Sun Yatsen in Cui Leng Village, Zhongshan, Guangdong.

He founded the Kuomintang (Nationalist Party) here in 1923 and trained the future Communist leaders at the Huangpu Military Academy. The theater inside the hall seats 5,000 people without a pillar to obstruct anybody's view. With good fortune you might attend a rare cultural performance at the time you are there.

There is an orchid garden, lakes and sports stadiums that sometimes hold interesting events. A day or night cruise on the **Zhujiang** (Pearl River) is a better way to see the city than cruising in a taxi through the constant grid lock of the streets. In the city, **Linhua Park** is next to the Dongfang Hotel, and **Cultural Park** huddles the Zhujiang. The Cultural Park has permanent exhibits and is the site for major events in the complex of exhibition halls, floral gardens, aquarium, opera house and concert hall.

The **Guangzhou Zoo** is reputed to be the largest in China with over 200 species including giant pandas. If temples are your cup of tea, **Liurong Si** (Temple of the Six Banyan Trees) is 5th century, serving currently as the headquarters of the Guangzhou Buddhist Association. **Huaisheng Mosque** is reputed to have been built by the first person to bring the Koran to China in the 7th century. The recently restored Gothic style **Roman Catholic Cathedral** was built in 1860 by a French architect. Services are currently held on Sunday.

A day in the life of a riverboat family.

For botanists and keen home gardeners, the **South China Botanical Gardens** is the largest in China (300 hectares) and is internationally respected. The best use of the park is to escape the city's smog and traffic for a morning or afternoon and relax on the pathways barricaded by the luxuriant greenery.

Guangzhou Environs

White Cloud Hills, 9 km from Guangzhou, is a scenic area often used for a weekend out of the city. The hill to climb is easy for those who have conquered the Emeishan and Huangshan. The peak Moxingling (Star Touching Peak) is 382 m, a leisurely half hour of mild effort. For a day trip the peak has pavilions and teahouses to rest in after the easy climb.

For a little self-indulgence, check into one of the 2 very luxurious hotels at the mountain, Shanzhuang and Shuangxi, with private villas, sunken spas, individual gardens and bamboo forests. They are used by important overseas Chinese and diplomatic VIPs from Hong Kong, Macao and Shenzhen. Weekends are usually fully booked, try a weekday and call direct.

Take a boat-trip to **Lotus Mountain** for a change of pace. It leaves early in the morning and gives you about 5 hours to lunch and roam the mountain before returning in the afternoon.

If you feel the need for a recuperative day or weekend, book a car to **Conghua Hot Springs** (81 km north of Guangzhou). The **Conghua Hot Springs Guesthouse** guarantees to relieve you of everything that ails you physically including headaches, stress and gynecological problems.

The side trips take a day; try going on weekdays. The 5 million residents of Guangzhou plus the thousands of well-heeled business travelers also use the getaways.

A Ride out of Guangzhou

The Guangzhou to Hong Kong thoroughfare is always busy whether by air, train, bus or hovercraft. The White Swan Hotel has a travel concourse to take care of your needs. All major hotels have travel desks or agents.

Zhenzhen is easier reached by train where you catch the electric trolley for Hong Kong. CAAC and Cathay Pacific fly daily to Hong Kong. A half-hour flight but an hour by taxi through traffic, 2-hour pre-flight and customs time leeway are about the time a hovercraft takes to make its multiple trips daily to Hong Kong. The water route, if you are not carrying too much luggage, is a way to escape the large crowds at the airport and train stations.

Another way to travel out of China in a leisurely manner is to hire a car and drive to **Zhuhai**, a 75-sq km Special Economic Zone across the waterfront from Macao. The 4 or 5-hour drive is a pleasant scenic tour of the lakes and canals of the Zhujiang Delta. Stop halfway at the small cobblestoned market town of **Zhongshan** or **Shiqi** (Shekkei) as it was once known. Non-tourist oriented markets are more natural and colorful and there is even a Ming Dynasty pagoda to visit.

Zhongshan Hot Springs Resort is an interesting stopover. More intriguing is the Zhuhai Sez Gongbei Hotel designed in the Qin Dynasty imperial style. Across the river is the gambling palace, Lisboa Hotel in Macao to get the adrenaline going when you tire of relaxing.

Zhangjiang – Guangdong Province

Zhanjiang, Guangdong Province is less than a day's drive east from Guangzhou. The aggressive China tourism moguls are taking advantage of this city port. Haibin Hotel is a reconditioned Hong Kong joint-venture affair with amenities and operated by Hong Kong staff. For overseas Chinese, Canton Bay Overseas Chinese Hotel is adequate. A scuba diving enterprise is developing and offers trips to the offshore coral reefs. A combined bus-boat ticket takes you to across the straits to **Haikou** on Hainan Island.

The less adventurous can return to Guangzhou. Depending on weather conditions, CAAC flies daily to Haikou

Trucks queue at Shenzhen to return to Hong Kong.

on hurricane-scarred Hainan Island. They fly by their own rules however. Canceled domestic flights do not give you a free hotel and first up on the next flight. CAAC's system of the-passenger-is-the-last to know becomes frustrating. Queue up with the other disconcerted travelers to find out when the next flight might leave and go back to the hotel for another night of fancy bed and good food.

Shenzhen - Guangdong Province

Shenzhen is often referred to as the backdoor of Hong Kong where raw materials are sent in to be turned into finished products before being sent back to Hong Kong again. Shenzhen is an area created to provide cheap labor and a business address within daily commuting distance to Hong Kong. The largest investors of joint ventures in Shenzhen are Hong Kong businessmen who recognize the labor pool and have the language and contact ability to work with the PRC's officials.

Shenzhen is a useful getaway for those who need to escape the hyperenergetic mayhem of Hong Kong for a weekend. They just cross the border into China and relax at one of the resort hotels. The Shenzhen Golf Co, Ltd on Shen Nan Road is a villa-style hotel, golf resort with Japanese baths, tennis, swimming and bowling facilities. Overseas

A relic from the Opium War at the mouth of the Zhuijiang.

Forum Hotel is a business-oriented joint venture and the Asia Hotel is a modern 33-storey building, well-equipped for a short stay.

Shantou - Guangdong Province

Off the beaten track, Shantou, once intended as a rival of Guangzhou, is an hour's flight away. At the Treaty of Tianjin in 1855, foreign concessions were granted to Great Britain at the end of the Opium War. The large population dispersed with the close of foreign trading with thousands of Hakka and Min emigrating to other parts of Asia. A large percentage of today's population has financial contacts with overseas relatives thus creating a kind of private network and the city is burgeoning with joint ventures from former residents.

Shantou, with this largess, is now a Special Economic Zone producing textiles, electronics, industrial, agricultural and aqua-cultural commodities. The fun and interest for visitors is to view the European colonial architecture almost as it was 150 years before. The balmy weather and a lovely beach resort on **Mayu Island** is a plus factor for an inexpensive getaway.

Less than an hour's drive away is **Chaozhou**, with a history dating from the Sui Dynasty (581-618). Quite untouched by the chaos of the Cultural Revolution, the Buddhist temple

Hong Kong

Hennessy Road in Hong Kong.

The gateway and financial funnel to China, Hong Kong is also the main tourist springboard into the Chinese hinterland. In 1997 Hong Kong will return to the fold of China, a stellar event which will take the center stage in world affairs when the time comes.

Major international airlines fly into Kaitak Airport, a narrow strip of repossessed land in Kowloon. Gleaming hotels provide a galaxy of star-studded accommodations. Hundreds of restaurants dish out the gamut of Chinese and international cuisine. A plethora of department stores, shops, stalls, boutiques and branches of mainland Chinese arts and crafts department stores parade the full panoply of international artware, jewelry, clothing, electronics, ad infinitum. It is said that if you can't buy it in Hong Kong, the thing probably doesn't exist.

A raging misconception is that greater Hong Kong is part of China. It is actually a leasehold of Great Britain, expiring in 1997. **Hong Kong** proper is an island with restricted space for the multi-million living and working population. **New Territories** is a 350-sq mile peninsula encompassing over 200 islands with the principal city of **Kowloon**. The major tourist action thrusts and throbs with shops, transportation agencies, the airport, multitudes of hotels and restaurants.

The famous Star Ferry, a tunnel and a subway system connects Hong Kong with Kowloon. Hovercraft and jetfoil Boeing boats link Macao and Guangzhou to the island piers. Daily trains, flights and coastal steamers also provide access to the mainland of China

At the height of tourism, 4 million visitors arrive annually in Hong Kong, thus the first concern is reservation of a hotel room. Tour groups have pre-booked allotments and travel agents have direct lines to the major hotel chains. Independent travelers have their frequent traveler membership cards and favorites depending on the degree of luxury, cost and location. Luxury hotels will cost more than US$150 per day. Heading the list is the venerable Peninsula, followed by the more flighty Regent, and Shangri-La in the Kowloon enclave called Tsimshatsui. The Kowloon, Hong Kong, Sheraton, Holiday Inn (Harbor View and Golden Mile), Marco Polo, World Trade are only a few of the better known hotels. All accept reservations with credit card guarantee, space permitting, and most have international telephone reservation services. Independent travelers will request the top 2 or 3 on their list and wait for an approval before selecting. (To note: Kowloon Hotel, another hotel efficiently operated by the Peninsula on an adjacent street, is modest in price and has tiny rooms but it offers good ambience and impeccable service and food.)

The CITS offices can ordinarily arrange your China visa and travel request within 48 hours. Do all your research, have your tentative schedule and itinerary well planned with 2 visa photos ready before you visit the office. Get there at the crack of the opening hour to avoid the long lines and frenetic hubbub. The hotels have travel agency desks if you care to use them but they will try to sell you packages.

Final note: 3 days in Hong Kong is the minimum without any sightseeing time allotted. Six days in hyper Hong Kong is dangerous to your nervous system.

Rice fields of the Zhujiang Delta, Guangdong Province.

Kaiyuan, built in the 8th century, and other secular art treasures and buildings are well-preserved. Reputed for its opera, a unique style of embroidery and porcelain, Chaozhou is a treasure trove. West Lake rivals the scenic and ancient beauty of Hangzhou's West Lake.

Chaozhou-Swatow cuisine is similar to Cantonese cuisine in the ample use of fresh vegetables in lightly fried and steamed dishes.

Shantou International Hotel, managed by the Lee Gardens Group of Hong Kong provide comfortable modern accommodations with facilities.

For a delightful wrap-up of this travel treasure, take the steamer Dinghu which sails every other day to Hong Kong.

Nanning – Guangxi Province

Nanning (see Guilin Section also) is strategically located for trade with Vietnam with access to the Gulf of Tonkin. There are daily flights to Guangzhou and Kunming. Train service is excellent north to Guilin and south to Zhanjiang, the coastal port to Hainan Island. An auto-tour can be arranged with CITS to circle west to the border town of Pingxiang, south to Dongxing, east to Zhanjiang. From there either return to Guangzhou or cross the gulf to Haikou on Hainan Island.

This adventurous trip takes you to the lovely southern countryside and the

2 border crossings to Vietnam. If you are game, wind up the tour in Guangzhou.

Free markets abound in Nanning, selling the border products from the south and imported gray-market goods from Hong Kong. Independent tourists always enjoy a bargain such as a sturdy hammock for 2 or 3 yuan, or a grimy wood-carving that portrays a finely carved Ho Ti when cleaned up. Nanning features Dragon Boat Races on the 5th day of the 5th lunar month (usually May or June) if you are lucky enough to co-ordinate a schedule.

The **Nanning Arts Institute** showcases colorful local crafts of bamboo, lacquerware and stone carving. Outside Nanning, the **Yiling Stalactite Cave** is a massive display of nature's underground wonders, augmented slightly with some artificial lighting.

Yongzhou Hotel is air-conditioned with modern amenities for general travelers. Yongjiang Hotel is reserved for overseas Chinese and is centrally located.

Due west from Nanning is the **Dietan Falls** on the Vietnam border, a magnificent sight with a surprise at the lower reaches. The Vietnamese have a pontoon bridge at this point and they bundle goods to an enormous market on the Chinese side. They bring in farm produce and craft merchandise to trade for the sophisticated manufactured goods of China. An interesting part of the road show is the trading in Vietnamese currency to the Chinese at about 2,000 to one. Counting bills would be laborious and inconvenient so they bundle the bills together in bricks, bound with string or metal staples.

Heading south, along the border, the next stop is **Shuikoujie** and then on to **Pingxiang**. At various points along the border, river boats ferry people back and forth for trading. It is possible to ride across, put the little toe onto Vietnamese soil and then return. Guard points are further inland at road crossings. Thread through **Friendship Pass**, where the mountain peaks form a narrow valley far below. Vestiges of the Sino-Viet war are still evident. Soldiers now guarding the pass while away their time watching television and amusing themselves in the current peace.

Nongyao is a new marketplace-town developed since the war by the exigencies of trade countenanced by the 2 nations. Over 10,000 people now trade through the area with unique goods that could have been bartered thousands of years ago. Baskets are laden with crabs, frogs, turtles and snakes.

Chickens, ducks and geese are common. Gamecocks and dogs, confined to cages are for gambling and eating and are not particularly friendly to western palates.

Dongxing is at the point of the gulf with an even larger market aided by its location at the Beilun River, emptying into the Tonkin. Goods come down river on scows still pummeled with rear oars and pushing poles. A motorized tug will pull some of them back upstream laden with Chinese goods. Actually both the Chinese and the Vietnamese use their side of the river to bring their wares to market. Pony carts, tricycle wagons, ancient trucks and buses come down inland to join the throng.

A side trip can be engineered at this point to **Mong Cai** inside the Vietnamese border with proper passports. It is a free port area on both sides with traffic flowing back and forth showing minimal identification. Modest huts have attractive furnishings and restaurants abound with appetizing foods. Markets are laden with produce. The sartorial cuts of the masses hint at a thriving economy.

Hainan Island – Hainan Province

During the days of dynastic rule, Hainan was a deserted island for mandarins who fell from grace. It is the southernmost territory of the Middle Kingdom and on its beach are 2 imposing boulders etched with the words, "The End of the World". The island has turned adversity to advantage. Its proximity to the booming economies of Southeast Asia makes it a gleaming prospect for Southeast Asian investors. And coupled with its inherent wealth of copper, titanium and rubber, the "Island of Exile" has metamorphosed to "Treasure Island" and earned its right to be a Special Economic Zone.

Fly or take a boat from Guangzhou or Hong Kong to **Haikou**, the capital of Hainan Island. The prevailing practice is to stay the first night in Haikou and put together a road trip to circle the island for the next few days. Plan on a minimum of a week because Hainan, the "Island of Coconuts" is a relaxing auto-adventure which includes staying at an assortment of resorts.

With the current push for tourism and business, the landscape of Haikou has been dotted with hotels. The Haikou Tower is quite new with 240 rooms and equipped with modern amenities. Qiao Fa Hot Spring Hotel provides hot mineral baths and a hot spring swimming pool with sauna facilities.

The food is some of the best in China, featuring seafood and Hainanese chicken, an international dish that is on most of Hong Kong and Singapore menus. The enigma is that it is served differently in Hainan. A claypot with a whole chicken in soup is their style, rather than the neat slices of boiled chicken breast served with a bowl of rice and chicken broth other Asian diners

The Bountiful Coconut Palm

Travelers visiting Wenchang County on Hainan Island are amazed at the large quantities of palm trees and coconuts involved, and the innumerable inhabitants employed in the cash crop yield. To most travelers the palm tree is valuable as shade on the beach or a beautiful backdrop for a photograph, and the shell often as a container for a refreshing mixed cocktail to sip in the tropical ambience. To the villagers, the coconut palm is a lifestyle affording income, shelter, food and drink.

The empty shells are fashioned into souvenir dishes, nut bowls, lamps and other attractive decorative art-crafted items to furnish the local homes and sell to the tourists. The husk fibers are traditionally used for ropes and ship hawsers, brooms, and other household maintenance items. Wrapping peeled from the trunks become the tapa cloth used throughout the islands for decorated ceremonial garments and wall hangings.

Palm fronds are used as covering for the cottages and woven into hats, baskets, lampshades and toys for the children. Trunks of the palm are the poles used to lift and support the homes above damp and flood endangered ground areas. Boards are laboriously cut by hand for the floors and walls. Dexterous carpenters fashion furniture for the palm tree culture of the islanders. Woven fronds are fashioned into sheets for wall dividers for the interior and sometimes used for sails for their watercraft.

The commercial production, termed as "cash crop", turns the processed white kernel into coconut milk and cream for delicious cooking additives. Copra, the dried meat of the coconut, is pressed for coconut oil. The sap is milked from the trunk, its sugar content is fermented into an alcoholic drink.

The next time you visit a beach fringed with swaying palm trees, look for the mature coconut which is blown down by a wind, half-buried in the sand. From the 3 small holes in the exposed end, green shoots appear and roots sprout underneath. Reproduction is endless and has stretched interminably for thousands of years. Take a green one that swishes with the milk inside and have a native splice open the top with his machete exposing the soft holes. Ice it down, stick a straw in it when cold enough and enjoy one of nature's finest cocktails, while lounging in the shade of your benefactor.

---

are accustomed to.

Hainan's capitalists hit the headlines in 1985. Hainan was provided with a multi-million dollar Federal fund to get transportation, massive tourist and food export industries started. The local bureaucracy decided to invest instead in automobiles, motorcycles, television and other electronic equipment to sell to the mainland provinces at a handsome profit. By the time Beijing caught up with and stopped the shenanigans, US$1.5b had gone into setting up the store. There is a plenitude of transportation on the island today; the new fancy resorts are still at the planning stage.

Around Hainan Island

One possible route on the island is to take the east coast to the bottom of the island and then work your way up north through the heart. The west coast is heavily militarized from the years of war with Vietnam, and is not open to normal travel.

Accommodations are tropic-comfort which means board-hard beds, mosquito netting, abundant seafood and unspoiled beaches. Hainan Island is not yet for the rich and famous but ideal for the adventurous traveler.

Heading south down the east coast, **Wenchang** is less than a 100 km away. Coconut plantations, Dong Jiao Ye Lin and Juan Hua Shan Ye Lin, are on an offshore island accessible from the village of Qing Lan Gang. Take swimsuits and towels if the weather is amiable. The beaches are some of the best in China and often deserted.

Xincun is a fishing and pearl diving port, occupied by the Danjia Minority people. Open markets in the small communities are always a stopover treat. **Monkey Island** is a 10-minute ferry ride from Xincun, a free monkey preserve if you are into an open zoo environment. Feeding times bring the creatures out of the woods in the morning and late afternoon.

Relax for a few days at **Sanya**, a bridge-connected peninsula at the southern tip of Hainan Island. Dadonghai Tourism Center Hotel is on the best beach 3 miles east of Sanya. Fancy tourist hotels are planned and may be ready by the time you get there. Inquire before leaving Haikou. Xinglong Resort Center is also on the southeast coast offering private villas in a tropical plantation setting. On the lower end of the budget, the Dadonghai Beach Village has spartan accommodations and backpacker facilities if you desire to be a beach bum for a longer stay.

Luhuitou Hotel on the **Luhuitou Peninsula** is the nicest facility, providing air-conditioned mini-villas, and various suites for modest prices. These fine facilities encourage the traveler to stay for a week and maybe return the next year for a month. The gardens and rocky beach are beautiful for daytime walking and evening firefly watching.

The name Luhuitou means Deer Turns the Head, a fanciful tale of a young handsome hunter chasing a young doe over hill and dale for days finally trapping it on the peninsula. The doe suddenly turns into a beautiful girl and they live happily ever after on the lovely peninsula.

Hainan Experimental Marine Research Station is there experimenting in the 4,000-year-old pearl industry. Cultured pearls were created far before Mikimoto's experiments, in the Song Dynasty 900 years ago. **Xidao Dongdaom** coral islands offshore may be ready for divers and snorkelers.

On the leisurely road back up the central spine of Hainan Island, stop for the night at **Tongshi**, capital of Li and Miao Autonomous Prefectures. The Tongza Holiday Resort, modern shopping mall and surprising highrises are the result of the largess mentioned before.

The road from Tongshi carves through a delightful thick forest to a small hill town called **Qiongzhong** for an overnight stay. The modest hotel and a chance to enjoy a lively market and a nearby waterfall at Baihuashan are worth the extra time. You could make it all the way back to Haikou in a day but that is no fun. Savor it slowly and relish the small villages and rural life spread leisurely along the route.

Three Gorges, Changjiang & Environs

ARTERY OF THE EAST

Variety is said to be the spice of life and nowhere is it more evident than in this particular part of China. The Changjiang (Yangtse) is considered the main artery of eastern China. Chongqing, the capital of Sichuan, is near the geographical heart of the nation, lying outside the autonomous regions of Qinghai and Tibet.

Book ahead with CITS as a FIT (Foreign Independent Traveler) or with one of the international travel agencies on one of the luxury passenger vessels which travel on the Changjiang between Chongqing and Wuhan through the Three Gorges.

Or, board a local steamer, the Jianghan, formerly called Big Red (or East is Red). Follow the Changjiang from Chongqing to Shanghai and stop at the small ports. Stop over for a few days at the major cities of Wuhan and Nanjing. From the port of Jiujang, take a side trip to Lushan Mountain Resort, summer retreat of the Politburo, or to Jingdezhen, the porcelain center of the nation. A month in this region would be none too long.

Sunrise, a silent drama on the Three Gorges of the Changjiang.

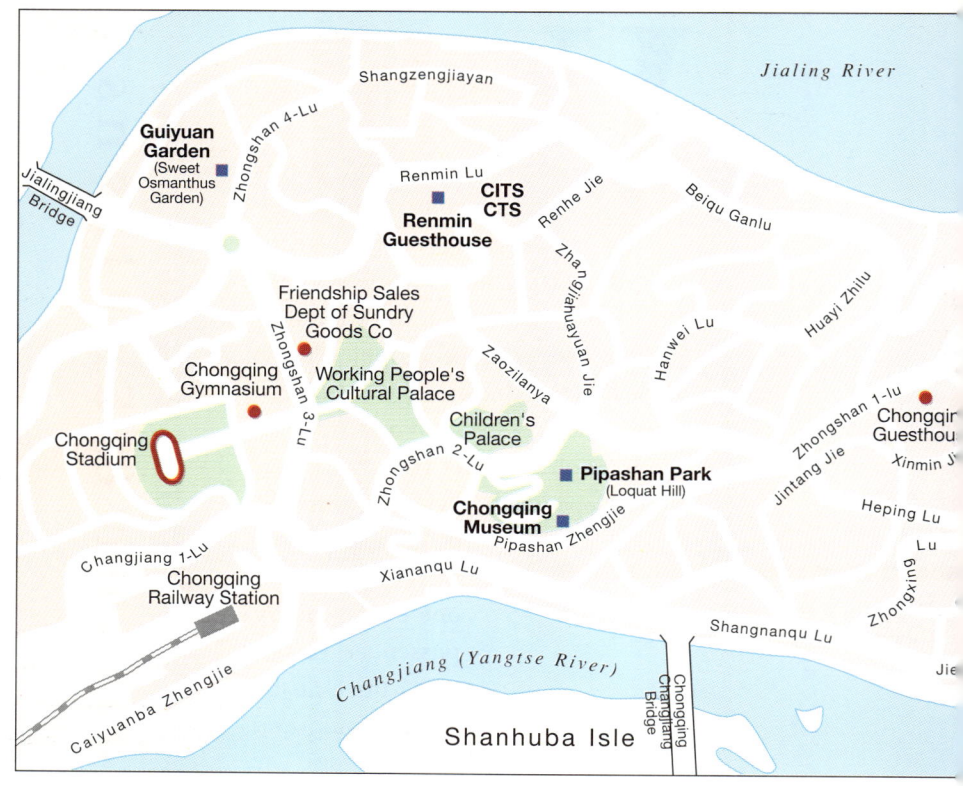

Chongqing – Sichuan Province

Chongqing has a volatile, interesting history, caught up as it was in China's many 20th century wars. It became China's capital when the Japanese pushed the Kuomintang government west. Chongqing translates as "twin fortune", named as such by Emperor Zhao Dun of the Southern Song Dynasty (1127-1279) when he succeeded to the throne in 1190 soon after he was made king of the region of Gong.

Fog often blankets the city during the winter months, leaving April through September as the best time to be there. Chongqing is accessible from most of the major cities in China and there are sometimes charter flights from Hong Kong. There is a train service but it is a long ride from Shanghai or Beijing. Be sure to specify Chongqing in Sichuan Province when you book the ticket. It can be confused with Changchun in Jilin Province, (see Northeast Section).

One of the largest cities in China, Chongqing has more than 6 million people. The city has been built on hills and sits on the edge of a cliff divided by 2 major waterways, the Changjiang and the Jialing River. Houses with black roofs nest on the sides of the mountain, often

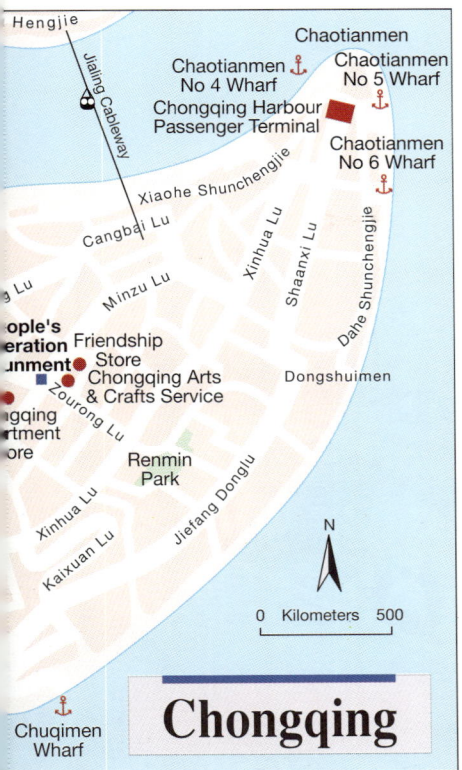

with their front doors on the top floor. At the top of the cliff you can get some of the best views of Chongqing encompassing the river from the river control command post and the busy **Chaotianmen Dock** below.

The Remin Hotel is a traditional guesthouse, one of the most beautiful in all China. Two wings surround a gallery with a 4000-seat auditorium. Tiered roofs, red-trimmed pillars, green tiles, turned up eaves with strange little animals designed to keep evil spirits away, are a welcome relief from the Hong Kong joint ventures and Russian style block buildings. It is one of the few times you will feel an aura of past oriental grandeur in a hotel residence, albeit one with modest room accommodations.

There are many other excellent hotels. The Chongqing Guesthouse and the Chongqing Hotel have been renovated and are ready for foreign guests. The Holiday Inn Yangtse Chongqing and a newer Holiday Inn Yangzijiang are on the international hotel reservation lists. For charm, the Xiao Quan Hotel near the Southern Hot Springs Park, an hour's drive from town, supplies piped-in spring water baths. VIPs are booked into the Yuzhou Guesthouse, a walled park-compound 20 minutes out of town.

Loquat Hill Park (Pipa Shan) sits on the highest hill point in Chongqing. The gardens include a bonsai nursery, while the paths and rest spots are often occupied by the old men playing chess or an unusual card game. The tea garden is pleasant for lunch or afternoon tea. You can have an overview of the city from the gardens and Chongqing after dark is a spectacle. **Chongqing City Museum** is in the park if you care to see some of their later exhibits including dinosaur skeletons unearthed in the region.

Be forewarned, Chongqing is as hilly as San Francisco. Three hundred steps up one side is the norm up Loquat Hill and it is another 300 steps down the opposite path to the dock area.

Either **South Spring Park** or **North Spring Park** is a pleasant day's outing. Walk the many trails through the wooded areas; rent a boat and paddle

A bridge across the Changjiang, the longest river in China, in Nanjing.

downstream. Bridges and tiny islands with pavilions decorate the meandering waterway.

A mineral spring swimming pool is available if you feel the need for an odiferous dip. Inside the locker room, individual hot or cold tubs are rented out by the hour to soak yourself in. As onerous as it may seem, try the mineral waters for the experience. The body will appreciate what the nose finds overpowering.

One of the best restaurants recommended is the South Springs Park with a

after which everyone sighs with relief, belches loudly and pockets the chopsticks for a souvenir. A meal at the time would cost Y16.50 (about US$4.00) per person.

Take a walk down the road outside the park through the local village. You will never tire of walking through small villages without guides, to mingle with the people and exchange a *"Ni hao, Ni hao ma"*, and wave goodbye with a *"Tsai jian"*. Language is no barrier to friendly spirits.

Jiefang Bei is the city square. Emanating from **Zongshan Lu**, intriguing shops draw you into their dark interiors offering treasures of old prints, water pipes, stone seals, porcelains and lacquerwares. On the other side, down **Shangqing Si** are the largest food markets and small restaurants with sidewalk tables where you can have tea and watch people. You can take the cable cars linking the banks of the river from **Yangtse Bridge**. The **River Control Peak** above the docks offer marvelous panoramas of the 2 rivers.

Chongqing Environs

Take time for a day's side trip out of Chongqing before you leave on the Big Red. **Dazu**, nearby **Beishan** (North Moutain) and **Baodingshan** (Treasure Moutain) together are less than 200 kms away. The countryside is lush with growing crops. Buddhist memorabilia dot the area as if they have been pep-

multi-course dinner offered for a flat fee. Share a table for 8 with other guests and spin the lazy susan as the first few courses fill you up. Hors d'oeuvres would include smoked fish, kidney slices, hot sliced radish (remember we are in Sichuan). Then come the main courses comprising substantial tasty local dishes. A light broth is always the last course

Navigating the gorges along the Changjiang.

pered by the great Sakyamuni himself. Beishan's famous site of Amitayus-Dyanasutra has 600 figures in honor of the Master of the Western Paradise, Buddha Amitabha.

On **Baodingshan**, 15 km from Dazu, massive sculptures are cut into cliffs and mountain sides. Guanyin (Goddess of Mercy) is depicted with 1000 arms and a 30-meter long reclining Buddha entering *nirvana*. Most travelers hurry to board the Changjiang boats and ignore the fun of wandering through the streets, to follow in the footsteps of Zhou Enlai, Mao Zedong, Chiang Kaishek and Emperor Zhao Dun. Remember, the emperor had good fortune twice and is willing to share it if you stay around long enough.

Sailing along the Changjiang

There are 2 ways of traveling up or down river. One is to book on one of the luxury cruise boats now engaged in shuttling tourists between Chongqing and Wuhan. This cruise is second only to the Xian Digs in popularity, after the Great Wall of course. On average the boats will take 5 days to travel downriver and 7 days up, stopping at specific cities for sightseeing.

The alternative is to go independently on the daily public steamer, originally called the Big Red (East is Red). The boats have been renamed for various cities and operate under the combined

On a Public Steamer along the Changjiang

Crowds hustle down the 300 odd steps in **Chaotianmen Dock** in the early dawn in order to depart at 5:30 am. A taxi and guide would have picked you up in the dark at the hotel two hours before. Departure is at first light. (You can board the night before for a small extra charge.) The dawn is damp and shivery, breakfast a roll and jam from the swagbag as it is too early for the hotel dining room. This is one time and place to have your guide arrange beforehand for a porter at a nominal cost. It is a hand-carry job when you approach the docks and traipse down hundreds of steps. The ship's ladders, external and internal, are impossible to navigate with your luggage through the crowds of passengers. Your cabin is well marked on the ticket for the porter to take it all the way. Don't worry if you lose track of him enroute to the ship. For whatever reason, transportation personnel in China will rarely assist you with your luggage.

Like all Big Red coastal steamers, a second class cabin is the best available but it is clean and adequate. The 2 or 3 first class cabins are reserved for the Captain and VIP guests. Blankets are folded in a traditional rose pattern, siesta straw mats rolled at the foot and a filled thermos is at hand on a rack. A wash basin is in the room and shared toilets and a shower stall are around the corner next to the hot water boiler.

Third class cabins bunk 4, the next 8, and so on down to the steerage compartments with 24 or 30. First and second class entitle you to use the lounge on the foredeck and meals will be served there. The steward exchanges your ticket for a pasteboard or metal chit bearing your cabin number when you come aboard. On departure you settle the bill and get your voucher back. The chit is your identification when you go ashore, so keep it with you at all times.

As to the cruise ships, there are various levels of luxury but all with attached toilet and bath facilities, sold as singles, doubles or suites, prices, commensurate.

When the vessel pulls out into the river, it will sail past the factories which fade off into the soft greenery of terraced paddies. On the Big Red, the freight and passenger port stops are always interesting, each stop lasting sometimes an hour and once in a while, overnight. You are allowed to go ashore most of the time but stay close enough to the docks to hear the 15-minute warning whistle from the ship. Local customs and immigration are non-existent for boat passengers. Your cabin chit is a boarding pass and you can come and go freely in the port area.

Fresh fruit is usually available in the port, cooked delicacies are chancy hygiene-wise, but a fresh fish (one that is still wiggling) or a tied-up bunch of squirming mudcrabs can be brought aboard. The steward will arrange to have it steamed for you at the next meal. Turn down all other suggestions about preparation: steam cook with ginger and spices, is the only way. Laoshan bottled water and beer are available on the ship and a snack shop will have packaged crackers, cookies and sweets.

Take a map and the detailed description of the journey with you (available at the hotel book counter), otherwise you will never remember the interesting stops and often told tales of the journey of the spectacles to be seen.

name of Jianghan, but everyone still calls them the Big Red. You can disembark at almost any port and catch the next boat down by pre-booking the segments to suit your own program.

Bookings should be made in advance with the International Travel Agency or the CITS. There are often last minute openings, however, should you happen to decide to "Do the Changjiang" when in Shanghai. For the public steamer, bookings can also be made in advance at the main booking office in Chaotianmen Dock.

For the independent traveler, one suggestion to get the most out of your

Changjiang voyage, is to book 4 segments: Chongqing to Wuhan, 2 or 3 nights on board; Wuhan to Jiujang, 1 night on board ship, 3 on shore; Jiujang to Nanjing, 1 night on board ship, 4 on shore; Nanjing to Shanghai, 1 or 2 nights back on the boat. The variation depends on whether the Big Red is on an express or a milk-run schedule. The first 3 segments are on board the Big Red and for the last segment from Nanjing, you have a choice between a quick air flight or the slow boat. There is not a lot of interesting scenery in the last segment because the Changjiang widens to several kilometers at the mouth and the deltas are mud flats. Even if you have booked all the way to Shanghai, you might want to throw away the rest of the ticket and fly instead. To avoid complications, we will describe the voyage downstream from Chongqing to Shanghai. The boat may not be able to stop at the same destination when traveling upstream as it would be on a different time schedule and it would take a day or two longer.

The luxury cruise boats usually arrange to pick their passengers up in a group by bus and they provide a guide. On board the boats are interpreters and lectures on the stopover points with video presentations of the sights often given.

It would be a good idea to take a supply of food with you if you decide to travel on the boat. Food can range from poor to adequate on the Big Reds, but it will never be wonderful. The cruise boats are better equipped for foreign tastebuds and they charge accordingly.

A boy riding a buffalo in the lush countryside of Yunnan.

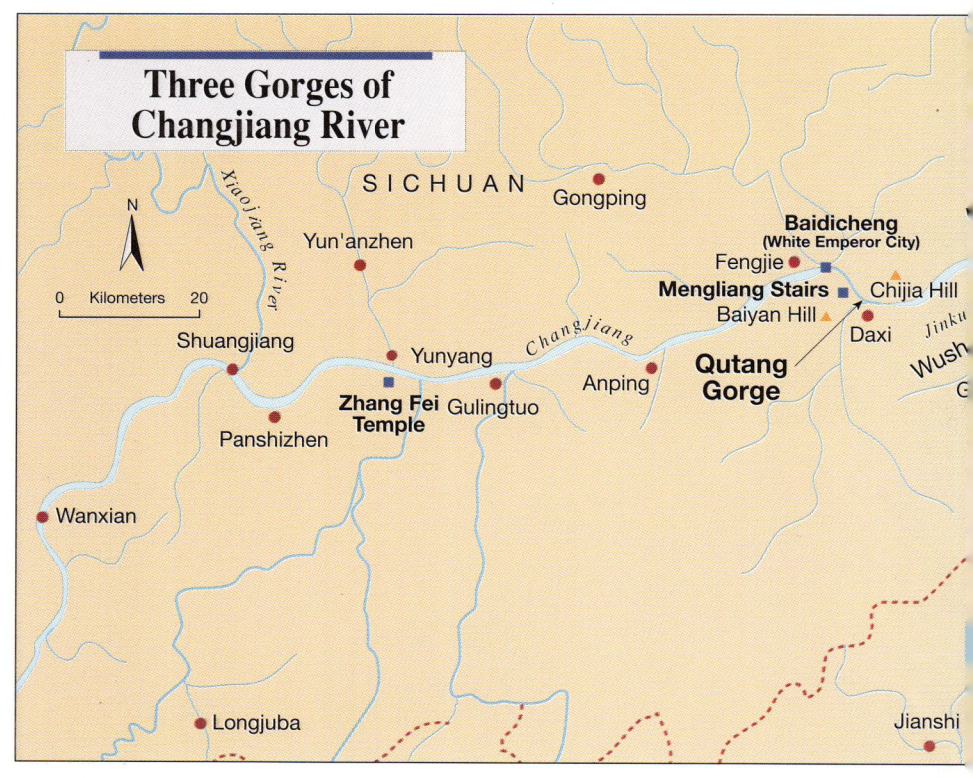

The Three Gorges

Each stop offers a fascinating view of everyday life along the river. Carry poles bent almost to the ground teeter on the shoulders of carriers. Families loaded with belongings, children backpacked or pushed ahead, merchants with high stacks of baskets, furniture and reed mats vie with each other to off-load their products.

Shibao Zai (Stone Treasure Stronghold) is the first overnight stop for the tour boats. A 90-meter high rock supports a mid-18th century Buddhist temple which an able-bodied can climb. The town has cobbled stone streets and thatched cottages which take you back in time. The boats leave late the next morning to arrive in Wanxian by early afternoon, docking there for the night.

On a shorter schedule, the Big Red boats dock at **Wanxian**, in the early evening of the first night. You have until 2 o'clock early the next morning to climb the long steps to the town, visit the man-made waterfalls and shop for souvenirs. The night market is waiting for the boat's passengers. You might want to try the delicious yellow grapefruit (pomelo). The town is famous for its oranges, tangerines and delicious peaches. Wanxian is also a big pro-

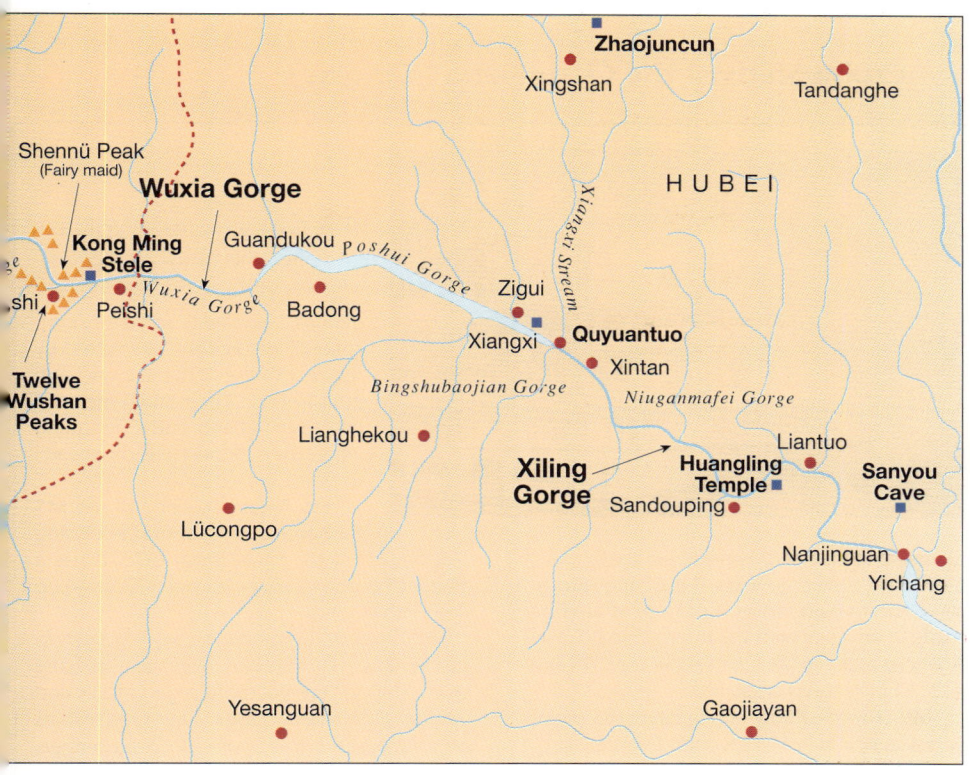

ducer of silk and leather.

If you have time to venture out, there are some historical sites in Wanxian's suburbs. Li Bai (701-762), a Tang Dynasty poet, is said to have read books on **Taibai Rock**. Forty cliff inscriptions, the Baiyan Academy and Taibai Temple are located nearby.

The Big Reds leave before dawn the next morning in order to negotiate the Three Gorges (Sanxia) by nightfall. They are the spectacular highlight of the trip, even if you have visited the Grand Canyon in the western United States.

Qutang Gorge, 8 km long, is the first of the 3 gorges to appear. Be up on deck and ready because in less than a half-hour the swift current will rush the boat through the opening at Kuimen Gate. Early morning fog creates an eerie ambience as the ship enters the narrow passageway. The waters froth from the eddies, the ship shudders as it heaves in the swells. Dawn is a mere glimmer of light in the deep bowels of the constricted corridor.

Qutang is considered the most spectacular gorge with the highest walls and narrowest passageway. The narrowest spots are only 100 to 150 m wide. Cliffs rise abruptly 500 to 700 m with the mountain peaks reaching as high as 1400 m. Some historical sites here include the **Meng Liang Staircase**, carved

Cruise Ships of the Changjiang (Yangtse)

A luxury cruise ship that plies the Changjiang.

Six passenger vessels, considered luxury class, and a few others now ply the Changjiang to serve the foreign visitor. Bookings should be made in advance with the International Travel Agencies as part of a China Tour or the CITS and CTS, China's travel agencies.

MV Yangzi Jiang, a 70-cabin, 65-meter vessel launched in 1983 is considered the largest and fastest (29 kph). It offers a 5-day cruise from either end of the Wuhan-Chongqing route or a 10-day return. The itineraries upriver and downriver vary to avoid duplication for the round-trip passenger. It is operated by the Wuhan Sub-branch of the Changjiang CITS.

MS Three Gorges (Sanxia) and sister ship **MS Goddess**, 70 m long, are the most comfortable and most luxurious of the Chinese vessels. All 26 cabins face outward with full length windows and the cruise ship is equipped with all amenities. The Chongqing Sub-branch of the Changjiang CITS operates these ships, offering 5 and 7-day cruises in either direction between Chongqing and Wuhan.

MS Bashan is Lindblad's newest cruise ship. She is operated as part of Lindblad's Asian Tours and accommodates a maximum of 66 passengers in single, double or deluxe suite accommodations. Lindblad tours feature educational lectures and are staffed by the best of the CITS personnel and interpreters. Their itineraries are between Yichang and Chongqing where they connect with other parts of China Travel Tours.

MS Emei is a clone of the **MS Bashan**, operated by the Chongqing Sub-Branch of the Changjiang CITS. It has a standard 5-day itinerary between Chongqing and Wuhan.

MS Kunlun resembles the Big Red ships in profile. It was refitted many years ago as a luxury cruise ship for the Politburo high officials and visiting dignitaries. Large suite-sized cabins accommodate a maximum of 36 passengers with a crew triple that size. Double promenade decks, multiple lounges, gourmet western and Chinese cuisine, a clinic, hair salon and an antique and curio store make the Kunlun a super luxury boat. They offer a 12-day cruise between Shanghai and Chongqing. Bookings are made by CITS through the Wuhan Sub-branch of the Changjiang CITS.

MS Xiling offers 6-day cruises stopping at Wuhan, Chongqing Shashi, Yichang, Wuhan, Shibaozhai and Wanxian enroute. There is accommodation for 178 passengers and it has all the deluxe entertainment facilities including a swimming pool and gift shops.

MS White Emperor is similar to the MS Xiling with accommodation for 160 passengers. It offers a 5-day trip between Chongqing and Wuhan with stops at Fengdu, Wanxian, Wushan, Yichang and Yueyang.

in the Song Dynasty a thousand years ago, the **Monk Suspended Upside Down** and the **Bellows Gorge**. The Meng Liang Staircase comprises holes 25 cms wide by 30 cms deep which had been cut into sheer cliff. They zigzag up the mountain 1 m apart.

Wu Gorge follows Qutang and is

Ethereal Moon Rock at Yangshuo.

44 kms long. It begins at the tributary Daning River, and passes the city of Wushan. Wu Gorge offers the most breathtaking scenery of the 3 gorges found in the **Twelve Peaks of Wushan**, the most well-known of which is Goddess Peak (Fairy Maiden Peak), the highest of all mountain peaks on the Changjiang. Atop the peak is a natural pillar of stone resembling a young woman. Therein lies a tale. The goddess is believed to be the youngest of 12 fairies, and when she emerges from the mist she confers good luck on all who travel the great river. At the foot of the Peak of the Immortals, is the **Kong Ming Tablet**. The Prime Minister, Kong Ming, of the Three Kingdoms period (220-280) declared his alliance with the states of Wu and Shu on a slab of rock.

The river narrows again, funneling through the long Wu Gorge. Hamlets and villages are seen on the slopes of the shore. The tour boats stop for a side trip at Wushan before they go up another spectacular series of gorges on the Daning River. Small launches are hired separately to journey up the river for 5 or 6 hours to view the **Three Little Gorges**. One unusal sight here are the coffins of the Ba tribe which hang in the caves on a sheer cliff of 500 m. A black boat in one of the crevices of the cliff is actually a coffin of an ancient tribe.

Back on the main course along the Changjiang, the boats now head for **Xiling Gorge**, the longest of the 3 gorges. Stretching 80 km it ends at the modern

Gezhouba Dam near Yichang. It is by far the wildest passage, said to be inhabited by the Dragon King's fiercest dragons who whip up the dangerous eddies with their tails. Rocks and boulders infest the area, the danger of the passage varying with the depth of the river. The Changjiang is known to vary 16 m during the flood and dry seasons making the river boat captains wary. None try the passage in the dark.

Orchards of oranges cover the hillside in between the 4 smaller gorges making up the Xiling. One gorge is called "the Sword and Book on the Art of War Gorge". Another has the intriguing name "Horse Lung and Ox Liver Gorge", followed by "Kong Ling Gorge" and the "Gorge of Shadow Play".

The Changjiang narrows again as it progresses through Xiling. Cliffs again appear to close ranks against the humans violating their privacy in their delicate craft. Shoals disappear, the river deepens, navigation guides appear and the waters widen again, as the massive **Gezhouba Dam** appears.

Passengers and crew line the decks when the vessels approach the locks to pass through the dam. Gezhouba Dam is usually reached late in the afternoon, in time to pass through to Yichang beyond. The tourist boats dock there for the night before continuing the journey to arrive at the Hankou part of Wuhan on the afternoon of the third day.

Yichang is an overnight stop for the cruise boat passengers to allow them to enjoy the city. The local tour encompasses a visit to the dam and a video of the construction. Yichang is an industrial city. Some of its historical attractions include the hometown of **Qu Yuan**, a great 4th century BC poet (Warring States Period 475-221 BC) and the hometown of **Wong Zhaojun**, the legendary Western Han imperial concubine who volunteered to marry a Xiongnu (Hun) chieftain to bring peace to her country.

Nearby is the **White Horse Cave** where you can walk through caverns of splendid stalactites and stalagmites. A short distance from the other end of the cave is the **Three Visitor's Caverns** which offers a view of the Changjiang.

The cruise boats stop at **Shashi** where you can visit nearby **Jingzhou** on a local tour. Jingzhou has a history of 2600 years. The Jingzhou Prefectural Museum displays artifacts from the Eastern Zhou, Qin and Western Han Dynasties and scattered around the city are burial grounds and tombs dating the same periods. The boats then stop over at **Chenglingji** before ending the 5 or 7-day voyage at **Wuhan**. Those aboard

The central market at Wuhan, "Chicago of China".

the Kunlun continue for another 5 days to Shanghai, stopping enroute at Jiujang, Wuhu and Nanjing.

Wuhan – Hubei Province

Wuhan, the Chicago of China, one of the Three Devils' Cauldrons (the other 2 being Chongqing and Nanjing), is the last city on the Big Red itinerary but another stopover port for other cruise ships. You need to spend at least 3 nights in this city because you will arrive late in the afternoon and will need at least 2 days to explore. The independent travelers will be met by the charming Wuhan CITS representatives with a private car and who would have arranged a small suite at the hotel of their request. You should carry a copy of the travel order, just in case there is a slip-up.

The tour groups and assembled luggage will be transported to the major hotel and given their itinerary for the area. The Qing Chuan will be the most probable accommodation, though the classic French Jianghan will be of interest to architecture enthusiasts. A new Holiday Inn will be available for business travelers and tourists alike. The occasional independent tourist arriving on the Big Red is somewhat of a curiosity to the CITS and will usually get a VIP welcome treatment. Enjoy it. Wuhan, actually composed of 3 cities, Hankou, Hanyang and Wuchang, is a vast industrial complex with over 4 million

The Sun Yatsen Memorial in Nanjing, capital for a brief period of the Republic of China.

people. **Hankou** and **Hanyang** are on the west bank of the Changjiang with **Wuchang** on the eastern bank. The Changjiang Bridge, built in 1957, connects Hanyang to Wuchang. In times of flood huge banks of levees attempt to contain the overflow.

Although Wuhan is highly industrial, and so often quickly passed through by the tour groups, it is an interesting city. Hankou is the center of Wuhan and is the most modern area with boulevards, modern shopping areas on **Zhongshan**, **Jiefang** and **Zongjia** Roads. The Friendship Store, Handicraft Center and antique store are marvelous for the curious shopper. You will see a fair amount of cloisonne on display, and a word to the guide should get you a visit to the factory. When you actually watch the meticulous detail performed by rows of artists, soldering the hundreds of cloison on the copper base, filling enamel in the trenches followed by the endless baking and polishing, there is far more appreciation of the unusual art.

The **Guiyuan Temple** from the Ming and Qing periods has a unique array of over 500 Buddhas in comical poses, showing a rare sense of humor from the era. They are reputed to have been carved by a lone carpenter and his son over a 9-year period. An unusual figure with 1000 hands and 1000 eyes sits on a lotus blossom.

The **Hubei Provincial Museum** has a unique display of ancient musical bells and an array of articles recently unearthed from a nearby tomb. The university is interesting to visit, especially if you have a trade or career in historical studies and paleontology.

Sun Yatsen (Zhongshan) Park, has a fine zoo and public swimming pool if you are hot and bothered by the humidity. **Red Hill Park**'s claim to fame is a 7-storey pagoda dating from the Yuan Dynasty 700 years ago. Painters gather at **East Lake (Dong Hu) Park** to replicate the **Endless Sky Pavilion**, the **Sparkling Lake Pavilion** and the **Reciting Pavilion** on the spot where the poet Qu Yuan was said to have received inspiration 2000 years ago.

For dining, try the Wuchang fish and a combination of eggs, prawn and rice called Triple Delicious. The Jinghan Hotel has the reputation of possessing one of the finest restaurants. Prices are modest so you can afford to try several dishes and order more of the ones you like. Replenish your swagbag and catch the next boat going south. If you need to stop adventuring and quit the country, Wuhan has excellent air connections to most major cities in China. The city is otherwise on the Beijing-Canton railway line.

Jiujang – Jianxi Province

Jiujang, one of the oldest ports on the Changjiang (Yangtse), dates from the 10th century. It is an overnight run from Wuhan, and 3 days from Shanghai if you are riding the Big Red on the Changjiang. The town has a hotel and several restaurants on the waterfront. The principal purpose of stopping at Jiujang is to visit an unbelievable Swiss-style resort at the top of nearby **Mount Lu (Lushan)**. You are now at the north peak of Jianxi Province as it tucks into the Changjiang.

There is an adequate hotel in Jiujang, the Nanhu Guesthouse if you need to stay overnight. We don't recommend the drive up the mountain after dark.

On your own, you can take a bus up a narrow twisting mountain road with magnificent scenery all the way which keeps you from worrying about falling over the cliff. CITS style, you will be met at the boat landing by the customary guide and private car with confirmed reservations at **Guling**.

The village square is on a lake with shops, restaurants and service facilities for the tourists. The town took on a more official status when the foreign diplomatic enclaves found it at the turn of the century.

The Central Committee of the Communist Party also used it to hold high security meetings in 1957 and 1959 attended by leaders such as of Mao Zedong and Deng Xiaoping. The town then became a vacation and conference hideaway over the years.

Visit **Mao Zedong's residence**, now a museum, to view the memorabilia of the early party hierarchy living a high life while projecting equality for all. A

Jingdezhen

Jingdezhen is the porcelain capital of China. It is an interesting cross-country ride from the Changjiang (Yangtse) city port of Jiujang, taking about 5 or 6 hours, depending on the condition of the roads, ferry connections, rise and fall of the river and the mood of the driver. River crossings are made on World War II, Landing Craft (LCT) which occasionally run into a tidal condition and leave the craft and passengers in the middle of the channel. At every river crossing you can buy a bundle of mudcrabs or a nice watermelon in season. Most overseas porcelain buyers take the train from Shanghai, Guixi or Yingtan and the company sends a van down to pick them up.

Jingdezhen is not on the regular tourist routes because of its isolated location. Porcelain buyers from around the world make the trek by train or boat and stay at the Jingdezhen Hotel in a park setting next to a small lake outside the town center. It is comfortable, the food is adequate and the shops in the compound are delightful to browse in. Walking around the area and through town in the crisp mountain air makes you feel like Marco Polo finding another wonder in the orient. This kind of isolated destination confers a great feeling of adventure.

A museum displays the history of kaolin clay that attracted the porcelain fabricators of past centuries. Some of the kilns are reputed to be 2000 years old. The village is composed of dozens of ceramic factories, some elaborate, others mere cottage industries which challenge the imagination and arouse temptation.

Fortunately the local foreign trade office has a system of arranging purchases from various sources into one shipment. Allow 4 to 6 months for delivery. It could take 2 months just to get the purchased item collected and packed. The item could be a one-off and the shopkeeper's only means of finding whether this particular sample would interest other buyers.

The rare egg-shell porcelain is especially fascinating, it is now being manufactured. Decorative figures of fishermen, temple lions, qilins, Guanyin on her lotus blossom or astride a fish, all rival the artware in De Hua, Fujian Province. Heavy iron-stone vases, reproductions of the blue artware of the Ming Dynasty, meter high fish bowls on wooden stands and assortments of porcelain eggs are just a few more of the tempting treasures.

Buying Tip. Always check the show rooms in the factories where prize-winning unique pieces are displayed, supposedly not for sale. With a little bit of subtle persuasion the manager will part with the treasure.

---

tour through the summer residence-cum-museum of the country's leaders reveals that even Mao was an ordinary person like the rest of us with a yen for practical comfort.

The sprawling ranch house has an enclave of gardens. Mao's bedroom, roped off, has a robe and his slippers on the bed, brushes, ink stones, water jug and rice paper ready for him to put down his thoughts and ideas in writing. The toilet has a western style commode and doors open to a lovely terrace facing the garden.

The other rooms of the house now contain museum cases of memorabilia of the Mao Zedong dynasty. If you see a "closed to the public" sign, Deng Xiaoping or his successor may be in residence, getting away from the pressures of daily politics. It has been rumored that Deng Xiaoping gave the go ahead for the unhappy event at Tiananmen Square while vacationing here that fatal June summer in 1989.

Lu Shan Hotel, colonial style, is the

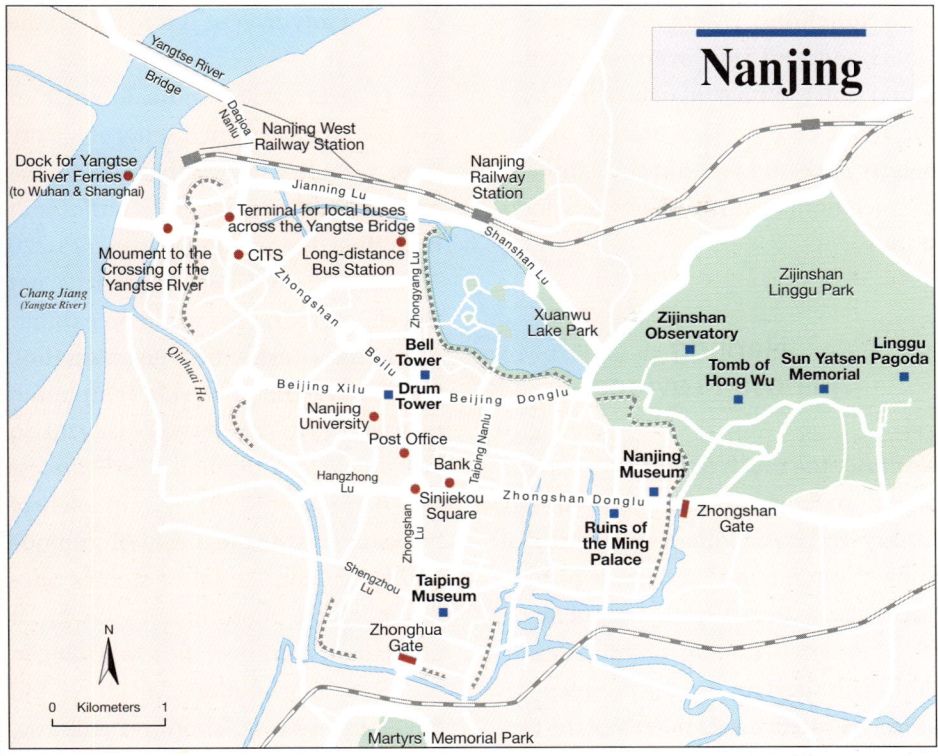

original destination for foreigners. Lulin Hotel is on Lulin Lake, a few kilometers out of the village. Uphill from the Lu Shan is the Yunshong Hotel. You might like to try the Lushan Villa Hotel, once the party grounds for Chiang Kaishek. Accommodations are spread around several buildings, make sure you get a room or small suite to yourself or else share the dormitory with international backpackers.

Another little known alternative is to be friendly to the local CITS office and inquire about the private villas for rent. These are European style large homes of stone in private gardens which have been taken over by various officials and generals not in residence. Have your friendly guide push a little and get you a deal for 3 or 4 days for a lump sum, including your driver and guide.

Around you the ambience is classic. The incense of fir trees fills the nostrils. Walk in the pine forests where you exit at cliff edges that automatically make you retreat when you find yourself looking a long way down. Clouds are often below, not above. Uphill labor is small effort when you find yourself drinking in the scenery insatiably at no extra cost. The food is good, the beds are comfortable and exercise makes you hungry and retire early.

Lushan is also accessible by car

from **Nanchang**. Fly or take a train into Nanchang and stay overnight at the Jianxi Hotel. With a bit of luck it will be the night of the open market in the nearby park and you can stroll among the merchants' stalls and hawkers' food stands.

Nanjing – Jiangsu Province

Nanjing, the much fought over capital of Jiangsu Province has a 5000-year-old history and has endured every disaster known to mankind. In current history Sun Yatsen, Father of the Republic of China declared Nanjing capital of China during his short time in the presidential office. He still oversees the city at the top of a magnificent memorial.

The **Yangste River Bridge**, which took 10 years and thousands of laborers to complete in 1968, spans the river as a 2-tier construction comprising railway and road. The Chinese are justly proud of the project that western nations proclaimed unfeasible and that the Russians abandoned half way through. The road is 4500 m long and the railway connection below 6000 m, the bridge itself spans 1600 m.

Nanjing has an array of attractions that could occupy a week both in the city itself and its suburbs that still show traces of the old Ming walls. Nanjing's history dates back 5,000 years but the written history goes back 3,000 years highlighting its importance at the delta of the mighty river as it forges onto the China Sea.

The **Nanjing Museum** dating from 1933 has an excellent display of history from Neolithic times through to the present. The famous jade burial suit from the Eastern Han Dynasty (25-220 AD) lies in state here when it is not traveling around the world on exhibit.

Linggu Park with its Beamless Hall, Pine Wind Pavilion, Linggu Temple and nearby Linggu Pagoda will easily take a half day to look through. The Beamless Hall dating from 1381, is built solely of bricks and has an architecturally unique vaulted ceiling. Buddhist statues once sat on a large platform in the center. It now is a memorial for those who died in the 1926-28 revolution. The Pine Wind Pavilion has a small shop and teahouse, if you need respite.

Nanjing is remembered for having been captured by Zhu Yuanshang in 1356 who made it the capital when he founded the Ming Dynasty. A huge palace was built followed by the construction of other buildings until the next Ming emperor, Yongle, moved the capital to Beijing. Nanjing then declined in importance and this was exacerbated by a series of natural disasters and the Manchu invasion in 1644.

Nanjing has remnants of the Ming gates and the Ming palace still has 5 marble bridges to evoke the memory of the once magnificent palace. The **Drum Tower** began its tour of duty in 1382 and the bell in the **Bell Tower** dates 6 years later.

Tree-lined avenue in Nanjing, whose history goes back 5,000 years.

It is inevitable then that you immerse yourself in history and at the same time, find yourself walking the streets of today. The food vendors have their baskets of live geese out on the sidewalk.

Noodle makers toss and twist the meters of dough in the air like an acrobat. The smell of fried food pervades the air and the venerable bearded ones sit around the minute tables in the tea shops. Cages of song birds hang over the sides of the bridge near the small park and the children drip the 2-fen ices over their clothes.

Hotels will vary from the 36-storey luxury Jinling Hotel in the center of town to the traditional Nanjing Hotel. It would be a good idea to check for yourself before advising your CITS guide of your preference.

Nanjing is a core tourist and economic center with transportation provided by the Big Reds which ply the Changjiang between Chongqing and Shanghai. Dozens of trains depart daily to all parts of China. There is a separate branch of CAAC, called Air Nanjing, which flies daily to all major cities.

Decide when you arrive, how you are going to finish the trip. The vast delta of the Changjiang from Nanjing out to the sea is not too interesting, though the final hours going up the Whangpoa (Huangpu) is always fascinating. It is a good time to review what you have seen of China and to decide on the next stage of your itinerary.

Sichuan, Yunnan & Xishuang Banna

The southwestern section of China is a world apart, in fact many worlds apart. **Chengdu** in Sichuan Province is an historic city and center of the giant panda's domain. Enjoy the nearby environs and a trek up **Emeishan**, another of the 5 famous mountains.

Kunming, **Yunnan Province**, the city of Eternal Spring, is the southern hub for exploration. **Simao** and the region called **Xishuang Banna** is further south where the 4 corners of China-Burma-Laos-Vietnam converge. Across the border one day visits are now possible for adventurous travelers.

China Southwest Airline (Branch of CAAC), serves Chengdu from Beijing, Shanghai, and Guangzhou which are also major points of entry into China. Connecting services to popular tourist points of Wuhan, Nanjing, Chongqing,

The giant panda, an endangered species, has several nature reserves specially allocated for its preservation.

Kunming, Xian and Guilin are available but not always on a daily basis. Of special interest is that Chengdu also has services to Lhasa in Tibet and Urumqi in Xinjiang.

Cathay Pacific and Dragon Air (both from Hong Kong), Malaysia Airlines and CAAC, now offer services from Chengdu and Kunming to Hong Kong, Kuala Lumpur (Malaysia) and Myanmar (Burma) for direct international routes.

Sichuan Provincial Airline provides a less expensive service to Xian and Kunming. The airline uses hand-me-down aircrafts and is therefore not for the timorous, as Captain Cook was wont to say.

Chengdu - Sichuan Province

Chengdu, translates as the "Perfect Metropolis". During its 2500-year recorded history, however, the region was subjected to fairly constant strife as the warlords, the Mongols and the Kuomintang fought over and controlled the territory. Deng Xiaoping was born here in 1904, giving credence to the reputation of the Sichuan-born as fighters and leaders.

Two and a half million people live in the Perfect Metropolis laid out with wide boulevards as in Beijing. The Fu, Xijao and Jin Rivers flow in sinuous

The aptly named Elephant Stone in the karst pillar Stone Forest in Kunming.

streams around the central district.

There are good hotels and a fine assortment of restaurants, tea houses and snack shops. The older Jin Jiang Hotel, located on the main boulevard Remin Nanlu, is the traditional headquarters for merchants and tourists with all facilities and services to meet their needs (including a CITS office). Across the street is the newer 21-storey Minshan Hotel, duplicating the services of the Jin Jiang. The main advantage of both hotels is their central location on **Remin Nanlu** boulevard, with a massive statue of Chairman Mao at the head, pointing the way back to your hotel if you get lost.

Shops, restaurants, food hawkers, tinkers, tailors and scales to weigh you for a yuan (2 fen for the locals) line the curbs of the boulevard. These are the new capitalists of China, allowed to use their free time and personal capital in the pursuit of making money. You will be immediately aware of the aggressive selling attitude they have, as against the normal iron rice bowl manner of their counterparts in assigned jobs.

Behind the giant statue of Chairman Mao, at the end of the boulevard, is the Exhibition Hall with 5 floors of Friendship Store merchandise to tempt you. Chengdu produces a wide range of brocade and filigree art goods in its factories. Of particular interest are the rare, magnificent and expensive 2-sided embroidery. This is the art of stitching on a screen to create a perfect rendition of a cat on one side, while a cat of

Children playing with a toy panda.

another color and in different position is stitched on to the other side. The finished product is then tightly framed on a swivel based hardwood screen. Unique reed-bound porcelain wares are available as are excellent jade and gemstone carvings.

The antique-curio counters, with inventories listing a decreasing number of the older items available, are patronized by the current generation of international tourists. Have your guide get permission for you to visit the various factories that produce new goods and replicas of the old to see how they are made, meet the artisans and listen to the manager proudly explaining the political or commune system. Prize winning items are available in the showrooms.

Between the Friendship Store and Donfeng Lu are short streets to look for *xio chi* translated literally as "little eats" meaning snacks. Pock-marked Grandma's Beancurd (Chen Maopo Doufu) is reputed the hottest meat sauce, of garlic, minced beef, salted soybean, chilli oil and peppercorn served on bite-sized squares of beancurd. The recipe and stall are over a century old. Boiled dumplings, noodle soups and rice balls are other specialties of the neighborhood, all needing substantial quaffs of beer to cool the tongue.

A stroll along the river next to the Jin Jiang Hotel can be very rewarding if you want to sample local food and do not have too many inhibitions about hygiene. More varieties of noodles, steamed buns, fried meats in little packets, sweet cakes and beancurd delights are sold from restaurants and hawker stalls at modest prices. Cross the bridges, visit the bird cage men, have an ice. Windows, porches and doors of the nearby apartments reveal the everyday lives of the local people. The **Remin Park** which has a teahouse is within walking distance.

Ask your guide to book for dinner and pre-order the menu at a vegetarian restaurant. Your guide may agree to join you if you invite him for dinner. Choosing the various dishes as they are being explained is the hors d'oeuvre before a meal. A select vegetarian-herbal meal is great to write home about. You may pay more in the special dining areas for foreigners, but the total cost is modest by international standards.

After dark, the artists appear on Remin Nanlu with their works pinned to clothes lines. Watercolors of scenery, pandas, celebrities and even while-you-wait sketches of yourself are fun to collect, roll in a tube and carry home with you. For the rest of the evening, you can prowl the Perfect Metropolis among the crowds of relaxed local Sichuanians.

Du Fu Cottage is the memorial to a Tang poet. Du Fu was a prolific poet in the 8th century and has been acknowledged a literary master to this day. The memorial is a pleasant park surrounding the original cottage to which Du Fu was known to have retired for 4 years when he was at the lower ebb of fortune.

Wenshou Monastery dates back to the Tang Dynasty.

He wrote more than 240 poems here reflecting on the misery of the people. A full day can be spent visiting the **Temple of Wuhou**, **Tomb of Wand Jian**, and the **Sichuan University Museum**.

The **Monastery of Divine Light** has 5 halls and endless bamboo and pool-decorated courtyards and a vegetarian restaurant. Originating in the 9th century, it is an active Buddist enclave containing a Burmese white jade Buddha, Ming and Qing artifacts and paintings, calligraphy and stone steles. Your guide may be able to persuade a friendly monk to allow you into the inner rooms to see hundreds of porcelain, ivory and gemstone treasures from the Eastern Han Dynasty (25-220 AD) to modern times. Tipping is not a custom but a 5 or 10

The Giant Panda

The largest panda sanctuary in China is at the **Wolong Nature Reserve**, 40 km from Chengdu. (Inquire when you are there if it is open for tourists.) In addition to the panda, golden monkeys, musk deer and the almost fictional snow leopard are protected in this half-million acre area.

Cuddly, round balls of wooly fluff, black eyes peering from white faces, clumsy and playful, the world-famous symbol of China is almost extinct. Pandas were first recorded in this area in 1896. Archeologists have traced the remains of the panda back a half-million years. Today the World Wide Fund for Nature estimates that there are less than a thousand pandas living today. Their food source, primarily tender bamboo, is fast disappearing. On top of that, pandas do not reproduce easily as frustrated zoo-keepers will affirm. Genetic defects, destruction of their forests and the age-old practice of poaching all contribute to the decline of the panda.

Pandas are shy and like to live and feed at around 2500 m altitude, away from inhabited areas. Visiting the preserve is no guarantee of seeing them in the wild. Custodians are said to have gone months without seeing any. Implanted tracking devices have increased the sophistication of research carried out on the pandas. Unfortunately ignorant or uncaring natives still trap them for commercial purposes.

The PRC donates pairs of the animal to various friends around the world as gifts. Their supply comes from the zoo residents, often artificially inseminated. A quirk in the nature of the boy and girl panda often renders them incompatible and they refuse to kiss and mate up. Thus you hear stories about the US male panda being sent on a vacation to visit the pretty female panda in Mexico City in the hope that they will have fun and produce a tiny pink hairless baby.

Souvenir wooly pandas however are available in great variety and quantity in Sichuan, rivaling the world's attention to the teddy bear. Every child should have one.

---

yuan FEC noticeably left in the contribution box will be accepted.

One of the halls (19th century) displays 500 life-sized figures of saints and Buddhist disciples, each with a distinct face and pose. One popular custom is to add the day of the month to your age, then start at any row and count the statues until you reach that number. The figure you arrive at is your "pre-incarnation". A card explains the nature and personality of the figure depicted which you would compare with your own. It is a fun form of "astrological lottery".

After touring China a few times, there is a tendency to shy away from monasteries, zoos and the thousands of parks. The rule of the thumb is to be selective. The **zoo** in Chengdu, for instance, is average, and includes a small train operated by child engineers and conductors.

However, this zoo has the largest population of **pandas** of any world zoo. The number varies from 8 to 10. They play like children and, despite the dismal cages, they are amusing and entertaining to watch.

Chengdu has considerable **night life**. The Minshan Hotel has a couple of bars and a lounge. The Jin Jiang Hotel sports a night club if you are lucky enough to get there in between renovations and rule changes. Bureaucratic dictators vary the policies fluctuating

The surroundings of Lixian Chang village in the countryside.

between what they consider good taste and contamination of the citizens. At times watching foreigners shake-a-leg is prohibited. At other times, they actually arrange dances for the masses. Foreigners can watch but not join in.

Chengdu has a 200-year-old opera tradition and is the headquarters of **Sichuan Opera**. Opera story lines are simple to follow with the good and bad guys well defined by costumes and headdress.

The opera is a tradition here so performances are frequent and of a high standard. One opera house is the **Jinjiang Theater** along Huaxinzhen Jie. You can also scout around for opera tours if you need a guide to initiate you into the art.

Chengdu Environs

The **Dujiangyan Irrigation Project**, about 60 km out of Chengdu makes an interesting day trip. Innovative methods of irrigating the plains of the Chengdu delta date back to the Jin Dynasty (265-420 AD). Dams were built, reservoirs created and channels were constructed to divert the Min River. The Min was known to flood disastrously, afterwhich the region was subjected to long periods of drought. There are blueprints of the early designs of the irrigation system and a Qing Dynasty map of the project in the **Two Kings Temple**. The two kings, Li Bing and his son Er Lang, both one time guardians of the project in the Kingdom of Shu, are memorialized in life-like statues. The temple and a tea house overlook the present domain of modern hydro-electric works. The territory has been expanded from the original 1,500,000 acres to the present almost 5,000,000 acres of productive soil.

Forty kilometers from Chengdu is the **Wolong Nature Reserve**, the largest of 13 nature reserves in China. The nature reserve has gained international official status as the United Nations has designated Wolong as an international biosphere preserve. The World Wide Fund for Nature is actively involved in research work on this reserve which protects a number of endangered species found in the area besides the panda.

It is a 9-hour bus ride to Wolong Nature Reserve via Guanxian.

Leshan – Sichuan Province

A 2 or 3-day side trip to **Leshan** and a partial climb up the famous **Mount Emei** is a good way to enjoy the probable wait for transportation to Tibet. Leshan is a typical small village with an historic claim to fame, the 71-meter high **Grand Buddha (Dafo)** in residence. Carved into a nearby cliff, the Buddha dominates the confluence of the Min and Dadu Rivers. Dafo is recorded as the largest Buddha sculpture in the world. Two persons can lie comfortably on the big toenail. Constructed during the Tang Dynasty (618-907) to control the fierce dragons beneath the surface of the rolling waters, it took 90 years to complete the sculpture.

Viewing the entire majestic Grand Buddha is best by boat, that way you can see the massive structure from different angles. The **Wulong Monastery**, at the foot and the **Grand Buddha Tem-**

Nature at its element in Sichuan.

ple near the head of Dafo, are close-up view points. You can also climb down a short way to look into the vast ears and peek into the eyes of this sculpture for a bug's view.

The town of Leshan has an adequate hotel and rural village streets to wander in. Pipe smokers use a unique bamboo stem with a tiny brass L-shaped bowl. The trick is to roll a leaf of unprocessed local tobacco into a slender cigar shape and insert it vertically in the bowl. Foreign visitors are still stared at by the children because they do not often wander this far into the interior. Travelers stop at Leshan for an overnight stay and rest after climbing nearby **Emeishan**, another of the 5 famous mountains.

Emeishan – Sichuan Province

You may wonder at the profusion of cane and umbrella vendors at the foot of the mountain. An hour into the climb will enlighten you on the wisdom of the entrepreneurs. The canes vary from ordinary bamboo or hardwood sticks to elaborately carved dragon-headed souvenirs.

Emeishan, like other famous climbs is a religious pilgrimage. Monks trek into isolated clefts to live as hermits for months or years at a time, withdrawing into prayer with a minimum of sustenance. Then to satisfy the logistical needs as well as prayer sources, temples were built at various stages, the earliest of which were built during the Eastern Han Dynasty (25-220). Emeishan, according to the records, was host to thousands of monks in past centuries who resided in more than a hundred temples on its slopes.

Stone steps were built for the less capable climbers, the elderly and the handicapped who were making pilgrimages to their favorite site. Caring custodians concerned with the high rate of lives lost in falling from danger points, exhaustion, lack of food or cover, built protecting rails, chains and guard ropes for the more dangerous passages. They provided housing and food for the pilgrims and hired porters to carry backbreaking loads of supplies. Enterprising entrepreneurs, even in past centuries, provided climbing assistance, water bottles and sedan chairs with porters for those unable to make the ascent on their own. It is a pleasant surprise when hot and tired, you turn a corner and find a watermelon vendor set up along the trail selling refreshing slices of the pink or yellow fruit. The temples provide food, tea and accommodation.

A rule of the thumb for the non-pilgrim. Enjoy the view as Mount Emei has been acclaimed as a "Beauty Under Heaven". For the day's outing, climb until noon, rest, have your lunch and go down in the afternoon. Even well-conditioned hikers climb slowly, take advantage of view points to see the magnificent vistas and pace themselves by counting steps. Good walking shoes or sandals are an absolute necessity. If you are a socks and sneaker wearer, carry 2 extra pairs of socks, and a small towel to dry the face and feet after cooling them in a stream. A plastic bottle of Laoshan Water (the non-carbonated variety), dried fruit and nut snacks are necessary contents for your backpack. As to the backpack, the lightest nylon available is the best. Reasonable comfort is the key to enjoying the climb.

Some of the better known mountains and scenic areas are the Crouching Tiger (Fuhusl), the Temple Of Ten

Thousand Years (Wannian) and Pure Sound Pavilion (Qingyinge). The monkeys you find enroute often tease the travelers, they love to steal your food or drag an unguarded backpack into the trees. Weary, limping on rubber-knees, you drop into the welcome seat of the car to journey back to Leshan.

Kunming - Yunnan Province

Kunming, the Eternal Spring City can be reached on domestic air flights from Chengdu, Shanghai and Beijing. CAAC and Dragon Air (Hong Kong) maintain international flights to Hong Kong, Bangkok and occasionally Rangoon, Myanmar (Burma). Because computerization of flights and reservations on CAAC are unreliable, it is wise to confirm your outgoing flight with a purchased ticket when you arrive.

Flights to **Jinghong** (Xishuang Banna) are often fully booked in advance. An intermediate airport in Simao is sometimes open. A pleasant stay overnight and a 4-hour car ride gets you to Jinghong. The best laid plans are a confirmed CITS independent tour, arranged when you get to Kunming. There is competitive jealousy among all Chinese bureaus including branches of the CITS. A locally arranged tour will have precedence over one booked in Shang-

The Stone Forest

A forest of limestone pinnacles.

CITS arranges a package of a 1 or 2-night junket to **Shiling** (The Stone Forest) which includes the 3 or 4-hour drive there. The countryside is jungle-lush beautiful and the village set into the hillside is picturesque. The Sani (Yi) people display their colorful woven crafts in the public square.

As the twilight comes in, the nearby forest of limestone pillars turn grey and forbidding. The paths become a maze and you suddenly wonder if you can find your way out. Laughing Chinese tourists, speaking no common oral language, join up and escort you back to the park.

The Stone Forest is a "forest" of towering limestone pinnacles distributed over an area of 27,000 hectares. Geologists proposed that 270 million years ago the movement of the earth's crust pushed the sea bottom up to become land. Made of limestone the protruding land mass was subjected to erosion, weathering and scouring over time. What remains today is a cluster of rocks with some of the most fanciful shapes imaginable.

Daylight is the best time to explore the forest. With good fortune, a lovely contralto voice may drift over from a nearby secluded nook. The strange echoing effect caused by the pillars tempts the visitor to sing in the jungle of stone.

Renaming nature's sculptures has been a custom dating some time back. Hence the fanciful names such as the "Phoenix Combing Its Wings", "Lotus Peak" or "Rhinoceros Looking At The Full Moon". The eeriness of the night before is gone, replaced by the wonder of daylight playing in the forest of stones.

hai or Beijing. Allow at least a week in Kunming, 3 or 4 days in Xishuang Banna and a direct flight to Hong Kong or Bangkok.

Kunming is 1,890 m above sea-level with the 40-kilometer long **Lake Dian** just south of it. This ensures a temperate climate year round, with the exception of the rainy season, thus its name, Eternal Spring City. The climate, excellent hotels, marvelous food, shops, restaurants and interesting central business district make Kunming an attractive place to visit. Kunming is an ideal center to wind up a tour through the far west, Tibet and Xinjiang. Rest a while, enjoy the fine food, take a side trip to the Stone Forest and Xishuang Banna before taking your international flight out of China.

Market activities in downtown Kunming.

Kunming has memories for World War II buffs and participants. The airport was the center for American planes flying in supplies over the mountains from India during World War II. The Amercians had an axe to grind with the Japanese who forced Vinegar Joe Stillwell the American General to lead his forces out of Burma on foot. Some of those aircraft can be seen rusting on the outskirts of the Kunming Airport.

The Green Lake Hotel across from **Green Lake Park**, though older is more charismatic than the modern hotels downtown. Early morning walks and participation in the *taijiquan* exercises make a good start for the day. After dinner, join the locals strolling the park and streets facing the lake. They are a friendly lot, the Yunnanians, given to laughter and camaraderie. One morning go out the back of the Green Lake Hotel to the raised roadway, and walk the sidestreets downtown. The bustle of the shops, smell of food and relative cleanliness exude a pleasant ambience.

Northeast of Green Lake Hotel is another pilgrimage haunt of devotees, known as **Yuan Tong Temple.** It is the largest Buddhist temple in Kunming. Behind the temple, located in very pleasant surroundings, is **Kunming Zoo.** You can get a good view of the city from here. For a more informed insight into the region, the **Kunming Provincial Museum** has an interesting exhibition on the minorities and a collection of relics from the region.

Yuan Tong Temple, the largest Buddhist temple in Kunming.

Kunming Environs

Just north of Kunming is the **Golden Temple**, a Taoist enclave in the middle of a pine forest. It appears to hang out from the cliff on the side of Phoenix Song Mountain. Ornate doorways, pretty gardens and a massive bronze bell take you back to the 17th century when a famous warlord set it up as a summer residence.

To get to the temple you may prefer to book with an organized tour as local

km northwest of the city, is the most intriguing. The temple was first built during the Yuan Dynasty and it contains 500 *arhats* (noble ones), created between 1883-90 during the Qing Dynasty, by the sculptor Li Guangxiu and his apprentices. These sculptures capture the expression of Buddha's disciples in varied poses so precisely and realistically that they have been known as "a pearl in the treasure-house of Oriental sculpture art". Some of the sculptures could also be caricatural portrayals of local models of the time.

You can take an express bus from Yunnan Hotel which is a direct service to the temple.

On a different aesthetic note is the **Xishan** (Western Hills) which lie on the western shore of **Lake Dian**, 15 km out of the city. From a distance these hills resemble a woman reclining with her long hair on the water. Hence the name "Sleeping Beauty Hills". A number of well-known temples cluster the hillsides. An express bus also serves this area.

Naturally **Lake Dian** will draw you to her shores with her scenic setting. Formed out of a fault, it has an incredibly bluish lake surface. The lake is 4 km south of Kunming and is a haven for exploration and hiking.

Xishuang Banna, Dai Autonomous Prefecture

Home of the Dai Minority, Xishuang Banna is geographically close to Burma,

transport, other than the express bus, is not efficient and is time-consuming. A tour will cover a number of sites outside the city. Both the Kunming Bus Service Company at Sun-Approaching Tower and the Yunnan Tourist Bus Company at Kunming Hotel offer tour services.

Among the attractions outside Kunming, **Bamboo Temple**, lying 12

The unassuming Bamboo Temple.

Laos, Thailand and Vietnam that the cultures and the people have intermingled from a long way back. Relatives of the same family may live in all 4 of the adjoining nations. The muddy Lacang (Mekong) River flows through the area, flooding often, serving as transportation for the locals and escape routes for fugitives fleeing from one country to the other. The New Year's Water Splashing Festival and the Dragon Boat Races are traditions still being practiced among these people.

CAS now flies Kunming-Jinghong several times a week in 2 hours. Kunming-Simao, about a 70-minute flight is an alternative route. This is an advantage if you care to stay overnight in **Simao** and see the lovely countryside in a 4 or 5-hour scenic trip by car to **Jinghong**. The 3-day bus trip over 733 km is for hardy travelers who may want to visit the small towns enroute.

By far, the most enjoyable route is to drive from Simao to Jinghong. The jungle is verdant, often overgrowths along the roadway. Varieties of bamboo lend their various shades of delicate green, difficult for an artist to duplicate though they try. Groves of coconut palms, oil palms, arecas (betel nut palms) line the roadway. Bamboo stilt homes are scattered on the hillsides with gardens of fruit trees including a variety of mangoes, papayas and bananas. The river banks are blankets of flowers. When you stop for a picnic in a palm grove, the overriding scent of the flowers wafts

Minority tribes people in Xishuang Banna.

over to create a romantic, poetic ambience.

Jinghong is alive with the colorful costumes and bright umbrellas of the Dai women. Long braids of hair are done up under real flower decorations or wound with scarves. Sarongs predominate as the outer dress, to cope with the heavy rainfall and temperate climate.

Bathing is done modestly in the river, by lifting the sarong gradually during immersion until it becomes a headdress, then reversing the procedure when emerging. The women undo their long tresses when bathing, creating lovely shiny reflections in the sun. It is said that rice water is saved from the cooking pots and used as an after-bath rinse. This is supposed to be healthy.

Young Dai people are romantics, free to make love before marriage. The women are sensual in thin sarongs, colorful head decorations, pretty jewelry and belts. They carry jaunty umbrellas in bright colors to ward off the sun and flirt with the young men.

Courting is an art, unlike the formal matchmaking in other parts of Asia. The lad on the ground below the bamboo porch sings or quotes a poem to his love who leans over to smile at him in true Romeo and Juliet style. If he is invited up to sit with her while she strips beans for the evening dinner, he must climb the pole and not use the regular ladder entrance. In the warm tropical evenings, the couple take long walks

Dai girls practise a dance at a festival in Jingzhen near Menghai.

along the palm forest paths, or along the river, singing plaintive songs or performing on a bamboo flute. They flirt during festivals, and when the wedding takes place, the whole village is invited to participate in the occasion.

Another important aspect in the life of the Dais is religion. Buddhism, the religion of the Dais, was introduced over a thousand years ago into the entire region including Burma, Thailand, Laos and Cambodia. Today young boys are still taught to be monks beginning with the endless chanting of the sutras and eventually graduating to reach the status of the Grand Buddhist Master.

On a more prosaic level, the highlight of the week for the Dais is the Sunday market, a wonderplace of fruits and vegetables, bright clothing, jewelry and woven products. Your hotel chef will willingly prepare the market produce you could not resist, bowing to the insistence of "steam cook, no oil please".

Puerh, the red tea reputed to be a heart stimulant of great merit is grown in Xishuang Banna. It is the oldest tea drinking area recorded, some of the bushes are over 800 years old and are still producing new tender leaves.

The area also offers some rather rare vegetation like a plant called Meindunmu which is supposed to cure cancer. Lotus leaves grow into giant sizes, large enough to be used as light skiffs on the lake.

Xishuang Banna is a wildlife paradise, a reserve spread over 3 counties,

Dinner at a Dai Farmer's

The bamboo log house is built generally of 32 thick logs extending from the ground up to the roof, 6 to 8 m high. Rarely is bamboo used now but the traditional name persists. The house is set back from the river on a hummock to protect it from the rain-induced floods of summer. Rice paddies surround the area. Shoes are left on the ground, the ladder climb is slightly rickety and the experience like that of climbing a child's tree house.

The family greets with giggles the clumsy entrance of the foreigners, after the climb up the ladder to the main floor, and wait to be introduced. Father, Mother, Granny and a gaggle of children are ready to be entertained. The upper level is a floor board room, divided into a living area with a sandbox fire pit in the center. The other half, concealed by a bead string curtain was the private sleeping area. It is not polite to ask to visit the bedroom. The area, like the hotel rooms, contains sleeping mats for the family with Mother and Father having a separate mosquito net to sleep under. Photographs and worldly possessions are displayed on the shelves. At dusk the home is delightfully cool with a light breeze airing the vented side walls. Seven people live comfortably here while the farm animals are kept in pens below on ground level.

Entertainment takes place on the porch which extends toward the river. Tiny backed stools are provided for the guests. A strong white corn wine is served in small cups, similar to and as fierce as Mao Tai. Sour chili snacks, hot enough to burn the tongue, are then served. Make for the communal bamboo rice basket on the table. It is the fluffy, sticky variety that you finger-roll into a ball and pop into the mouth. Let it roam around the mouth for a moment to absorb the chili. Hot food is prevalent in most of the Asian countries because it kills certain germs and stimulates the gastric juices to aid digestion. After 2 or 3 refills of the wine, you will be laughing along with the family at your antics.

Dinner may start with "fried moss" tasting like potato chip and "sour meat" looking like raw pork and which is very sour and very hot. "Roast chicken in lemongrass" is more palatable to the taste as is roast fish and rice cooked in a bamboo tube. With many balls of rice in between, the courses will continue until you are filled to the brim.

The farmer is interested in the world you come from, as your guide will translate. The conversation on both sides becomes more garrulous with the succeeding cups of wine. Food continues course by course, each dish more spicy than the last. Fortunately the rice bowl is handy to calm the fires. Farmer Dai is the only family member at the meal. The women fuss about bringing the food, the children go off in a corner to play.

Growing rice is pleasant now as the farmer can keep his surplus for sale on the free market. His teenage sons will soon be gone for three months as novices at the monastery. Birth control measures are not taken seriously in this province as the farmers need strong sons and daughters to cultivate the crop. Flood years are disastrous, but life in general is good.

At the end of the evening, promise to send pictures and hold tight while going down the ladder which may appear to be swaying. Congeniality has brought the distant travelers together with a worldly camaraderie both families will remember.

Jinghong, Menghai and Mengla south of the southernmost tip of Yunnan. The tropical rain forest has over 300 varieties of trees and over 1100 species of wildlife including birds, land vertebrates, reptiles and fish. Herds of wild elephants numbering over 300 are recorded, all protected.

The golden monkey is considered a distinguished citizen. The reserve is a rare place on earth for botanists, geologists, lovers to walk hand in hand in, and anyone desiring to see one of the most beautiful localities in the world.

All China Minority Nationalities Athletic Meet

In November 1991, 5000 minority nationalities opened the ceremony of the Fourth All China Minority Nationalities Athletic Meet in Nanning, Guangxi Province. Fifty-six minorities from 31 provinces put up magnificent original song and dance performances.

Tianjin hosted the first event in 1953; Hohote in Inner Mongolia sponsored the second in 1982; far west Urumqi took over the third in 1986 and Nanning in 1991. The event is now scheduled every 4 years, similar to the Olympics. Kunming will host the 5th meet in November 1995.

A summary of the Nanning meet reported over 200 events which were divided into 2 major groups: competition events and performance events. Competition events included snatching fire iron rings, swing, archery, rolling pearl balls, polo, wrestling minority style, horse racing, martial arts, and dragon boat racing. The wrestling competition included Mongolian, Tibetan, Yi, Uygur and Manchu/Hui styles.

A hundred and twenty performances were scheduled including such colorful dances as the "Dance of the Chinese Unicorns", "Phoenixes and Egrets", "Ancient Martial Plank-Shoe Dance", "Tremendous Momentum of the Lusheng Dance", "Powerful Comely Young Warriors" (100 teenagers dressed as warriors mounted on small ponies), "Playing Football on Stilts", "Dance of the Bronze Drum", to mention a few. Acrobatics, magnificently colorful costumes and traditional esoteric music brought thousands of visitors from all over China.

The success of the event promises a two-fold turnout in Kunming where facilities for the greater national and international crowds are being planned.

Mid-April is the Buddhist New Year celebrated with the Water Festival, a mardi-gras of delightful proportions. Home made rockets, peacock and red deer dances, all bring the crowds out in an umbrella-waving frenzy of color. Fun water fights in the river drench everyone. They are meant to wash away the past year's ills and provide a good clean start in the new year.

The rockets, filled with lucky amulets, zoom up like space launches before they explode in the air raining amulets on the lucky people below. Hot air paper balloons become lanterns in the sky, dispensing good luck around the countryside when they eventually fall.

Boat races in dragon-shaped water craft are the sport of the event causing as much celebration as a winning soccer match. Water washing spreads to the Buddhist temple where all the statues are meticulously cleaned in honor of the New Year.

A unique tourist adventure is to have your guide wangle you accommodations in a Dai Bamboo Hotel, often booked full far in advance. (CITS often blocks a few openings.)

The log houses are on stilts, duplicating the farmers' houses, scattered in wooded areas. They come in different sizes, some for a honeymoon couple, others for 6 persons. The floors are mat covered and the beds are kapok mattresses with fresh sheets, quilts and mosquito nettings. The open structure is cool, provided a favorable breeze is blowing. A toilet and a well for bathing are nearby.

China-Burma-Laos-Vietnam - The Corners Of Four Nations

A unique travel expression for the more adventurous are day trips from Xishuang Banna across the borders of the nations that join geographically at this point. The entire border between Yunnan Province and the other countries is over 4000 kms but the junction funnels to less than 100 kms. Tourism is beginning to sprout with the need for cash dollars and the minority population that transcend the borders. Special border passes are obtained in Jinghong, seat of the Dai Autonomous Prefecture.

Myanmar

The new name of Myanmar is used more by map-makers and the rarified politicos of the nation. Burma is still the common reference of travelers and locals. The border can be crossed at 3 different places for 1-day tours: **Daluo** in Menghai County, in Xishuang Banna at **Dehong Dai** and **Jingpo** crossing via Wandang or Nongdao in Ruli County.

According to recent travelers the border via Nongdao is the most interesting. A diesel-powered wooden craft takes the travelers across the **Ruli River** in a 10-minute ride from China to Burma. As in all of Burma, Buddhism is a dominant feature here. A temple is the first stop, requiring worshippers to sit in front of Sakyamuni. A White Pagoda stands outside, and behind that stretches a line of realistic full-height sculptures of Sakyamuni leading 28 disciples.

Lunch is provided in the bamboo house of Namhkam Overseas Travel Service and the streets of the village offer wonderful treats for the casual visitor. Markets contain the manufactured products of China and the produce of Burma. The Dai people are the most prevalent, with Han Chinese who emigrated from across the border in previous generations, now merged into the Dai society and adopted language.

Laos

The Sino-Laos border is reminiscent of the old Sino-French crossing being the boundary line between the Qing empire and the French occupiers of Laos. The crossing starts at Mengla County in Xishuang Banna to Namtha in Laos. According to travelers' reports, **Namtha** looks like a remote Chinese mountain village. The single road is lined with houses and the market place comprises rough stalls containing the same products as in the Burmese counterparts. A Chinese family provides food and drinks for visitors at a Sino-Laos thatched-roof restaurant. The tour includes a visit to the largest building in the area, a 2-storey government center and a square in the center of town. The Yaos minority are counterparts of the same group in Yunnan in dress and language.

Early morning landscape of the Luoshuo River at Menglun, Xishuang Banna.

Vietnam

Hekou is a small border town in the Yao Autonomous District of Yunnan, situated across the river from Vietnam. Traders cross the river freely to set up stalls on the main avenue of Hekou called Vietnam Street.

The Vietnam border town of **Lao Cai**

is the crossover point attracting eager and enterprising peddlers from Hanoi and Ho Minh City for the communal open marketplace. The railway bridge, blown up on the Vietnam side during the 1979 Sino-Vietnam war, should hopefully have been repaired by the time you visit this region. This should allow easier access to Vietnam across the river.

Nearby **Mount Silian** in Hekou offers a view of the city and Lao Cai in Vietnam on the other side of the Song Hong River.

Inner Mongolia & the Ancient Capitals

There is an air of the unexpected, stepping into the rarefied ambience of **Inner Mongolia** otherwise known as Nei Monggol Zizhigu. You somehow expect a tribe of horse-mounted fierce warriors to meet the train, an anxiety which soon dissipates when, not camels or horses, but a humped CITS Toyota van and a representative arrive to take you to their new Inner Mongolia hotel. Backpackers, both Chinese and foreign are more in evidence than typical tour groups.

Sculpture in the Yungang Caves reflect both Buddhist and Hindu influence.

The Grasslands

Arrange a 3 or 4-day road trip to the outer area called the **grasslands**. CITS will try to group you, but check the price for an independent car tour instead of a group tour by van. If it is not too unreasonable, opt for the extra flexibility and comfort. They will offer a nearby overnight trip or a longer distance to a remote area taking 3 or 4 days. Take the longer one and fill up your swagbag

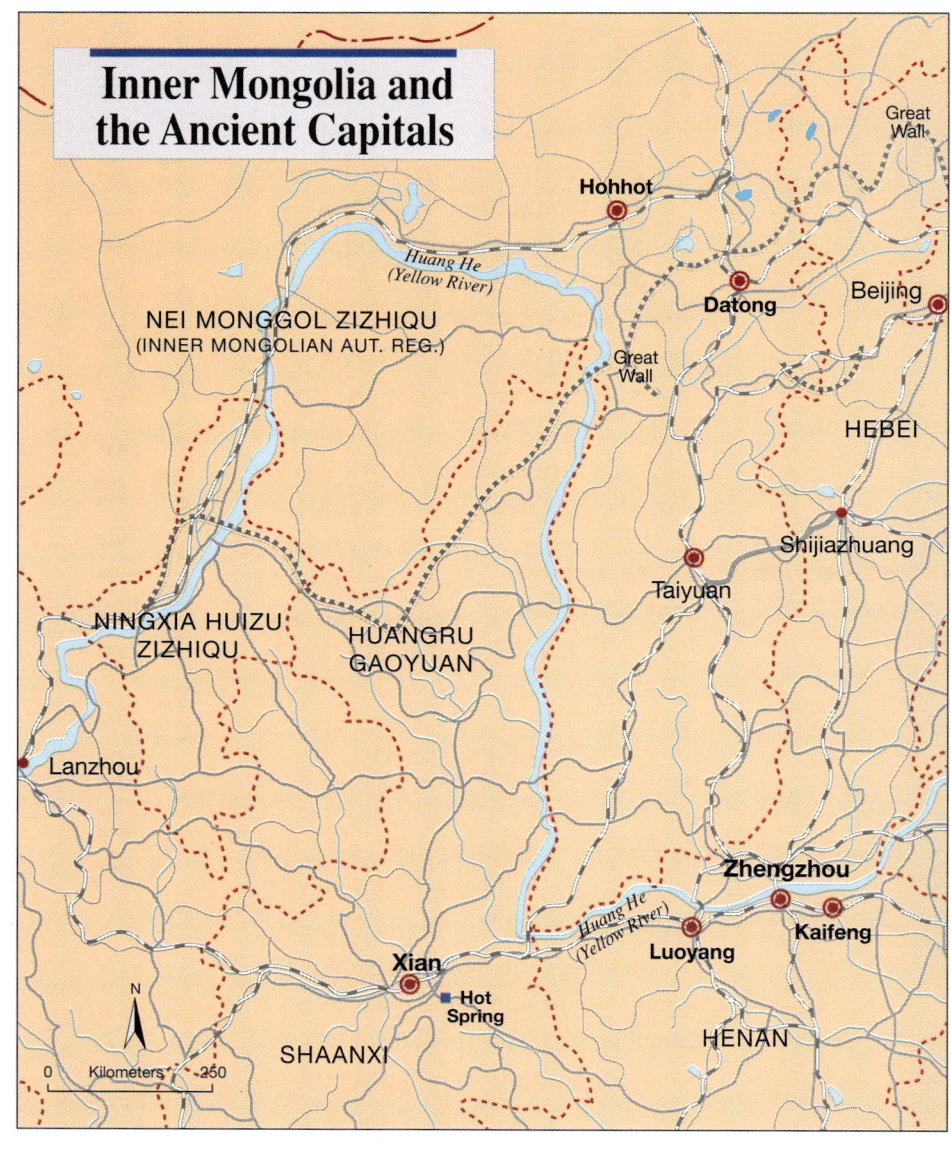

Inner Mongolia and the Ancient Capitals

with trail food.

Road travel increases the eerie feeling. The first part of the journey takes you through mud hut villages and rural farming and you will stop by a pleasant small town to have lunch. In the late afternoon, you suddenly notice that the dirt road has disappeared. Your driver appears to be following telephone poles over an unmarked dry grass flat land. Low hills can be seen in the distance. Your guide may scare you with tales of tourists disappearing forever when storms obliterate the landscape. A herd of grazing camels appear over a slight rise stopping to stare. An untended herd

An entire home, the yurt, is moved by a yak-drawn cart in Mongolia.

of Mongolian horses is surprised or an arrogant stallion defiantly challenges your car before he stampedes his charges out of danger.

The monotonous roll of miles and miles of grassland lulls the senses until a remote civilization appears like a mirage in the distance. Round mounds of desert *yurts* pop out of nowhere lined up like motel rooms to accommodate the tourist and a short line of tin-roofed ghost town stores remind you of western cowboy movies. An incongruous brick building houses an office reception and a dining hall about the size of a gymnasium. The staff escort you to the first *yurt* in the line, an igloo-shaped mound of hide and wool with a midget-sized door. The inside is surprisingly cozy with sleeping pallets and a fire box in the center. Familiar hot water thermos flasks are waiting with tea paraphernalia on a low table. Pillows are stacked around for seating.

Washing facilities consist of a bowl and a pitcher and a night pot stands in the corner. The toilets are in an open shed away from the *yurts* to be endured stoically when the need arises. One trick is to squat with the nose pinched. Again eerie fascination takes over as the nomadic life of the Mongols emerge. A tiny 5-year-old boy, leading camels on a tether to the water hole, stares at the strange visitors. Tin-roofed huts with fenced corrals behind them belie the ancient ways. *Yurts* are for the visitors, the locals live in farm houses.

The Loess Plateau

The mighty **Huanghe** (Yellow River) bends at the intersection of Henan, Shaanxi and Shanxi Provinces. To the west Ningxia adds to its territory the vast plateau called Loess which extends through the center of Gansu and stretches a finger into Qinghai.

"Loess" is a fine yellowish brown loam which consists of tiny mineral particles found in deserts and former glacial areas.

The Chinese call the Loess Plateau "The Sea of Yellow Sands". In some places an aerial view is similar to the photographs brought back by the astronauts of the US space flights. There are lakes, deep gorges, fanciful formations of cliffs, cities, and villages where the residents built their homes into the mountains. Various names have been given to the area considered the origin of Chinese civilization, the culture of the ancient capitals, the Silk Road and the Han people's homeland of the Dragon race.

Officially it extends from **Xining** in the west to Zhengzhou, Xian in the south to the tip of Shanxi near Datong. Adventurous travelers can join camel tours in various areas. Those with less time and unable to take the sea-sick rolling gait of the dromedaries can view the area by car or take a train from its principal cities.

Civilizations are thought to have been in the area millions of years ago. From a mountain top the silted waterways flow in twisted streams, barred by retaining walls from overflowing the city, crowded against the mountain.

Many of the people live in the traditional cave abodes carved deep into the side of a hill. They build a normal facade on the outside with porches and gardens. Some of the homes creep up the side of the hill at various levels like an apartment house. A distinct advantage, the main reason for the lifestyle, is protection against the weather. Vicious sandstorms, stifling heat of the summer in the low lying areas, cold and bleak winters of below zero temperature are all offset by the safe and temperate lodgings. Domestic animals are often kept in a side room in the cave-homes as they need the same protection as their owners.

The **Tang Pagoda** dominates a hill and the **Ten Thousand Flowers Hill** is famous for its peonies in season. Tourists are few and far between, thus the local people often invite the travelers into their homes for a meal. Paper cutting was a hobby adopted by the locals to while the time away during inclement weather but which has now developed into an art. Principal formal entertainment in the provinces are operas of shadow play using elaborate figures and traveling troupes.

Loess Plateau exploring is possible from Xian, Shaanxi; Taiyuan, Shanxi; Yinchuan, Ningxia; and Lanzhou in Gansu Province.

Camels, horses, sheep and cattle are the local industry. The herds graze in vast areas because of the stumpy coarse grass. Low hills roll into the distance on one side while the other is a flat table as far as the eye can see and at dusk the bright red ball of the sun disappears behind a straight horizon. There is suddenly an awareness of why the ancients thought the world was flat.

Dinner is roast mutton served on the shank that looks like a quarter of a sheep. You will find an odd billing system when checking out. The price of a whole slaughtered sheep costs some 50 yuan. The locals thank you for giving the rest to them. Cut your own hunk and gnaw away with rice and vegetables on the side for the 2 nights you are there. Beer is available but steaming hot glasses of tea are more palatable in the rarified atmosphere.

The hills are adorned with waving pieces of prayer cloth. You are invited to ride a camel and a fast trotting Mongolian pony. With good fortune an actual

Mongolia People's Republic

China and what was once the USSR compress Mongolia along its enormous length. It spreads like peanut butter along the entire northern border of Inner Mongolia. Gansu Province touches it briefly and the northern border of Xinjiang Province finishes the sandwich.

Communism is Mongolia's forte, in a brotherhood with Russia it was awarded membership in the United Nations and is now recognized by over 100 nations. The political future of Mongolia is in the same turmoil as the other former Russian conglomeration. We bring it in this text for travelers as a massive neighbor of China and certain adventurers may want to cross over the border, taking a flight from Beijing to Ulaan Bataar (Ulan Bator).

750 years have passed since the days of Ghengis Khan. The **Gobi Desert** comprises a good deal of the territory. Temperatures can drop to -25°C in the winter and 17°C in the summer. The people retain the living style called *gers*, the round felt tents similar to the *yurts* of Inner Mongolia.

Ulaan Bataar

The city is located in the Tuul River Valley, the *gers* circle the hillside around the typical city blocks of apartments and low rise government buildings. Once a Tibetan Buddhist stronghold with thousands of lamas and hundreds of monasteries, the faithful have but one existing working monastery left, **Teghinlen**. Teghinlen translates as the "great vehicle of complete joy". It is peopled by the Yellow Hats known for using the traditional yak butter lamps and who prostrate in obeisance.

Temples and museums around give the history of the area. Mongolians excel in horsemanship, archery and wrestling, thus it is an important part of local entertainment. There is an opera house to show off the fine ballet troupe and perform operatic Mongolian folk tales.

Terelji is a *ger* camp less than an hour's drive from the capital. **Karakorum**, 300 km west, is famous for being Kublai Khan's capital before he moved it to Beijing. The Gobi Desert occupies immense tracts of sand dunes. Grasslands similar to Inner Mongolia provide forage for sheep, horses and camels.

Hotel accommodations are adequate, the Hotel Ulan Bator is preferred by most international travelers. Mongolian shopping is limited to camel hair caps and jackets, leather riding boots and some art and craft wares.

Mongolia is for the "Around the World in 80 Days" travelers seeking the thrill of a Marco Polo or a Mount Everest challenger. You can name drop to listeners about flying from Beijing to Ulan Bator to Novosibirsk to Moscow. Be sure to obtain all visas before leaving.

caravan will pass by and you can see the folded *yurt* on a cart piled high along with the other necessities like cooking pans and bundled clothing.

Mongolian courtesy requires the headman to invite you to his social *yurt* with the other dignitaries to discuss politics. Conversation is a complicated process with the local interpreter converting the native patois into Mandarin for your guide, who in turn translates for you. Feel free to talk directly. It is surprising how often tone and manner become a communication link. Hot camel-butter milk-sweetened tea, that takes a bit of getting-used-to, is served, when the courtesies are toasted endlessly.

Inner Mongolia is an autonomous province, thus they can raise as many children as they wish and do not come under strict control of the central party in Beijing. Flock-tending families move

A young Muslim smile.

their charges far into the grasslands following the forage supply. Their caravans set up camps in the far reaches wherever water is available and when they return to the village a year later with an enlarged flock, it results in a celebration. Music, dancing, and bright colored clothing replace the dull practical layers of everyday garb.

Money is of little consequence as barter is the exchange medium which takes place in the form of the herds of live animals, skins and meat. The Mongolians do not bathe or shave often but then the dry cold air eliminates sweat-generated body odors.

The return ride to **Hohhot** could be nicely interrupted by an overnight stay in a hotel.

The 3 blocks of shoplined dirt streets are interesting souvenir opportunities. Unlike the friendship stores, you can acquire such treasures as hand-hammered cooking utensils and serving pieces in the open market. A Mongolian wooden saddle would be a wonder in your living room along with the woven woolen shawls and covers. The open vegetable stall displays a tempting array of freshly picked vegetables.

Hohhot, the Capital

It means "green city" and is especially so in the summer. Peopled by a dozen nationalities including the Mongolians, Hans, Manchus and the Huis, Hohhot looks back on 400 years of history. It is also one of China's major woolen textile centers, producing carpets, tapestries and other woolen goods. There is an interesting Equestrian Cultural Performance on the polo grounds. A polo team demonstrates the elite sport of kings, rarely seen in our worlds. The dressage exhibition is a remarkable show of horse training. Mongolian trick riders thunder by, over and under their horses, to impress you with circus riding that would exceed the fame of Barnum and Bailey.

Wuta (Five-Pagoda) Monastery. Also named the Cideng (Lantern of Compassion), this monastery was built in 1727 at the base of a 3-storey structure and is built with glazed tiles bearing niches of Buddhist images and astronomical maps in Mongolian, the only example of their kind in the country.

Nine kilometers south of Hohhot, on the south bank of the Dahai River is the **Zhaojun Tomb**. It is 33 m high and covered by green grass, hence the appellation the "Green Tomb", one of the 8 views of Hohhot. The tomb was built in memory of a Han girl, Wang Zhaojun, who volunteered to marry a Xiongnu (Hun) Chieftain Huhanye during the reign of the Western Han Dynasty (Emperor Yuandi 48-33 BC). She was made Ninghu Empress and did much to improve relations between the Xiongnu tribe and the reigning dynasty in China.

The **Old Town** is located directly north of Zhaojun's Tomb and is worth exploring when your guide wishes to have an afternoon off.

The 11th grand living Buddha resides in the **Xiletuzhao Temple**. He dresses informally and is very much a part of the 20th century scene. Further north is the **Great Mosque** which is in disrepair, but it reminds one of the region's colorful ethnic diversity.

The main activity in town is centred around **Dazhao Temple** and extends along Tongdao Lu and Xinhua Lu where you find some of the more interesting markets. A government department store on Xinhua Lu offers a good selection of minority clothing. Bolts of unusually woven cloth, sold by the meter, can be found here. They are rarely tourist priced, therefore modest.

The **Inner Mongolian Museum** is a treat even for those sated with museums and temples. The museum houses artifacts and weapons, the Mongolian heritage from a colorful history. A whole mammoth skeleton is there for readers of Jean Auer's Cave Bear stories. Ask if the curator will open the 3rd floor for you, normally closed to the regular traffic. The **Minority Handicraft Factory** has hand-hammered copper ware, daggers, boots and saddles. For authenticity buy one of the knives in a leather sheaf with matching chopsticks. Please remember to bury it in your checked luggage before going through the security checks at the next international airport. A fancy letter opener can look like a lethal weapon in the X-ray machines.

Access to Hohhot is by train or plane. Then, as the distances are great, it is advisable to continue by train to

Ningxia Hui Autonomous Region

Ningxia, the geographical heart of China, is composed of the Ningxia Plain, the Helan Highland, the Loess Plateau and the Liupan Mountains (Longshan). Rarely visited by tourists, the capital city of **Yinchuan** is located in the northern tip of the smallest province in China.

A large oil painting in the Ningxia Museum at Chengtian Temple in Yinchuan depicts the fierce horse-mounted figure of Li Yuanhao, founding emperor of Western Xia Dynasty (1038-1227). One claim to fame is that the mighty warrior Genghis Khan failed to capture Ningxia before he died in 1226. Three days later, unaware that the Great Khan had died, the king surrendered.

Travelers desiring to stray from the normal paths will find the strange sight of the blue waters of the Huanghe (Yellow River) at **Shapatou**, west of the capital. Yellow sands float on the hills above green forestry in what is termed a Sea of Sands. According to local lore there was once a city of Prince Gui which was inundated over the centuries by the drifting sands of the Tenger Desert. Like the famed city of Atlantis supposedly buried in the sea, the floating sand dunes are now 70 to 100 m deep.

Sand Lake Recreational Garden, an hour's drive north of the city is actually on a farm. Methods have been used to control the Sea of Sand and reservoir water from the Huanghe (Yellow River) to create farmland and a pretty lake. The clear water attracts waterfowl and contains a plentiful supply of carp. Migratory white cranes and wild geese from Siberia stop to feed on the fish in season. Like the birds, domestic tourists soon found the lake a pleasant place to visit for relief from the summer heat. Other activities on the lake include boating, swimming and fishing from May to October. The nearby sand dunes are used for sledding when the surface cools enough to play on. Sheepskin rafts ferry passengers across the river, and camels form a safari across the sea of sand for the entertainment of visitors.

The distinctive life styles of the Hui people have changed little over the centuries; they are of modest dressing with little animation of jewelry or color. They adopted the Islamic faith in the 7th century. The Ming Dynasty seeking elimination of the Hui decreed they could not intermarry with their own tribes. This forced the integration with the Han, but the belief in Allah survived. Two hundred kilometers south of Yinchuan Tongxin is a **Grand Mosque** constructed in traditional Chinese style with tiered roofs and sweeping eaves, reputed to be the site of the first mosque in China. The large worshipping area can accommodate over 700 people in prayer at one time, though the community has a modest population.

Datong, first of the ancient capitals, rather than by car. As always, on long train rides, carry your own reserve snack packs and avoid the dining cars.

Datong - Shanxi Province

The Northern Wei Dynasty made **Datong** their capital in the 4th and 5th centuries AD. It was located just inside the Great Wall thus protecting it from the Mongols. It became the center of an advanced culture in irrigation, trade and the advancement of Buddhism.

Datong is a 5 or 6-hour train ride from Hohhot. The Yungang Hotel is adequate, certainly better than what the traveler would have had in the 5th century. Restaurants are minimal, the hotel food adequate but there is always hope for an unexpected delicious meal.

Outside Datong are the **Yungang Caves,** overflowing with sculptures of

Gaomiao Temple in Zhongwei, dating from the early 15th century, is known as the Temple of Three Religions, celebrating Taoism, Confucianism and Buddhism. The large compound has a marvelous array of halls and pavilions. The inscription on a stone at the entrance could be a lesson for all mankind: "In this place, Confucianism, Buddhism and Taoism free the souls of men from hell. Within these walls, nature and man enrich each other."

The wide panorama of the Loess Plateau unfolds in the south and focuses on the city of **Guyuan** (Yuanzhou), a favorite stopping place on the Silk Road. The Guyuan Museum displays Persian relics from the tomb of Li Xiang, of the Western Zhou era (1100-771 BC). The **Mount Sumeru Grottoes** contain sculptures from the Tang, Northern Wei and Sui Dynasties and the Liupan Mountains, where Ghengis Khan died 700 years ago, are south of Guyuan.

Hohhot is 12 hours away by express train. There are air flights twice a week from Beijing to Yinchuan. The hotels listed in the directory are clean and modest. The Ningxia Hotel is a delightful Chinese style hotel with red column entrance gates and a white marble bridge next to a calm water pool. The Yinchuan offers facilities for meetings with a 700-person conference room, in case you wish to organize your own safari to the Loess Plateau.

Sakyamuni and his disciples in the sheltered rocks. The capital was moved to Luoyang in 494 AD at about the time the last cave carvings were made. The art of carving the huge caves and turning out the sculpture out of solid sandstone rock is reputed to have come from India.

Historians regale in the narrations depicted by the different images of Buddha, the gathering of disciples, likenesses of the rulers, with their Greek, Byzantine and Persian influence. Chinese concepts are depicted by dragons and strange animals and Hinduism is revealed in the images of Vishnu and Shiva. The knowledge of the world around them by these artisans of 1,500 years ago is amazing when you consider the travel systems available in those days.

Everyone visits the **Nine Dragon Screen**, 2 storeys high and a block long, originally protecting the palace of a Ming royal descendant. The most fun is exploring within the ancient city walls, parts of which are still intact.

There is a **silk factory** in Datong, producing the threads from the cocoon to the multi-strand yarn. Conditions in the room where the cocoons are unwound is an experience likened to the sweat shops of large manufacturing centers. Women mostly, work in rolled up pants and shirt sleeves, heads wrapped in the sauna steam atmosphere. What is most impressive is the amount of thread used to manufacture the thousands of spools of silk. Noodle sized hanks are piled high on skids ready to be shipped to cloth producing factories.

Datong Environs

The most interesting site outside of Datong is the **Xuankong** (Hanging Temple) on the fall side of a massive dam controlling the man-made lake on **Jinlong Canyon**. From the parking area,

Magnificent sculpture is carved out of solid sandstone rock in the Yungang Caves.

cross a swinging bridge to the opposite side of the dry channel below the dam. Narrow steps that are more a ladder than staircase curve around the wall to the temple entrance a few hundred feet above. The temple extrudes about 5 m from the wall attached and is supported by timbers driven into the rock.

One way traffic through the maze of chambers is carefully monitored by the resident monks. Ancient and suspicious iron rails supposedly protect you from the sheer drop below. An unsettling feeling pervades. Dating back some

The road to an ancient city.

1,400 years, the essence of the temple and monastery is its rare combination of Taoism, Confucianism and Buddhism.

The narrow entrance is foreboding as is the narrow walkway from chamber to chamber. Studded metal steps give a small vote of confidence. Sculptures are carved flat against the walls; meditation caves appear dreary and cell-like. It is said that the temple originated because a golden dragon was believed to be the cause of the annual floods inundating the valley. The monks could thus ward off evil in complete safety from the ravage of storms and waters.

You have to climb a few hundred steps up alongside the sheer wall of the dam target to the dam site and lake above. Just the idea of this alone has discouraged those suffering from acrophobia.

Most of the tourists climb to the top of the dam after leaving the temple, while the fainted-hearted make their way back to the car to commiserate with each other and wait for the crowd to return.

Xuankong Temple perched precariously on the side of a dam for 1,400 years now.

Taiyuan - Shanxi Province

Taiyuan is the capital of Shanxi Province. Like Suzhou it is known to be 2,500 years old and was on Marco Polo's route. In his day he described it as a prosperous city and center of trade and industry. It takes 8 or 9 hours by train between Datong and Taiyuan without having to camp by the wayside enroute.

The Shanxi Grand Hotel is indeed grand with spacious rooms and hot water bath guaranteed at least once a day. Across the wide avenue is a lovely park where you can go for your morning exercise or a stroll when you have an hour or two of leisure before dinner.

The **Provincial Museum of Shanxi** consists of 2 buildings : a Confucian temple and another building of Taoist origin built during the Ming and Qing period. A day trip out of Taiyuan is the **Shaunglin Monastery** of the same period, containing over 2,000 figures from earlier dynasties. The complex is well worth the visit even though travelers may be shy of temples by this time.

The **Jinci Buddhist Temple** is an interesting composite of halls, gardens, bridges of the Song, Zhou, Ming and Qing Dynasties. It is a half-hour drive outside the city. You may get back in time for a late lunch. In particular, cross the canal inside the temple complex on the **Huixian** ("Meet the Immortals Bridge"). Eleventh century cast iron fig-

The Museum of Shanxi is a modern example of Tang Dynasty architecture housing tomb artifacts.

ures stand waiting for your greetings. It is always nice to meet your own immortals, you never can tell when you will need their assistance.

For a special innovative treat, arrange a dinner in the subterranean air raid shelters cum food storage and an array of shops. The dinner is a unique travel treasure because of the ambience. The white tile entrance looks like a subway system, the long halls with storage niches emanates the fear that China once had of enemy bombing. Taiyuan throughout its history has been the victim of central location, a nerve center secondary to Beijing. The communists converted the coal deposits nearby the city into a vast industrial center. All energy hubs feared being bombed out by the Nationalists, the Russians or whoever else might want to replace the Politburo and take over China. When you sit back in your chair after a sumptuous dinner, staring at the assortment of soiled dishes, empty beer, orange crush and wine bottles, you will appreciate the incongruity of the location.

The strategic importance of Taiyuan is also evident when you have to make a decision as to the next stop. Due east is **Shijiazhuang**, the capital of Hebei Province on the rail link to Beijing. South is **Zhengzhou**, with access to the old capitals of Kaifeng and Luoyang. Southwest is **Xian**, where the buried terracotta army is slowly emerging from their 2000-year-old burial crypts. There is air access from Taiyuan to any of these destinations as well as exit from China via Beijing or Shanghai. Smart travelers will get back on the Iron Rooster, pass up Shijiazhuang (nothing of great interest), and head south to Zhengzhou, thence west to Xian.

Another alternative is to hire a car and driver from CITS to drive south to Yuncheng through Shanxi's less important but very interesting cities, on the way to Zhengzhou.

Linfen (Yao's City) was a capital city 5,000 years ago when a legendary tribal chief by the name of Yao commanded this territory. **Yao Temple** (Eastern Jin Dynasty 264-420) and **Dayun Monastery** (Tang Dynasty 627-649) are in the area. Dayun displays a 33-meter iron bust of Buddha and a towering pagoda. **Dongyue Monastery** is about 60 km away on **Dongshan Mountain**, a massive complex of over 300 buildings dedicated to Dongyue, a king known as god of destiny. He is still worshipped as the divine being who decides your hell or heaven fate. Every section of this province appears to have memorabilia temples, pagodas and old palaces of former rulers. There is a magnificent waterfall near the border of Shanxi and Shaanxi Provinces (it is difficult keeping the double "aa" Shaanxi apart from the single "a" neighbor Shanxi) called **Hukou** (teapot spout). The **Huanghe (Yellow River)** narrows into a gorge and spumes over a 30-meter falls.

Yuncheng is known as a place where Chinese culture began in early mythology. Yu the Great supposedly started the fabled Xia Dynasty and controlled the forces of the Huanghe. At **Changping** to the west, Guan Yu, a famous general of the Three Kingdoms Period (220-280) is memorialized. A traditional Chinese palace, started in the 6th century was renovated and enlarged during the Ming Dynasty (1634-1911). Surviving even the Cultural Revolution, it is in excellent condition from the animal decorated eaves to the gilded statue of General Guan sitting in a meditative position, long dangling pigtails dangling from sideburns, chin and mustache. The complex has 3 main sections, all with high ceilings and open pavilions dedicated to the master. He is further memorialized in the classic novel ***Romance of the Three Kingdoms***.

Side tours by car are the essence of travel treasures taking the traveler off the touted paths of the tours and the tourist crowds, to allow them to soak in the ambience of history and the great artistry of the ancients.

Kaifeng – Henan Province

Kaifeng, capital during the Northern Song Period can be a day trip east from Zhengzhou; however, it is well worth staying a day or two because of the historical attractions. The Eastern Capital Hotel is the newest and the Kaifeng Guesthouse is adequate. Another may be available by the time you arrive.

Kaifeng was the capital of Wei during the Warring States Period (465-211 BC); of Liang, Jin, Han, and Zhou during the Five Dynasties (907-960). The empire claimed it as capital during the Northern Song (960-1127) and the Jin Dynasty overlapped from 1115 to 1234. Even when the Mongols and the Manchus conquered the empire and moved the capital to Beijing, Kaifeng was a threatening thorn, subject to constant sieges and invasion.

During its heyday, Kaifeng's population exceeded 1 million in the 11th and early 12th century and was thought to be the largest city in the world at the time.

Song Capital Street, now known as **Zongshan** is a wide avenue leading to the Imperial Palace. Gray-tiled roofs, 2 and 3 storey red-shuttered buildings line the busy thoroughfare. Shops vending the classic calligraphy art, seal-carving, porcelain ware, antique curios, food shops and many others fill the lower floors.

As in all celebrated cities, there is always one classic area that inevitably arouses interest and endless comment. Located in a 3-storey building, the Alum is the most famous. The **Alum** was once the center of entertainment by singsong girls. Hearsay claims that more than a thousand vendors of the flesh worked in the pleasure palace. The figure given is of course logically impossible. The multitude of windows facing the street however, lend a certain veracity to the ease of advertising in those ancient days. In a classic novel **Outlaws of the Marsh** is a story about a Song Emperor Huizong and his singsong girl Li Shishi. Her room was in the Alum Building.

Drum Tower Square sports a night market every evening that, by tradition, lasts until the early morning hours. By dusk the hawkers would have set up dozens of food stalls hustling noodles, dumplings, deep fired whatevers, and banana leaf wrapped rice. Rows of stalls display the endless variety of local goods, imported goods and black market goods with their vendors shouting the wares.

Iron Pagoda is one of the most beautiful sights in the area, newly rebuilt from its 1000-year origin. The 13 storeys stand over 50 m high; the facade is of brown glazed tiles and decorated with mythical animals. **Dragon Park** and **Dragon Pavilion** date from the Song Dynasty (960-1279) when Kaifeng was the capital.

Yanqing Temple is in the southwest part of Kaifeng. It memorializes the Quangzhen Sect of Taoism's founder Wang Chongyang.

Religious history is centered in the **Dong Da Mosque** and **Xiangguo Si Monastery** and Kaifeng boasts an interesting sidelight of history, a small tribe of Hebrews. Their origin is uncertain but their existence was recorded in the diary of the Jesuit priest Matteo Ricci in 1615. Chinese missionaries recovered the scrolls and prayer books from floods in 1642 and 1850.

Xian is a 12-hour train trip from Zhengzhou or you can fly there in an hour. Air transportation is also avail-

Shaolin power.

able to Beijing and Shanghai.

Zhengzhou – Henan Province

Zhengzhou boasts of the comfortable Henan International House which is a pleasant place to stay. It conveniently contains the CITS offices. Food service is good and special treat dinners can easily be arranged by your guide at the Shaolin or Shushang Restaurants, in their upstairs private facilities. The antique and curio section of the Friendship Store has or did have at one time, a nice collection of snuff bottles and jade amulets. Ask to see the vault room that displays a remarkable collection of antique fine imperial jade for sale. Some of the pieces compare with items in the jewelry section of the Forbidden City, at prices that would impoverish an Emperor.

Zhengzhou is a large city, built up mainly after the Communists took over. Like Taiyuan, the large tour groups pass it up in favor of Xian. Therefore you will find the CITS more amenable, the hotel personnel affable and anxious to visit with you.

Henan Provincial Museum is negligible but the **Shang City** ruins outside the city is interesting as a warmup for the Xian and Banpo digs to be visited later. You get to go into the tombs and see the coffins still intact. The ruins around the area give a hint of village life thousands of years ago. A visit to the **Huanghe** and its irrigation projects, **Mengshan** (*shan* means "mountain") and the nearby **Yellow River Park** is a nice morning's drive.

A 3-day southern loop side trip through Henan Province covers **Luoyang** and the **Longmen Caves**, **Sangyang Academy of Classical Learning** and the **Shaolin Monastery** in Deng Feng county, the highlight of the Zhengzhou stop. As always the individual trips by private vehicle are the most enjoyable. When you return from the loop you can take a side trip for the day or overnight to Kaifeng, once the imperial capital of the Northern Song Dynasty (960-1127AD).

The first night's stay is at Luoyang and the second night at a remote hotel on the edge of a small village, the closest thing you will get to a motel in China. Apparently built to accommodate independent travelers, the closet-sized rooms are clean, ensuite toilets, and showers down the outside arcade. The menu is table d'hote but better than the formal hotel in Luoyang.

Luoyang Loop – Henan Province

Luoyang was founded in 1200 BC, the capital of 10 dynasties. It was the door through which Buddhism entered China from India. The first temple, **White Horse** (67 AD), saw the translation of Indian Sanskrit scriptures into Chinese. The present day Ming and Qing buildings are on the site of the original temple. During the Northern Wei Dynasty (386-534 AD) hundreds of temples were built. The ambitious monks and their disciples dug caves into the sandstone

A narrow corridor along the side of cave grottoes.

cliffs and carved massive sculptures in them. The sculpting was cleverly done to leave pictorials on the walls and ceilings, nooks and crannies. Succeeding generations added more caves with thousands of carved figures in them.

The **Longmen Caves** are an interesting historic site. One of the caves has over 10,000 small carved Buddhas in little niches. It is said that they were once made of solid gold and replaced with gilt replicas by subsequent dynasties. According to the records there are 97,000 carved statues in 1,400 caves plus 750 small shrines and over 40 pagodas. It is the highest concentration of Buddhist art work in the world. You are guaranteed to get a fill of statues and

The Martial Arts of the Shaolin Monastery

Devotion to martial arts requires discipline and training.

The all time favorite Chinese movies like "The Shaolin Monastery", "The Sons of Shaolin" and "The Wudang Mountains" are re-run year after year in the cinemas and television. Soap opera style series based on patriotic themes and classical martial arts are shown wherever television or video presentations are available. Small children, sporting wooden sword replicas leap and prance in the streets to emulate their TV heros equivalent to Batman or Spiderman. Morning *taijiquan* and *qigong* exercises are a prevalent feature the length and breadth of China.

Aficionados of *kung fu, karate, taekwondo* or *judo* from all over the world journey to their mecca, the Shaolin Zen Buddhist Monastery in the Songshan Mountains of Henan Province, as pilgrims to attend training courses. The arts all originated in China as techniques in physical exercise which turned into martial combat or competitive training.

Changquan, long boxing, is taught as the art of speed and dexterity. *Xingyiquan*, imitation boxing has graceful, balanced, dance-like movements, favored as the years take their toll on muscle and bone. The southern style of boxing, *nanquan*, attempts to simulate the movement of animals like the slinking tiger or the high-stepping crane.

Recorded history of Shaolin begins in the 6th century with the monk, Bodhidarma, who founded the monastery. It started as a method of exercise for the sedentary meditating monks and became a military adjunct under a Tang Emperor (Li Shimin, 626-649). *Jiujitsu* is the Japanese art of self-defence which merged with the Shaolin systems to create *judo* (the Soft Path), *karate* and *aikido*. Korea adopted a form called *taekwondo* and *tangshoudo*. Thailand's is called *siamqu* and the Philippines adopted stick fighting.

Bruce Lee's films made a household word of *kung fu*, which is not a style but a description of one's ability. Lee was *kung fu* when he practiced karate, for instance.

Taijiquan is by far the most popular offering an "inner approach" to shadow boxing. The style is reputed to have been formed from observation of a snake and a crane fighting. The crane strikes hard fast blows, while the undulating snake avoids being struck by dexterity. Bodhidarma taught that flexibility is superior to strength. His method is encircling to break the momentum of harsh blows. Movements must always flow like water, upstream or downstream (forward or back) with great concentration on breathing. "Taiji", means the highest point in the sky and therefore the principle around which the world revolves, thus the navel becomes the fulcrum for the exercises.

Qigong is the breathing technique and medical practitioners in China relate it to health curatives. *Taijiquan* and *qigong* are reputed to have a positive effect on metabolism; they lower cholesterol, prevents arteriosclerosis if done on a regular basis.

Taijiquan is also an art based on the evasion of a fight, said to make one supple as a child, healthy like a woodcutter and calm as a sage.

Posturing their prayers.

ancient massive art works, enough to last for the rest of the trip. Fortune will be with you if it is a hot day in the summer and the sellers of watermelons are standing ready with their slicing knives.

Shongyan Shu Yuan (Academy of Classical High Learning) is on an off road from Luoyang towards Shaolin Monastery. It is a winding unpaved succession of hairpin curves up the mountain, frequented by the occasional donkey cart of a local farmer. The village is small and the streets too narrow for the car so one must wend one's way uphill to the gates of the academy. Shongyan Shu Yuan is the oldest school of higher learning in China. There is a 3,000-year-old cypress where Confucius is said to have taught his disciples. The local lore is that when you touch the gnarled ancient branches you will have joined hands with the scholars and thus gained some of their wisdom.

Shaolin Monastery is the last major stop on the loop, with its nearby forest of stupas on **Song Shan** (Middle Mountain). There is not a lot to see, but a walk through the historic ambience of the monastery listening to the story of the founding Indian monks is memorable. Their devotion to Buddhism by cultivating moral character with prayer and physical fitness is exemplary. Stiff limbs, arising from hours of sitting cross-legged during prayer time, needed the exercise to keep them fit; thus was born the martial arts called *kung-fu*.

Damo, one of the monks started

Jun Porcelain, Luoyang tri-colored Glazed Pottery

The tri-colored glazed pottery of the Tang Dynasty was fashioned in Luoyang 1,300 years ago. Figures of camels, horses, kings and people were decorated with the red, green and white glazes softly blended into each other. A modern research factory continues to experiment with the system to replicate the original works. Modern adaptations have added black, purple, yellow, and blue among other colors to the selection.

Jun porcelain, far older, is said to originate in the Xia Dynasty (21st to 16th century BC) and is still produced in Henan Province. Like the Tang period, its claim to beauty is in the magnificent colors of the blended glazes. Blue glaze was introduced in the Song Dynasty and the introduction of copper into the process produced unique results. The copper also produced a hardness that would ring and a solid texture. The art work serves as functional pieces such as vases, complicated serving trays and wine vessels. Descendants of the original potters are again working up the international reputation of the Jun porcelain urged and supported by the government's desire for exports.

Both the Tang and the Jun porcelain are spread throughout the heartland of the Silk Road and the ancient capitals. Visit the factories and showrooms in Luoyang and Zhengzhou to find the one-of-a-kind prizewinning show piece.

---

with boxing, developing an intense variety of styles. Records of the 5th century Northern Dynasties tell of the special fighting abilities called martial arts taught by the monks of Shaolin.

Next to the temple complex is the **Pagoda Forest**, literally a cemetery for distinguished leaders of Shaolin. Some of the kung fu movies were filmed here for background. The adversaries leaped, spun, kicked and fought to the end among the grove of pagodas. To the Chinese tourists who come in droves, it is the JR Ewing Southfork Ranch of "Dallas" television fame. The Chinese are addicted to the fast action films showing actors flying through the air, kick-tossing and pounding each other to the ground for hours at a time (without a bruise or drop of blood!).

A story evolving from Shaolin is of the white snake transformed into a beautiful maiden. She or it, had an exquisite love affair with her hero who fought hordes of villains to rescue her. The tale has been made into a favorite movie. Dozens of similar tear-jerkers with amazing fighting grace were filmed without the greased bodies and fierce weapons of modern day Stallone and Schartzenagger.

The village, streets leading up to the temple, smoke-belching buses, the proliferation of graffiti and resulting litter are typical of those scenic wonders of the masses. Hopefully the government's Department of Tourism will have it cleaned up before you get there.

On the way back to Zhengzhou, your guide will undoubtedly pause at **Aongyue Temple**, the largest of the Taoist temples and the **Han Tombs** in Mixian County. The site is an antitheses of Shaolin, clean and neat with a tea shop for respite. The deep passageway down into the burial area is lighted.

CARGOS & CULTURE

Xian & The Silk Road

The legendary Silk Road dates as far back as 2000 years and came about with the advent of the well-known trade route from China through Central Asia to Europe, the main item transported along the route being silk.

Starting from **Xian** (ancient Chang'an) the original road traverses Shanxi and Gansu Provinces, the Tarim Basin in Xinjiang, Central Asia, Iran, Iraq and Syria to the east coast of the Mediterranean Sea. In all, it covers a distance of 7,000 km, more than half of which is in China.

Sprawling along the Silk Road today are some well-known historical sites such as the buried terracotta army of China's first emperor, the Famen Temple, Sakyamuni's Shrine, the world renowned Mogao Grottoes in Dunhuang, Jiayuguan the starting point of the Great wall; majestic Ta'er Monastery and Gaochang, once an important town.

The several dozen minority nationalities living along the way take

The Bell Tower in Xian is an imposing reminder of its history.

A Muslim cherub.

the traveler back to another era of a time long past with their song, dance and varied festivities.

Xian, Ancient Chang'an – Shaanxi Province

Chang'an, as it was once known, is in the center of the vast Shaanxi Plain. Twelve dynasties, from Western Zhou (1,000 BC) to the days of the Tang, 1100 years later, built their capitals here.

At the height of the Tang Dynasty, Chang'an was the capital of the empire populated by a good number of courtiers, merchants and foreign traders. It was a cosmopolitan city and foreigners were allowed to take up residence for commerce, education and other cultural exchanges. Being the hub of the empire it was linked to the rest of China by canals and roads. Roads radiated from Chang'an and extended to sea ports and caravan routes which connected China to the rest of the world, thus making Chang'an an international trade centre. It was from here that Chinese envoy, Zhang Qian, set out on the historic mission to the west and thus the Silk Road came into being as a viable and important trade route linking the east to the west.

Xian, the City

Xian and the surrounding area, after

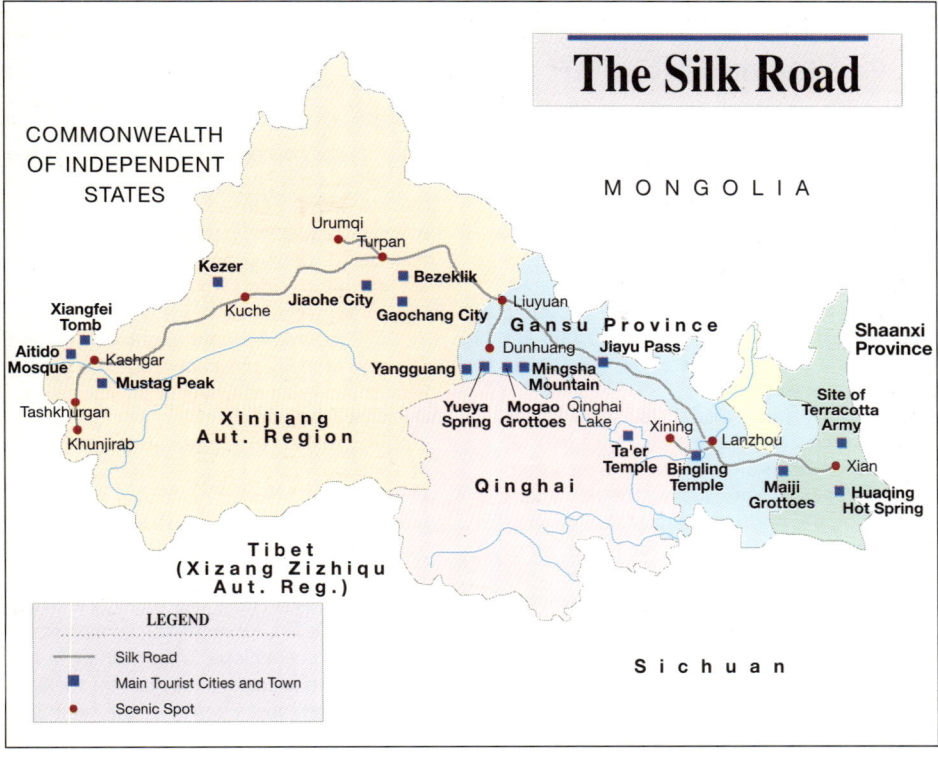

The Silk Road

the Great Wall, attract China's greatest number of tourists. It is surrounded by a rectangular wall with a circumference of 14 km. The walls had been rebuilt and date as far back as the Tang Dynasty, if not even earlier, and some parts have completely disappeared.

Xian itself is a large bustling city that has a university and a pleasant town square featuring a massive **Bell Tower** and **Drum Tower**, both evidences of the communication process of another era. The Temple of Confucius is now the **Shaanxi Provincial Museum**, containing relics of many dynasties, dating as far back as the Zhou Dynasty.

The **Forest of Stele**s is engrossing even if you cannot read all the ancient script. It is the largest stone library in China comprising steles and engraved stone tablets. It was built to preserve the 13 classics including the Confucian Analects.

Standing as a reminder of Xian at its height of cultural importance is the **Big Wild Goose Pagoda** (Ci'en Temple) and the **Little Goose Pagoda** found a few kilometers apart outside the gates of Xian. Both had been built to store the Buddhist scriptures and writings brought back from India by the traveling monks. 1335 volumes of translated scripts by Xuan Zang are stored in the Big Wild Goose Pagoda. You can also get a good

Passage of Silk and Art Treasures

For hundreds of years till today, just the mention of the Silk Road would be catalytic, sending the imagination reeling with visions of fabled cities and serpentine camel caravans crawling across vast open deserts and climbing difficult narrow mountain passes to carry silk and other Chinese luxuries to the imperial courts of Rome, Arabia and India. The Silk Road stretched 7,000 km between the great empires of the age, China and Rome, Persia and India.

It all began more than 2,000 years ago in 138 BC when Zhang Qian (Chang Chien) set out on a secret mission to the west, to secure aid for Emperor Han Wudi against the barbarians threatening the north of China. As he traveled west, Zhang Qian discovered the kingdoms of Central Asia and learnt about the great empires of Persia, India and Rome. The news aroused untold curiosity; stories were rife on either side of the world. In the east, the reigning emperor decided to establish trade relations with the kingdoms of the west. The route taken by Zhang Qian became established over the years linking China to the west and was named the Silk Road by European scholars.

The original Silk Road began in the ancient Chinese capital of Chang'an (now Xian) and led through the corridor west of the Huanghe in Gansu Province, passing Langzhou, Jinquan, Jiayu Pass and Dunhuang. However, the term is misleading for many roads led west from Chang'an. Principal routes pass through Gansu Province to Xinjiang going either north or south around the Taklamakan Desert, the Pamirs (then called Congling), Central Asia, Afghanistan, Iran, Iraq and Syria, ending at the eastern shores of the Mediterranean Sea, more than half of the distance being in China. Other routes include the southwestern route through Yunnan and later another that transported the cargoes by ship from the port of Guangzhou (the Sea Silk Road).

The Silk Road was memorable for the treasures that were transported on heavily burdened camels across hazardous terrains. Silk was the most valued cargo, hence the name of the route "the Silk Road". Other cargo included furs, ceramics, lacquer, bronzeware and rhubarb, all these being items exported from China. On their return trip traders would bring gold, linen, ivory, coral, precious stones and glass into China. The Silk Road also brought about a significant exchange of ideas and knowledge. Buddhism for example, entered China in the 1st century AD via the Silk Road.

After a millennium, trade on the Silk Road lost its momentum. Europe discovered silkworms when silkworms were smuggled from China. Silk was then produced domestically and this affected trade adversely. Travel along the Silk Road, which had always been long and hazardous (the elements took their toll with the Taklamakan Desert, for example, claiming many lives), now grew perilous. Tribal warfare in the western region decreased the odds for survival. Gradually China lost interest in the west and trade on the Silk Road practically ceased, the Silk Road faded into a myth.

Interest in the Silk Road revived in the late 19th century, this time by the Europeans. A search for antiquities and the mood of the day: the search for something new and exotic, a thirst for adventure and the need to concretise what was now the chimerique Silk Road brought a new flock of travelers on the Silk Road.

Adventurers and European scholars explored the great heartland of Eurasia discovering the lost mythical cities of the Silk Road and taking with them vast amounts of art treasures to the museums of Europe, India and Japan. Starting from Xian, some of the historical sites include Dunhuang, Jiayuguan, the Turpan Depression, Urumqi and Kashgar.

The Silk Road is even more accessible now to travelers. In ancient times camels were the only means of transport. Today, there are the trains and buses apart from the basic camels, horses and bicycles.

view of the countryside and the city from the outstanding Buddhist structure here which has become the symbol of the city of Xian.

Northwest of the Drum Tower is the **Great Mosque**, one of the largest Is-

The Big Wild Goose Pagoda stores Buddhist scriptures and writings brought back by monks returning from India.

lamic mosques in China. It was substantially expanded during the Tang Dynasty and renovated a number of times during the latter dynasties. The murals and 600 ceiling panels are rare ancient art works rich in color and design.

Xian Environs

The Tomb of Qin Shihuang. The province of Shaanxi keeps a record of the imperials and their lifestyle. Along with the luxurious chateaus of their realms

The Buried Terracotta Army

At the age of 13 Ying Zheng ascended the throne of the Qin Dynasty and became the first emperor, Qin Shihuang (259–210 BC) in 246 BC. He began his tomb when he first ascended the throne and continued its construction during his lifetime.

At the age of 22, Zheng declared himself the First Emperor of Qin after he united China by conquering other warrior states and introducing education, currency, weights and a written script. Qin revealed a paradoxical streak of cruelty in his dealings with his own people. Exorbitant taxes were levied and the records show he conscripted 700,000 peasants to build his Afang Palace and the Mausoleum. Hundreds of thousands more garrisoned the frontiers and built the Great Wall. Uprisings and other conquering hordes eventually destroyed the empire, burned the palace and robbed parts of the vast underground mausoleum. That was 2,500 years ago. Qin died in 210 BC at the ripe old age of 50.

Farmers uncovered the buried army of terracotta soldiers in March, 1974, while drilling a well. The Shaanxi Provincial Museum under the leadership of Shaanxi Provincial Committee for the Protection and Preservation of Historical Relics and the Cultural Centre of Lintong County took over. Eventually 2 more pits were discovered in a site area of 6,500 sq m. Viewed under an immense skeletal building, a small section of the underground city in the first pit is mesmerizing. At present 2 vaults are open to visitors.

The first vault is thought to have 6,000 terracotta warriors when the entire area of 14,629 sq m was exhumed from the rammed earth walls. The soldiers and cadres of officer led units stand row upon row fitted with armor, their armament, horses and war-carts. Look carefully at the faces of the soldiers, only a few uncovered. Each is different, a sculpture of an actual human, with an assortment of individual features.

The test excavation shows that these underground vaults were originally a huge construction of earth and wood work, at one time burned in a fire and collapsed. On the east side there are 5 passages. The excavation you will see is the western part of the middle passage, 7.5m long, 3.7/4.2m wide, and 0.5-4.0m deep. The earth on the slope is very hard, rammed earth construction. The passage was stopped up by beams standing in dense rows, wrapped outside with a layer of mats. The standing beams were burned leaving traces of the mat patterns and charred holes where the beams once were. Corridors are laid out for the lines of the figures. In between every 2 corridors are earth ridges seeming to symbolize the walls.

This data reveals how the vaults were built. The weight was borne by the pillars, covered with mats and then clay. Red soil, loess and drab soil were then laid on top to cover the entire site. Generations of earth movement domed the sites. After the early pillages, the tombs were forgotten until the farmers' drilling activities uncovered the stupendous ancient works.

Over 500 warriors, tall life-sized pottery figures, are exposed, the bulk of them crushed during the period of the burning. There are 2 kinds of warriors, those wearing short coarse clothes, the foot soldiers, and warriors clad in armour who wear waist bands, puttees and shoes in the shape of a square in the upper and unpointed toes. Hair is put up in buns all turned to the right side. Judging from the various gestures of hands and arms plus the real weapons unearthed beside them, some carried arrows and bows with quivers on the back. Others bore spears and swords, crossbows and arrows.

Twenty-four horses, 4 abreast lead 6 chariots. They are with decorated gold, bronze and

The buried terracotta army in full attendance.

stone. Fire burned out the wooden parts of the harnessing, leaving the debris of the decorations and metal pieces. Work continues to restore each figure, wagon, pottery and equipment to close to the original state.

Overall, the lines of warriors and horses with chariots depict an army full of power and grandeur as you can imagine the Qin Emperor surveying his domain. The youthful commander swept away 6 other states as a tiger would sweep any living thing before him. Panoply and ceremony are recorded as Qin returned to the capital, a conquering hero.

Both men and horses were made of the gray pottery and clay, baked in high temperature leaving a hard surface. Observations revealed they were made in molds but sculptured one by one.

The heads, hands and bodies were made separately, then assembled with mud before firing. Heads, bodies and arms are hollow, whereas the feet, legs and hands are solid. Apparently the feet and legs were made first, then dried. Bodies were constructed using strings of clay, heads usually made in 2 halves and then joined.

After the clay was applied for the second time, details of the mouth, nose, eyes and marks of clothes were sculpted. Hair was applied by dividing it to the ears, combed across the temple and then pigtails were added, plaited in 3 strands to a tail. The pigtails were then coiled into a bun and fastened with the help of a hairpin. Each figure varied as if an individual model posed for his own reproduction in clay.

Originally the pottery figures were painted with bright colors, almost all deteriorated in the fires and through time. Enough residue remains to provide the myriad of colors available: green, delicate pale green, bright red, delicate pale-pink, orange-yellow, black and white, grey white, reddish brown and others. This attention to detail is intriguing to the viewer; that is why we suggest a second or even a third visit to appreciate the grandeur.

The souvenir shop at the digs are loaded with replicas of the Tang horses and camels. Printed literature, slide sets, postcards abound and they will probably have video tapes by the time you get there. The literature is good depending on your penchant for collecting. Pass up the handicrafts because the local minorities have set up roadside outdoor shopping fairs with much more interesting clothing items. The Tang pottery replicas in Guangzhou and Hong Kong are much better.

As to visiting the many sites surrounding Xian, our recommendation is to spend the money and have CITS organize a non-group tour for you in a private car. The regular package tours leave you too little time at each site. You need a minimum of 2 visits to the terracotta warriors locale at different times to absorb the scope of the digs. It is more than a burial tomb, an incomparable window into the past.

are hectares of tombs where they constructed underground palaces to spend their afterlife.

The celebrated digs of the first emperor of the Qins is the ultimate in burial grounds, now 1 of the 3 most important sites in China for local Chinese and international visitors.

Qin Shihuang (259–210 BC), China's first emperor, had this tomb constructed from the time he ascended the throne. The tomb, found at the foot of **Lishan (Li Hill)** in Lintong County comprised basically an inner and outer city. Three vaults housing 6,000 terracotta warriors and horses are located 1.5 km east of the emperor's tomb.

The largest vault contains about 1,000 warriors of an average height of 1.8m and several dozen live-size horses. These figures are well-shaped and proportioned, highly realistic and have great artistic appeal.

Banpo Village

Even older than Xian is the 6,000-year-old **Banpo Village** located 6 km outside the city. Treated more modestly than the digs, the village is, however, the second attraction in Xian after the buried terracotta legion.

It is one of the earliest known agricultural villages in China covering an area of 50,000 sq m.

It has a museum displaying primitive villages, the tools of production and artifacts for daily use.

Banpo Village

Six kilometers outside of Xian, Banpo Village is a fascinating view into life as it was 6000 years ago. Banpo was a communal village in the Neolithic Age. Excavation discovered it to be a matriarchal society which survived by farming, fishing, hunting and raising livestock. They created kilns to make earthenware products and to build permanent homes. Very simply, the village was divided into a residential area, a pottery area and a burial ground. The village was surrounded by a moat with plank bridges withdrawn at night for protection. A museum was built on the actual digging site and it displays evidences of the civilization: hatchets, scythes, knives, arrowheads carved from stone, fine needles and other household tools made from bone. Pottery shards proved the baking of clay with decorations and art forms of the period. Faint colors with incised lines depicting a tiger or warrior are visible on the pottery.

Women were believed to wield great influence because valuables were buried with the females, interred separately from the males. Archeologists believe polygamy was the way of life. Homes were for the mothers and children while the men went on long hunting trips. Banpo is supposed to be a village of women, visited occasionally by the nomadic men.

Huaqing Hot Springs

Not far from the Qinling terracotta figures at the foot of **Lishan**, the **Huaqing Hot Springs** is an excellent retreat. You can bathe in the mineral baths as did the emperors' concubines, in public bathhouses serviced with water from the hot springs. You will not be able to resist stopping along the roadside to shop at the stalls of colorful native clothing and souvenirs.

For a special treat, adventurous

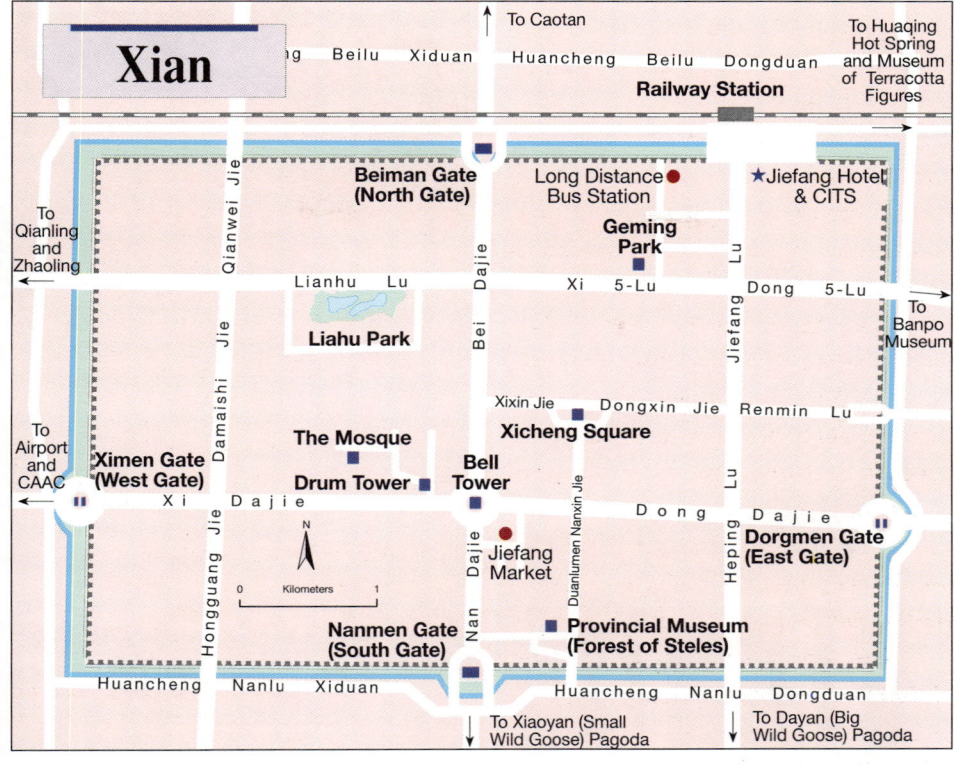

travelers can arrange to stay a night or two at the hot springs in classic Ming ambience. It is an excellent place from which you can visit the famous digs, a few minutes away.

Xian is such a popular destination now that charters fly directly from and to Hong Kong and there are many direct flights connecting Xian to many Asian cities.

There are at least 4 five-star hotels in Xian to choose from, all highly priced (see Directory). They will take international reservations by facsimile in case you want to make a direct trip from Hong Kong or a domestic flight from any of the major cities in China.

Lanzhou

Lanzhou lies along the **Huanghe** between 2 mountains. It became a major city on the ancient Silk Road and was a center for caravan traffic till World War II because of its strategic geographical location. Lanzhou is the capital of Gansu Province and became a major industrial city with a fine railway network and air system linking the city to the rest of the country.

Though the city itself offers little in terms of major attractions it is a very pleasant place. The **White Pagoda Hill** lies on the north bank of the Huanghe,

The emperor and his concubines took their retreat in the Huaqing Hot Springs which contained mineral baths.

just opposite the city. It is a beautiful park named after the temple White Pagoda, a 17-meter rectangular structure built during the Yuan Dynasty. Across the street from Friendship Hotel is **Gansu Provincial Museum** displaying exhibits native to Gansu Province and the **Biling Si Caves.**

Remember that you are in the river valley: fruit is abundant, particularly the Bailan sweet melon and the Dongguo pears. Gansu art-craft products are also much sought after, such as the luminous wine cup, carved lacquerware,

hotels in town, with the latter being used by visiting dignitaries. Alternatively, the Lanzhou Hotel is more strategically located in town and in terms of accessibility.

Lanzhou Environs

Certainly a sight not to be missed are the stupendous **Biling Si Caves**. The 183 caves built over 2 kms of sheer cliffs, contain 694 stone statues, 82 clay sculptures and 900 sq m of murals. They date as far back as 420 AD, though two-thirds of the art were completed during the Tang Dynasty. The sculpture and murals display high artistic skill revealing ideas taken from both folk and foreign art.

There are organized tours to Biling Si Caves, 110 km from Lanzhou and not easily accessible. From Lanzhou you can either take a minibus from the Victory Hotel (book in advance) or book on a minibus tour with CITS.

The whole tour takes about 12 hours, travel time being equally divided between travelling on the bus and the boat. Though the long journey is worth the experience, you should not spend more than an hour at the caves themselves, even if they seem impressive.

An alternative to the organized tour is to take the public bus from Lanzhou to Yonqing where you can join a tour boat to the Biling Si Caves. During spring and summer floods may render the caves inaccessible.

inkslabs and carvings on pebbles from the Huanghe. A further expression of art is found in the highly recommended Dance Ensemble of Gansu Province (enquire at the hotel information desk).

Accommodation on the whole, in Lanzhou, is rather inexpensive. The Jinchen Hotel and the Ninwozhuang Guesthouse are 2 of the more expensive

A treasure trove of art was uncovered in the Mogao Grottoes just outside Dunhuang.

Xining – Qinghai Province

From Lanzhou, you can take a 5-hour train ride to **Xining**, the next stop on the Silk Road. Xining lies on the Tibetan Plateau and is the capital and only large city of vast Qinghai Province. The city is a stopover for travelers heading for **Ta'er Monastery** and **Qinghai Lake**.

Various minority groups and the Hans live in this region. You will find an expression of this colorful ethnic mixture in the busy **Great Mosque** on Dongguan Dajie and the **Beishan Temple**, a short hike up the mountainside. Look for the huge market, near the **West Gate**, which is well worth a visit if you need to shop for basic essentials. Some of the best restaurants are located around the market such as the Peace Restaurant on Dong Dajie. The Qingken Daxia on Shengli Lu and the Rongyuan Fandian are equally good, but are located further from the city center.

Accommodation to date ranges from the posh Qinghai Hotel to the Xining and the Xining Daxia.

Other than the train, Xining is also accessible by air from Beijing, Lanzhou and Taiyuan.

Xining Environs

Ta'er Monastery was built in the 16th century at the birthplace of its founder,

Bird Island on Qinghai Lake is a breeding ground for migratory birds.

Zonggeba. It is located in **Huangzhong**, 25 km from Xining and is one of China's 6 large lamaseries of the Yellow Sect Buddhism.

The monastery is 400,000 sq m comprising several temples and immense halls and is a miniature town. Ta'er is also well known for certain artistic works: butter sculpture, wall painting and "piled" embroidery. Butter sculpture originated in Tibet and they are figures and landscapes carved skilfully out of yak butter.

An attractive feature of this visit is that you can stay at the monastery itself which provides accommodation for guests at Y10 for a bed in a 3-bed room. The extensive monastery grounds and its surrounding area are well worth exploring. You can always take a walk down the hill towards town. To add to this attraction, food at the monastery is good and there are regular buses to Huangzhong from Xining.

Qinghai Lake

From Xining you can also take a trip to **Qinghai Lake** or "green lake", 300 km west of Xining. It is the largest salt water lake in China, surrounded by snow-capped mountains and good pastureland. To add to this idyllic nature scene, the many islands on the lake become breeding grounds for migratory birds from April to September.

The most popular of these islands is

Bird Island, northwest of Qinghai Lake. Over recent years, rain and water shortage have made the island a peninsula.

Bird Island is not easily accessible, the closest town having regular transport to Xining is **Hemaihe**.

From Hemaihe take the bus heading towards Bird Island. To date the occasional bus that runs in this direction stops at **Shinaihai** (40 km). From here it is another 13 km to the Bird Island Hotel and you either walk there or hitch a ride.

Alternatively there are organized tours with CITS or you can rent a minibus in a group through the Peace Center.

Jiayuguan

Jiayuguan (Jiayu Pass) lies essentially between the snow-capped peaks of **Qilianshan** and **Black Mountain** (Mazon Range). In 1372 the reigning Ming emperor had a fort built here and since then the pass has been considered to mark the end of the Great Wall. In reality, the wall extends beyond this point.

The fort is enclosed by an inner and outer wall 10 m high. Two 17-meter high towers on either side of the inner wall overlook the fort. The fort was also called the "Impregnable Pass Under Heaven".

Apart from accommodation, Jiayuguan Hotel would be a useful landmark from which to find one's bearings. You can get either a minibus or a bus

from the hotel to the railway station and the fort proper itself. To board the bus to Dunhuang, however, you have to take a 20-minute walk from the hotel.

The choice of accommodation is limited in Jiayuguan. The Jiayuguan Hotel is the more popular of 2 hotels as it is strategically located in town while the more recent Chang Cheng Hotel is

Jiayuguan on the Mazon Range supposedly marks the end of the Great Wall extending westwards.

not as conveniently located and it takes about 35 minutes to walk to the railway station.

Jiayuguan town lies on the Lanzhou-Urumqi railway line and there is a regular train service on this line. Another possibility is to take flights into Jiayuguan from Lanzhou and Dunhuang but these are subject to the tourist trade and may not operate during the slow tourist season. The airport is 14 km from the city and bus rides to Dunhuang take a good 7 hours from Jiayuguan.

Jiayuguan Environs

Jiayuguan's out of this world surroundings inevitably tempt the traveler to explore outside the town. The **Overhanging Great Wall**, 7 km away, links Jiayuguan to Black Mountain. It was reconstructed in 1987 from remnants dating back to the 16th century. Nine kilometers northwest of Jiayuguan are the **Black Mountain Rock Paintings** which date back to the Warring States Period (476-221 BC), a platter for enthusiasts.

If you have come as far as this, you may just want to make a trip to the **Xicheng Underground Gallery**, euphemistic for the original wall paintings of ancient tombs found on this site, which date as far back as the 2nd century. This immense site of tombs is in the desert 20 km east of Jiayuguan.

Further afield is the **July 1st Glacier**, 120 km southwest of Jiayuguan in the **Qilianshan**.

The glacier is 4300 m high and you can hike up the side of the glacier on a 5-kilometer long path. You need to take a taxi there which would cost at least Y200.

Similarly, there is no public transport to the other sites outside Jiayuguan. You can either organize a trip on a minibus (if you can get a group together) or hire a taxi. A possible alternative for the sites nearer the town is to hitch a ride on a tour bus with a little gift for the driver.

Dunhuang

Dunhuang is a shock of green in the midst of the barren unchanging scene of the desert. The sight of this town by the oasis is certainly a welcome change for all travelers after a long haul in the desert. In ancient times Dunhuang was a key town along the Silk Road where

Sculptures of Sakyamuni and his disciples abound in the caves along the Silk Road.

Chinese traders would hand over their goods to Central Asian caravan masters.

Reminders of Dunhuang's heyday can be seen in the ruins of the **Yangguan**, lying 76 km southwest, and the **Yumen**, lying 98 km northwest of the town. They were strategically important passes along the active south and north routes of the Silk Road respectively. Today Dunhuang is more of a stopping point for its remarkable attractions: the **Mogao Grottoes** and the desert "wonders" of the **Mingshasan** (Singing Sand Hill) and the **Yueya** (Crescent) **Spring**.

Dunhuang is more easily accessible by rail and bus. The town **Liyuan** lies on the Lanzhou-Urumqi railway line and is the jumping off point for Dunhuang. From Liyuan you can take a bus to Dunhuang, a 3-hour ride over 130 kms. The bus station is a short distance from the railway station.

Alternatively, there are direct buses from Jiayuguan to Dunhuang. It is a stiff 7-hour ride over 380 kms. There are also flights into Dunhuang from Lanzhou and Jiayuguan and charter flights from Beijing (between July and October).

The town does not offer a wide selection of hotels. The better known, however, is the large Dunhuang Hotel which is strategically located near the CAAC office and the CITS and is the point from which to hire taxis to visit the sites outside the town. It also offers good, reasonably priced food.

Take note that there is another Dunhuang Hotel which is a lot smaller and located near the bus station. Facilities here are somewhat lacking though its location is convenient. Another hotel to be considered is the Silu Hotel, located just behind the large Dunhuang Hotel and Feitian Hotel. On a warm summer evening, take a walk downtown and head for the traffic circle by the post office. Find yourself a table among the multitude set up specially for dinner and try the local fare of your choice.

The town itself has little to offer in terms of attractions. There is the **Dunhuang County Museum** along Panxuan Lu which displays ethnic scriptures and relics unearthed from the sites around the city.

Dunhuang Environs

Standing out in the stern desert landscape is the **Mingshashan (Singing Sand Hill)**. Lying 6 km out of Dunhuang, it comprises numerous dunes and ridges, the sandy slopes giving the impression of rippling waves.

When the wind blows over the sand or if you slide down the sand from the hilltop, you can hear a pleasant sound as if the sand is "singing".

This dramatic scene terminates in a delightful crescent-shaped pool **(Yueya Spring)** found at the foot of Mingshashan. Despite lying in the desert surrounded by sand, the spring has never dried up nor been buried by sand. There is one bus daily, in the evening, to the sand dunes.

Mogao Grottoes

At the eastern foot of the Mingshashan, 25 kms southeast of Dunhuang, lies one of China's 3 brilliant troves, the **Mogao Grottoes.** Five tiers of caves had been hewn in the steep desert cliffs of Mingshashan out of which only 492 caves remain, the rest having been badly damaged by the weather over time and erosion.

The caves contain 45 000 sq m of murals and over 2,000 statues mainly of Buddha and his disciples, many of them colored. These sculpture and murals have been highly acclaimed as works of

The murals in Dunhuang.

art. They reveal the different emphases relevant to the dynastic periods during which they were built such as the various interpretations of Buddha, his deeds and life stories, portraits and lifestyle of the nobles of the various dynasties. These grottoes appearing against the setting of an arid desert landscape accentuate even more, the high workmanship of this extensive work of art.

For over 10 centuries these caves made Dunhuang the center of Buddhist culture on the Silk Road. When traffic on the Silk Road declined, they slipped into anonymity and were gradually abandoned. Interest in the grottoes revived in the early 20th century when the explorers, Sir Aurel Stein and a Frenchman Pelliot, fell upon a treasure trove of ancient classics, documents and silk paintings which were stored in a cave guarded by a monk. The ensuing deal made by these explorers and the monk, Wang Yuan, a venture quickly taken up by others, remains a controversial issue. Stein, for example, bought up a substantial part of this ancient find for the British Museum in return for restoring some of the grottoes.

A public bus leaves Dunhuang for the Mogao Grottoes twice a day. It is a half hour trip one way leaving you about 2 hours at the caves before the bus returns to town. You can also take a taxi to the caves but you need to arrange for the driver to wait for you. For the enthusiast, there is a good hotel at the caves where one can stay for the night.

Xinjiang & Environs

Turpan, **Urumqi** and **Kashgar** mark the Central Asian reaches of the silk route. Imagine Zhang Qian's astonishment and awe as he ventured on this unmarked road with his entourage: the harshness of the land, a people with Caucasian features in bright costumes and their unusual customs, and so forth. The area is outside China proper, classified as the Xinjiang Uygur Autonomous Region.

The native people, called the Uygurs, look more Caucasian than Chinese. They speak Russian, Turkish and a local patois mixed with Mandarin. The women dress flamboyantly and wear glittering earrings. Their cultures date back over 2,000 years when the oases around which they live became important stopover points on the Silk Road.

Where the region was once dominated by the minority nationalities, it is now being gradually overwhelmed by

A mudhouse outside Kashgar, Xinjiang.

Uygur father and son from Kashgar, Xinjiang.

the influx of Han Chinese. They started settling here when the Lanzhou-Urumqi railway line opened the region to industrialization. In the south, however, the Muslim Uygurs still predominate.

Xinjiang has been declared autonomous by the Chinese government but in reality, the struggle for independence continues. Historically, the Han Chinese have always been invaders, hence intruders in this region. The relationship between the 2 has been one of uneasy calm interspersed by uprisings among the predominantly Muslim minority nationalities in the late 19th century and the occasional show of force by the government to establish control over the region. Like Tibet, the area may not be opened to travelers at the time you wish to go. The political situation is volatile and borders can be closed unexpectedly. Contact the nearest Consulate or CITS office for current information before planning a trip there.

Turpan

Turpan is 154 m below sea-level and is reputed to be the hottest place in the China in June-July. In the summer it is a veritable sauna with the temperature reaching as high as 49°C. In winter the temperature dips as low as -30°C.

Turpan Basin lies on the southern side of the **Tian Mountain** in central Xinjiang. It was an important town on the old Silk Road and a center of Bud-

Katakh home on the range on Mount Bagda.

dhism until its conversion to Islam in the 8th century. It is the center of Uygur culture and nearby **Gaochang** was once the capital of the Uygurs.

The Uygurs predominate comprising 75 per cent of the inhabitants here, the rest being mostly Han Chinese. The center of life is the large Turpan oasis which comprises a few main streets with all facilities within walking distance. Trees and mud houses line the streets of the quaint little town where open channels of flowing water run down the side of the streets serving the daily needs of the people.

One of the most colorful and lively scenes here is the market, situated just across the bus station. The **Turpan Bazaar** is second only to Kashgar's. Brightly clad customers haggle over prices; all sorts of tools, knives and ornate items are an eyeful. Travelers should try the local fare here: delicious flatbread, Hami melons, seedless grapes and grape wine.

Mosques scattered all over town reveal Turpan's Muslim culture. The **Emin Minaret** or **Sugongta** date back to the 18th century and was designed in a simple Afghan style. The minaret is a 44-meter tower with an adjoining mosque.

Accommodation-wise the Turpan Guesthouse is still the most popular hotel offering an irresistible ambience and good food. The Oasis Hotel, however, is more modern. Food here is good but it is more reasonably-priced at Silk Road Restaurant.

Busy, frenzied, noisy trade of live stock and produce in the Sunday Great Bazaar in Kashgar.

Turpan is not easily accessible. The nearest airport is at Urumqi and the nearest railway line is the Urumqi-Lanzhou line. The railway station closest to Turpan is at **Daheyan** and from here you would need to take a bus to Turpan. If you are traveling between Turpan and Ürümqi, the direct bus or minibus is faster and more convenient than the train.

Turpan Environs

Inevitably the fascinating contrasts of Turpan's surroundings beckon. Hire a minibus for a full day (10 hours) to see the sights outside Turpan and normally it is not difficult to find other travelers with whom to share the expense. The drivers will approach you to offer their services, but be selective. It would be a good idea to prepare a program for the driver listing out the sights you want to see.

The ruins of the ancient city of **Gaochang** could be your first site of call. It lies 40 km east of Turpan and was once the capital of the Uygurs. Gaochang was built in the 1st century BC by a Han emperor as a defense base and was reconstructed in the 7th century during the Tang Dynasty when it became a major town on the Silk Road. It covers 2 million sq m and consists of an inner and outer city and the palace city. The city was abandoned in the 13th century.

The Flaming Mountains were so named because in summer one would think that the mountains were on fire.

Just northwest of this ancient city of Gaochang is the burial ground for its residents dating as far back as the 3rd century. Known as the **Astana Tombs**, excavations have unearthed tombs, mummies, silks, embroidery and other funerary objects.

Further on, standing defiantly against the passage of time are the **Flaming Mountains** which lie to the north of Gaochang. Composed of red sand store, the mountains look like raging flames in the blazing sun and in mid-summer the temperature could reach 80°C.

The Flaming Mountains were made famous in a classic novel in Chinese literature, *A Journey to the West*. They were portrayed as a formidable barrier confronting the monk, Xuan Zang and his followers, who were on a pilgrimage to the west.

Following the Flaming Mountains is the next site **Bezekelik Thousand Buddha Caves** which lie on its western flank. The caves contain statues and murals depicting stories from Buddha's life. Many of these caves have been destroyed through pilferage, wilful vandalism and the lack of care in the face of the elements.

Along the western side of Flaming Mountain, is **Grape Valley**, which lies in a valley and is 8 km long and half a kilometer wide. It is a little paradise of greenery and fruit in this sheer vast desert of Xinjiang. Grape is abundant and Xinjiang is particularly known for

Journey to the West, Then and Now

Twenty-five-year-old Buddhist monk Xuan Zang left Chang'an (now Xian) in 627 AD as a Tang Dynasty traveler with an itch to see the world of the west and study with important teachers in India. Nineteen years and 25,000 km later he returned home to a celebrant audience with a camel safari laden with Buddhist statues and *sutras*.

In his time he wrote the "Records of Western Regions" documenting his journey through 24 countries, as did Marco Polo 600 years later, reversing the direction. **Journey to the West** is a collection of fanciful tales written during the Ming Dynasty, based on the adventures of the monk, Tripitaka, (characterization of Xuan Zang), 2 disciples, the Monkey King, Devil Ox King and Princess Iron Fan. Their adventures, based on Zang's report are as famous in China as Dorothy, Toto, Cowardly Lion and Tin Man traveling the yellow brick road to the Land of Oz in the West.

Read **Journey to the West** and follow Zang's route from Hami to Aksu and Korgas spanning the province of Xingjiang. Feast on the famous Hami melons, swelter near the Flaming Mountains in the Turpan area, while visiting the remains of Gaochang City, site of the Ancient Tombs, and the caves of the Thousands Buddhas.

The Gobi Desert threatens to dry you to a frazzle while traversing the road from Korla to Kuga. While re-hydrating in Kuga, visit the bazaar which stretches from one end to the other of the new section of town. Roasting meats and other local dishes at the fast food stands tempt the palate; yoghurt is big with the Uygur women. Copies of the Koran and other Muslim religious artifacts attest to the switch from Zang's Buddhist day to the present and worship of Allah. Donkeys, camels, cattle, are for sale here. If you need a new harness gear or saddles, the trading is fierce bartering for other goods more important than money. The farmers arrive early, donkey carts loaded with food produce.

Journey to the West speaks of the **Kingdom of Women** in the area. Kuga is noted for the beautiful women of Xingjiang. Long braids swirling, elegantly garbed in colorful period costumes, the lovely women dance and perform, as noted by Monk Zang 1400 years before. There are more Thousand Buddha Caves near Kuga, as are the ruins of an ancient city called Subash. All that remains are pagodas and pavilions on both sides of the river.

Zang then traveled, as he reported, 600 li to the kingdom of Baluka. This is the vast desert of the Tarim Basin, hundreds of kilometers of eerie land formations. Today the poles of modern communications are the only evidence of change from the monk's time. Zang wrote of the kingdom of Baluka, which is now the modern city of Aksu. Travelers now see wide streets, dine on Sichuan cuisine, play trader in the night market, or see a Shaolin film at a movie theater, a welcome change from the austere territory just passed through.

The route then turns north over the Tianshan mountains at altitudes near 8,000 m to Zhaoshu. On the other side, grasslands beckon, Mongolian herdsmen with their flocks of sheep decorate the green plateaus and a large marsh is a breeding ground for white swans. Nomadic Kazaks live as they did centuries ago in *yurts* without the modern conveniences of electricity.

Korgas is the end of the Xinjiang journey, the last city before crossing over into what was once the Soviet Union. Reading Monk Zang's account and his mythological counterpart Tripitaka in **Journey to the West** and then traveling through the ancient country reminds the traveler of how little the country has changed in 1200 years.

the seedless white *manaizi* and rosy species. However, there are also other temperate fruit like peaches, apricots, apples, pomegranates, pears, water melons and musk melons. However tempting, these fruit *cannot* be picked by the tourists.

Turpan keeps in touch with life

The Kizil Thousand Buddha Cave has one of the biggest group of grottoes dating back to the 3rd century.

2,000 years back in a curiously unique way, through the *karez*, an underground irrigation system, which has remained a vital part of the life support system in the region today. This system consists of wells ("Karez"), underground channels or ditches and dams. Water from the melting snow is collected in wells sunk into the ground. The underground channels then conduct the ground water to the valley below. Channels built "underground" reduce the loss of water in Turpan's extremely hot and dry climate. There are 1,600 wells in Xinjiang. Today, the karez is considered the third great construction project of ancient China after the Great Wall and the Grand Canal.

Urumqi

In contrast to the quieter, more remote and more rural Turpan, **Urumqi** is a bustling city, a 20th century outpost with all the facilities of a modern city including an airport! The capital of Xinjiang, it came into existence 2,000 years ago when it became an important crossroads for ancient caravans. Its fortunes however, followed that of the Silk Road: when trade on the Silk Road

Jianhe was once an important city lying along the Silk Road.

declined, Urumqi languished. With the opening of the railway from Lanzhou across the Xinjiang Desert, the city boomed.

With greater industrialization and development came an influx of Han Chinese into what was once a predominantly Muslim area. Thus Urumqi has an interesting representation of the minority nationalities, particularly the Uygurs, and the Han Chinese. Brightly clad they stand in great contrast to the grimly-clad Han Chinese.

An exhibition hall in the **Xinjiang**

Urumqi evolved from a trading post along the Silk Road into a bustling 20th century modern city.

Autonomous Region Museum is devoted to the display of architectural styles, production tools, costumes and daily necessities highlighting the culture and life-styles of the different minority nationalities. The museum also displays artifacts and reliefs in its historical section.

In the center of town is the popular **Renmin Park**. It is a beautiful park filled with trees interspersed with pavilions and a lake. It is an exercise ground in the morning and on Sundays, the whole of Ürümqi seems to descend to the park.

A 3-hour bus ride from Urumqi is **Tian Chi** (Heaven's Pool), situated half way up **Mount Bogda** in the middle of a desert. The edenic scene is unreal: one of the bluest lakes nestling in the hills surrounded by alpine nature. Even the name, Tian Chi, betrays the awe of those who beheld it. Higher peaks look over the lakes, blending in with the scene and showing off their snow-capped tops.

You may want to spend some time by the lake if you are unable to resist the call of the surroundings. There is a hotel by the lake, the Heavenly Lake Hotel Bogdashan, which may not be as appealing as it sounds. Accommodations are rural but the sunset and daybreak views are spectacular and well worth the inconvenience. By the time you get there the locals may be willing to share their yurts for an up-market stay over.

A public bus leaves for the lake

A gathering of women and children in the Xinjiang Valley.

early in the morning and makes a return trip in the evening. Alternatively, you may prefer to hire a taxi.

Back in the town of Urumqi, there is a limited choice of accommodation. The Kunlun Guesthouse is an adequate hotel, renovated to suit the need of tour groups. However, the hotel is not strategically located in town. The Bogda Hotel is more favorably located but a star or two down from the Kunlun. You will probably not get your choice. (CITS assistance is necessary in all of Xinjiang for transportation to scenic sights in the environs.)

Though seemingly isolated Urumqi is connected by rail and air to various cities in China. There are also long-distance buses travelling to other cities particularly Turpan, Yining and Kashgar.

Kashgar

Kashgar, the commonly used name for Kashi, is a 2-hour flight from Urumqi. It is the second city in Xinjiang Autonomous Region, close to the Russian, Afghanistan and Pakistan borders. Monk Xuan Zang took the route through Kashi on his return trip and stopped by the large trading city bisecting the Silk Road..

The Kashgar Hotel is adequate, not quite in the star rating but considering the area, the rusty warm water bath and the inside room toilet are modern. The Seman Hotel was once the Russian dip-

A Chinese Muslim reading the Koran in Id Kah Mosque, Kashgar.

lomatic residence if you wish for the ambience of what was once the outpost of civilization.

The north and south routes of the Silk Road converged in Kashgar as the vortex of east west trade. Camels laden with wool and silk headed west, returning months later with sugar, spices and Russian cigarettes. It took 5 or 6 months for the camel caravans to go from Kashgar to Beijing and several weeks to the trading bazaars of India and Russia. Early adventurers such as Marco Polo reported on passing through the huge marketplaces, sometimes joining the caravans for safety.

Kashgar, according to history was an important trading center 2,000 years ago and today 50,000 or more traders come from hundreds of miles each week for the Sunday Great Bazaar seemingly to continue a tradition.

Donkey carts, the principal vehicle of transportation, create traffic jams along the roads on entering the city. In the city they are used as taxis and are often seen lined with carpets and decorated in gay colours transporting the locals and visitors to the bazaar grounds which extend to more than a kilometer in length and half in width.

The crescendo of noise reaches a high level heard all over the market area from the section dealing in sheep, camels, horses, goats and cattle. Sorry, no elephants in modern times. Small gestures signal the successful completion of deals, a system that has existed

The Tomb of Abakh Hoja was the burial ground of a ruling family in Kashgar.

for centuries.

Eating stalls abound and the aroma of fried, broiled and stewed foods permeates the air. Nang bread baked like bagels in round doughnut shapes and they are stacked on skewers or hung in raffia tied bunches. Lamb shish kebabs, apparently the most popular "eat while you walk" food is irresistible even to foreigners wary of standards of hygiene.

The holiday air of the locals is contagious with the giggling unmarried girls showing their age by the number of braids, dressed as brightly and colorfully as their personalities. Double braided matrons shopping for beautiful bolts of cloth harangue the vendors for a better price. Areas of food vending vary from the bizarre displays of butchered animal parts to the lovely Hami melons, the most delicious in all Asia.

Bright clothing, rolls of cloth, rare and beautiful rugs, fur hats, parkas and boots of decorated leather attract the bartering crowds. Yengisar knives, sharp as razors with etchings on the blades despite their hardness, are displayed in rows with their fancy leather sheaths to fit at the waist or boot, both treasure and necessity for travelers.

Rare jade in imperial emerald green or the traditional mutton fat is exchanged instead of money. Dealers sit cross-legged on mats or beautifully woven rugs surrounded with their goods, pockets and sleeves containing the rare and more valuable items. Bolts of cloth are stacked like walls around the silk and cotton vendors, to be scattered in half-unrolled piles when a customer begins to bargain for garment materials.

Rows of stringed instruments are displayed in all their gaudy splendor of inlaid designs; glittering gilded trunks gleam in the sunlight. Furniture, a highly decorative craft, are stacked high on the carts heading towards the market; they have a prominent position on the buyer's cart heading home.

The handful of foreign tourists gawk at the din and hubbub, and snap their cameras at disinterested merchants and children, who shyly turn their faces to hide at the point of a lens. There is more bartering than money exchange and sometimes fierce altercations appear between the traders unable to reach an agreement on the value of a goat or a fur hat.

Kashgar is the great **Sunday Bazaar**. For the rest of the week, there is a regular wet market located a short distance from the site of the Sunday Bazaar. It has comparatively less excitement but it is the center of activity in Kashgar.

A day's tour includes the **Id Kah Mosque**, built in the traditional Russian style with onion-shaped domes and minarets in stark contrast to the Chinese versions. The huge open center hall accommodates 500 or more people during the prayer times. The **Tomb of Abakh Hoja** is the only other major scenic site, burial ground for 5 generations of a ruling family.

Locals also call it the Tomb of the Fragrant Concubine and tell the story of the beautiful daughter, of the Hoja clan, Xiang Fei, who was sent unwillingly by her father to marry the Qing Emperor Qianlong for political reasons. Refusing to bed with the ruler she died of longing for her home and her own lover. The body was returned to her family who entombed and praised her steadfastness.

Side trips can be arranged to **Hotan** better known as the silk capital of Xinjiang. A tale exists about a Tang princess concubine sent to marry the King of Qusadana (ancient Hotan). Silk worms and mulberry seeds were smuggled in her trousseau. The result of this young woman's innovativeness started the Hotan family cottage industry of sericulture and silk weaving.

Hotan also boasts a market of which the main treasures are jade. The nearby river was said to have an unusual alluvial trove of the precious material, discovered by wading bare foot in the streams. Decorative fine daggers are also found in the market place, products of the small village of Yengisar between Kashgar and Hotan.

To summarize, the adventurous traveling of Xinjiang Province, the most fun is to be had in prowling the markets of the various trading centers, just as native predecessors did in centuries past.

With the proper visas obtained beforehand, you can continue over the border to Pakistan, Afghanistan, India or what was once known as the USSR.

Tibet

Romantics picture Tibet coming over the pass into the green valley of Shangri-la, life in a state of extended animation. The rarified Himalayan air allows the essence of beauty to last forever in the mind. Folks who seek far-reaching itineraries dream of Tibet as the ultimate quest. Today Tibet is politically an autonomous region, **Xizang Zizhiqu**.

In 1984 the Foreign Tourist Bureau of China, anxious to provide more destinations to generate free-flowing cash, opened the province for group and independent travel. Hotels were built to accommodate the persnickety foreigners desiring clean beds, boiled water and western toilets. Toyota Land Cruisers were imported for the few independent travelers desiring personal tours. Guest houses, designed for government VIPs admit the up-market groups who agree

The towering Potala Palace is symbolic of Buddhism's place in the lives of the Tibetans.

to spend a sizeable per diem, per person.

By 1987 however, Tibetan anti-Chinese sentiments resurfaced and almost led to a revolt. The Chinese government clamped down, claiming the barbarians were causing all the trouble, fomenting unrest among the natives. Only a few well-chaperoned tours were allowed in and they were restricted to **Lhasa** and **Xigase**. By 1989 Tibet was closed entirely.

Lhasa

Lhasa Holiday Inn has 500 rooms awaiting guests; reservations are possible via the International Holiday Inn system. Two deluxe presidential suites are offered, a Chinese restaurant provides a familiar menu and the coffee shop serves Yak-burgers. The hotel operates a small farm and greenhouse to maintain food supplies. Likewise, Tibet Hotel and Tibet Guesthouse are down the street from the Holiday Inn offering western-type accommodations. Lhasa #3 CITS Guesthouse is the most interesting being normally reserved for VIPs. It is set in a compound out of the city. Lhasa's altitude does not lend itself to long exhausting walks so the city hotels are more convenient.

Other historical centers like **Xigase** and **Gyantse** have smaller recently built hotels. Mountain climbers from around

Tibet

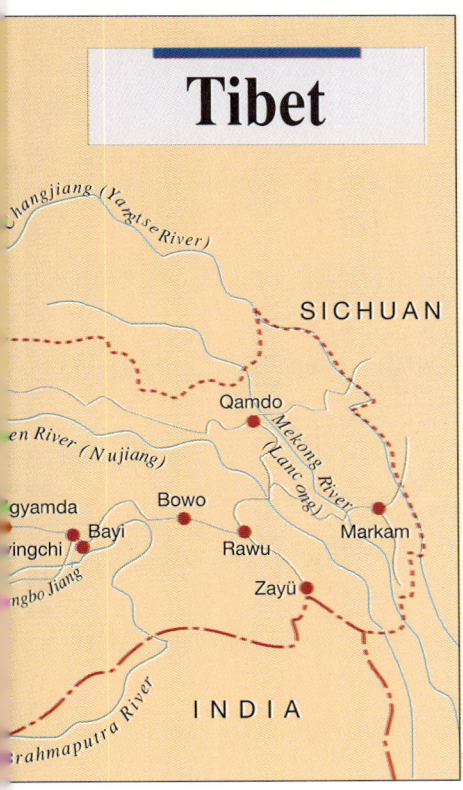

pendent tour leave 3 or 4 days' leeway. This does not present an insurmountable problem as there is so much to see in Sichuan Province, Southwest China while you are waiting. Xian also provides a large scale of sightseeing.

For hardy adventurers it is possible to enter Tibet from Nepal. A highway runs from Lhasa via **Xigaze** to the border town of **Zham**, thence to Kathmandu in Nepal. Emphasizing "hardy", the thousand kilometer road crosses the Himalayas passing by Mount Everest (Qomolangma). Views are often blotted out by low hanging clouds; snow storms block the road, and jeep-style vehicles are not known for their comfortable seating. Plus this, the "fit" must have the stamina to confront the bureaucracy issuing permits for this route in China and Nepal.

On arrival in Lhasa, groups as small as 2 or 3 are allowed to travel together in some semblance of comfort in the Toyota Landcruisers with Beijing University student translator/guides. CITS has an efficient staff to oversee the visitors. Independent travelers usually make arrangements with the Chengdu CITS for their adventure in Tibet.

Lhasa is best known for the "old culture" air, as you might savor the historical aura of the remnants of Rome, Pompeii or the Acropolis. Tibet's altitude at 4,000 m creates all the physical discomforts they warn you about that you many face when you first arrive: lassitude, nausea, headaches and sleepless nights take about 3 days to recover

the world still desire to conquer Everest from the Tibetan side. History will no doubt repeat itself, Tibet will open and close its borders with the rise and fall of internal problems. Experienced travelers will keep the region on the list and await the opportunity to journey to Shangri-la, the much fantasized ancient civilization on top of the world.

Generally, when Tibet is open for travel, air access is from Chengdu, Sichuan Province (daily) and Xian, Shaanxi Province (twice weekly). Even if the traveler has confirmed reservations on a pre-sold tour plan there are often flight delays. Weather and the arrogant CAAC often postpone flights, causing a stack-up of passengers. On an inde-

Pang La Pass Village is almost lost in the vast terrain at the foot of Mount Everest.

from. Portable oxygen is available in green canvas underarm canvas balloons. Take it slow, visit the temples first thing in the morning when you are fresh and when the exhibits are most likely to be open.

Jokhang Temple is the easiest place to start with, being in the center of the **Barkhor**, the business section of downtown Lhasa. Take your best flashlight with an extra battery. Pilgrims will show you the way, first by prostrating themselves full length before entering the temple. There are unlit electric lights strung around the ceiling apparently for use only during paid photography sessions. Take your snaps outside, leave your camera in the case when you enter. You can purchase postcard photos, books, slides and probably video cassettes by the time you get there. The halls are hazy, lit and odorized by yak butter lamps. Pilgrims outnumber the foreigners a hundred to one on an average day.

A gold statue of a 12-year-old Sakyamuni is in the central hall. Tapestries from the Tang and the Ming Dynasties hang from the pillars. There are 5 big copper pots for making tea for 5000 people in front of the temple. Tea makers use ladders to brew the tea and then to clean the pots. The Jokhang Temple is the favorite spot for worshipers in all of Tibet.

The lamas are everywhere chanting prayers in groups, staring at the pilgrims, rolling balls of *tsampa* (barley

The Potala Palace

The truncated pyramid style building was originally built over 1000 years ago. The latest rehabilitation began in the 17th century and the palace now occupies an area of approximately 160,000 sq m.

The immensity of the construction becomes evident when you approach the foot of the steps and look up. As you ascend, the aura of the past ages grows. Thousands of tons of stone blocks were chipped into identical sizes to form the walls and steps towering over you. There were no fork-lift or giant earth moving machines available then. Leverage, blocks and pulleys, the backs of thousands and thousands of workers created it. Architects planned it so precisely that except for pure erosion, the edifice has survived in its original form.

The White Palace was built first, followed by the Red Palace 50 years later, to house the Dalai Lama. Thirteen floors hold about 1000 rooms consisting of ceremonial halls, chapels, meditation niches and vaults for the departed Dalai Lamas. The Fifth Dalai Lama has the most splendiferous chapel decorated with an estimated 4 tons of gold, diamonds, turquoise, coral, pearls and other semi-precious stones.

The current Dalai Lama's private apartment, empty since his departure in 1959 can be reached through narrow hallways. It is a 1920's style apartment with radio, overstuffed furniture, a modest bath and toilet, greeting rooms for official meetings and a tiny cot equipped bedroom.

The apartment is kept clean and ready for the moment of return, hoped for by every Tibetan, like the second coming of the Lord. Each day thousands of adherents file through the private chambers leaving gifts of yak butter, prayer flags and bits of money. They believe the Dalai Lama or his next incarnation will eventually re-occupy the Potala Palace and they wait with great anticipation for this day.

The Dalai Lama's residence is on the highest floor of the Potala Palace.

The golden-roofed Jokhang Temple in Lhasa is one of Tibet's holiest shrines and 1,300 years old.

and butter) in their palms. The array of Buddhas, Buddha's disciples and Buddha's protectors set in millions of dollars of precious gems is endless. Before each is a picture of the current Dalai Lama; the pilgrims prostrate themselves time and again before both images. Piles of coins and soiled paper money are scattered throughout the statues until one wonders if they are ever collected and spent for the upkeep of the temple.

Eventually you will surface on the roof. The saffron-robed lamas are inclined to stop and talk to you if you are away from the crowd. They yearn for any contact with the outside world, even if just to pass the time of day. The fresh air reaffirms your assurance of continued life though the odor of the yak butter lamps stays on the clothing for hours.

The view across the Barkhor, teems with pedestrians, bikes, tourists, dogs and endless arrays of hawkers. The **Potala Palace** in all its magical splendor dominates the plain. For the moment you are on the top of the world in a temple begun in 700 AD, overlooking the city of Lhasa. The temple has existed through cycles of civilization and has been devastated time and again. The most recent destruction was the result of the Red Guard frenzy during the Cultural Revolution when the number of ancient temples were reduced from hundreds to a mere 20.

Tibetans claim the region as their country and vow never to be completely

Barkhor Square, the business district of Lhasa, with Potala Palace in the distance.

conquered. They wait for the day when the Dalai Lama returns in splendor to restore their way of life. The Han Chinese declare Tibet is just another province of the PRC granting it dubious autonomy.

The pilgrimage circuit around the Jokhang Temple is known as the **Barkhor**, which is lined with shops and stalls. The colorful blend of minorities, nomads, religious devotees, each with an intrinsic dress and hairstyle decorated with silver, turquoise and coral jewelry, is awesome. The smell of yak butter is overpowering and the sight of ice-block sized bricks of the pale yellow stuff is definitely not encouraging. The display of goods varies in a fascinating array of food, carpets, clothing, and almost-antique treasures. Silver gongs and bells tinkle, small children dash around while you check your money

An altar in a Buddhist monastery.

belt. Copper and brass pots are replicas of the monstrous ones you just saw in the temple. A merchant holds up a pair of silver clappers on a leather string barely touching each other. The sweet sharp chimes ring and echo as fine as in the Sydney Opera House. Only a stomach groaning for sustenance would cause you to leave with a promise to return.

The current Dalai Lama renewed the **Norbu Lingka** as a summer palace in 1956. An entourage journeyed 5 km each summer from the Potala Palace to Norbu Lingka in pompous splendor. The potentate was transported in a sedan chair accompanied by the palace guards, notables, and musicians. Throngs lined the streets, prostrating themselves like dominos falling as the procession passed. Gardens flourished, an informal ambience was maintained for the short summers. Summer vacation pleasures were short indeed as 3 years after the Norbu Lingka was renewed, the Dalai Lama elected exile to escape the Communists, leaving his people to suffer under the iron hand of Han Chinese generals. The Dalai Lama now languishes in India. The palace and the surrounding park are now enjoyed by a small group of maintenance retainers and the occasional tourist.

At the time of the Communist invasion, or rescue, depending on which side of the eternal question you vision, the vast **Drepung Monastery** just outside of Lhasa had a reputed 7,500 to 10,000 resident monks. Currently less than 250 reside in the relatively deserted area.

Drepung is more of a spiritual city than a monastery. Narrow streets, 2 and 3-storey apartments are tiered up the low mountainside. Drepung was built in 1416 by Jiangyang Qujie, a disciple of the monk Zongkaya, founder of the Yellow Sect Buddhism.

The monastery consists of a number of grand halls and chambers, and the Dalai Lama's palaces used before the Potala Palace. The Grand Hall of Guoqin has 190 huge pillars and can accommodate 10,000 lamas at one prayer session. Many relics are displayed in the smaller chambers and a statue of Buddha Jiangba is enshrined on the second floor.

Drepung is one of the 3 monasteries of the Yellow Sect Buddhism standing in the eastern, western and northern sectors of Lhasa. **Gandan Monastery** is on the slope of **Mount Wanpur** and looks like a castle from the distance. It was built in the early 15th century by the monk Zongkaba. **Sera Monastery** is named after the Sera flower (wild rose), built by Zongkaba's disciple, Xiajia Yixi. Inside are 16 *arhats* (Buddhist saints) carved out of sandalwood from the Ming emperor, over 10,000 golden copper Buddhist statues and the Holy Prayer Scripture Ganzhuer written in cinnabar.

The Potala Palace is too vast to cover in one visit. The proper and intelligent approach to this vast edifice is to leave it until you have become acclimatized. Bring your flashlight, your bottle of water and start early.

River on the Roof

The highest river on earth is said to be the **Yarlung Zangbo,** flowing from west to east north of the Himalayan range. On an average the river flows on the Tibetan Plateau at 4,500 m above sea level for a total length of 2,000 km inside Tibet. Another 1,000 km is added to its length as it becomes the Great Brahmaputra of India, eventually flowing into the Bay of Bengal.

The Yarlung is known as a "holy river" to the Tibetans and begins in the glaciers and the melting snow north of the Himalayas. With constant floods, glacial debris and other deposits, the Yarlung Valley becomes excellent farmland. Grains, vegetables, some fruit such as tangerines and peaches grow abundantly, endangered only by winds. To this end fruit trees are planted to windward sides of the fields to protect them and the homes of the farms existing on a corner of the plateau.

Part of the Yarlung is navigable in the flat areas, broadened by sandbars and funneling off into tributaries. Yak hide coracles, a tub-like craft, are used for people transportation; other scows are poled. As it moves down to the lower reaches the shores turn to evergreen trees and other runoffs join it to hasten the waters.

Namjagbarwa, a 7,500-meter mountain then splits the mighty river forcing it to make a deliberate "U" turn, called the "big bend". The confluence of the waters, narrowing of the channels now make the Yarlung a raging torrent falling fast to sea level.

Lhasa Environs

With an area of 1,200,000 sq kms, Tibet occupies a not inconsiderable one-eighth of the total territory of the whole country of China. The average altitude above sea-level is over 4,000 m, which makes it the highest plateau in the world, commonly known as the "roof of the world". A 1984 census shows that the popula-

Waiting for customers in a street market in Lhasa.

tion of Tibet is 1,966,800 with 1,870,000 Tibetans. They make up 95 per cent of the population, while the rest are the Han, Menba, Luoba, Hui, Naxi, Yidong, and Xiarba minorities.

There is an endless array of monasteries throughout Tibet and more major mountains and rivers than any place in the world. The number one peak on earth is Mount Everest with a height of 8,848 m, attracting mountaineers and tourists from all over the world. Eight of 14 peaks in the world over 8,000 m are in Tibet. Its neighbors are Burma, India, Sikkim, Bhutan, and Nepal, all to the southwest.

Tibet is full of rivers and lakes, providing an abundance of hydroelectric power and a little known source of fish.

The **Yangzongyong Lake**, for instance, has a coastal line of 250 km; the deepest point is 60 m. Tourist information brochures estimate that the lake has a self-replenishing reserve of 300 million kg of fish and is called "the Fish Store of Tibet". Namu Lake has an area of 1,940 sq km, the second largest salt lake in the world. The Tibet Plateau is frozen at least 6 months of the year, but boasts surprisingly of over 300 hot springs, some boiling enough to cook your breakfast eggs.

The above miscellaneous data should give you some idea of the immensity of **Xizang**, the province of Tibet. Travelers do well to visit the following 3 cities after spending some days in the capital Lhasa.

Xigaze - Gyangze - Zhanang

Road travel in Tibet is a literally gripping experience. One learns to grip the hand holds in the landcruiser tightly. The route from Lhasa to **Xigaze** via Gyangze rises to 4,794 m at the **Kampa-La Pass**. Far below are the amazingly clear waters of **Lake Yamdrok**. The driver will stop to catch a breath and give you time to run the video for standard snapshot cameras do not record the vastness of the area well. Looking back from the heights you can see the valley of the **Yarlung River**. The next stop is even more spectacular as the altitude reaches 5,045 m.

Gyangze, Tibet's third largest city, was the trading center for Bhutan, Sikkim and India, and is famous for its **Fort Dzong**. Only traces of the walls can be seen today. **Palkhor Monastery** and Dzong are the travel treasures in Gyangze, now a rural and relatively untrammeled small village south of Lhasa. The 360 km trip to Xigaze is arduous and time consuming, therefore you only stop for a short picnic lunch at Gyangze.

The **Tashilhunpo Monastery**, built in the 15th century, is the main attraction in Xigaze, the second largest city in Tibet. It is known as the seat of the Panchen Lama, second in religious command. Tourists are shown a short video of the last visit of the 10th Panchen Lama who was escorted to Beijing, and treated as an official emissary of Tibet before his death in 1989.

The once busy monastery hosted over 4,000 lamas in its heyday, but now only attended by less than 10 per cent of that number. A 27-meter Maitreya, (Buddha of the Future) is visualized from different levels inside the building. The fourth Panchen Lama left a fortune in gold and precious jewels to decorate his 11-meter memorial. The total is said to be 3,000 ounces of gold, 15 tons of silver and thousands of precious stones to astonish the current tourists.

Scores of *tangkas* hang in its halls and chambers. Statues of Sakyamuni, Zongkaba, murals of the 4 heavenly kings all are in remarkably good condition and clarity. The Hall of Buddha Maitreya is in the best known hall displaying a 30-meter statue donated by the 9th Panchen Lama in 1914. Another sitting statue of Maitreya is a mere 27 m tall and contains 29 kg of gold with 115 tons of copper. This location was often used for conferences with emissaries from the imperial courts of the Ming Dynasty. They would travel for months to arrive, and then hold weeks of discussion, often arriving at no decision!

The Xigatze Hotel on the outside of town gives an adequate amount of physical comfort. Eating in Tibet is always subject to supply, the mood of the chef and the degree of your hunger. Beer always seems available and the always present pot of rice is help-yourself until you are full. A loaded swagbag in these areas is a friend indeed. For supplemental feeding, canned mandarin oranges,

Prayer flags fluttering in the Tibetan mountains.

lychee and peaches are usually available in the local department or Friendship Stores.

Zhanang, south and east of Lhasa, in the general direction of the airport, is a fascinating side trip. It is located on the banks of the **Yarlung** (Bhumapatra), the headwaters of the Mekong and Changjiang Rivers. **Samye Monastery** is located on the opposite side of the Yarlung. The local water taxi service is a scow poled across the turbulent waters in flood season, around emerging islands of sand in its quiet times. Other passengers are the Tibetan devotee tourists visiting the monastery, farmers with a dragon tractor perched precariously on the snout of the scow and probably monks returning to their station.

Local land taxi service is a dragon tractor pulling a metal wagon bed in which the standing travelers rattle against each other over the rutted roads. The 5-kilometer ride is a tooth shaking endurance test, similar to being inside a pin ball machine. If they offer a horse for saddle-wise transit, take it.

Samye's interest is in the small complement of novices, lamas and workers rebuilding an 8th century edifice reputed to be the oldest monastery in Tibet. Watching 2 laborers hand sawing a 10-meter wood plank in half, lengthwise, is a lesson in ancient construction methods. A picnic lunch on a balcony, a conversation with the local head Lama delighted to have visitors or a leisurely stroll through the halls and galleries

The Himalayan Mountains, the backyard of Tingri, Tibet.

without crowds is delightful. Outside the children of the nearby village play on the shores of the stream, naked, screaming at each other as they all do around the world.

The 3 cities are mentioned as choices of overnight stops and a full day's road journey by car through the autonomous region of Tibet. All interior travel is at the whim of the Foreign Tourist Department, unless you want to backpack. They control the hotels, vehicles and guides. The landcruiser winds up and down mountains reaching altitudes of 7000 m, the air so rarefied that you wonder if you are really breathing. Earthen bridges are often put up forging the gullies and streams. Mesas resemble Mongolia's grasslands making the earth appear flat. Caravans of small donkeys pass by, carrying loads 3 times higher and twice as heavy. Prayer flags wave from peaks and piles of rocks indicate a funeral or religious site. Vistas from the mountain heights stretch into infinity. Remains of ruined monasteries strain the reason for senseless destruction by modern history as the profusion of rubble of former magnificent edifices remind you of the millions of hours of antlike labor, and the burdening of the workers, builders, artisans, and patrons of Tibet's religious art and architecture over the centuries. Flying out over the 7,500-meter mountains in an airplane at 10,000 m brings the snow-covered peaks very close to your window, a final memory of Shangri-la.

Cuisine

From the beginning of chronicled history, every celebration be it for the living or the dead, have all centered around food. National holidays, birthdays of the immortals, anniversaries, entertainment of dignitaries, offerings to one's ancestors - they culminate in the ultimate banquet. Since ancient times, the banquet consists of a multitude of chefs working for weeks in advance to prepare an unending array of fascinating dishes.

A street vendor selling deep fried fritters, xio chi, in Datong.

The variety consists partially of exotic and rare foods obscure to the western gourmet: shark's fin, bird's nest, deer penis, rhinoceros horn, quail and sparrow, eel and snake, duck and goose, camel hump in Mongolia, bear claws and moose nose in Heilongjiang, to name just a few. Then there are the varieties engendered by the 58 minority groups living in the sprawling territories of China. Archeologists claim that Peking Man roasted sabre tooth tiger meat in his cave. The Banpo Village near Xian

Swirling noodles.

turned up interesting evidence of steam cooking and the bones of elephant, chicken and carp.

With the advance of civilization, the imperials demanded new food experiences and more variety. The Silk Road vendors brought spices, garlic, dried fruits and unique vegetables from the Middle East. Concubines who craved exotic fruit, had their liege lords order fresh lychee and mangoes – rushed fresh by horseback from the southern estates. Carp raised in ponds provided fresh fish for those cities far from the seas. For centuries they have been cultivated in aquatic farms because they cannot breed fast enough in the wild to satisfy the Chinese appetite for them. The art of food preservation was written in stone, as the purveyors learned how to cure meat with salt and preserve the fish in oil after cooking. Vegetables and herbs were dried and sold along with the hundreds of medicinal plant yields of roots, leaves and berries.

Food and eating are linked closely with healing and maintaining an inner harmony. All foods are seen to possess the *yin* and *yang* which are opposing qualities in the nature of things as in male and female, negative and positive. The constant interplay between these opposing forces is seen to control bodily harmony and good health. Thus ingredients in recipes are often kept balanced with this concept in mind.

Rival warlords competed with generals on the battlefield and chefs in the

A whole goat banquet in Kunming, Yunnan.

kitchen, each trying to out-entertain the other on the few occasions when negotiating treaties. Steamed, stir fried, roasted and boiled foods were arranged on the serving platters to represent images of dragons and butterflies, birds and flowers, beautiful mountains and green valleys.

Each area specialized in food styles, limited to what was available locally. Thus Beijing, Shanghai, Guangzhou, Kunming and Chongqing developed identifiably different wok cultures. In the north, for example, food style has a particular character dictated by the weather and the rustic environment. The Siberian winds make the region unbearably cold in winter and modern transport of food to supermarkets are unknown even today to the average citizen. Hence easy to store cabbage, corn, lentils, sweet potatoes and turnips along with grain and mutton are the staples needed for the masses to survive the winter. The hot dusty summers bring floods along the Huanghe (Yellow River) and the Changjiang (Yangtse) irrigating, and then sometimes overrunning, the planted fields. Produce also flood the cities as truckloads of vegetables and fruit are brought in, literally heaped on the sidewalks.

Beijing Cuisine

The elitist dining once known in the Forbidden City, presents a different story.

A delicious tea-smoked duck course from Chengdu, Sichuan.

During the 60-year reign of Emperor Qianlong (1736-96) of the Qing Dynasty, there were 2,000 chefs at work in the imperial kitchens. They fed the thousands more of the entourage comprising advisors, administrators, concubines, soldiers and families. The cuisine reflects the Muslim heritage of the conquerors, the horsemen of the north. Mutton and lamb are the meats while stews and hot pots prevail. Beijing Duck, hung out to dry, then roasted, is known and served internationally in all Chinese communities. Mao Tai, White Lightning, served by the thimblefuls is reflective of the Mongol hordes' fierce nature.

Shandong Province, bordering the sea, adds prawn and fish to the menus, shipping daily truckloads to the capital. Sweet potatoes, the vegetable that came to China from the Americas via the Philippines is a staple. Fortunate climate providing a bountiful agricultural harvest adds to the wealth of sea food, making Shandong a gourmet's paradise. **Tsingtao** *pijiu* (beer), a smooth concoction, has won many medals around the world. Shandong also boasts of the best wines of export quality from the vineyards begun during the European occupation.

Shanghai, Center of Fish and Rice Land

Shanghai, surrounded by Jiangsu, Anhui and Zhejiang is credited with the title, "gastronomical jewel of all China". The 3 provinces in the delta of the Changjiang, blessed with lakes and river and moderate climates, provide a wealth of fish, grain, and vegetables to the most popular city in China.

Eat-and-run food shops, the forerunner of western junk-food enterprises serve twisted fried bread, steamed buns, and bowls of rice gruel to early morning customers on their way to work. They stand or knee-sit by the curbs handling the food adroitly and rapidly with chopsticks, rarely taking more than 3 minutes. The general workforce bring their rice bowls to the office and an in-house kitchen prepares simple menus of rice and vegetables. Lunch is a quick meal and a long siesta.

The elite lunch atop the Peace Hotel overlooking the Huangpo, a 20-page menu lists hundreds of delectable dishes serving foreigners and local business persons in a rapid table turnover. A list of Shanghai restaurants would fill a 100-page book. Everyone who has ever gone to the Paris of the East has a half-dozen favorites. A surge of joint-venture, splendiferous highrise hotels has brought in another wave of international style cuisine.

Secretive gourmets, however, keep to themselves the "one dish to die over" for which they would schedule meetings and fly in from Tokyo or Hong Kong. The Shanghai Hairy Crab is harvested for a controlled short period in September-October, from Yengcheng Lake, up the river toward Nanjing. About the size

As hot as they look, chillis dried on the roof of a Dai house in Xishuang Banna.

of an average man's hand, covered with a black furry coat, the crab is steamed and served in its shell.

Pork and poultry are also favorites of Shanghai cuisine, featuring slow braising instead of stir frying. The food tends to become more oily, laced with Shaoxing's yellow wine and soy sauce mixtures with a pinch of sugar or honey.

Bamboo baskets of steamed dumplings are on every table, filled with tiers of the assorted delicacies. If the dumpling is small, put it whole into your mouth. Take a bite, sample the exquisite texture and aroma of the filling inside, and you will understand why the Chinese take to dumplings in the same way as an American to hotdogs. Shanghai cuisine absorbs the style of its

Dim Sum Teahouse

A typical *Dim Sum* Teahouse is a chaotic, noisy experience that one must enjoy (endure) before going to Chinese heaven. An absolute rule of thumb is to arrive before noon and the bedlam crowd, to assure a sufficiently large round table to handle your group. Grouping is the only way to go, otherwise you have no chance to compete in the din and sharing of the delectable morsels.

Soup and special dishes are ordered at once and tea selection if you desire something different from the regular Jasmine or Oolong. Waitresses start their interminable cart-filled circuits among the tables, each cart filled with a specialty of dumplings, *wontons*, steamed pork-filled buns, spring rolls, stuffed rice noodles, shrimp bonnet, pork turnovers, spareribs, chicken feet, curried chicken wings, seafood turnovers, medallion mushrooms, mini stuffed potato pancakes, and a thousand other possibilities depending on the ingenuity of the chef of the day.

One of China's most famous teahouses is the Rich Spring Restaurant, in the city of Yangzhou. The dough recipe for the restaurant's steamed buns is reputed to be over 1,000 years old and the buns are famed for their unfailingly light texture.

Bun fillings can be sweet or savory. The ingredients are chosen in harmony with the seasons: bamboo shoots in spring, salted vegetables in summer, crab in autumn and pork in winter. One of the restaurant's most exclusive offerings is "Five Treasure Buns". Legend has it that this bun was devised at the whim of an Emperor's eunuch who had a weakness for steamed buns. Using the emperor's name, he ordered the chefs to devise a five treasure filling. When the buns were served to the Emperor, he asked how they came to be made. When he realised the request was made falsely in his name, he had the eunuch executed. The recipe, however, lived on.

Sip your tea after savoring every bite-sized delicacy, relax, discuss the merits with your companions. With each selection the waitress will provide enough for each guest to sample, counting by the size of the serving dish. Don't ask for the table to be cleared, that's your tab when you are ready to go. Nearby tables will approach a crescendo of noise as the diners prepare to take off and return to the office. Never mind the arguments, it is customary to fight over the check vociferously and aggressively, then shake hands as the winner pays up.

---

neighbors, the 3 provinces surrounding it make it a national enclave of good food and drink.

The Deep South - Cantonese Cuisine

The Chinese, both Hakka and Han from Guangdong, Fujian, Hainan Island, and other southeast ports emigrated to the Golden Mountain of America, the sheep lands of Australia and New Zealand, neighboring Asian lands and islands. They took with them the art of Canton-

ese food preparation and endeared the world to their cuisine. Each country required an alteration of form and substance in the process of assimilation, therefore Bamboo Chicken will be different in San Francisco or Sydney. Acceptance of the Chinese chef or small restaurant owner is world-wide and he is a familiar figure found in a tin shack roadside seafood eatery in rural Malaysia or in replicas of the Hong Kong Jade Garden's impressive and busy dining rooms around the world.

Guangzhou (Canton) has its own reputation for eccentric and exotic

Chicken Culture

The lowly chicken, snubbed by the more elegant members of the poultry tribes of duck, geese, swan, pheasants, quail, and other wild birds has been, is and will be, the staple of good eating in China as it is around the world. Who can ignore the medicinal qualities of a hearty chicken broth when the throat tightens, chest rales, and headaches threaten? What civilization did not leave the bones of chicken in its residue, sifted by the archeologists?

China, the Beautiful Cook Book, a combination of magnificent photography of China's wondrous scenery and taste tempting assorted cuisine entitles the following chicken recipes:

Chicken Ball and Pea Soup (Beijing)
Steamed Whole Chicken with Glutinous Rice and Delicacies (Sichuan)
Braised Chicken with Lemon (Shanghai)
Chicken and Ginkgo Nuts (Sichuan)
Chicken in a Lantern (Beijing)
Phoenix Breast with Sour Sauce (Sichuan)
Fried Chicken Legs (Shanghai)
Braised Chicken Legs in a Lotus Shape (Shanghai)
Chicken Rolls with Sesame Seeds (Beijing)
Mandarin Diced Chicken (Sichuan)
Sliced Chicken and Seasonal Vegetables (Sichuan)
Steamed Whole Lantern Shaped Chicken (Sichuan)
Diced Tomato Amidst Chicken Snow (Sichuan)
Chicken Shreds and Garlic Chives (Sichuan)
Chrysanthemum Fire Pot (Shanghai)
Chicken Braised in Soy Sauce with Two Kinds of Meatballs (Guangzhou)
Wengchang Chicken, Guangzhou Style
Sliced Chicken with Scallion Oil (Guangzhou)
Dong Jiang Salt Baked Chicken (Guangzhou)
Boned Chicken with Crab Roe (Guangzhou)
Steamed Chicken Wings with Filling (Shanghai)
Shredded Chicken and Tender Celery (Sichuan)
Stewed Chicken Li Kou Fu Style (Guangzhou)
Chicken Wing and Frog Leg Tapestry (Guangzhou)
Velvet Chicken with Shark's Fins (Beijing)

And the list goes on through hundreds of cook books, the names alone tempting the palate. Modern dieticians and health gurus shout the cholesterol free advantages of skinned chicken, merely reiterating what Chinese chefs have known for millenniums.

Leave us not forget the famous **Beggar's Chicken**, once considered a lowly dish, now acclaimed in restaurants throughout the world: An early version of its recipe says "First go out and steal a chicken. Stuff it with herbs and vegetables, encase it in mud and throw in the coals of a tramp's fire. When the aroma drives you to distraction hammer it open and eat the feast of the Emperor."

dishes. The people of this province have developed a simple though distinctive philosophy on food: "to turn an unlikely ingredient into a cherished delicacy, all that is needed is the proper seasoning and cooking."

Wild Buffet

It is not a popular misconception that the locals eat any animal that walks, flies or swims. When elephants were abundant, they feasted on barbecued trunk, the flavor of which they compared to pork. The great python is a renowned dish finely sliced and dipped in vinegar.

In Guangdong, the Snake Restaurant specializes in food prepared with wild animals, particularly snakes. The chefs in this restaurant take great pride

Essence of the Wok

You start with a stainless steel wok of substantial thickness. The new greasy appliance must be scrubbed down, debrided, and boiled for a half-hour before it can become your true friend. Thoroughly clean and soak it after each cooking experience and then massage your friend lightly with salad oil to keep its gloss and rust-free state.

Of all the metals, stainless steel retains the heat best, the bowl shape requiring heat at the bottom, which spreads in varying degrees upwards. Heat the wok, using the wide rim of the holder up to keep the base closest to the heat source. A small amount of oil will attest to the proper temperature as it sizzles, then maintain the same heat during the cooking cycle.

The wok chef will surround the cooking area with the separate ingredients, diced and sliced, to be stir fried, each in order of its delicacy frying time. Preparation means the slicing and dicing all done beforehand, the guests at the table ready to eat. Nothing is left to chance, and no cooking begins before everything is ready.

Only when the surface of the oil shimmers, is it ready for stir-frying. The chef adds the first of his ingredients – to flavor the oil, 2 smashed cloves of garlic. A quick sizzle results. The oil must be just hot enough to sear ingredients, sealing in natural flavors and juices.

As soon as the chef smells the fragrance of the garlic, he adds the first of the stir-fry ingredients; rapidly he tosses, lifts and turns them. As he works, he moves the wok backwards and forwards over the fire to maintain the necessary quick sizzle. He must now add seasonings to the wok. The heat brings out their fragrance and the chef responds by adding a dash more rice wine. Now the 'big heat' flame explodes over the stir-fry.

The last task is to make the sauce, one that will lightly coat each slice of meat and shine each sliver of vegetable. To do so, the chef slides the stir-fry out into a dish, then ladles stock into the center of the wok. It boils instantly; a light binding of cornflour is stirred in. The sauce is cooked in seconds.

Now he tosses the stir-fry back in, it boils and he puts in the rest of the ingredients. It is a matter of minutes before the dish is ready to be whisked onto the table.

in their establishment: they see themselves as providers of fine cuisine that also benefits the health of patrons who regard the snake as a rejuvenator. They also believe that the more poisonous the snake, the more potent its effect.

Unusual animals are found on other specialized menus: wild birds, parrots, cockatoos and owls compete with bred-for-food chow dogs. Anteaters, sloths, and all manner of game are touted to the tastes of the Cantonese gourmets.

The essence of Cantonese food is fresh preparation by stir-fry, or steaming with light sauces of ginger and green onion. The gypsy-like Hakka have their style, Fujian, Taiwan and Hainan Island compete with the major use of treasures from the sea. Vegetables are lightly cooked with little oil, often *shuang* style (steamed), to retain the freshness. Temperate weather provides several growth cycles within each year and rice is the reigning basic dish. Fried rice, is probably the best known international dish, fried lightly with pork, chicken, shrimp, scallions and whatever is in the kitchen for the chef.

Chicken soup, prepared from a bottomless stock pot in most homes has a variety like the *mille-fleur* designs in cloisonne. Hainan chicken is a well-

Cossack men frying up a meal outdoors.

known course served in its home territory, whole, in the pot with ginger and spices. Hong Kong and Singapore versions serve it as steamed white meat of chicken with a bowl of clear broth and a side of ginger spiced rice. McDonald's of America may be everywhere today but the Chinese restaurant serving Cantonese fried rice and egg flower soup was there first.

The Hot Stuff - Sichuan Cuisine

Sichuan is the garden basket, geographic center of China, feeding over a hundred million people. Sichuan (Szechuan) means 4 rivers and is in debt to those 4 rivers that beget the tremendous yield of garden vegetables. Since ancient times, rulers have harnessed the rivers with dams, diverting the waters to the fields in a divide-and-conquer system of irrigation.

Rivaling Cantonese cuisine, Sichuan has its own restaurants often combined with the other Asian countries of similar origin. Thai, Malaysian, Vietnamese, Kampuchean, and some Indian cultures are said to have originated in Sichuan and its southern neighbor Yunnan.

Food styles are similar using the ubiquitous pepper in its infinite variety to heat up the action. Don't worry about the larger bell peppers and the long pinnochio-nose-like red and green ones.

It is the little red ones, sliced and added to soy on the table that are dangerous. A bit of the liquid or a stray piece in the soup bowl seem at first sip palatable, and then the unquenchable fire sets in. The Friends of the Pepper Society claim it quickens the blood (it does), stimulates the taste buds (sure does, one can't taste a thing after chewing on the little red devil), and aids digestion (yes it does, one can feel it all the way through the system).

Sichuan cuisine boasts of the 7 flavors: *tien* (sweet), originating with honey or sugar; *suan* (sour), from vinegar; *tien* (salty), using soy sauce or salt; *xiang* (fragrant), the use and aroma of garlic and ginger; *ku* (bitter) from green onions and leeks; *ma* (nutty), from the pervasive sesame seeds; and *la* (hot) from the infamous tiny red chili.

Yunnan's Smorgasbord

Food style discussions cannot ignore the stew pot of Yunnan and its border cornucopia of Xishuang Banna territory. For centuries, the tribal minorities mixed and matched their societies with the Burmese, Siamese, Vietnamese, Cambodian, and Indian nationalities. The names have changed in some instances but the family ties and heritages remain.

Thus, particular food habits and cuisines resulted from this pot-pourri. The climate is temperate, Kunming is the "city of eternal spring". There are 3 or 4 vegetable harvests a year so, the Buddhist vegetarians are satisfied. Sheep are plentiful to cater to Muslim cuisine which require lamb. Rice and other grains, aided and abetted with the muscles of the water buffalo, grow almost everywhere in the valleys. The Zhuangs, on their feast days, make a giant pyramidal dumpling made of sticky rice

A street restaurant, an essential aspect of Chinese life.

stuffed with pork, set to stew in a sealed pot for hours. Rivers and lakes provide an abundance of fish and mudcrabs. A Dai Farmer in Xishaung Banna will take you into his stilt home and regale you with local wines, sticky rice, and a variety of spicy dishes.

As the region is fairly remote the food that evolve from the intermingling of the people living on its borders would develop a particular character of its own, rich in variety with a distinctive flavor reflective of its diverse people and their heritage.

Shopping

Souvenirs, collectibles, art, crafts, antiques, jewelry, books, posters, clothing, furniture, carpets, and whatevers are the inevitable acquisitions for the traveler in China. Each purchase recalls an experience, an adventurous place, or a chance meeting with a unique person.

Shopping involves personality quirks of people: the "look but don't buy" and the "I'll think about it" attitudes; the impulsive spender; or the serious investigative selective buyer. Looking without any intention of buying is fun. No-spend shopping is like reading a library book. One can learn a tremendous amount about the nature and history of this ancient country by looking through the shops as one might a museum. Absorb the endless variety, wonder about the unknown artist who spent a lifetime carving a village

A vendor in Kunming selling joss-sticks and candles.

The Arts and Crafts Center in Shanghai.

of people on a block of soapstone or on a whole ivory tusk and the circumstances that surround his works.

"I'll think about it" attributes are an expression of repressed desire for an item without the urge to actually acquire it. In China, this is a very difficult problem resulting in a lifetime of "I wish I had bought that pair of cloisonne vases when I was in Beijing, they were half the price of the Chinese art dealer in San Francisco and were infintely more beautiful."

The impulsive shopper is often a victim of bargain-hunting greed. "The jade ring in the antique-curio shop is so cheap, I can probably sell it for twice as much when I get home." A jeweler friend at home informs him that the stone is actually adventurine, worth about what he paid for.

Then there is the serious collector of carved netsukes who has a library of books on the subject, and 3 curio cabinets at home displaying the collection. He (rarely a she) carries a jeweler's eye trained to minutely examine each and every possible purchase. The collector has a different touring schedule as he wants to spend more time prowling the antique shops in Beijing's Liulichang district.

The fun shopper purchases a bunch of cloisonne bangle bracelets for her (women have a greater tendency for fun-shopping) several nieces' Christmas gifts, or a pretty rose quartz carving of Ho Ti, the laughing Buddha because it reminds her of Uncle Jake.

Each chapter in the Follow That Bug section, delineates interesting art, crafts, antiques and other local products. The chapter on Crafts explains briefly most of the potential harvest of treasures. Visits to museum exhibits of Oriental artifacts and Chinese artifact stores will familiarize, to a degree, what the shopper will see in China.

For the serious shopper, book stores and libraries have a store house of information on every artform ever produced. Literally thousands of books have been written on everything from netsukes, jade, cloisonne to paper cuts or kites. Reading will give the background to the item and spark an interest to be pursued. A pre-conceived objective makes shopping a treasure hunt.

Friendship Stores are found in main cities in China.

Cloisonne

Cloisonne is a prolific craft form found almost all over the Orient and especially China because the tourist shoppers love it. Try to seek out specific items to make your collection impressive, memorable and important.

Miniature vases, for instance, in mirror-image pairs on their wood-carved stands can be a delight if you look carefully at selections. Boxes is another idea. The Chinese love interestingly shaped boxes to hold valued items, give a gift in, or keep favored medicinal herbs in.

Jewelry for the woman who loves to jingle-jangle is a delight. Bracelets alone are available in dozens of styles and a myriad of colors. Cloisonne beads abound that can be worn as or collected to re-string in personally created designs for the talented hobbyist bead-stringer.

Antique cloisonne requires more study and expertise to tell the truly old from the current prolific Beijing production. The rewards are great, however, for the supply is becoming limited and their value are constantly increasing. For this collectible you must scrounge every antique corner of Friendship Stores and every antique-curio shop. Especially rewarding are off-beat stores in small towns not hounded by the tourist. Don't forget, emigres with very interesting collections are in Hong Kong, Singapore, Malaysia, Indonesia and Taiwan if you

Suni tribe women determined not to lose any opportunity in selling handicraft.

are also visiting those nearby areas.

Porcelain

Ceramic arts are discussed in the various locations they are found in and the Crafts section. The non-professional shopper can readily be interested in small easily carried items such as soup spoons and small saucers, rice bowls and lidded tea cups, miniature tea sets and tiny wine bottles.

The best and most fun sources for these items are the People's Department Stores. In the large cities, they are ranked by number. Prowling Wanfujing and Xidan in Beijing or Nanjing Road in Shanghai can occupy a day each at least.

For serious porcelain vases, sculpture, covered jars, and dinnerware you are on your own, guided by personal taste and expertise.

Lacquer Products

Cinnabar and weightless **lacquer** artforms are discussed in detail elsewhere but here again the acquisition can take a specific bend. House decorative items abound from tiny miniatures to massive vases, bowls and mysterious looking urns.

Southern areas like Fujian Province specialize in the weightless lacquer formed into highly-decorated boxes, trays, vases, and hundreds of miscellaneous items. Beijing and the northern provinces accomplish the endless hours of work in detailed carving of multi-layers of lacquer products. They make magnificent wedding gifts for favored friends, as their lasting qualities make heirlooms out of the product.

The List Goes On

Kites for flying or room decoration.
Tea cans in their myriad of design and colors.
Embroideries with panels showing the Hundred Children, or expensive and very valuable 2-sided works of art.
Posters and books in the Xinhua Book Stores.
Pocket knives. The Chinese love decorated pocket knives for peeling fruit. Department stores have full cases of them.
Clothing: silks, cottons, cashmere, beaded fancy eveningwear, articles abound everywhere you turn. You will find international brand names, the overrun from exported products.
Art in traditional form and by the modernists.
Snuff bottles in an infinite variety of materials, old and new.
Calligraphy art supplies: slates, inks, brushes, water jars and an infinite variety of papers to paint on.
Chopsticks. The ordinary bunches of decorated bamboo, personal sets in beautiful cases, old ivories, new

An antique-curio shop in Beijing.

cloisonne-tipped.
Tea. Puerh, Jasmine, Oolong, Cloud Mountain, Dragon Well, and a thousand other local varieties, packaged in beautiful tins and decorated bamboo boxes, or also in cheap plastic bags in the villages.
Music cassette tapes, and now videos, of modern and traditional songs.

The list goes on, subject to your own discovery of a unique or unusual item that few people collect. Or, you can easily stumble upon a rare item while exploring one of the little towns tucked in a corner of China.

Shopping is fun and games, or serious and technical, as you make it. Ingenuity and a specific field make it far more interesting. Happy Hunting!

TRAVEL TIPS

CLOTHING

Travel light. Take practical everyday washables that are broken in and comfortable. Three or four changes are enough as the hotels all have inexpensive daily laundry service. Anticipate the weather. Light, waterproof, lined jackets over a sweater or sweatshirt make a good hedge against unexpected cool days or evening walks. You may have heard that China manufactures the whole world's denims and tee shirts which is probably true. You can replace or augment any of your clothing including a cashmere sweater at a modest price. Murphy's law says you will return with twice as much as you came with.

In moderate weather, experienced travelers take foot-shaped sandals like Birkenstocks and 1 pair of lightweight walking sports shoes. A pair of slip-on loafers for dinner is enough.

CHINA INTERNATIONAL TRAVEL SERVICE - CITS (Luxingshe)

CITS and CTS. It is important that you know the exact function of this bureaucracy. They have offices in every city, town or village that has access to foreign visitors. Their job is to arrange accommodation, transportation, translators and guides. The function is to meet you, see to your local needs and then see you off to the next destination. In some cases of extended travel a national guide is assigned to travel with you as a companion. For the most part, they are young men and women, trained in Beijing University. CITS charges a fee for the paper work, a daily rate for the guide, a mileage rate for the car and driver and a fee for meeting or seeing you off. They purchase for you, bus, air, rail and boat tickets. All other charges for hotel, food and auto transportation are pay as you go. The service is offered, not required. Use at your own discretion.

In the rare instance you find the guide incompatible, it is in order to **diplomatically** request a replacement. Remember China's personnel are not rewarded for extra effort or excellence. Don't worry. Most of the CITS personnel are friendly, competent and delight in contact with the outside world.

Tipping is not required and frowned upon by the government. A nice thank you letter from home, enclosing photographs taken enroute, is much appreciated.

COMMUNICATIONS

Facsimile services have replaced telex in all of the major city hotels. Include your credit card number and expiry date to guarantee the first night. Be sure to cancel 48 hours in advance if you change plans.

Take a friend's fax number if you don't have a machine yourself to send messages home. Telephone service from major centers like Shanghai are good, direct dialing available in some hotels. Letters and postcards are great because you can select pretty stamps. If your luggage loads up, take a carton to the nearest international post office (available in all major cities). Present it open, for customs inspection and a local attendant will help you paper cover and seal it for shipment. Seamail takes 6 to 8 weeks in the Pacific area, about double that to the United States and Europe. It is very reliable, confounded only by your own country's customs regulations. A phone call to your post office department in charge of incoming foreign packages, before you leave, will give you shipping guidelines and duty costs for unaccompanied luggage, as the authorities call it.

EQUIPMENT AND APPLIANCES

Look before you plug in. The current is 240 and most of the plugs are slanted prongs like in Australia. Frequent travelers carry a kit of plugs including a converter (US travelers) for 240/110.

It is prudent to carry a camera that thinks for itself and is small enough to carry in a shirt pocket. The yield with an average 200 color film is usually 36 plus with good results.

However, scenery is not possible with a pocket camera. Every scenic location sells postcards, photos, slides and now some video tapes to augment your memory book. Camera bugs with the 12-inch lenses and video devotees that require back up back-ache carryalls are on their own. Pocket-sized binoculars are handy to have for the long vistas. Film developing in China is adequate. The lead bag for exposed or raw film is important because Hong Kong and some Chinese X-rays will definitely damage the film. Also carry a hot rod or two cup water heater. In some out-of-the-way places, it is always safer to boil your own water.

FOOD AND DRINK

Ordinary everyday eating can be fun. Tour-group food is the most criticized aspect of organized travel in China. Numerous unidentifiable dishes are served family-style at tables catering for 8 or 10. The food rarely is hot, sauces disguise the contents and often surly attendants ignore a request for bottled water or more rice.

Independent everyday dining can be fun with an effort on your part to decipher the menu. Write down favorite dishes in your conversation book (in Mandarin and pinyin, dining room personnel are always happy to oblige). All hotels now have a menu in English/Mandarin, most of the time the same menu printed in some secret tourist supply house. The difference is how the local chef prepares the same selection.

There is always a steamed rice pot for general serving. There will also be Shanghai or Tsingtao beer. Organize the trick of ordering vegetables steam cooked if excessive oil bothers your cholesterol. Pork is a staple, palatable beef is rare. Hard-boiled eggs for breakfast is common tourist fare. Crisp duck and crisp chicken are favorites because they are well cooked. Fresh fruit is often available, to be peeled before eating.

The dessert can vary from a cold fruit soup to a clear no-taste broth. Canned fruit is a staple all over China. Most hotels have an adequate supply for you to order lychee or peaches as a western dessert. When staying more than one day in a hotel, order something special for the evening meal at breakfast or lunch time like steamed mandarin fish or Mongolian hot pot (Steamboat).

HOTELS

In the major cities of China, there are older Chinese or European style hotels dating from the 1920s when the land was opened to foreigners. For instance the Beijing (Peking) Hotel on Chang An Avenue in Beijing, has an old wing (20's) and a new wing (40's). The rooms are commodious compared to the new hotels, furnished with heavy well-worn furniture. On the corner of the same block is the new tower hotel of the Beijing, Hong Kong style with all of the modern conveniences. The original section has the lobby, various restaurants, shops and, yes, the smells of the old business world. Old China hands still prefer the 1940's section of the Beijing Hotel.

In Shanghai, the same is true of the older Jin Jiang Hotel with its North Wing or the new sumptuous tower nearby. Each city is also starred with dozens of international hotels, available on international reservations systems with a credit card guarantee.

Wherever you travel in China, there are wide-spread price levels. If you have engaged a CITS guide to meet you with no hotel specified, the room will be where their office is, usually the best. It is perfectly in order to negotiate the room price and location. If the hotel doesn't suit for any reason, ask to be taken to another. Special hotels and preferred locations are noted in the area discussed. When making your own reservations, consult the directory. We have listed only the better ones, CITS will assist in getting economy accommodations if you desire.

INDEPENDENT TRAVEL (FIT)

If you are more adventurous, desiring a freer schedule you will only need to define the general itinerary and original landing point. The destination sections are written with this in mind. The segments define an area of travel that can leisurely be covered in 3 or 4 weeks. You need only to book the international flight ticket and your arrival hotel in advance. Ongoing arrangements are made as your time and inclination suit. We suggest the use of China International Travel Service (CITS) or China Travel Service (CTS) for internal travel arrangements. CITS is the general travel service for foreigners, CTS for overseas Chinese.

First time travelers to China may elect to arrange a pre-planned independent tour (FIT) to feel more secure. Compare the tour offers by the local agents and CITS for price and detail. Then ask the one that is more knowledgeable to make an IT (independent tour) to the precise area you want to see. Local scenic and side trips are arranged when you get there. The rule of thumb is "more days, less movement".

An example is a 21-day visit to the Beijing area, touring Beijing, Tianjin, Beidaihe or Chengde and maybe Guilin on the way back to Hong Kong. You would be in and out of Beijing 2 or 3 times, visit the Great Wall and Forbidden City when the weather is nice. Make the summer capital or a seaside resort a leisurely visit, wander the streets of Tianjin and leave China from its most picturesque spot of Guilin still fresh in your mind. Thus 3 or 4 days of major travel leaves 17 good days of the 21 for actual viewing pleasure.

An alternative is to have your local travel agent or CITS book your international air ticket, first arrival hotel reservation and assist with the visa. On arrival in Beijing, contact the CITS office or hotel concierge for local tours and the ongoing reservations for your side trips. A well-selected hotel is within walking or short taxi distance from the Forbidden City, Tiananmen Square, shopping streets, Coal Hill and Beihai Park. Enjoy each at your leisure, endurance, and the whims of the weather.

The third method for the adventurous and confident traveler is to book a flight and hotel reservation into Shanghai or Beijing direct. By following the destination chapters, you then contact the local CITS and proceed city by city. On subsequent trips to China, confidence will dictate your own arrangements with less and less scheduling.

LOTIONS AND POTIONS

Take only essentials. Your favorite Panadol or Tylenol and a stomach distress like Lomotil are essential. The rest of the "must haves" and "what ifs" from your medicine chest are better left home. In China, you buy Essential Tiger Balm which is a cure-all. You will be surprised to find Crest Toothpaste and Johnson's Baby Powder on the shelf in your hotel. If you get a cold, stay in bed, drink noodle soup and tea with honey and lemon just like your family doctor used to advice. All kinds of tea are plentiful, coffee sometimes scarce, especially if you like decaffeinated. Imported powdered coffees are available in the hotel stores, expensive and not always your favorite brand. Sugar is available, powdered cream not always. Hygiene is generally good now due to government intervention.

Medical attention is adequate, though not with the ambience you are familiar with. Persistent cold viruses are familiar to the doctors. Broken bones are set. Emergency air transportation to Hong Kong is rarely more than a few hours away, though getting a seat may be a problem. Check with your local health department about shots necessary. Gamma globin (hepatitis protection) is recommended. If you have physical problems such as heart trouble, carry the latest data from your doctor's office with you. The most common problem is weariness and common colds. The essence is don't worry.

LUGGAGE

Expandable nylon or canvas duffles that take abuse are more practical than formal suitcases. Hand trolleys or built-in wheels are an absolute necessity. Porters must be pre-arranged and are rare. There are long walks in airports and train depots. Except for the 5-star hotels, floor attendants do not carry luggage. Be sure the handle straps on duffles are one piece that go all around the bag. Torn handles are a nuisance.

Avoid the bigger sizes that tempt overfilling. For 2 people we suggest one medium for each and one smaller together for shoes, mechanical gear, books and whatever else you cannot do without (the heavy stuff). When you take side trips, check in the medium ones at your hotel. Use the smaller one with a minimum of clothes and gear for the junket. A small, very light, extra foldaway nylon case is handy for shopping excess acquired. Surplus can always be shipped home (see Communications).

Take a durable, light, carryall backpack as an extra for short trips. Even on a day trip, you will find it useful for a light jacket, camera, films, binoculars and other basic necessities. On trains, buses and long auto trips pack the swag bag with a good supply of snacks. Bottled water and snacks are available in the bigger hotel lobbies or department store food counters. At the first available department store, buy one of their folding pocket gadgets with the can-bottle opener, spoon, fork, and knife. It is a universal tool in China.

MEDICINE

Acupuncture is the technique of inserting thin stainless steel needles into various nerve points of the body, primarily an anaesthesia, not a cure for ailments. Surgery is routinely performed in many hospitals where doctors use several of 150 basic points to numb the affected area. In some instances a low voltage electric current is applied to augment the insertion. There are over 2000 points identified for possible treatment.

Western medicine has accepted acupuncture to some degree and acknowledge its benefits in treating ailments such as migraine headaches and back pains. The theory of Chinese proponents are that the insertion point relates to a particular part of the body, an organ, a joint, a gland etc. They believe an energy channel, converted by Westerners as a nerve meridian, blocks the pain sensations of the sensory system. In principle, acupuncture is used widely in China because of the low cost and lack of side effects from other anaesthetic drugs.

Herbal medicine can best be described by repeating excerpts from an article in China Reconstructs, a national magazine:

"It was harvest time in the Golden Bridge brigade in Kiangsu province's Yicheng county on the north bank of the Yangtze. While other brigade members were picking cotton and reaping mid-season rice, its barefoot doctors and health workers were harvesting their medicinal herbs in a special plot near the brigade clinic. The young men and women were gathering seeds from the Job's Tears plant (used in Chinese medicine as a stimulant to the digestive system), cultivating other herbs and turning up the soil in preparation for planting lovage, an herb used to treat gynaecological disorders... The "Garden of a Hundred Herbs" actually grows 240 varieties on a rotation process in the 800 sq m plot. They include well known flowers like the cockscomb and gladioli, the globe amaranth with red ball-like blossoms, locally known as *Red for a Thousand Days*, a medicine for asthma and dysentery.

In addition to the usual stock of drugs and ampules, inside the 110-sq-meter pharmacy were 2 cabinets of small drawers, each labeled with the name of the herb or other Chinese medicine it contained, 86 kinds of western drugs and more than 360 Chinese medicinal ingredients."

Medicine for the masses ranges from modern hospitals in the larger cities to a proliferation of local doctors in the rural areas. Local doctors receive from 6 months to a year's training, and are then sent out as teams to learn on the job. The PRC promulgates research, training, hygiene, and education in every corner of the country.

In rural areas, at open markets, there is always a herb seller, his wares spread in bowls, trays and gunny sacks. Snake and other animal extracts are hustled as cures, in bottles and sometimes alive. The stands are busy, the vendors acting as doctors spouting their technical knowledge. Raw pictures are shown of before and after conditions of their patients.

Exporting packaged medicines, dried herbs, medicinal teas, ginseng roots and a host of others is a large cash-flow business for China. Walking through the streets after dinner is a sensory sensation of restaurants, food shops and especially the pharmacology stores.

MONEY

Question #1: What will it cost? Everyone spends in a different manner. For the best hotels, general dining, domestic transportation of taxis, trains, boats and planes, plan US$150 per day per couple times the number of days you will be in China. International air tickets are extra. Most tourists travel as a couple, in pairs or *en famille*, thus we talk in terms of 2 persons. Tour packages always quote per person with a supplement for privacy.

As in all international travel, the big cities can cost US$200-250 a day with taxis, expensive dining, and side junkets. Joint-venture 5-star hotels in Beijing and Shanghai average US$125 for standard doubles, a nice hotel in Ningbo will cost US$25. A crowded bus tour to the Great Wall will be a tenth of what a comfortable independent taxi will cost. Tourist air tickets are double the domestic fare but not in excess of other parts of the world. When accompanied by a CITS guide, you pay for their fares, food and lodging but at local prices. Despite advertising to the contrary, most package tours are equal to or more than FIT, except for the international air fare. If booking your own, shop around. There are special competitive fares to Hong Kong, and sometimes to direct entry points in China saving an expensive Hong Kong stopover.

It is best to take cash or traveler's checks. The credit card companies have invaded China but the systems of charges are varied and often expensive.

Some areas will charge you 4 per cent to use your credit card. The rule of thumb is pay as you go whenever possible. Make as few advance payments as possible. Changing or trying to get a refund on a prepaid hotel or Great Wall Tour is a lesson in time-consuming frustration, in most cases impossible. If a travel agent says, the only way you can travel in China is prepaid, get another agent. They earn a commission for their efforts, therefore desire to sell you as much of the package as possible.

China issues Foreign Exchange Currency (FEC) Yuan to all tourists in exchange for most international currency or traveler's checks. Don't worry if you accumulate a few pieces of *reminbi* (people's money) enroute. Some free-market traders will try to give you *reminbi* in exchange for a large bill. Refuse it, take back your bill and start walking away. Proper FEC appears magically. The Bank of China maintains cash-counters at all major hotels, airports and tourist stores. They trade fairly, respective of the international quotes and exchange unused currency on your departure, provided you keep the encashment certificates when you change. They will not cash more than you bought. *Reminbi* and FEC Yuan have no international exchange value outside China.

Black market is a No No in any country, especially China. There is no justification in circumventing laws, especially in militaristic China. Wave off all of the "Change Money?" requests.

One side light to the above rule. When you travel with a guide to Confucius' birth place, Qu Fu, for instance, the custom is to pay for his or her costs. The easiest way, is to entrust a sum of FEC to the guide. Let her or him pay all the transportation, hotel, food and whatever out of the kitty. At the end, they will give you a stack of receipts and the change. Guides can and will negotiate better prices than you and pay considerably less for their accommodation and meals than you. The guide may spend some of his own *reminbi* for the expenses where he can and keep your FEC. That's a prerequisite for her or him to purchase imported products such as Kodak Film and Coca Cola, for personal use. Gray market, not black.

TOUR PACKAGES

China International Travel Service CITS has offices in most capital cities, (see Directory). Qantas, has its travel associate Jetabout ready to help. Singapore Airlines and Cathay Pacific use their own friendly helpers as do many other major international airlines. The walls of most Asian-oriented agencies are plastered with special deals. Your school alumni, professional association, sister city organization, propose tours from time to time. Ask yourself the big question: where do we want to go first? If you are planning on going to Tibet, the Hong Kong-Beijing-Lhasa package may be just the right itinerary for you.

A typical commercial China tour: every day is scheduled in detail, weather and physical stamina not withstanding. The net result can be a tiring, physically demanding trip, inhibited by the tour group herding instinct of the operators. Study the itinerary carefully and compare with others before you decide.

Consult the various brochures; read them with your wall map to check the relative distances covered. The formula to determine value of a package: tour days minus travel days divided into land cost equals viewing cost per day. Obviously the least number of stops is the best value.

TRANSPORTATION

Most of the major airlines fly into Beijing or Shanghai, the principal ports of tourist entry. Singapore Airlines, Cathay Pacific, Japan Airlines, Northwest and Qantas are just a few. The rates are relatively uniform but it pays to call to see if there are any current round trip promotions. Make your plans first, then look for a package that fits. Around The World and Circle Pacific special rates benefit long distance travelers, using Hong Kong and Singapore as hubs.

Domestic flights on CAAC, China's national carrier now has many sub-branches serving special areas. All are part of the CAAC computerized system. The general axioms of domestic travel in China are: surface by car up to 8 hours; surface by train up to 12 hours; by boat whenever possible; otherwise fly. Chinese aircraft, schedules and attention to travelers are improving.

Private car traveling between cities is always interesting because you can stop along the way for the scenic splendors, visit small villages, shop, and sample local foods.

Trains are inexpensive and expeditious. More than 8 hours requires a sleeping berth and dining on board, both unnecessarily tiresome and frustrating. For privacy and comfort, book a compartment all to yourself.

Coastal steamers and river passenger boats are exciting, reasonably comfortable and out of the tourist traffic in most cases. The fun is mixing with the locals, stopping at small port cities and taking time for a relaxing journey. Overnights cost much less than the average hotel.

VISA

Obtain the information yourself direct from the source. Even if your travel agent is arranging your trip and getting your Visa, take the time to call the nearest Chinese consulate or embassy for an application form. They will tell you exactly what a tourist from your country must do to obtain a visa, length of stay allowed, the cost and how long it will take to process. You have to surrender your passport of course and do check the visa "stamp" when you get it back.

Two passport-sized photos are required and it is best to have some spares made at the same time. You may want to make a side trip to Bhutan or Nepal while in the area.

It would not be difficult to obtain a single entry 6-month travel visa, starting from the date of issue. Apply within 30 days of your intended trip. Any other arrangements must be specifically applied for before entry. Changes can be made internally but it takes time and often frustration with bureaucracy.

Make sure the dates and time limit are what you need. If you mail your passports, use registered-receipt mail systems. The visa normally reads single entry visit. If you exit Hong Kong, you cannot return to China on the same visa. A common mistake is to confuse Hong Kong as part of China. It is now a British colony and will revert to the Chinese only in 1997.

GLOSSARY

LANGUAGE

The Chinese phonetic system is called pinyin, merely the way it sounds to the westerner's ear. The basic written language, referred to as Mandarin evolves from the original pictorial letters and contains over 50,000 characters.

    The English speaking visitor is in luck as the majority of the young people and a host of educated elders speak understandable English. They learn it in school, over the radio from the constant BBC broadcasts and through their own initiative. CITS offices have a rota of guides, about half are English speaking, others in French, Italian, German and so on. Friendship Stores always have people that can converse in various languages. Notwithstanding it is common courtesy to speak the few words of Hello - Goodbye - Thank You. If you garble a word, the humorous Chinese will laugh and assist you with the tongue twisters.

    A simple conversation book (pocket size) will cover all but the most unusual communication situations. Eurasia Press's China Traveler's Conversation in existence since 1980 is excellent as it is easy to find what you want in it. Berlitz is comprehensive but the print is very small. Many others are in book stores all over the world. Spend a little time looking over the selection for these important points: size of type; arrangement for easy access; empty pages to add your own special needs; good food coverage; and a 4-way listing: English - Pinyin - Pronunciation - Characters in Chinese. The pronunciation is especially important to assist you in learning acceptable phonetics. Practice writing numbers to make them easier to recognize, at least 1 through 10. It is fun to know a price before the clerk tells you.

BRIEF GUIDE TO THE VOWELS AND CONSONANTS

Variations from normal spoken English:

a	ah as in far
ao	ow as in cow or allow
c/ci	ts aspirated as in its; "cao" is "tsao"
ch	as in chew
e	eh as in her
g	hard g as in go
h	guttural, aspirated as in huh or her
i	ee as in eek when used with the common syllables

Like "c" "ch" "r" "s" "sh" "z" and zh:

j	ch, as in jeep
o	aw as in flaw
q	ch as in cheek
qi	ch, softly as in cheese
qu	ch, as in chew
u	oo as in clue
x	hs as in "Xiao" = shao
z	ds as in suds or adze
zh	j as in the j for jeep

BASIC PHRASES TO PRACTICE ON

ENGLISH	PINYIN	PHONETIC
How are you?	ni hao	knee how
Hello, how are you?	ni hao ma	knee how mah
Good, fine, well	hao	how
Thank you	xiexie	shee-ah shee-ah
Good, thank you	hao xiexie	how, shee-ah shee-ah
Please	qing	ching
Don't mention it	bu keqi	boo ker-chee
Sorry!	duibuqi	doo-ay boo chee
Good morning	zao, zao an	dsow, dsow ahn
Good evening	wan, wan an	whan, whan ahn

English	Pinyin	Phonetic
Goodbye	zaijian	dsai jee-en
Goodbye	zaiwei	dsai way
Hot water	kaishui	kai-shway
Cold water	lengshui	lung kai-shway
Good	hao	how
Very good	hen hao	hun how
Best	tsui hao	zoo-ee how
No good	bu hao	boo how
Slow	man man	mahn mahn
Fast	kuai	koowhy
Toilet	cesuo	tse-swo
Men's	nan	nahn
Ladies	nui	nwee
Bath	xizao	shee-dsow
Laundry	xiyidian	shee-yee-dee-en

FOODS AND ACCESSORIES
(Enough to get breakfast and room service)

ENGLISH	PINYIN	PHONETIC
Breakfast	zaofan	dsow-fahn
Lunch	wufan	woo-fahn
Dinner	wanfan	wahn-fahn
Chopsticks	kuaizi	kwhy-zee
Fork	cha	chah
Knife	dao	dow
Spoon	shao	sh-ow
Cup	bei	bay
Bowl	wan	wahn
Beer	pijiu	pee-jew
Mineral water	laoshan	l'ow-shan
Soda	qishui	chee-shway
Tea	cha	chah
Coffee	kafei	kah-fey
Milk	niunai	knee-o-nye
Juice	shiguo zhi	shway-qwaw-jir
Wine	jiu	jee-oh
Rice	mifan	mee-fahn
Bread	mianbao	mee-ahn-bow
Steamed buns	miantou	man-toh
Potatoes	tudou	too-doh
Eggs	jidan	jee-dahn
Fried eggs	jian jidan	jee-en jee-dahn
Scrambled eggs	chao jidan	chow jee-dahn
Boiled eggs	zhu jidan	jew jee-dahn
Beef	niurou	knee-o-roh
Pork	zhurou	jew-roh
Chicken	ji	jee
Duck	ya	yah
Fish	yu	yew
Shrimp	xia	shee-ah
Boil	zhu	jew
Fry	jian	jee-en
Steam	zheng	juhng
Ginger	jiang	jee-ahng
Garlic	suan	soo-ahn
Oil	you	yoh
Salt	yan	yen
Pepper	hujiao fen	hoo-jew-ow fun
Soy	jiangyou	jee-ahng-yo
Soup	tang	tahng
Vegetables	shucai	shoo-tsai
Green Vegetables	qincai	chin-tsai
Bean curd	doufu	doe-foo
Fruit	shuiquo	shway-gwaw
Toast	kao mianbao	cow mee-ahn-bow
Porridge	zhou	joe
Noodle soup	tangmian	tahng mee-en

PRACTICE THE NUMBERS
(Learn to write the first ten)

ENGLISH	PINYIN	PHONETIC
One	yi	yee
Two	er	erh
Three	san	sahn
Four	si	see
Five	wu	woo
Six	liu	leo
Seven	qi	chee
Eight	ba	bah
Nine	jiu	jew
Ten	shi	shir
Eleven	shiyi	shir-yee
Twelve	shier	shir-erh
Thirteen	shisan	shir-sahn
Twenty	ershi	erh-shir
Thirty	sanshi	sahn-shir
Fifty	wushi	woo-shir
One hundred	yibai	yee-bye
One hundred one	yibailingyi	yee-bye-ling-yi
One thousand	yi qian	yee-chee-ahn

AND THE MONEY

Foreign Exchange Currency		FEC
Money	qian	chee-en
Yuan	kuai (yuan)	kwhy (yoo-

		ahn)
Jiao	mao (jiao)	mao (jee-ow)
Fen	fen	fun
Change money	huan qian	hwahn chee-en

WEIGHTS AND MEASURES

1 Kilogram = 2 catties = 2.205 pounds
1 Catty = 0.5 kilograms = 1.102 pounds
1 Pound = 0.454 kilograms = 0.907 catties

1 Kilometer = 2 li = 0.621 miles
1 Li = 0.5 kilometer = 0.311 miles
1 Mile = 1.609 kilometers = 3.219 li
1 Meter = 3 Chinese feet = 3.281 feet
1 Chinese Foot = 0.333 metres = 1.094 feet
1 Foot = 0.305 meters = 0.914 Chinese Feet
1 Hectare = 15 mou = 2.47 acres
1 Mou = 0.065 hectares = 0.164 acres
1 Acre = 0.405 hectares = 6.070 mou

DIRECTORY

DIRECTORY/REFERENCES

NAN-SOUTH BEI-NORTH
DONG-EAST XI-WEST
ZHONG-MIDDLE
LU-MAIN ROAD JIE-ALLEY

USE "0" PREFIX DOMESTIC AREA CODE
DELETE "0" PREFIX WHEN CALLING FROM OUTSIDE

CITS - CHINA INTERNATIONAL TRAVEL SERVICE OFFICES

Beijing
Head Office
6 Dong Chang'an Dajie, Beijing
Tel: (01)55-1031

2 Dong Qianman Dajie
Tel: (01)212-2211

8 Dong Jiamen Xang,
Dongchenchu,
Beijing 1000005
Tel: (01)512-9933
Fax: (01)512-9008

Australia
Level 2, 724-728 George St.,
Sydney, NSW 2000
Tel: (02)211-2633
Fax: (02)281-3595

Canada
PO Box 17, Main Fl. 999
W. Hastings St.
Vancouver
B.C. V6C 2W2
Tel: (604)684-8787
Fax: (604)684-3321

France
10 Rue de Rome,
75008, Paris
Tel: (1)45-22-92-72
Fax: (1)45-22-92-79

Hong Kong
Central Branch,
2nd Floor China Travel Bldg.
72 Queens Rd., Central
Tel (5)853-3533
Fax (5)541-9777

Kowloon Branch
1st Floor Alpha House
27-33 Nathan Road
Tsimshatsui
Tel: (3)721-1331
Fax: (3)721-7757

Japan
Nihombashi-Settsu Building
2-2-4 Nihombashi, Chuo-Ku,
Tokyo
Tel: (03)273-5512
Fax: (03)273-2667

Macao
Hotel Beverly Plaza,
Avenida do Dr. Rodrigo Rodriquez
Tel: 388-922

Philippines
489 San Fernando St., Binondo,
Manila
Tel: 40-74-75
Fax: 40-78-34

Singapore
Ground Floor, SIA Bldg.
77 Robinson Rd.
Tel: (65) 224-0550
Fax: (65) 224-5009

Thailand
460/2-3 Surawong Rd
Bangkok 10500
Tel 233-2895
Fax 236-5511

United Kingdom
24 Cambridge Circus
London WC2H 8HD
Tel (071)836-9911
Fax (071)836-3121

United States of America
2nd Fl. 212 Sutter St.
San Francisco, CA 94108
Tel (415)398-6627
Fax (415)398-6669

Los Angeles Branch, Suite 138
2223 E. Garvey Ave.
Monterey Park, Ca 91754
Tel (818)288-8222
Fax (818)288-3464

COMPLAINT HOT LINES
For serious problems of service with any of the tourist connected

organizations such as CAAC, CITS, CTS, hotels, restaurants and the like. Copy and put in with travel documents.

BEIJING - (01)5130828
GANSU PROVINCE - (0931) 26860
GUANGDONG PROVINCE - (020) 677422
GUILIN - (0773) 226553
JIANGSU PROVINCE - (025) 301221
SHAANXI PROVINCE - (029) 711480
SHANGHAI - (012) 4390630
TIANJIN - (022) 318814/318812
ZHEJIANG PROVINCE - (0571) 556631

HOTELS AND RESTAURANTS

The better hotels and some restaurants are listed below for general reference and for direct reservations when desired. In the more popular destinations of Beijing, Shanghai, Guangzhou, Hangzhou, Xian and Guilin, prices can run from US$100-US$150 (Superior doubles) per day. In the general tourist areas, US$50-US$75 per day for doubles or small suites. Most of the off-tour cities the rates will vary from US$15-35 per day, doubles. See Travel Tips for further information regarding hotel selections.

AREA CODES - ADD (0) PREFIX FOR DOMESTIC USE

BEIDAIHE, HEBEI PROVINCE
Zhong Hai Tan (Central Beach) Guesthouse
30 Xijing Road.
Tel: 2398/2445 - Ext 626
100 rms. + Villas
JINSHAN GUESTHOUSE
4 Jingshanzui Road
Tel: 41338

BEIJING, Capital - Area Code (86+1)
Beijing Hotel (East Wing)
33 East Chang An
Tel: 513 7766
Fax: 513-7307

Beijing Hotel (Guibinlou)
Distinguished Guest Building
33 East Chang An
Tel: 513 666
Fax: 513-0048

China World Hotel (Shangri-la)
1 Jianguomenwai De Bei Yao
Tel: 505-2277
Fax: 505-0818/38
699 rooms.

Great Wall Sheraton Hotel
6A Donghuan Bei Road
Tel: 500-5566
Fax: 500-3398
1007 rooms.

Jianguo Hotel
5 Jianguomenwai Dajie
Tel: 500-2233
Fax: 500-2871

Jinglun (Beijing-Toronto) Hotel (Nikko GP)
3 Jianguomenwai Dajie
Tel: 500 2266
Fax: 500 2022
659 rooms.

Kunlun Hotel (Jin Jiang GP)
21 Laing Ma Qiao
Chaoyang District
Tel: 500-3388
Fax: 500-3228
1005 rooms.

Minzu (Nationalities) Hotel
51 Fuxingmennei Avenue
Tel: 601 4466
Fax: 601 4849
615 rooms.

Palace Hotel
8 Goldfish Lane
Tel: 512 8899
Fax: 512 9050

578 rooms.

Peace (Heping) Hotel
3 Jinyu Hutong (Goldfish Alley No. 3)
Tel: 512 8833
Fax: 512 6863

Shangri-la Beijing
29 Zishyuan Road
Tel: 841-2211
Telex: 222-322 SHABJ CN
666+76 rooms.

CHANGCHUN, JILIN
Changbaishan Hotel
Tel: 883551

Chunyi Guesthouse
2 Sidalin Dajie
Tel: 35951

CHENGDE, HEBEI PROVINCE
Chengde Hotel
Chezhan Lu
Tel: 227373

Duja Village, Mongolian Hotel
Inside Imperial Compound
Tel: 2269

Qiwanglou Hotel
Inside Imperial Compound
Tel: 4385

CHENGDU, SICHUAN PROVINCE
Chengdu Hotel (Luxury)
Dongfeng/Sanduan Road
Tel: 43312
 258 rooms.

Jin Jiang Guesthouse (Luxury)
36 South Renmin Road
Tel: 24481
467 rooms.

Minshan Hotel (Luxury)
17 South Renmin Road
337 rooms.

Shaanxi Huiguan (Inn)
36 Shaanxi St.
Tel: 22687

35 rooms.

CHONGQING, SICHUAN PROVINCE
Chongqing Guesthouse
Minsheng Lu
Tel: 45662

Chungking Hotel
Xinhua Lu (near Chaotianmen Pier)
Tel: 49301

Remin Hotel
Zhongshan Sanlu
Tel: 351421

DALIAN, LIAONING PROVINCE
Banchuidao Guesthouse
Coastal Road
Tel: 235131
10 bldgs. inc. villas

Dalian International Hotel
9 Stalin Road
Tel: 238 238
380 rooms.

Furama Hotel
74 Sidalin Lu
Tel: 230888

Holiday Inn
18 Shengli Square
Tel: 808888
226 rooms.

FUZHOU, FUJIAN PROVINCE
Foreign Trade Center Hotel
Wusi Lu
Tel: 50154

Overseas Chinese Hotel
Wusi Lu
Tel: 557603

GUANGZHO, GUANGDONG PROVINCE - HOTELS
China Hotel
Liu Hua Lu
Tel: 666888
1200 rooms.

Dongfang Hotel
120 Liu Hua Road
Tel 669900
400 rooms, old wing/700 rooms, new wing

Garden Hotel (Peninsula GP)
368 Huanshi Dong Lu
Tel: 773388
1000 rooms.

White Swan Hotel
1 South Street Shamian Island
Tel: 886968
1000 rooms.

GUANGZHOU RESTAURANTS
Banxi (Friendship) Restaurant
151 Xangyang Yi Road
Tel: 885655

Beiyuan North Garden Restaurant
202 Xiaobei Road
Tel: 332307

Datong Restaurant (Top Floor)
63 Yanjiang Road
Tel: 888988

Guangzhou (First House In Canton) Restaurant
2 Wengchang Wan Lu
Tel: 862439

Nanyuan (South Garden) Restaurant
120 Qianjin Road
Tel: 448380

Snake Restaurant
43 Jianglan Road
Tel: 883811

GUILIN, GUANGXI PROVINCE
Banyan Lake Hotel
17 Ronghu Bei Road
Tel 3811/2647

Holiday Inn, Guilin
14 Ronghu Nan Lu
Tel: 3950
259 rooms.

Sheraton Guilin Hotel
9 Binjiang Nan Lu
Tel: 225588/223855

HAIKOU, and HAINAN ISLAND
Area Code (86)+750
Haikou Tower Hotel
Binghai Avenue, Haikou
240 rooms.
Tel: 23962

Seaview International Hotel
6 Hai Xiu Road
Haikou
Tel: 23386/23377/26618
Fax: 22900/33101

Dadonghai Toursim Hotel
Sanya, southeast coast
Tel: Contact Haikou CITS

Luhuituo Hotel
Luhuituo Peninsula, southeast coast
Tel: 74659

Tongda Villa Resort
Li & Miao Aut Dis Tongda
Tel: Hong Kong 3-659003

HANGZHOU, ZHEJIANG PROVINCE
- Area Code (86+571)
Dragon Hotel
Shugang Road
Hangzhou, Zhejiang 310007
Tel: 554488
Fax: 558090
557 rooms

Friendship Hotel Hangzhou
53 Pinghai Road
Hangzhou, Zhejiang 310006
Tel: 777888
Fax 773842
224 rooms.

Hangzhou International Mansion
157 Tiyuchang Road
Hangzhou, Zhejiang 310006
Tel: 556224, 555724
Fax: 574201

296 rooms.

Hangzhou Overseas Chinese Hotel
15 Hubin Road
Hangzhou, Zhejiang 310006
Tel: 774401, 774953
Fax: 774978
300 rooms.

Hangzhou Xihu State Hotel (Liuzhuang Villa-West Lake Garden)
Usually reserved for special tours and VIPs
7 Xishan Road
Hangzhou, Zhejiang 310007
Tel: 776889
Fax: 772348
113 rooms.

Huajiashan Hotel (Garden Style)
12 Faxiang Lu, Xishan Road
Hangzhou, Zhejiang 310007
Tel: 771224
Fax: 773980
196 rooms.

Huagang Hotel (Garden Style)
4 Xishan Road
Hangzhou, Zhejiang 310007
Tel: 771324
Fax: 772481
200 rooms.

Shangri-la Hotel
78 Beishan Road
Hangzhou, Zhejiang 310007
Tel: 777951
Fax: 773545
387 rooms.

Xin Qiao Hotel
176 Jie Fang Road
Hangzhou, Zhejiang 310001
Tel: 776688
Fax: 772768
381 rooms.

Xizi Guesthouse (Wangzhuang Villa-Mao Zedong's Fmr Res)
Usually reserved for Special tours and VIPs

37 Nanshan Road
Hangzhou, Zhejiang 310007
Tel: 23577
Telex: 351085 XICI CN
120 rooms.

Zhejiang Guesthouse
68 Santaishan Road
Hangzhou, Zhejiang 310007
Tel: 777988
Fax: 771904
175 rooms.

HARBIN, HEILONGJIANG PROVINCE
International Hotel
Xida Zhije and Hongjun Jie
Tel: 31441

Swan Hotel
73 Zhongshan Lu
Tel: 220201

JINGHONG, XISHUANGBANNA AREA, YUNNAN PROVINCE
Banna Hotel
Tel: 2969

KUNMING, YUNNAN PROVINCE
Golden Dragon Hotel
575 Beijing Road
Kunming, Yunnan 650011
Tel: 33104, 33015
Fax: 31082
302 rooms.

Golden Peacock Hotel
Daguan Park
Kunming, Yunnan 650032
Tel: 41334, 42512
Fax: 41087
104 rooms.

Green Lake Hotel
Across from Green Lake Park
6 South Cuihu
Kunming, Yunnan 650031
Tel: 22192
Fax: 53286
172 rooms.

LUSHAN MOUNTAIN RESORT (GUILING), JINGXI PROVINCE
Lulin Hotel
Tel: 282424

NANJING, JIANGSU PROVINCE
Hongjiao Hotel
202 Zhongshan Beilu
Tel: 633931

Jingling Hotel
Nanjing Central
Tel: 742888

Nanjing Hotel
259 Zhongshan Beilu
Tel: 639831

NANNING, GUANGXI PROVINCE
Area Code (0771)
Mingyuan Hotel
38 Xinming Road
Nanning 530012
Tel: 28923
Fax: 28583
248 rooms.

Xiyuan Hotel
38 Jiangnan Road
Nanning 530031
Tel: 29923/22075
Fax: 24864
350 rooms.

Yongzhou Hotel
59 Xinming Road
Tel: 28323
Fax: 25032
450 rooms.

NINGBO, ZHEJIANG PROVINCE Area code (0574)
Asia Garden Hotel
Mayuan Road
Ningbo, Zhejiang 315000
Tel: 366888
Fax: 352138
172 rooms.

Golden Dragon Hotel
Nanshan Square
Ningbo, Zhejiang 315000
Tel: 318888

Fax: 312288
304 rooms.

Ningbo Hotel
65 Maiyuan Road
Ningbo, Zhejiang 315000
Tel: 366334
Fax: 366301
114 rooms.

NINGXIA PROVINCE
Helan Mountain Hotel
1 Choufang Street
Yinchuan 750021
Tel: 77301
175 rooms.

Ningxia Hotel
3 Park Street
Yinchuan 750001
Tel: 45131
300 rooms.

QINGDAO, SHANDONG PROVINCE
Sea-And-Sky Hotel
36 Zhanshan Avenue
Tel: 366888

Yellow Sea Hotel
75 Yanyi Road
Tel: 270215
450 rooms.

Badaguan Guesthouse
15 Zhanshan Road
Tel: 62800
30 villas.

QUFU, SHANDONG PROVINCE
Confucius Mansions Hotel
Confucius Mansions
Tel: 412374/412686

Queli Hotel
1 Queli Street
Tel: 411300/411303

SHANGHAI HOTELS
Area Code (86) + 12
Hua Ting Sheraton Hotel
Tel bet airport and Bund
1200 Cao Xi Bei Lu
1008 rooms average

Jing'an Guesthouse
Colonial-nostalgic very modest
370 Huashan Road
Upper Nanjing Road
Tel: 255-1888
Fax: 255-2657

Jin Jiang Hotel
Central 15 min to Bund
59 Maoming Road
Tel: 433-1694
Fax: 433-1694

Jin Jiang Tower
161 Changle Road
Tel: 58-2582
Fax: 58-4567
728 rooms slightly below average.

Nikko Longbai Shanghai
2451 Longbai - near airport
Tel: 259-3636
Garden style 419 rooms average.

Peace Hotel
20 Nanjing Dong Lu at the Bund
Tel: 321-1244
Fax: 329-0300
180 rooms modest.

Portman Shanghai Hotel (Shangri-la)
1376 Nanjing Road W.
Tel: 58-2582 ext. 58645
Fax: 33-2813
700 rooms.

Shanghai Hilton International
15 min to Bund
250 Huashan Road
Tel: 255 0000
Fax: 55-3848
800 rooms expensive

Shanghai Jin Cang Mandarin Hotel
1225 Nanjing Road W. Central
Tel: 33-5550
Fax: 33-5405
600 rooms expensive

SHANGHAI RESTAURANTS
Chengdu - Sichuan
129 Shunchang Road
Tel: 28-3767

Moslem
710 Fuzhou Road
Tel: 22-4273

Sichuan (SavorySpicy)
457 Nanjing
Tel: 22-1965

Renmin - Suzhou and Wuxi
226 Nanjing Road. W.
Tel: 320-1763

Shanghai Laofandian (Local Specialties)
242 Fuyou Road
Tel: 328-2782

Treasure Island (Taiwanese)
981/985 Yan'an Road
Tel: 437-4941

Yangyunlou (Beijing)
755 Nanjing
Tel: 322-3298

Yangzhou (Regional)
308 Nanjing
Tel: 322-5826

Yueyanglou (Hunan)
28 Xizangan Road
Tel: 327-9494

Xinya (Cantonese)
#719 Nanjing
Tel: 322-3636

SHENYANG, LIAONING PROVINCE
Friendship Hotel
#1 Huanghe Beidajie, Huangugu
Tel: 466581

Liaoning Mansions Hotel
#1 Huanghe Dajie, Section 6
Tel: 462536

Phoenix Hotel
109 Huanghe Nandajie

Tel: 466500

TIANJIN
Area Code (86) + 22
Crystal Palace
Youyi and Binshui Roads
Tel: 33-1337

Tianjin Garden Hotel
337 Machang Road
Tel: 286 5353

Tianjin Hyatt
219 Jiefang Beilu
Tel: 318888

Tianjin Sheraton
Zi Jin Shan Road
Tel: 33-3388
Fax: 31-8740
282 rooms.

Victory Hotel (Nendels Hotel GP)
11 Jintang Road
Tel: 984984/985833
U.S. 800 547-0106
350 rooms.

TIBET, XIZANG PROVINCE
Lhasa Hotel (Holiday Inn)
1 Minzu Road
Tel: 22221
468 rooms.

Tibet Hotel (Tibetan decor)
Nation Road
Tel: 24966

Tibet Guesthouse (Potala Pal Dec)
Minzu Road
Tel: 23738/23729

Lhasa CITS Guesthouse (VIP)
Quo San Suo Compound
Tel: 22225

Xigaze Hotel
13 Jiagang Road
Xigaze
Tel: 2519

WENZHOU, ZHEJIANG PROVINCE
Area Code (86)+571
Jingshan Hotel
35 Xueshan Road
Tel: 25901
100 rooms. Lux

Overseas Chinese Hotel
17 Xinhe Road
Tel: 23911
100 rooms.

Wenzhou Hotel
Chaiqiao Alley
Tel: 24981

WUHAN, HUBEI PROVINCE
Jinghuan Hotel
245 Shengli Jie
Tel: 21253

Qing Chuan Hotel
Qingchuan Jie
Tel: 441141

WUXI, JIANGSU PROVINCE
Hubin Hotel
Liyuan Road
Tel: 668812
360 rooms.

Millido Hotel
2 Liangxi Road
Tel: 665665
Fax: 668660
251 rooms.

Shuixiu Hotel
Liyuan Road
Tel: 26591/668591

Taihu Hotel
Meiyuan
Tel: 667901

XIAMEN, FUJIAN PROVINCE
Xin Qiao Hotel
Xinhua Lu
Tel: 38388

XIAN, SHAANXI PROVINCE
Golden Flower
8 Changle Xilu

Tel: 332981
200 rooms.

Holiday Inn
8 Huangcheng Donglu Nanduan
Tel: 333888

Hyatt Hotel
Dong Dajie & Heping Lu
Tel: 712020

Jianguo Hotel
Dongguan Zhengjie
Tel: 3388888

XINJIANG AUT REG
Kashgar Hotel
Tawahose Road
Kashgar
Tel: 2367/2368

Turpan Guesthouse
Turpan
Tel: 2907/2301

Kunlun Hotel
Youhao Road
Urumqi
Tel: 42411/43801
350 rooms.

Xinjiang Friendship Guesthouse
Yan'an Road
Urumqi
Tel: 22940/23991
150 rooms.

YANTAI, SHANDONG PROVINCE
Yantai Hill Hotel
Tel: 24491

PHOTO CREDITS

Antiques of the Orient : 19, 108, 120 (bottom), 212
Beijing Slide Studio/China National Tourist Office in Singapore : 158, 159, 331, 334, 337, 338, 345, 347, 350/351, 352, 353, 359, 365, 367, 368, 372
Bio Foto/Arthur Christiansen : 59 (top)
Randa Bishop : 36, 66, 186, 242, 250, 260, Backcover (top, right)
Hans Deumling/Stockphotos : 384
Van Goubergen : 84/85, 201, 363, 364, 369
Nigel Hicks : xii, xiii, 24, 45, 50, 57, 58 (top), 58 (bottom), 199, 218, 221, 233, 234, 235, 236/237, 240/241, 252, 256 (bottom), 257 (bottom right), 261, 264, 265, 267, 285, 310, 312, 316/317, 336, 379, 393
Image Bank : Front cover
Image Bank/Anthony Boccaccio : 54/55, 80, 82, 83, 194, 227, 230/231
Image Bank/John Bryson : 128, 130
Image Bank/W L Chin : 162
Image Bank/Michael Coyne : 32
Image Bank/Tom Owen Edmunds : 31, 35, 69, 72, 131, 133 (bottom)
Image Bank/Jay Freis : xvi, 76, 311, Backcover (top, left)
Image Bank/Fong Siu Nang : 39, 74, 81, 216, 280/281, 297, 302/303
Image Bank/Fotoworld : 48
Image Bank/Larry Gatz : 52, 262
Image Bank/Larry Dale Gordon : 102/103, 150
Image Bank/Peter Hendrie : 245, 256 (top)
Image Bank/Tadao Kimura : 328/329
Image Bank/Don Klumpp : 64, 71, 110, 244, 248, 362, 329
Image Bank/Lee Man You : 26
Image Bank/Romilly Lockyer : 2, 86
Image Bank/Terry Madison : 43, 99, 169, 247
Image Bank/Arthur Meyerson : 251
Image Bank/Marvin E Newman : 88
Image Bank/P & G Bowater : 8/9, 40, 174, 178, 181, 182/183, 266, 340, Backcover (bottom)
Image Bank/Anne Rippy : 51, 371
Image Bank/Guido Alberto Rossi : Front end, 4/5, 70, 190, 249, 397
Image Bank/Marcel Isy-Schwart : 398/399
Image Bank/Ivor Sharp : 92/93
Image Bank/Paul Slaughter : 44, 111, 184, 276/277, 381, 404
Image Bank/Harald Sund : 7, 68, 90, 106, 132/133, 135, 139, 374, 378, 380, 386, 387
Image Bank/Nevada Wier : 298, 301, 321, 360, 370, 382, 388
Image Bank/Jules Zalon : 211
Leong Ka Tai : 21, 153, 206/207, 224, 391, 392
Pateman : xi, 6, 10, 12, 14, 16/17, 46/47, 56, 96, 112, 113, 117, 119, 136, 140, 141, 145, 146, 147, 154, 160, 165, 167, 170, 173, 198, 272, 278, 284, 287, 288, 293, 324, 330, 354/355, 390, 405, 406, Back end
Christine Pemberton : xiv, xv (top), xv (bottom), 38, 65, 105, 116, 124, 137, 180/181, 187, 203, 205, 217, 257 (bottom-left), 299, 318, 342, 356/357
Morten Strange : 59 (centre), 59 (bottom), 60 (top), 60 (bottom)
Scholars' Studio : 91, 95, 109, 120 (top), 121
Bill Wassman : x, 62, 73, 306, 307, 308/309, 400

INDEX

1911 Revolution, 260

A

A Journey to the West, 365
Acrobatics, 92
Afghanistan, 50
Agriculture, 19
Alum, 333
Analects, 77, 79, 81
Anhui Province, 214
animal husbandry, 12
Antique, 7
Aongyue Temple, 339
Ape Man (Yuanmou Man), 11
Archeologists, 12
architecture, 101, 104, 179, 207
arhats, 309
arts and crafts, 7, 14, 110, 188, 350
Arts and Crafts Industry Factories, 187
Arts and Crafts Institute, 188
Astana Tombs, 365
autonomous regions, 5

B

Ba tribe, 285
Badaling, 143, 144
Bai, 68
Bai Chongxi, 181
Baita, 138
bamboo, 5, 100, 113, 240, 268, 300, 310
Bamboo Temple, 309
Bangladesh, 50
Banpo, 11
Banpo Village, 37, 348
Baochu Pagoda, 204
Baodingshan, 277, 278

Baoquo Temple Complex, 222
Barkhor, 378, 381
beaches, 238, 271
Beidaihe, 148
Beihai, 137
Beijing, 3, 5, 28, 51, 55, 125, 128, 129, 151, 152, 391
Beijing Duck, 151, 153
Beijing Opera, 88, 89
Beijing Zoo, 140
Beilun River, 269
Beishan, 277, 278
Beishan Temple, 352
Bellows Gorge, 284
Bezekelik Thousand Buddha Caves, 365
Bhutan, 50
Bicycles, 45
Big Red, 273, 278, 279, 280, 282, 283, 284, 287, 293
Big Wild Goose Pagoda, 343
Biling Si Caves, 350, 351
Bird Island, 354
Birth Control, 66
Bisquit, 120
Black Mountain Rock Paintings, 356
blanc-de-Chine, 112, 121, 227, 229, 241
border, 268, 269, 295, 315, 316, 323
Boxer Rebellion, 21, 31
British, 20, 255
bronze, 12, 40, 107, 108, 112
Brunei, 50
Buddha, 80, 278, 288, 302, 327
Buddhism, 3, 18, 71, 77, 80, 81, 82, 277, 292, 312, 314, 315, 325, 326, 327, 335, 336, 338

Buddhist scriptures, 343
Bund, 179, 181, 182, 183, 187, 191
Burma, 18, 50, 309, 312
butter sculpture, 353

C

Cactus, 240
Cambodia, 312
camels, 321, 322, 323
canals, 197
Canton, 20
Cantonese, 257
caravan, 323, 324, 342, 349
carpet, 151, 187, 325
carved figures, 336
cash crop, 39, 270
Cathay, 19
cave abodes, 322
cave carvings, 327
caves, 335, 336, 351
ceiling panels, 345
celadons, 229
Celestial Caves, 239
Central Asia, 16, 18
ceramics, 19, 118, 120, 225
Chang An Avenue, 25
Chang An Boulevard, 128
Chang'an, 13, 20, 51
Changjiang, 3, 7, 37, 44, 56, 64, 195, 202, 273, 274, 278, 279, 284, 285, 286, 288, 290
Changjiang Bridge, 288
Changping, 332
Chaotianmen Dock, 275, 279
Chaozhou, 265
Chengde, 147
Chengdu, 295, 296, 297
Chenglingji, 286

423

INDEX

Chiang Kaishek, 22, 23, 24, 30, 32
Chiangs, 24
Children's Palace, 183
China Silk Museum, 208
China Tea Museum, 208
Chinese Communist Party (CCP), 3, 5, 30, 33, 186
Chinese language, 9
Chinese Revolution, 22
Chinese Tea Museum, 212
Chongqing, 51, 274, 275, 277, 278, 280
Chongqing City Museum, 275
Christian, 20
Christianity, 3, 83
Cinnabar, 404
civilization, 11, 12, 18, 52, 322
Cixi, the Empress Dowager, 136, 140, 142
clay figurines, 199
clay sculptures, 351
climate, 3, 54, 55, 57
cloisonne, 7, 43, 109, 110, 118, 288, 402, 403
Commonwealth of Independent States, 49
commune, 25, 39, 183
communications, 44
Communism, 22, 23, 24, 25, 28, 34, 42, 64, 261, 323, 335
Communist Party, 33, 178
concessions, 20, 255
Confucian, 3, 14, 18, 76, 77, 78, 80, 81, 82, 327
Confucius, 78
Conghua Hot Springs, 263
cormorant fishermen, 246, 248
crafts, 107, 108, 109
cruise, 278, 280, 284, 286
cuisine, 193, 213, 229, 248, 257, 267
cultivation, 37
Cultural Park, 261
Cultural Revolution, 25, 29, 33, 35, 178
culture, 3, 13, 18
Currency, 3

D

Dadu River, 302
Dagoba, 101
Dai, 68, 311, 312, 315
Dai Minority, 309
Dalai Lama, 67, 71, 379, 381
Daluo, 315
Daning River, 285
Danjia Minority, 271
Daqing, 42
Datong, 326
Dayun Monastery, 332
Dazhalan, 152
Dazhao Temple, 325
Dazu, 277
De Hua, 112, 121, 227
Dehong Dai, 315
Deng Xiaoping, 25, 29, 33, 34, 35, 290, 296
Dietan Falls, 268
Dim Sum, 394
Dong Lu, 181
Dongfanghong, 201
Dongxing, 269
Dongyue Monastery, 332
dragon, 109, 112, 138, 142
Dragon Boat, 251, 268, 310
Dragon Lady, 23, 24
Dragon Park, 333
dragon symbol, 121
Dragon Well, 209
Dragon Well Tea, 204, 212
Drepung, 383
Drepung Monastery, 382
Drum Hills, 226
Drum Tower Square, 333
Du Fu, 95, 96
Du Fu Cottage, 299
Dujiangyan Irrigation Project, 301
Dunhuang, 355, 356, 357, 358
Dunhuang County Museum, 358
Duxiufeng, 245

E

Earthenware, 119
Echo Wall, 138
Economic and Technical Development Zone (NETDZ), 45, 222
Economy, 3, 41
Edgar Snow, 28
Elephant Trunk Hill, 244
Elephant Trunk Rock, 246
Emeishan, 54, 304
endangered species, 5, 302
Eternal Spring, 5
Ewenki, 73
exploration, 19

F

FEC (Foreign Exchange Currency), 3
Federal Government, 5
Feilai Peak, 204, 209
Fenghua River, 221, 223
feudal society, 13
feudal system, 71
fine arts, 87
First National Congress, 22, 185
First Republic of China, 13, 31
fish farming, 199
Five Dynasties, 19
Flaming Mountains, 365
flea markets, 192
flora and fauna, 5
flowers, 114
Forbidden City, 1, 20, 129, 133
foreign concessions, 265
foreign investment, 222
Forest of Steles, 343
Fort Dzong, 385
Free Economic Zone, 221, 222, 226
French, 20, 175, 255
Freshwater Pearl Industry, 187
Friendship Pass, 268
Friendship Store, 192, 288
Fu, 117, 119
fu lions, 117
Fuel and Power, 41
Fujian, 56, 57, 225, 228, 394
Fuzhou, 225, 226, 227, 228, 232

G

Gang of Four., 28
Gansu Province, 349
Gansu Provincial Museum, 350
Gaochang, 364
Gaomiao Temple, 327
Gaotian, 246
Garden of the Humble Administrator, 196
Geological Museum, 249
Germans, 20
gers, 323
Gezhouba Dam, 286
giant pandas, 261
Gobi Desert, 18, 323, 366
Gold fish, 112, 116
Golden Age, 18

golden monkey, 313
Golden Temple, 308
Government, 3
Grand Buddha (Dafo), 302
Grand Buddha Temple, 302
Grand Canal, 7, 18, 44, 52, 195, 198, 199, 202
Grand Mosque, 326
Grand View Garden, 135, 188
Grape Valley, 365
grasslands, 6, 58, 319, 324
Great Britain, 266
Great Hall, 131
Great Hall of the People, 129, 131
Great Khan, 1
Great Leap Forward, 25, 29
Great Mosque, 325, 344, 352
Great Wall, 14, 15, 19, 20, 143, 144, 354
Green Lake Park, 307
Gross domestic product, 47
grottoes, 18
Guangdong, 27, 29, 30, 45, 57, 394, 395
Guangdong Historical Museum, 260
Guangdong Province, 255, 263
Guangxi Province, 267
Guangzhou, 6, 45, 253, 254, 255, 256, 259, 262
Guangzhou Trade Fair, 258
Guangzhou Trade Fair Complex, 258
Guangzhou Zoo, 261
Guanqian Jie, 198
Guanyin, 76, 81, 112, 223, 227, 278
Guilin, 243, 247, 251
Guiyuan Temple, 288
Gulang Yu, 235, 236
Gulang Yu Island, 241
Guling, 289
gun powder, 18
Guyuan, 327
Gyantse, 376, 385

H

Haikou, 263, 269
Hainan Experimental Marine Research Station, 271
Hainan Island, 5, 253, 254, 263, 269, 270, 271, 394
Han, 3, 13, 16, 17, 64, 68, 80, 304, 315, 325, 339
Han Fei, 14
Han Suyin, 98
handicraft, 7, 19
Hangzhou, 18, 19, 201
Hankou, 288
Hanyang, 288
Harbin, 5, 55
Heavenly Peace, 24
Hebrews, 333
Heilongjiang, 49, 55
Hekou, 316, 317
Hemaihe, 354
Henan Province, 332
Henan Provincial Museum, 335
herbal, 9
Himalayas, 3
Hinduism, 327
Hohhot, 324, 325, 327
Hong Kong, 5, 35, 44, 45, 253, 264, 266
Hongkong Park, 184
hot spring, 53, 226, 254, 348, 349
Huqingyutang Pharmacy, 210
Huaihai Zhong Lu, 192
Huanghe (Yellow River), 3, 7, 12, 37, 52, 64, 322, 326, 332, 335, 349
Huangpu River, 175, 188, 191, 220
Huangshan, 54, 177, 213, 214
Huangzhong, 353
Huanqiu, 139
Huaqing Hot Springs, 348
Hubei Provincial Museum, 288
Hui, 3, 64, 68, 72, 326
Huishan Clay Workshop, 199
Huishan Hills, 200
Huixian, 330
Hukou, 332
Hundred Flowers Movement, 25, 28
hutongs, 232, 256
Hydro-electric, 42

I

Id Kah Mosque, 373
imperial parks, 135
India, 18, 50
Indonesia, 50
Industrial Economic Transformation, 40
Industrial Revolution, 41
Inner Mongolia, 7, 55, 72, 319, 323
Inner Mongolian Museum, 325
Inner Mongolian Plateau, 51
Iron Pagoda, 333
Iron Rooster, 332
irrigation, 12, 37, 326
Islam, 3, 83, 326

J

jade, 110, 112, 114, 116, 117, 187, 335
Jade Buddha Temple, 184
Japan, 20, 32, 50
Jesuits, 20, 27, 83, 333
Jialing River, 274
Jiang Qing, 25, 28
Jianghan, 273, 279
Jiangsu Province, 202, 292
Jiangxin, 225
Jianxi Province, 289
Jiayuguan, 354, 355
Jichang Garden, 200
Jiefang Bei, 277
Jinjiang River, 232
Jin Dynasty, 301
Jin Jiang, 177
Jin Jiang Hotel, 175
Jinci Buddhist Temple, 330
Jingdezhen, 120, 121, 229, 290
Jinghong, 305, 310, 311, 313, 315
Jingpo, 315
Jingshan, Park (Prospect Hill), 139
Jingzhou, 286
Jinhua, 210
Jinjiang Theater, 301
Jinlong Canyon, 327
Jiujang, 289
Jiulongbi, 138
Jokhang Temple, 378, 381
Journey to the West, 366
Judaism, 85
Juyongguan, 143

K

Kaifeng, 19, 51, 332, 333, 335
Kaiyuan, 267
Kampa-La Pass, 385
Kangxi, 20, 30, 38, 110, 147
Kaoshan, 73
Karl Marx, 32
Kashgar, 370

Kazaks, 71
Kirgiz, 71
Kong Ming Tablet, 285
Korea, 49, 64, 73
Kowloon, 266
Koxinga Memorial Hall, 237
Kruschev, 29, 31, 33
Kublai Khan, 1, 19
K'ung Futse, 78
kung-fu., 338, 339
Kunming, 5, 305, 306, 307, 398
Kunming Lake, 137
Kunming Provincial Museum, 307
Kunming Zoo, 307
Kuomintang, 21, 30, 261

L

Lacang (Mekong) River, 310
lacquer, 227, 228, 229, 404
lacquerware, 202, 227, 228, 229, 268, 350, 404
Lake Dian, 306, 309
Lake Dianshan, 187, 188, 189
Lake Taihu, 199, 200, 201, 202
Lake Yamdrok, 385
Langshan, 12
Lantian, 11, 13
Lanzhou, 349, 351
Lao Cai, 316, 317
Lao Shouxing, 76, 114, 199
Lao Tze, 14, 77
Laojunyan, 233
Laos, 50, 310, 312, 315
Leshan, 302, 303
Lhasa, 376, 377, 383
Li, 69
Li Garden Island, 200
Li Po, 94
Li River, 245, 246
Li Shixian, 210
Lijiang, 244
limestone pinnacles, 306
Lin Biao, 29
linen industry, 43
Linfen, 332
Linggu Park, 292
Lingxiang grass, 251
Lingyin Temple, 203, 209
Linhua Park, 261
Lishan, 348
literature, 14, 18, 92, 98
Little Goose Pagoda, 343
Liuha, 209

Liuzhou, 249
Liyuan, 357
Loess Plateau, 18, 51, 322
log houses, 314
Logouqiao (Reed Gully Bridge), 145
Long Gallery, 137
Long March, 23, 28, 34
Longmen Caves, 335, 336
Longquam, 229
Lop Nor, 51
Loquat Hill Park, 275
Lotus, 113, 312
Lotus Mountain, 262
Lotus Nunnery, 237
Lu Xun, 96, 97, 184
Lu Xun's Tomb, 184
Ludiyan (Reed Flute Cave), 245
Luhuitou Peninsula, 271
Lulin Lake, 291
Luoba, 71
Luohan fruit, 251
Luoyang, 13, 18, 51, 327, 335, 338
Lushan, 289

M

Mahjong, 202
Maitreya, 81, 203
Malaysia, 50
Manchu, 5, 20, 32, 64, 71
mandarin, 38
Mao Tai, 392
Mao Zedong, 22, 23, 25, 28, 31, 32, 33, 38, 178, 186, 289, 290
Mao Zedong Memorial Hall, 129, 132
Marble Boat, 137
marble-carving, 233
Marco Polo, 1, 2, 19, 330
Marquise Liu Park, 249
martial arts, 338, 339
Marxism-Leninism, 22, 97
Matriarchal clan, 11
Matteo Ricci, 20, 27, 333
medicine, 18
Mei Lanfang, 88, 89, 91
Meiyuan, 199
Menba, 71
Mencius, 14, 76
Meng Liang Staircase, 283, 284
Menghai, 313
Mengla, 313
Mengla County, 315

Mengshan, 335
Miao, 64, 69
Middle East, 16
Middle Kingdom, 6, 27, 51, 52
migratory birds, 353
Min River, 226, 301, 302
mineral spring waters, 226, 276
Ming, 13, 19, 20, 24, 27, 229, 232, 292
Ming Tombs, 141, 142
Mingshashan, 357, 358
minorities, 247, 248
minority groups, 69, 70, 72, 73, 352
Minority Handicraft Factory, 325
minority nationalities, 64, 68, 314, 341
Mo Tse, 14
Moganshan, 213, 216
Mogao Grottoes, 357, 358, 359
Monastery of Divine Light, 299
Mong Cai, 269
Mongol, 6, 19, 64, 72, 321, 324
Mongolia People's Republic, 323
Monk Suspended Upside Down, 284
Monkey Island, 271
Monument to the People's Heroes, 129, 131
Moon Lake, 222
Mount Bogda, 369
Mount Everest, 3, 50
Mount Fubo, 245
Mount Silian, 317
Mount Sumeru Grottoes, 327
Mount Wu Yi, 228
mulberry, 12, 196, 198
murals, 345, 351
Museum of Chinese Revolution, 129, 131
Musical Instruments, 91
Muslims, 84
Mutianyu, 143, 144
Myanmar, 315

N

Namjagbarwa, 383
Namtha, 315
Nanjing, 210, 273, 280, 292
Nanjing Lu, 193
Nanjing Museum, 292
Nanjing Road, 189, 192

Nanning, 250, 253, 267, 268, 314
Nanning Arts Institute, 268
Nanputuo, 238
Nansha Islands, 49
Nantai Island, 226
Nanxi River, 225
National People's Congress, 3
National Revolutionary Army, 22
Nationalists, 21, 22, 23, 24
Nepal, 50
New Territories, 266
Nine Dragon Screen, 327
Ningbo, 221, 222, 223
Ningxia, 322
Ningxia Hui Autonomous Region, 326
nirvana, 81
Nongdao, 315
Nongyao, 268
Norbu Lingka, 382
Northern + Southern Dynasties, 13
Number 1 Department Store, 191
Number 1 Silk Factory, 199

O

Observatory, 136
Old Town, 183
opium, 20
Opium War, 20, 30, 179, 265
Oracle bones, 13, 93
Oroqen, 73
Overhanging Great Wall, 356
overseas Chinese, 238
overseas Fujians, 238

P

Pagoda, 101, 104, 209, 339
Pagoda Forest, 339
Pailing, 211
Pakistan, 50
Palkhor Monastery, 385
Pamirs, 49
pandas, 300
paper making, 43
papercutting, 202
pearl, 189, 228, 271
Peasant uprisings, 17, 18
Peking, 1, 13, 20
Peking Man, 11, 125, 146
People's Republic of China, 3, 13, 24, 25, 31, 128
People's University in Beijing, 9
Period of the Three Kingdoms, 13
Persia, 18
Philippines, 50
phoenix, 112, 121, 142
pilgrimage, 304, 307
Pingxiang, 268
Population, 3, 64, 69, 70, 72, 73
porcelain, 7, 19, 43, 119, 120, 121, 229, 241, 267, 290, 333, 404
Pornography, 66
Portuguese, 235
Potala Palace, 379, 380
President Nixon, 24, 35
Primitive man, 11
Prince of Shi Jinhua, 210
Provincial Museum of Shanxi, 330
Pu Yi, 21
Public Steamer, 278, 279
Puerh, 312
Purple Cloud Rock, 241
Putuoshan, 222

Q

Qaidam Basin, 51
Qi Baishi, 100
Qiandao, 210
Qiandao Lake, 213
Qianlong, 29, 30, 38, 110, 147, 203, 205, 228
Qianmen, 128
Qiatou Village, 225
Qilianshan, 356
Qilin, 104
qilin, 112, 117
Qin Dynasty, 11, 13, 14, 226, 346
Qin Shihuang, 14, 15, 143, 144, 346, 348
Qing Dynasty, 13, 20, 24, 202, 210, 226, 228, 229, 232
Qing Tombs, 142
Qingdao, 31
Qinghai, 51, 52
Qinghai Lake, 50, 353
Qinghai Province, 352
Qinghai Tibetan Plateau, 50
Qiniandian, 138
Qiongzhong, 271
Qu Fu, 78
Qu Yuan, 286, 289
Quanzhou, 229, 232
Quemoy, 237
Qutang Gorge, 283

R

rain forest, 58, 313
Red Guards, 25, 29, 33, 178
Red Hill Park, 289
red-headed crane, 5
Religion, 3, 75
Renmin Park, 299, 369
renminbi, 3
Republic of China, 21, 292
revolution, 255, 292
River Control Peak, 277
Roof of the World, 50
Ruli River, 315
Russia, 31, 32, 33
Russian Revolution, 22
Russians, 20, 292

S

Saga of the Gang of Four, 33
Sakyamuni, 18, 82, 203, 278, 315, 327
Samye Monastery, 386
Sand Lake Recreational Garden, 326
Sangyang Academy of Classical Learning, 335
Sani (Yi) people, 306
Sanskrit scriptures, 335
Sanxia, 283
Sanya, 271
science, 18, 19
scramble for concessions, 20
Sculpture of the Five Goats, 259
Sea of Sands, 326
Sericulture, 12, 39, 196, 208
Seventeen-Arch Bridge, 137
Shaanxi Plain, 342
Shaanxi Province, 11, 23
Shaanxi Provincial Museum, 343, 346
Shamian Island, 255, 256
Shang, 12, 13
Shang City, 335
Shang Yang, 14
Shanghai, 5, 28, 30, 41, 44, 51, 175, 177, 178, 179, 185, 273, 280, 392
Shanghai Arts and Crafts Exhibition Center, 192

Shanghai Arts and Crafts Export and Import Corpora, 187
Shanghai Arts and Crafts Service Department Store, 191
Shangqing Si, 277
Shantou, 265
Shanxi Province, 326, 330
Shaolin, 335, 338, 339
Shaoxing, 193, 213, 214, 223
Shaoxing Opera, 208
Shaoxing wines, 213
Shapatou, 326
Shashi, 286
Shatian pomelo, 251
Shaunglin Monastery, 330
She, 73
Shenzhen, 45, 253, 254, 264
Shibao Zai, 282
Shijiazhuang, 331
Shiling, 306
Shinaihai, 354
Shongyan Shu Yuan, 338
shopping, 256, 258, 288
Shuikoujie, 268
Sichuan, 397, 398
Sichuan Province, 304
Sichuan Opera, 89, 301
Sichuan Province, 296
Sichuan University Museum, 299
Sikkim, 50
silk, 12, 17, 39, 42, 110, 196, 198, 208, 327
Silk Road, 16, 17, 18, 42, 84, 109, 341, 342, 349, 352
Sima Qian, 17
Simao, 310
Six Dynasties Period, 13
Six Harmonies, 209
Six Harmonies Pagoda, 204
Six Hills, 205
slave labor, 12, 13
Snake Restaurant, 395
Socialism, 24, 28
Solitary Hill, 206
Song, 13, 221, 274
Song Hong River, 317
Song Shan, 338
Songs, 19
Soong, 21, 22, 24
Soong Qingling, 185
South China Botanical Gardens, 262
South Spring Park, 275, 276

Spanish, 235
Special Economic Zone, 45, 263, 265, 269
Spring and Autumn period, 13
St Ignatius Catholic Church, 181
state-owned enterprises, 47
Stone Forest, 306
Stoneware, 120
Stupa, 101, 338
Sui, 13, 52, 195
Summer Palace, 136, 147
Summer Palace at Chengde, 81
Sun Yatsen, 21, 31, 184, 292
Sun Yatsen Monument and Memorial Hall, 260
Sun Yatsen Park, 289
Sunlight Rock, 237
Suzhou, 195

T
Ta'er Monastery, 352, 353
taijiquan, 203
Taiping Rebellion, 21, 210
Taiping uprising, 30
Taiwan, 24, 31, 32, 50, 233, 234, 237
Taiyuan, 330, 331
Taklamakan, 51
Tan Kah Kee, 238
Tang, 13, 18, 64, 80, 96, 221, 226, 238, 302, 342
Tang Pagoda, 322
Taoism, 3, 77, 78, 80, 327, 308, 333
Tashilhunpo Monastery, 385
tea, 192, 199, 212, 239, 312
Teghinlen, 323
Temple of Wuhou, 299
Ten Kingdoms, 19
terracotta warriors, 348
textiles, 19, 42
Thailand, 50, 310, 312
Thousands of Rock Lotuses Temple, 241
Thousands of Rocks Reservoir, 239
Three Gorges, 273, 282, 283
Three Kingdoms, 18
Three Little Gorges, 285
Three Visitor's Caverns, 286
Tian Chi, 369
Tian Mountain, 362
Tiananmen, 128, 129, 130
Tiananmen Incident, 25, 35

Tiananmen Square, 25, 129, 130, 131
Tianfeng Ta Pagoda, 222
Tianjin, 5, 8, 43, 149, 151
Tiantan Park, 138
Tianyi Ge Library, 221
Tibet, 64, 70, 71
Tieyingbi, 138
Tiger Spring, 209
Tinglinguan, 137
Tomb of Abakh Hoja, 373
Tomb of Qin Shihuang, 345
Tomb of Wand Jian, 299
Tongshi, 271
trade centre, 342
Travels of Marco Polo, 1
Tuancheng, 138
Tujia, 73
Turpan, 362, 364, 366
Turpan Basin, 362
Turpan Bazaar, 363
Turpan Depression, 51
Twelve Peaks of Wushan, 285
Two Kings Temple, 301

U
Ulaan Bataar, 323
underground palaces, 348
Unemployment, 47
Urumqi, 364, 367, 368
Uygurs, 64, 71

V
Vietnam, 50, 268, 269, 270, 310, 316

W
wall painting, 353
Wang Changling, 94
Wang Hungwen, 33
Wang Wei, 51, 94
Wang Zhaojun, 286, 325
Wangfujing, 152
Wanxian, 282
warlords, 18, 20
Warring States Period, 13
Water Festival, 314
Weddings, 232, 312
Wenchang, 271
Wenchang County, 270
wenren, 3
Wenzhou, 220, 223, 224, 225
West Gate, 352
West Lake, 193, 201, 202, 205,

208, 209
West Lake Park, 226
Western Han, 15
Western Jin, 18
White Cloud Hills, 262
White Horse, 335
White Horse Cave, 286
White Pagoda,, 350
White Pagoda Hill, 349
wildlife, 312, 313
Wolong Nature Reserve, 300, 302
Woodblock printing, 18
woolen textile centers, 325
World War II, 307
World Wide Fund for Nature, 300, 302
Wu Gorge, 284, 285
Wu Yi, 54
Wu Yi Mountain, 239
Wuchang, 288
Wuhan, 41, 273, 278, 280, 286, 287, 289
Wulong Monastery, 302
Wulongting, 138
Wushan, 226, 285
Wusuli River, 49
Wuta (Five-Pagoda) Monastery, 325
Wuxi, 198
Wuxing Teahouse, 183, 184
Wuzhou, 247, 248

X

Xia, 12, 13
Xiamen, 45, 232, 233, 234, 239, 240, 241
Xian, 11, 20, 37, 109, 331, 332, 333, 341, 342, 343, 344, 349
Xibo, 71
Xicheng Underground Gallery, 356
Xidan Avenue, 152
Xigaze, 376, 377, 385
Xihui Park, 200
Xiletuzhao Temple, 325
Xiling, 143, 286
Xiling Gorge, 285
Xinanjiang River, 213
Xincun, 271
Xingping, 247, 248
Xining, 322, 352
Xinjiang, 55, 368
Xinjiang Autonomous Region

Museum, 368
Xinjiang Uygur Autonomous Region, 71
Xishan, 200, 250, 309
Xishuang Banna, 5, 309, 312, 315, 398, 399
Xizang, 384
Xizhu Garden Nunnery, 248
Xu Beihong, 100, 101, 117
Xuan Zang, 343, 365
Xuankong, 327
Xuhui, 181
Xunpu, 232

Y

yak butter, 323, 353
Yanan, 23
Yandang Mountains, 225
Yangguan, 357
Yangshao, 11
Yangshuo, 246, 247
Yangste River Bridge, 292
Yangtse, 273
Yangtse Bridge, 277
Yangzhou, 202
Yangzongyong Lake, 384
Yanqing Temple, 333
Yao, 68, 316
Yao Temple, 332
Yaos minority, 315
Yarlung Zangbo, 383
Yellow Dragon Cave, 204, 209
Yellow Hat Sect, 67
Yellow Hats, 323
Yellow River, 37
Yellow River Park, 335
Yellow Sect Buddhism, 353
Yi, 69
Yichang, 42, 286
Yiheyuan, 135, 136, 137
Yiling Cave, 250
Yiling Stalactite Cave, 268
Yin and yang, 118
Yis, 64
Yongguansi, 226
Yongjiang River, 221
Yuan, 1, 3, 13, 19
Yuan Shikai, 21
Yuan Tong Temple, 307
Yuanlu, 232
Yuanmou, 13
Yuantouzhu, 200
Yudaiqiao, 137
Yuehuayuan, 135

Yuexiu Park, 259
Yumen, 357
Yuncheng, 332
Yungang Caves, 326
Yunnan, 5, 56, 57, 305, 313, 315, 316, 398
yurts, 321, 323
Yushan, 226
Yuyao, 221, 223
Yuyuan, 183

Z

Zengmu Reef, 49
Zhanang, 386
Zhang Qian, 342
Zhanjiang, 263
Zhaojun Tomb, 325
Zhejiang Province, 210, 216, 223
Zhengzhou, 331, 332, 334
Zhenhailou, 259
Zhenjiang Provincial Museum, 205
Zhenzhen, 263
Zhongquo, 6, 9, 11
Zhongshan, 181
Zhongshan Dong Lu, 191
Zhongshan Hot Springs, 263
Zhou Enlai, 13, 25, 30, 33, 34, 186
Zhoukoudian, 11, 125, 146
Zhuang Tse, 14
Zhuangs, 64, 68
Zhuhai, 45, 254, 263
Zhujiang (Pearl) River, 44, 64, 255, 261
zoo, 226, 245, 300

NOTES

NOTES